CRITIQUE OF JUDGEMENT

IMMANUEL KANT (1724–1804) was born in Königsberg, the capital of Eastern Prussia, and spent his ⸻⸻⸻ ⸻⸻⸻ ⸻⸻ teacher, and academic in his home city and it⸻⸻  and the natural sciences at the ⸻ He spent the succeeding years as a private lecturer, publishing ⸻ treatises on scientific and phil⸻ period. Kant finally became P⸻ at the University of Königsberg in 1770. Ov⸻ ⸻ which Wilhelm Dilthey described as the 'silent decade', Kant radically revised his earlier ideas and developed an entirely novel conception of the proper method of philosophy, which culminated in his epoch-making *Critique of Pure Reason* in 1781. He extended his 'transcendental' approach in the *Critique of Practical Reason* of 1786 and the *Critique of Judgement* in 1790, the work which Kant himself saw as completing the entire 'critical enterprise'. Throughout the 1790s Kant also produced an abundance of dense contributions to eminently topical questions of ethics, politics, and history, and religion. Kant retired from lecturing in 1796 and died at the beginning of 1804. The *Critique of Judgement* has proved particularly influential in the continental philosophical tradition and also remains a central point of reference for the contemporary renewal of interest in Kantian thought as a whole.

NICHOLAS WALKER has published articles and essays in the field of German philosophy and literature and has translated texts by Adorno, Habermas, Heidegger, and Gadamer.

OXFORD WORLD'S CLASSICS

*For over 100 years Oxford World's Classics have brought
readers closer to the world's great literature. Now with over 700
titles—from the 4,000-year-old myths of Mesopotamia to the
twentieth century's greatest novels—the series makes available
lesser-known as well as celebrated writing.*

*The pocket-sized hardbacks of the early years contained
introductions by Virginia Woolf, T. S. Eliot, Graham Greene,
and other literary figures which enriched the experience of reading.
Today the series is recognized for its fine scholarship and
reliability in texts that span world literature, drama and poetry,
religion, philosophy and politics. Each edition includes perceptive
commentary and essential background information to meet the
changing needs of readers.*

OXFORD WORLD'S CLASSICS

IMMANUEL KANT

Critique of Judgement

Translated by
JAMES CREED MEREDITH

Revised, edited, and introduced by
NICHOLAS WALKER

OXFORD
UNIVERSITY PRESS

OXFORD
UNIVERSITY PRESS

Great Clarendon Street, Oxford OX2 6DP

Oxford University Press is a department of the University of Oxford.
It furthers the University's objective of excellence in research, scholarship,
and education by publishing worldwide in

Oxford New York

Auckland Cape Town Dar es Salaam Hong Kong Karachi
Kuala Lumpur Madrid Melbourne Mexico City Nairobi
New Delhi Shanghai Taipei Toronto

With offices in

Argentina Austria Brazil Chile Czech Republic France Greece
Guatemala Hungary Italy Japan Poland Portugal Singapore
South Korea Switzerland Thailand Turkey Ukraine Vietnam

Oxford is a registered trade mark of Oxford University Press
in the UK and in certain other countries

Published in the United States
by Oxford University Press Inc., New York

British Library Cataloguing in Publication Data

Data available

Library of Congress Cataloging in Publication Data

Kant, Immanuel, 1724–1804.
[Kritik der Urteilskraft. English]
Critique of judgement / Immanuel Kant ; translated by James Creed Meredith ; revised
and edited by Nicholas Walker.
p. cm.
Includes bibliographical references and index.
ISBN-13: 978-0-19-280617-8 (alk. paper)
1. Judgment (Logic) 2. Judgment (Aesthetics) 3. Teleology. I. Walker, Nicholas. II. Title.
B2783.E5M47 2007
121–dc22
2007001270

ISBN 978-0-19-955246-7

18

Typeset by Cepha Imaging Private Ltd., Bangalore, India
Printed in Great Britain
on acid-free paper by
Clays Ltd, Elcograf S.p.A.

CONTENTS

Introduction   vii

Note on the Text, Translation, and Revision   xxiv

Select Bibliography   xxviii

A Chronology of Immanuel Kant   xxxii

Analytical Table of Contents   xxxv

CRITIQUE OF JUDGEMENT

Preface to the First Edition, 1790   3

Introduction   7

PART ONE. CRITIQUE OF AESTHETIC JUDGEMENT

FIRST SECTION *Analytic of Aesthetic Judgement*   35

  First Book. Analytic of the Beautiful   35

  Second Book. Analytic of the Sublime   75

SECOND SECTION *Dialectic of Aesthetic Judgement*   165

PART TWO. CRITIQUE OF TELEOLOGICAL JUDGEMENT

FIRST DIVISION *Analytic of Teleological Judgement*   190

SECOND DIVISION *Dialectic of Teleological Judgement*   213

APPENDIX *Theory of the Method of Teleological Judgement*   245

Appendix: The 'First Introduction' to the *Critique of Judgement* 315

Explanatory Notes   357

Bilingual Glossary   365

Analytical Index   375

INTRODUCTION

HEGEL famously claimed, if the student transcripts of his lectures on the history of philosophy are to be believed, that 'Kant spoke the first rational word concerning the beautiful' and had thus made a fundamental, and indeed epochal, contribution to what it was now customary to call 'aesthetics'. But in fact the *Critique of Judgement*, to which he was specifically alluding, is both more and less than what we would commonly understand by the term aesthetics. And in certain crucial respects the enormous influence which this work in particular exercised upon the first generation of German idealist thinkers who succeeded Kant, and upon nearly all of the most important artistic and literary figures of the period as well, lay almost as much in his philosophical treatment of organic nature as in his interpretation of the realm of aesthetic experience. In order to understand the eventual conjunction or coordination of these apparently rather distinct areas of interest and concern in Kant's mature thought, it is helpful to recall in outline something of the development of his philosophy before the publication of the first edition of the *Critique of Judgement* in 1790.

Although Kant had never been an uncritical or unqualified adherent of the rationalist metaphysical tradition associated with Leibniz, and especially with the historically influential codification of broadly Leibnizian views on the part of philosophers like Christian Wolff or Alexander Gottlieb Baumgarten, this tradition of thought furnished the initial parameters for the development of his own views on the central philosophical issues of the epoch: the precise relationship of reason and the senses in the acquisition of our theoretical knowledge of nature; the ultimate character of the good and the demonstrability of practical, i.e. ethical, principles; the possibility of our knowledge of God by recourse to natural reason and the defence of the essential interests of humanity traditionally associated with such presumed knowledge; the reality of human freedom, the nature of the soul and the hope of immortality; the proper status of judgements concerning matters of beauty and taste—in short: the 'objectivity' or otherwise of the claims that had been raised concerning the central questions once addressed by classical metaphysics under the threefold rubric of the 'true', the 'good', and the 'beautiful'.

In fact it is Baumgarten who is generally credited with expressly introducing the term 'aesthetics' as the 'science of the beautiful' into philosophical currency in the early eighteenth century through his treatise on *Metaphysics* (1742). For Baumgarten the discipline implied a study of the 'sensitive' or percipient activity of the mind in recognizing beauty as an intrinsic feature of certain objects, one which he wished to vindicate as a distinctive and valuable aspect of human experience but nonetheless continued to regard as a kind of 'lower' or rudimentary cognition in relation to conceptually transparent philosophical knowledge based upon perspicuous principles. This rationalist tradition was also broadly continued by thinkers like Moses Mendelssohn who also emphasized the apparently 'disinterested' or non-utilitarian character of our typically aesthetic judgements of things. But Kant was also familiar with the alternative intellectual tradition of British empiricist thought, not merely with regard to the theory of knowledge as developed by John Locke and David Hume in particular, but also with respect to the influential reflections on 'moral sense', taste, aesthetic pleasure, and the nature of the sublime that were developed, amongst others, by Francis Hutcheson, the Earl of Shaftesbury, Hume, and Edmund Burke. It is, however, somewhat misleading to regard these respective rationalist-metaphysical and the empiricist-naturalistic strands of thought as rigidly or entirely divorced from one another since there were many thinkers who drew on both traditions or tried to mediate between their respective insights and emphases. Thus Mendelssohn was instrumental in spreading knowledge of recent British philosophy in the German lands and the ethical thought of Shaftesbury in particular was strongly indebted to the tradition of classical philosophy.

Kant had already responded to some of the central themes explored in the broadly empiricist tradition of aesthetic thought, with its characteristic emphasis upon the social, moral, and psychological aspects of aesthetic experience, and attempted to integrate its insights in the context of his own developing reflections in his *Observations on the Feeling of the Beautiful and the Sublime* of 1764. It is perhaps already worthy of note that in this early work, Kant's only published contribution to aesthetic questions apart from the *Critique of Judgement*, he is principally concerned with our aesthetic relation to nature in general and human nature in particular, rather than with art in the narrower sense of the word. And in his early lectures on philosophy Kant had also repeatedly touched upon the status of the aesthetic perception of 'the beautiful' as a fundamental question for the theory or 'critique' of taste as he sometimes described it. In the general culture of the time the German expression *Critik* (or *Kritik* as it is written today)—a term taken over from French during the seventeenth century—often signified what we would recently still understand by the term 'criticism' in a literary and artistic context: a reflective assessment of the intrinsic merits or aesthetic value of a specific work of art or corpus. It is true that it eventually became almost a motto of the German Enlightenment in a variety of different contexts, independently of Kant's subsequent work, and was explicitly applied to social practices and political and other institutions as well as texts and artistic products. In its original and most general sense the word simply indicated the art of distinguishing appropriately between the true and the false and furnishing a carefully considered judgement, based on justifying grounds, upon any contested subject matter whatsoever. Of itself the word signifies neither a positive nor a negative assessment of the object in question. When Kant uses the expression 'critique' in his own earlier (i.e. 'pre-critical') writings it denotes the systematic philosophical attempt to determine whether, as leading metaphysical thinkers of the time claimed, there are indeed rational principles involved in our response to or our perception of the beautiful and, if so, to explicate and clarify their distinctive character and status.

As his own dissatisfaction with rationalist metaphysics in all areas of its alleged competence continued to gather pace, partly under the explicit influence of Hume's objections to the idea of demonstrable but substantive *a priori* knowledge, Kant's entire conception of the task of philosophy and its appropriate methodology was also fundamentally transformed and this in turn eventually led Kant to a complete reformulation of all its central problems and questions in a new conceptual framework. Kant laboriously developed his new approach to the method of philosophy between 1770 and 1780, seeking to mediate the insights of the rationalist and empiricist traditions on an entirely new level that avoided the eclectic accommodations and problematic compromises of other contemporary thinkers.[1] This new approach—'transcendental' philosophy as a metaphysics of experience rather than a 'transcendent' metaphysics as presumed *a priori* knowledge of supersensible objects and realities—establishes the idea of 'critique' in a new and rigorous sense of a meta-theoretical enquiry into the very conditions of the possibility of objective knowledge and principled action. In the *Critique of Pure Reason* (first edition, 1780) and the *Critique of Practical Reason* (first edition, 1788) Kant undertakes to examine the range and competence of the human mind itself, to clarify its distinctive faculties or powers, and thus to elucidate and define our capacity for acquiring theoretical knowledge of the world of appearances, the only world that is cognitively available to us as finite rational beings, and for determining our wills in accordance with an objective moral law on the basis of a freedom which that law first properly reveals. The critiques are thus primarily dedicated to uncovering and exhibiting the *a priori* principles of the mind and the rational structure of experience and moral practice in general. When Kant came to elaborate the argument of the first *Critique* he no longer believed that it was possible to identify any rational principles governing the 'aesthetic' domain in the modern sense of the term. There Kant offers only a 'transcendental aesthetic' which lays out the *a priori* structure that precedes any experience of particular objects, namely the framework of space and time as the two 'pure forms of intuition'. These forms are 'aesthetic' in the literal and original sense of the Greek word from which our expression ultimately derives: they pertain to the sensibility or receptivity that is presupposed by any experience through the senses and thus make no specific reference to particular forms of perception, like that of the beautiful in nature or art, for example. Questions concerning the latter are naturally still of interest to Kant in an anthropological and psychological sense in the context of the empirical study of human beings in general, but they do not form a special part of the 'science' of philosophy understood in the strict sense as the systematic elucidation of the *a priori* concepts and principles governing experience or human conduct as such.

---

[1] For a differentiated account of the evolution of Kant's thought in relation to other contemporary thinkers and schools of thought and of the eventual emergence of his own distinctive project of transcendental philosophy, see Lewis White Beck, *Early German Philosophy. Kant and His Predecessors* (Bristol: Thoemmes Press, 1996) ch. 17, esp. 438–69.

By the time he came to compose the *Critique of Judgement*, nearly ten years after the publication of the first, Kant's thought had evolved considerably in this and in other related respects and he was able to take up once again, in a correspondingly transformed manner, some of his own earlier concerns with taste, beauty, and the sublime, and indeed with the 'teleological' perspective on nature as an apparent manifestation of order and design in relation to our own cognitive and practical purposes. Kant had come to believe that the activity of judging itself requires further clarification as a process of rendering the detail of our experience coherent and intelligible. In the first *Critique* to make a 'judgement' involved applying concepts to particular instances or rules and principles to particular cases. But he had concentrated there on the way in which we apply concepts or rules that we *already* possess, rather than on the way we come to form or discover relevant concepts. The application of concepts that subsume the objects that fall under them is described by Kant as a matter of 'determining' judgement, but he now explicitly distinguishes from this the process of 'reflective' judgement where only the 'particular' is given and the appropriate 'universal' must still be discovered for the former. In place of merely applying a law or principle to a range or group of empirical data, we may need to seek out and discern a previously unknown or unrecognized law or principle that can organize the relevant givens in an appropriate and systematic way. Here we must seek out the concepts under which the particulars in question may fall. If his first *Critique* had established to Kant's satisfaction that the general lawfulness and regularity of phenomena, their thorough causal interconnectedness, was a condition of the possibility of the kind of experience we actually enjoy and is already presupposed by the practice of scientific enquiry into nature, this general prerequisite is itself too general to define the specific content or procedures of a special science. The particular laws of a specific science are not merely directly derived from the lawfulness of nature in general. We also need in turn to comprehend the immense variety and complexity of the natural world within the broader perspective of an ever more comprehensive theory or system of all specific laws. The development of such a perspective requires the active and creative contribution of thought on our part but it could never proceed with any hope of success without the presupposition that nature as a whole, considered as the sum of all possible phenomena, will ultimately cohere with our own cognitive needs in pursuing its order and intelligibility. It is in this sense that Kant regards nature, the order of appearances, as conformable or appropriate to our own faculties, as 'purposive' for the latter, in investigating its character, and when this general accordance is verified in our actual investigations Kant claims that we also feel a particular kind of pleasure or satisfaction that reflects the universal constitution of the human mind in general. We 'rejoice', he says, to find that it is so purposive—as if 'by a lucky chance that favours us'. Kant insists that this does not license us to regard nature in a dogmatic sense as deliberately contrived, teleologically fashioned by God, for example, for our cognitive or other purposes, but it allows us to regard the world we inhabit as hospitable in principle to such ends.

This is one side of the 'concord' between our faculties and the world of experience we inhabit, and the one which Kant discusses first in the published 'Introduction' to the third *Critique*. The other side to which he turns first in the first division of the work concerns 'aesthetic' judgements in the broadest sense, though this too will involve, in a different way, the distinction between the 'determining' power of judgement that is directly oriented to objective knowledge of things and events and merely 'reflective' power of judgement that does not simply subsume its objects under given concepts. In the 'Introduction' Kant distinguishes, here following the philosophical tradition, between three basic faculties of the mind: the faculty of cognition in general, the faculty of feeling (of pleasure or its opposite), and the faculty of desire (or will). Kant now wonders, as he had not in the first *Critique*, whether this intermediate faculty of 'feeling' might not perform some kind of mediating role between the other two faculties and now asks whether there might not be a special *a priori* principle that governs this faculty in its own right and is common to all human beings as creatures that are simultaneously rational and sensitive in character. This thought provides Kant with the key to an analysis of aesthetic judgement that is not merely psychological or empirical in character but can claim a certain distinctive kind of rational status or quasi-objectivity. It is above all to this question that the first, and substantially longer, part of his book is devoted.

If at first sight the general structure of the book is clear, the specific order and internal organization of the topics discussed is frequently less than perspicuous. The skeletal table of contents which Kant himself supplied ('division of the entire work') is signally unhelpful in this respect and this edition is therefore prefaced by an analytical table of contents indicating the various subdivisions and numbered sections of the text. In general accordance with his systematic procedure in the other two critiques, Kant basically divides both parts of the third *Critique* into an 'Analytic' and a 'Dialectic'. The analytic of Part One is further divided into two books discussing the 'beautiful' and the 'sublime' respectively, although in fact a substantial part of Book Two is given over to a 'deduction' of aesthetic judgements and a discussion of 'genius' and the specific character of 'fine art'. As the name itself implies, the analytic undertakes to clarify the essential internal structure of the kind of judgement in question and elucidate its ultimate grounds. It might seem that Kant simply assumes from the start that there are indeed 'judgements' of a specifically aesthetic kind concerning the beautiful, but this impression results at least in part from the systematic mode of presentation which he chooses to deploy his basic arguments. He famously organizes his analysis in terms of four 'moments' of the judgement of taste, each of which is supposed to contribute something essential to the complete exposition of the problem, and this part of his text has probably received more comment and interpretation than any other section of the work. It may appear paradoxical that Kant should model his analysis on the four types or groups of cognitive and theoretical judgements that he presented in the first *Critique* since his first emphatic point is precisely that the 'aesthetic' judgement of taste is not a cognitive judgement at all. But it nonetheless *resembles* a judgement, and will reveal itself to be both more and less than a standard propositional judgement concerning the truth of an object or state of affairs, in so far as it raises a universal claim and potentially addresses all of us. Kant uses his fourfold categorization of cognitive judgements as a clue or guide to clarifying the peculiar character of aesthetic judgements and here calls them 'moments' to indicate that they present different aspects or dimensions of a single complex thematic and need to be gathered together in order to unfold the full character of such judgements. Each of the moments yields a partial 'definition' or 'elucidation' (*Erklärung*) that captures an essential feature of the latter. We work through the analysis in each case towards the resulting 'definitions' which have not inappropriately been described as the four 'paradoxes' of aesthetic judgement.[2]

The first moment tells us that taste is the capacity for judging something to be beautiful on the basis of an entirely 'disinterested' delight. This is one of the most celebrated claims of the third *Critique*, although in one form or another it had almost become a commonplace of aesthetic reflection in the later eighteenth century. Kant's distinctive contribution lies in the way he clarifies this idea in relation to specific kinds of interest and relates it in complex ways to the other essential features he attempts to disclose. Thus Kant distinguishes between the satisfaction or delight we take in the *agreeable* (the sensuously pleasurable or gratifying), in the *good* (the morally good as well as the instrumentally good or the useful) and in the *beautiful*. The agreeable is what contingently pleases us individually with respect to our own subjective feeling but raises no claim to general agreement on the part of others, the good claims universality on the basis of objective concepts of things or through objective rational principles springing from the moral law, while the beautiful enjoys a curious intermediate position in so far as, like the former, it is directly bound up with subjective feeling (the state of the percipient subject) but nonetheless appears, like the latter, to make a universal claim. Kant describes it as a 'free' delight because it is not enforced upon us either by the demands of immediate sensuous need or by other moral or pragmatic interests. The language of 'disinterestedness' is potentially misleading in so far as it might suggest a purely detached objectivity, but what Kant has in mind is a relation in which we are addressed by something in a unique way. Cognitive judgements about objects in general also have a sensuous dimension as objects of sensible perception, but the distinctively aesthetic character that belongs to the judgement of taste refers to the way in which the subject is affected and enhanced in its own feeling of life. The relation involved is not a neutral one, as in a standard cognitive judgement, but one that engages our entire subjective being as rational and sensitive creatures in a way that is both active and passive. Similarly Kant's emphasis upon our 'indifference' to the 'reality' of the object is a rather obscure formulation of the thought that we are here principally concerned with the 'showing' or emphatic appearing of the object as such in relation to

[2] Bernard Bosanquet, *A History of Aesthetic* (London: Allen & Unwin, 1904), 263.

ourselves, but without any direct instrumental or cognitive interest. In an aesthetic respect we thus enjoy a special kind of disinterested interest in the object in so far as it affects us in a certain way, and thus in *dwelling* upon it in its own right.

The following moments supplement and deepen this initial orientation, seeking out and exposing the hidden grounds, conditions, and ramifications of aesthetic judgement. The second moment tells us that the beautiful pleases 'universally but without a concept'. The judgement of beauty presumes but cannot demand, on grounds of proof, universal agreement since it is not directly based on determinate concepts at all. Kant argues that the non-demonstrable but nonetheless binding claim involved here can only be grounded in a 'free play' of our universally shared faculties of understanding and imagination. This refers to our powers of cognition 'in general' which are here suspended, as it were, and liberated from the need to terminate in a determinate judgement or subsumption of the individual content of experience under concepts. The third moment introduces the crucial notion of a 'purposiveness that is perceived without any representation of purpose' where Kant emphasizes the perception of the form, rather than the matter, of the object as giving rise to our specific pleasure independently of any judgement of the 'perfection' or fitness of the thing to any presumed end or applied concept, although he here also distinguishes and acknowledges cases of 'dependent beauty' as well as the 'free beauty' which properly characterizes pure judgements of taste. The fourth moment, finally, asserts the 'necessity' of aesthetic judgements and appeals to the idea of a 'common sense' underlying our capacity to communicate aesthetic judgements. But the necessity that others agree with our judgements remains an exemplary one that can only be expected and never demanded of others, unlike the universal acknowledgement required by theoretical or practical principles.

It is characteristic of the modernity of Kant's approach that he should turn directly from the beautiful to a striking consideration of the problem of the 'sublime' and assign the latter a distinctive and complementary importance of its own alongside the more traditional classical emphasis upon beautiful 'form'. His approach is not traditionally 'theological' in so far as he essentially treats the sublime in relation to the exercise of our own powers or faculties of mind, as testifying to our own autonomy, rather than as a direct expression of divine power for example. There are certain objects, and Kant here concentrates principally on objects of nature, which strongly engage the imagination and thereby lead our reason to entertain and reflect upon 'ideas' that actually surpass the capacities of imaginative visualization. Kant's examples of the sublime are largely standard ones, like the vastness of the heavens or the overwhelming violence of natural phenomena, sights which excite thoughts of infinite magnitude and infinite power (the mathematical and the dynamical sublime as Kant describes them). Our response to such manifestations of nature suffers a characteristic reversal, however, which ultimately throws us back upon ourselves through the conspicuous contrast between our physical frailty and insignificance considered as merely natural beings in the totality of the cosmos and our moral calling or vocation (a perspective which Kant expressed with exemplary pathos in the famous peroration that concludes the second *Critique*). Although we immediately tend to ascribe the sublime to nature itself, it is ultimately the pre-eminence of the power of reason, in its practical dimension, which merits the predicate of sublimity. For in the last analysis it is reason and the idea of humanity in us which surpasses the capacity of imagination fully to capture or represent in sensible terms the full significance of our own 'place' in the world as the only being that can lend it any ultimate sense. Thus in Kant it is the moral law, the 'fact of reason', that is the principal instance of the sublime and which for him characteristically attracts the religious rhetoric of 'awful' elevation and ultimate inscrutability (a metaphorics characteristic of the critical philosophy in general but particularly evident in the third *Critique*).

Although it has generally been observed that Kant's concern with aesthetic judgement is primarily directed towards natural beauty, and his examples usually drawn from natural phenomena, it is by no means the case that he simply neglects 'art' in the sense of expressly fabricated products with aesthetic intent. In fact Kant assigns a distinctive role to art that cannot be discharged by the experience of natural beauty (although it is ultimately bound up with the latter in a complex and indirect manner) and includes an extensive discussion of the character of 'fine art', as distinct from craft, towards the end of Book Two. One of the most remarkable aspects of Kant's thought in this regard is the degree to which he is capable of opening up such fecund lines of enquiry and reflection for succeeding thinkers and artists despite the fact that his own first-hand acquaintance with, and aesthetic response to, significant art of the recent or distant past, or of his contemporary world, was notoriously limited.[3] Some of Kant's most productive and influential observations are precisely to be found in this section of the *Critique* where he broaches the question of 'genius' and what he calls 'aesthetic ideas'. With his own non-rationalistic insistence that there are no 'rules' for taste that could be formulated as cognitive judgements, and that the beautiful cannot be defined in determinate conceptual terms, Kant is only drawing the appropriate conclusion when he here goes on to claim that the individual who 'makes' significant works of art through the power of genius also 'draws forth' something in a hitherto unanticipated and unparalleled way. Such exemplary creations give rise to a new measure or standard that cannot simply be reproduced or imitated by others on the basis of acquired rules or skills, however diligently they may study their predecessors, although they can furnish models that encourage fresh creativity in turn.

In the first *Critique* Kant had claimed that there are concepts of reason which inevitably transcend empirical experience and to which no object of the senses could ever be adequate. In the third *Critique* he introduces the parallel case of sensuous representations produced through the imagination in the form of images or symbols that evoke the strictly unrepresentable without any determinate concept being able to capture or exhaust their full significance. He describes these as 'aesthetic ideas' and they are a distinctive contribution of art as such. Kant's condensed and highly suggestive discussion has much of interest to say about signs, symbolism, and the 'rendering of ideas in sensuous form' and perhaps also reveals the degree to which he was particularly responsive to certain baroque conceptions of allegorical and figurative expression that were already coming to appear outmoded in his own time. In this connection Kant also provides a tentative sketch of a 'division' of the several arts that was not without influence on the more ambitious and detailed 'systems' of the art

---

[3] Adorno provocatively remarked that Hegel and Kant 'were, to put it bluntly, the last who were capable of writing a major aesthetics without understanding anything about art'. Adorno, *Ästhetische Theorie* (Frankfurt: Suhrkamp, 1970), 495. There is a specific discussion of Kant's knowledge of particular arts and works of art in the classical older biography by Karl Vorländer, *Immanuel Kant. Der Mann und das Werk* (1924), 3rd edn. (Wiesbaden: Marix Verlag, 2004), 370–405.

forms that would subsequently be offered by Hegel, Schelling, and Schopenhauer.

In the shorter second part of the *Critique* Kant turns directly to the problem of teleology, or 'design' as it had generally been described in British philosophy, and the associated themes he had already adumbrated in the 'Introduction' to the text. This part of the work has generally attracted far less interest and comment, at least since the beginning of the nineteenth century, than the part devoted to aesthetic judgement and related topics. If Kant had attempted to explain the judgement of taste in terms of the perception of form, or 'purposiveness without purpose' or 'subjective' purpose oriented to the play of our faculties independent of any theoretical cognitive interest, he now addresses the problem of 'objective' purposiveness, of a purposiveness with a purpose, or that design that we may be tempted to ascribe to certain objects of nature and perhaps to nature as a whole. It is immediately evident that this entire question is fraught with fundamental implications for metaphysical philosophy in general and traditional theology and religious thought in particular. Kant starts by discussing the case where we are most likely to entertain teleological considerations concerning the intrinsic character and possibility of certain kinds of natural things, namely the organism as the primary datum of biology. He thinks that we do have to consider organism in terms of ends if we examine the typical processes of formation, growth, and reproduction that characterize such things: the apparent self-organization of the object in maintaining its structure and preserving its own existence through time. Although the words 'organism' and 'organization' are ultimately related to an ancient Greek word originally denoting a 'tool' or 'implement', the natural forms in question exhibit, like works of art in this respect, a different and more internal kind of purposiveness and appear to exist for their own sake, and that of their species, whereas an instrument serves something entirely beyond and independent of itself. An organism is a whole which results from the functioning of the parts, while the parts in turn depend on the functioning of the whole. Kant famously claims that we cannot imagine 'a Newton' who will explain a simple blade of grass on purely mechanical principles of cause and effect like those governing the material and inorganic world. Yet he also insists that we can only make use of such ideas in a regulative or heuristic fashion in relation to our ongoing scientific investigation of nature. Kant argues that although we must always seek to push causal explanation of things as far as we possibly can, we cannot altogether forgo the idea of internal self-organization on the part of living things. As in his other *Critiques* and in the first part of the present one, Kant attempts to negotiate the apparent contradictions between these two perspectives through a discussion of the relevant 'dialectic' and the 'antinomies' involved.

But this understandable propensity to interpret certain things of nature in teleological terms may also be extrapolated to things as a whole and combined with an appeal to God as the divine ground and creator of the world. In this connection once again Kant returns to the theological 'argument from design' that he had already criticized, together with the other traditional arguments for the existence of God, in the *Critique of Pure Reason*. Many of the considerations he marshals here are reminiscent of Hume's equally critical observations regarding the traditional claims of natural theology in so far as the latter attempts to establish a relevant theistic conception of God on the basis of the purposiveness of nature both in itself and in relation to human needs and requirements. In short Kant argues that our ideas of God in this respect are inevitably anthropomorphic in character and are entirely insufficient to establish the desired conclusion concerning an all-wise or all-powerful divine being anyway. Many things effectively serve human ends, although we cannot claim that they were objectively created to do so, but it is equally obvious that many features of the world frustrate our purposes as well. The only non-dogmatic way that we can make sense of the concept of God as author of the world, as a source of design, is as an 'idea of reason' which orients our own search for system and coherence in the world of experience. And Kant thinks that the concept of God as first cause or origin of things, as the alleged conclusion of a metaphysical argument, is not necessary to the fundamentally 'practical' (moral) perspective that should govern our reflection on 'religious' questions. The only finite being that could be an absolute 'end' of creation is the human being, considered not merely as a link in the chain of natural causality but as a moral being capable of grasping itself as such. This is Kant's moral theology for which we already possess within our own self-conception the immanent source of the idea of God in a practical respect and which thus requires no further external 'evidences' of nature or any such additional support. The conclusions of the third *Critique* return us to the basic convictions already expressed in Kant's

practical and theoretical philosophy as articulated in the first two
Critiques. We must content ourselves with the thought that nature
reveals itself as at least adapted to our theoretical desire to know it
and above all to the potential practical realization of what the moral
consciousness enjoins upon us.

Ever since its publication the third *Critique* has exercised a powerful
influence, in direct and often indirect and subterranean ways, upon
subsequent continental and Anglo-American thought, and indeed,
despite its technical difficulty, upon artistic practice and reflection
far beyond the confines of philosophy in the narrower professional
sense. It is understandable that the initial philosophical reception of
the work concentrated largely on its relation to the rest of Kant's
mature thought and on the question whether, as its author believed,
it successfully brought the structure of the critical philosophy to systematic completion. For those like Hegel and Schelling, who attempted
to resolve what they saw as the persisting but avoidable aporias of
that philosophy and its apparently dualistic implications, the complex
argument of the third *Critique* seemed to open up especially fruitful
lines of enquiry. In different ways they both strove to develop a
dynamic non-reductionistic account of nature on the basis of Kant's
analysis of teleology and to articulate a comprehensive philosophy of
art in a richer and more historically sensitive manner than Kant himself, acknowledging but attempting to mitigate his sharp contrast
between the beautiful and the sublime. Schelling was particularly
influenced by Kant's account of the relation between art and genius,
while Hegel characteristically emphasized the capacity of art to
symbolize and embody spiritual content in a distinctive manner.

    At the same time, writers like Friedrich Schiller and Johann Wolfgang
von Goethe likewise saw the third *Critique* as a means of mediating
the felt opposition between freedom and nature within the experience
of the human subject itself. Schiller's *Letters on the Aesthetic Education
of Man* of 1795 envisaged the aesthetic dimension as potentially healing
the rift between inner and outer nature and the fragmented character
of the human faculties accentuated under modern conditions of the
radical division of labour and the concomitant specialization of human
life. In his reflections on tragedy Schiller also explored Kantian ideas
concerning the relation between morality and the sublime. Although
Goethe had precious little time for the technicalities of the critical

philosophy, and was wary of the traditional religious implications of some of Kant's later work as he saw it, he responded throughout his literary and scientific work to the idea of an inexhaustible fullness of experience that could never be rendered wholly transparent to human understanding, thus retaining much of the characteristic pathos and modesty of Kant's attitude to nature and human existence.

Schopenhauer derided the systematic ambitions of his idealist predecessors and contemporaries like Hegel and Schelling, and especially their tortuous efforts to redeem the true content of Christianity in philosophical form, and claimed to return in many ways to the original Kantian perspective. But the older historians of philosophy were not entirely unjustified in regarding Schopenhauer's thought as an important coda to the classical idealist tradition that had more in common with the latter than he either realized or acknowledged. By combining Platonic and Kantian strands of thought he developed the idea of aesthetic disinterestedness in conjunction with a pessimistic moral philosophy that emphasized freedom from the bondage to desire, and ascribed an almost redemptive role to the aesthetic in overcoming a purely calculative and instrumental attitude to the world in general. It was originally through the work of Schopenhauer that a number of transformed Kantian motifs found their way into the thought of the early Nietzsche in particular.

But by the middle of the nineteenth century the continuing influence of Kant's work was more commonly registered in an expressly anti-metaphysical mode of thought that interpreted his approach to aesthetic questions in naturalistic terms by appeal to the data of psychology and physiology. Thinkers such as Johann Friedrich Herbart, followed by Hermann Helmholtz and Wilhelm Wundt, attempted to recover Kant's apparent emphasis upon the autonomy of aesthetic experience and explored the subjective conditions and structures of perception that made judgements of form possible in the first place. These approaches initially helped to encourage broadly 'formalist' interpretations of aesthetic experience that ignored or abstracted from the social-historical conditions and specificity of the categories through which we make sense of both nature and the cultural world. The story of Kantian influence on aesthetics is subsequently deepened and complicated later in the century with the emergence of explicitly 'neo-Kantian' schools, which opposed the complete naturalization of human experience and sought to reassert Kant's interest in discerning distinctive principles governing different spheres of cognition, action, and aesthetic feeling and perception. In this context Hermann Cohen in particular developed an elaborate threefold system that sought to recapture the authentic orientation of the critical philosophy. In fact neo-Kantian philosophy of the late nineteenth and early twentieth centuries also entered into a complex symbiosis with the hermeneutical approach of thinkers such as Wilhelm Dilthey and Georg Simmel, who drew freely on Kant and German idealism in an attempt to transcend the ahistorical bias of positivistic philosophy pre-eminently oriented to the explanatory method of the natural sciences. A historicized Kantian perspective had already inspired important early theorists of art history like Heinrich Wölfflin, who tried to explain how specific and shared structures mediated our understanding of artistic form and expression in different epochs, but it was probably through Ernst Cassirer that freely developed Kantian themes came to exercise their most significant influence on early modern art history and theory in the work of Erwin Panofsky and the Warburg School.

Despite its emphatic repudiation of the pure aesthetic standpoint of the individual feeling subject as the appropriate perspective for understanding the phenomenon of art, the ontological hermeneutics pioneered by Martin Heidegger and developed by Hans-Georg Gadamer can nonetheless, despite immediate appearances, be plausibly read as a creative 'repetition' of central themes of Kant's third *Critique*. Heidegger would liberate Kant's insights from his narrow interpretation of cognition in terms of judgement and open up the conception of attuned faculties by reference to his own concept of hermeneutic 'understanding' as a concrete orientation already given along with the structure of our being-in-the-world as the shared field of our theoretical, instrumental, and practical involvements.

But the promising and problematic heritage of Kant's reflections on the aesthetic relations of both art and nature is probably most explicitly addressed in the aesthetic theory which Theodor Adorno developed in critical and productive counterpoint with Hegel and the dialectical tradition in general. Adorno both returns the thematic of natural beauty to a central place in relation to the claims of art and refuses a purely formalist and non-cognitivist reading of Kant's contribution without subordinating the aesthetic dimension in an intellectualist manner to the 'higher' truth of philosophical conceptualization. In a highly differentiated way Adorno thus returns us to some of the earliest questions of Kant's immediate successors concerning the aesthetic as a possible intimation of an uncoerced reconciliation between reason and nature in the human subject that freely acknowledges its ineliminable dependence upon what it has not itself created or fully constituted and must therefore thankfully receive.

As far as much of the twentieth century Anglophone reception of Kant is concerned, the emphasis lay for a long time on his contributions to the theory of knowledge and, to a lesser extent, on his moral philosophy. Within analytical aesthetics Kant's treatment of pure aesthetic judgements has naturally been much discussed, but until fairly recent times the full wealth, range, and implications of Kant's interest in the aesthetic dimension of experience were somewhat neglected by comparison. In this regard there has been a veritable renaissance in the English-language literature on Kant which has come increasingly to focus once again upon the place of the third *Critique* in the economy of his thought as a whole. Much of the current discussion addresses the emancipatory self-understanding of the critical system with specific reference to Kant's related reflections on history, politics, and religion. The *Critique of Judgement* has perhaps never seemed a more seminal text and indispensable point of reference than it does today.

NOTE ON THE TEXT,
TRANSLATION, AND REVISION

JAMES CREED MEREDITH's translation of Kant's *Critique of Judgement*, the second complete English version of the text to appear, was originally published in two volumes, in 1911 and 1928 respectively, with extensive introductory essays, accompanying notes, and an analytical index for each volume. The translation was reissued in a single volume, without the introductory matter and notes, in 1952. Like all subsequent translators, Meredith based his edition on the text presented in the standard German edition of Kant's writings, published under the aegis of the Prussian Academy of Sciences (the 'Academy Edition'). The *Critique of Judgement* was edited by Wilhelm Windelband and first appeared in 1908 in volume V (text: pp. 165–485; apparatus: pp. 512–44). Windelband took Kant's second edition (1793) as the basis for the Academy edition and indicated variants and disputed textual issues in his apparatus. The marginal pagination provided in Meredith's text refers to that of the Academy Edition, which is also generally reproduced in other translations and editions of Kant's writings.

The present edition of Meredith's translation has been supplemented by a new translation of Kant's substantial 'First Introduction' which, it seems, Kant had originally intended for the third *Critique*, but eventually decided to replace with the shorter and less complex text that was actually published as the 'Introduction' to the work. The marginal pagination in the translation of the 'First Introduction' refers to that of the text published in volume XX of the Academy Edition (pp. 195–251) and edited by Gerhard Lehmann.

Meredith's translation has been revised in a number of respects in accordance with a more contemporary literary style and with certain current terminological conventions in the field of Kant studies in English. The changes in question are of broadly two kinds. First, certain words and expressions, turns of phrase, and orthographic features that were not particularly unusual at the beginning of the last century but are now antiquated or obsolete have been adapted or replaced in the light of contemporary usage and vocabulary (thus terms like 'metaphysic', 'fancy', or 'affection' have been replaced by 'metaphysics', 'fantasy', and 'affect'). Secondly, a number of specific changes have been introduced with regard to certain important technical terms deployed throughout the text: (i) Meredith's translation of Kant's *beurteilen* and *Beurteilung* as 'estimate' or 'estimation' has been replaced by 'judge' and 'judging' respectively in order to retain the connection with the terms denoting a specific 'judgement' of whatever kind (*Urteil*) and the faculty or power of judgement in general (*Urteilskraft*). When the term 'judgement' is not qualified by the definite or indefinite article in the text it translates the latter sense of the word. If there is any danger of ambiguity, the relevant meaning has been spelt out as the 'power of judgement'; (ii) Where 'estimate' or 'estimation' is retained in the text, as in the second book of Part One, it translates Kant's use of *schätzen* and *Schätzung*; (iii) Meredith's old term 'determinant judgement' for Kant's *bestimmende Urteilskraft* has been replaced by the more current 'determining judgement'; (iv) Meredith's capitalization of 'Object' to translate Kant's *Objekt*, as distinct from 'object' to translate *Gegenstand*, has been dropped since, in this text, Kant does not consistently deploy these two terms in significantly distinct senses; (v) Lastly, Meredith's use of 'final' and 'finality' to translate Kant's terms *zweckmäßig* and *Zweckmäßigkeit* has been replaced throughout with the now standard terms 'purposive' and 'purposiveness' respectively. There is nothing intrinsically wrong with 'final' and 'finality', terms commonly used in philosophical literature at the end of the nineteenth and the beginning of the twentieth centuries, especially with reference to Kant and German Idealism, but they have largely fallen into desuetude in modern philosophy and may therefore easily mislead a contemporary reader. It is also preferable, generally speaking, to render one semantic field (in this case *Zweck* and its cognate forms) with as few different expressions in the translation as possible. No readable version of Kant is able to manage without deploying both 'end' and 'purpose', according to context, as the most appropriate rendering of *Zweck* (and the same is true for *Erkenntnis*, which must be rendered as 'knowledge' or 'cognition' according to context). When the adjective 'final' is retained in the text it serves to translate Kant's *Endursache* or 'final cause'. It should be noted that the term 'finality' will frequently be encountered in a large body of the secondary literature on Kant and German Idealism in English composed before fairly recent times. It is worth remembering that Meredith's translation pre-dated Norman Kemp Smith's

classic translation of the *Critique of Pure Reason* of 1929, a version
which strongly influenced the rendering of Kant's terminology that
subsequently became standard in English. A detailed bilingual glossary
of Kant's most important terms and otherwise significant and characteristic vocabulary has been provided in the present edition. The
German terms are given here in their modern forms, which sometimes
diverge slightly from the orthography of Kant's time.

Apart from the aforementioned cases, intervention in Meredith's
text has been kept to a minimum in order to preserve the general
fluency and literary quality of his version. There is little point in
revising an old translation if the cumulative effect of a host of alter-
ations effectively distorts its rhetorical tone and drastically alters its
stylistic physiognomy as a whole. If we really find an earlier translation
not so much inevitably 'dated' in certain respects as intrinsically inadequate (through technical inaccuracy, stylistic infelicity, or syntactical
clumsiness), we should take Hamlet's advice to the players and 'reform
it altogether' and therefore undertake an entirely new translation.
Although there is probably no such thing, for good hermeneutic reasons, as a 'definitive' translation of any literary or philosophical text
of note, any more than there are definitive and unchangeable perform-
ances of great works of art, there can certainly be 'exemplary' ones, to
borrow Kant's expression, that set new standards and encourage further exploration of a challenging and productive text. Meredith's
version is a remarkably readable and often eloquent version of a work
that even its first English-language translator described as 'repulsive'
in style.[1] The translation can especially be recommended for those who
would like to read the work straight through with (arduous) enjoyment as a classic of philosophical literature in its own right in spite of
its forbidding technical complexity. Meredith admirably communicates the rhetorical pathos of the text and captures the vividness of
Kant's metaphors in a way that can easily escape more allegedly 'literal'
translations. On those occasions where Meredith did introduce an
image or metaphor that is not strictly represented in the original,
although such cases usually accord closely with the spirit and tone of
Kant's writing, the text has been adapted to reflect the German more
closely. It should also be mentioned that Meredith, like Kemp Smith

---

[1] See Immanuel Kant, *Critique of Judgement*, trans. J. H. Bernard (Mineola, NY: Dover,
2005) (reprint of the 1914 edition), p. x.

after him, felt free to rearticulate and break up some of Kant's more tortuous and serpentine sentences in the interest of clarity, elegance, and readability. This is advisable, and often necessary, for a grammatically gendered language with a different semantic structure from English and serves to clarify the reference of potentially ambiguous pronouns in complex periods.

A similar approach has been followed with regard to my translation of the 'First Introduction' which is one of the densest and thorniest of Kant's texts. The terminology is consistent with that of the revised Meredith text of the third *Critique* and a broadly similar style has also been attempted throughout. The primary texts have been kept entirely free of editorial insertions, brackets or footnotes to facilitate continuous reading and all numbered footnotes in the text are Kant's own.

The explanatory notes that have been supplied serve principally to clarify various references and allusions on Kant's part and are indicated with an asterisk at appropriate points in the main text. Kant employed a variety of conventions for marking emphasis in his texts, especially enlarged lettering and spaced print. The translation reflects such emphasis in the original text by the use of capitalization or italics.

SELECT BIBLIOGRAPHY

The following is an extensive bibliography of secondary literature in English on the interpretation, context, and reception of Kant's third *Critique* (excluding individual articles in books and journals, but including translations, international collections, and special journal issues dedicated to the subject). For detailed bibliographies of the literature, including foreign language publications, the reader might consult the works listed by Henry Allison, Paul Guyer, Angelica Nuzzo, and John Zammito.

General Discussions of Kant's Life and Thought

Ameriks, Karl, *Interpreting Kant's Critiques* (Oxford: Clarendon Press, 2003).

Cassirer, Ernst, *Kant's Life and Work* (New Haven and London: Yale University Press, 1981).

Goldmann, Lucien, *Immanuel Kant* (London: NLB, 1971).

Guyer, Paul, *Kant* (London: Routledge, 2006).

Höffe, Otfried, *Kant* (Albany, NY: State University of New York Press, 1994).

Kuehn, Manfred, *Kant: A Biography* (Cambridge: Cambridge University Press, 2001).

Lindsay, A. D., *Kant* (London: Ernest Benn, 1934).

Introductions to Part One of the Third Critique

Burnham, Douglas, *An Introduction to Kant's Critique of Judgement* (Edinburgh: Edinburgh University Press, 2000).

Kemal, Salim, *Kant's Aesthetic Theory: An Introduction* (London: Macmillan, 1992).

Wetzel, Christian Helmut, *An Introduction to Kant's Aesthetics: Core Concepts and Problems* (Oxford: Blackwell, 2005).

Discussions of All or Part of the Third Critique

Allison, Henry, *Kant's Theory of Taste: A Reading of the 'Critique of Aesthetic Judgment'* (Cambridge: Cambridge University Press, 2001).

Baldacchino, Lewis, *A Study in Kant's Metaphysics of Aesthetic Experience—Reason and Feeling* (Lewiston, NY: Edwin Mellen Press, 1992).

Cohen, Ted, and Guyer, Paul (eds.), *Essays in Kant's Aesthetics* (Chicago: Chicago University Press, 1982).

Coleman, Francis, *The Harmony of Reason: A Study in Kant's Aesthetics* (Pittsburgh: University of Pittsburgh Press, 1974).

Crawford, D. W., *Kant's Aesthetic Theory* (Albany, NY: State University of New York Press, 1974).

Crowther, Paul, *The Kantian Sublime* (Oxford: Clarendon Press, 1989).

Funke, G. (ed.), *Akten des Siebenten Internationalen Kant Kongresses 1990*, 2 vols. (Bonn and Berlin: Bouvier, 1991).

Gibbons, Sarah, *Kant's Theory of Imagination: Bridging Gaps in Judgment and Experience* (Oxford: Clarendon Press, 1994).

Ginsborg, Hanna, *The Role of Taste in Kant's Theory of Cognition* (New York: Garland, 1990).

Guyer, Paul, *Kant and the Experience of Freedom: Essays on Aesthetics and Morality* (Cambridge: Cambridge University Press, 1993).

——*Kant and the Claims of Taste* (Cambridge: Cambridge University Press, 1997).

——(ed.), *Kant's Critique of the Power of Judgment. Critical Essays* (Lantham, Md.; Oxford: Rowman & Littlefield, 2003).

Harper, Alfred, *Essays on Kant's Third Critique* (London: Mekler & Deahl, 1989).

Henrich, Dieter, *Aesthetic Judgment and the Moral Image of the World: Studies in Kant* (Stanford, Calif.: Stanford University Press, 1992).

Kemal, Salim, *Kant and Fine Art: An Essay on Kant and Philosophy of Fine Art and Culture* (Oxford: Clarendon Press, 1986).

Kirwan, James, *The Aesthetic in Kant: A Critique* (London: Continuum, 2004).

Kukla, Rebecca (ed.), *Aesthetics and Cognition in Kant's Critical Philosophy* (Cambridge: Cambridge University Press, 2006).

McClosky, Mary A., *Kant's Aesthetics* (Albany, NY: State University of New York Press, 1987).

McFarland, John, *Kant's Concept of Teleology* (Edinburgh: University of Edinburgh Press, 1970).

McLaughlin, Peter, *Kant's Critique of Teleology in Biological Explanation: Antinomy and Teleology* (Lewiston, NY: Edwin Mellen Press, 1990).

Macmillan, R. A. C., *The Crowning Phase of the Critical Philosophy. A Study in Kant's Critique of Judgment* (London: Macmillan, 1912; repr. New York: Garland, 1976).

Meerebote, R., and Hudson, R. (eds.), *Kant's Aesthetics* (Atascadero, Calif.: Ridgeview Publishing Company, 1991).

Nuzzo, Angelica, *Kant and the Unity of Reason* (Indiana: Purdue University Press, 2005).

Parret, Hermann (ed.), *Kants Ästhetik, Kant's Aesthetics, L'Ésthetique de Kant* (Berlin and New York: de Gruyter, 1998).

Robinson, Hoke (ed.), *System and Teleology in Kant's Critique of Judgment* (*Southern Journal of Philosophy* 30 [Supplement], Memphis State University, 1992).

Rogerson, Kenneth, *Kant's Aesthetics: the Roles of Form and Expression* (Lantham, Md.: University Press of America, 1986).

Schaper, Eva, *Studies in Kant's Aesthetics* (Edinburgh: Edinburgh University Press, 1979).

Uehling, Theodore, *The Notion of Form in Kant's Critique of Aesthetic Judgment* (The Hague: Mouton, 1971).

Zumbach, C., *The Transcendent Science: Kant's Conception of Biological Methodology* (The Hague: Nijhoff, 1984).

Historical Context and Earlier Reception of the Third Critique

Ameriks, Karl, *The Cambridge Companion to German Idealism* (Cambridge: Cambridge University Press, 2000).

Beck, Lewis White, *Early German Philosophy: Kant and His Predecessors* (Bristol: Thoemmes Press, 1996).

Beiser, Frederick C., *German Idealism. The Struggle against Subjectivism 1781–1801* (Cambridge, Mass.: Harvard University Press, 2002).

Bernstein, Jay (ed.), *Classic and Romantic German Aesthetics* (Cambridge: Cambridge University Press, 2003).

Cassirer, Ernst, *Rousseau, Kant and Goethe* (Princeton: Princeton University Press, 1945).

Caygill, Howard, *The Art of Judgement* (Oxford: Basil Blackwell, 1989).

Dickie, George, *The Century of Taste: The Philosophical Odyssey of Taste in the Eighteenth Century* (New York and Oxford: Oxford University Press, 1996).

Henrich, Dieter, *Between Kant and Hegel: Lectures on German Idealism* (Cambridge, Mass.: Harvard University Press, 2003).

Huhn, Tom, *Imitation and Society. The Persistence of Mimesis in the Aesthetics of Burke, Hogarth and Kant* (Pennsylvania: Pennsylvania University Press, 2006).

Saville, Anthony, *Aesthetic Reconstructions: The Seminal Writings of Lessing, Kant and Schiller* (Oxford: Blackwell, 1987).

Sedgwick, Sally (ed.), *The Reception of Kant's Critical Philosophy: Fichte, Schelling, Hegel* (Cambridge: Cambridge University Press, 2000).

Zammito, John H., *The Genesis of Kant's Critique of Judgment* (Chicago: University of Chicago Press, 1992).

Legacy and Later Reception of the Third Critique

Banham, Gary, *Kant and the Ends of Aesthetics* (New York: Macmillan, 2000).

Bernstein, Jay, *The Fate of Art. Aesthetic Alienation from Kant to Derrida and Adorno* (Cambridge: Polity Press, 1992).

Bowie, Andrew, *Aesthetics and Subjectivity from Kant to Nietzsche* (Manchester: Manchester University Press, 1990).

—— *From Romanticism to Critical Theory: The Philosophy of German Literary Theory* (London: Routledge, 1997).

Budd, Malcolm, *The Aesthetic Appreciation of Nature: Essays on the Aesthetics of Nature* (Oxford: Clarendon Press, 2002).

Cheetham, Mark, *Kant, Art and Art History: Moments of Discipline* (Cambridge: Cambridge University Press, 2001).

Courtine, Jean-François, et al., *Of the Sublime: Presence in Question* (Albany, NY: State University of New York Press, 1995).

De Duve, Thierry, *Kant after Duchamps* (Cambridge, Mass.: MIT Press, 1996).

Derrida, Jacques, *The Truth in Painting* (Chicago and London: University of Chicago Press, 1987).

Ferretti, Silvia, *Cassirer, Panofsky, and Warburg: Symbol, Art, and History* (New Haven: Yale University Press, 1989).

Gasché, Rudolf, *The Idea of Form: Rethinking Kant's Aesthetics* (Stanford, Calif.: Stanford University Press, 2003).

Horrowitz, Gregg M., *Sustaining Loss. Art and Mournful Life* (Stanford, Calif.: Stanford University Press, 2001).

Kirwan, James, *Sublimity: The Non-Rational and the Irrational in the History of Aesthetics* (London: Routledge, 2005).

Lyotard, Jean-François, *Lectures on the Analytic of the Sublime* (Stanford, Calif.: Stanford University Press, 1994).

Makreel, Rudolf A., *Imagination and Interpretation in Kant. The Hermeneutical Import of the Critique of Judgment* (Chicago: Chicago University Press, 1990).

Mothersill, Mary, *Beauty Restored* (Oxford: Clarendon Press, 1984).

Myskja, Børn K., *The Sublime in Kant and Beckett* (Berlin: Walter de Gruyter, 2002).

Podro, Michael, *The Manifold in Perception: Theories of Art from Kant to Hildebrand* (Oxford: Clarendon Press, 1972).

Saville, Anthony, *Kantian Aesthetics Pursued* (Edinburgh: Edinburgh University Press, 1993).

Schaeffer, Jean-Marie, *Art of the Modern Age: Philosophy of Art from Kant to Heidegger* (Princeton: Princeton University Press, 2000).

Further Reading in Oxford World's Classics

Berkeley, George, *Principles of Human Knowledge and Three Dialogues*, ed. Howard Robinson.

Descartes, René, *A Discourse on the Method*, trans. Ian Maclean.

Hume, David, *An Enquiry concerning Human Understanding*, ed. Peter Millican.

A CHRONOLOGY OF IMMANUEL KANT

1724   Immanuel Kant born in Königsberg on 22 April.

1732   Birth of Haydn.

1732–40 Attends the pietistic Friedrichskollegium.

1737   Death of Kant's mother.

1740   Death of Frederick William II and accession of Frederick II ('Frederick the Great').

1740–6 Enrols at the University of Königsberg and studies mathematics, natural science and theology.

1746   Death of Kant's father; he presents *Thoughts on the Estimation of Living Forces* at the University (published in 1747).

1747–54 Employed as a private tutor for families in the environs of Königsberg.

1749   Birth of Goethe.

1755   Publishes *Universal Natural History and Theory of the Heavens*; obtains his Doctoral Degree with the Dissertation *On Fire*.

1756   Publishes three essays on the Lisbon earthquake, the *Physical Monadology*, and *New Observations on the Theory of the Winds*; unsuccessfully applies for a professorship in logic and metaphysics at the University of Königsberg; birth of Mozart.

1759   Birth of Schiller.

1762   Publishes *The False Subtlety of the Four Syllogistic Figures* and *The Only Possible Basis for a Demonstration of the Existence of God*. Rousseau publishes *Émile* and *The Social Contract*; birth of Fichte.

1763   Publishes *An Attempt to Introduce the Concept of Negative Quantities into Philosophy*.

1764   Declines offer of Professorship of Poetry; publishes *Observations on the Feeling of the Beautiful and the Sublime* and the *Enquiry Concerning the Distinctness of the Principles of Natural Theology and Morals*.

1765   Posthumous publication of Leibniz's *New Essays on the Human Understanding*.

1766   Publishes *Dreams of a Ghost-Seer*.

1768   Publishes *On the Ultimate Ground of the Differences of Direction in Space*.

1769   Declines offer of Professorship in Erlangen.

1770   Declines offer of Professorship in Jena; appointed Professor of Logic and Metaphysics in Königsberg; publishes the Dissertation *On the Forms and Principles of the Sensible and the Intelligible World*; births of Hegel and Beethoven.

1770–80 The so-called 'silent decade' during which Kant elaborates the first *Critique*.

1775   Birth of Schelling.

1776   Death of Hume; the American 'Declaration of Independence' and the 'Declaration of the Rights of Man'.

1778   Declines offer of Professorship in Halle; deaths of Rousseau and Voltaire.

1781   Publishes the *Critique of Pure Reason* and dedicates the book to Karl von Zedlitz, Prussian Minister of Education; death of Lessing.

1783   Publishes *Prolegomena to Any Future Metaphysics*. Kant buys a house.

1784   Publishes *Idea for a Universal History* and *An Answer to the Question: What is Enlightenment?* Death of Diderot.

1785   Publishes *Groundwork of the Metaphysics of Morals*.

1786   Publishes *The Metaphysical First Principles of Natural Science* and *The Conjectural Beginning of Human History*; elected Rector of the University of Königsberg and becomes external member of the Berlin Academy of Sciences; death of Frederick the Great and accession of Frederick William II; death of Moses Mendelssohn.

1786–7 Reinhold publishes his *Letters on the Kantian Philosophy*.

1787   Second edition of the *Critique of Pure Reason*.

1788   Publishes the *Critique of Practical Reason*; death of Hamann; von Zedlitz replaced by J. C. Wöllner as Minister of Education.

1789   Civil unrest in Paris and the beginnings of the French Revolution.

1790   Publishes the *Critique of Judgement*.

1792   France declared a republic; execution of Louis XVI; Fichte's *Essay towards a Critique of All Revelation* appears anonymously and is widely ascribed to Kant.

1793   Publishes *Religion within the Limits of Reason Alone* and *On the Common Saying: That may be Right in Theory but is not Valid in*

Practice; second edition of the *Critique of Judgement*; Schiller publishes *On Grace and Dignity*.

1794   Elected member of the St Petersburg Academy of Sciences; comes into conflict with the Prussian Censor and receives royal reprimand for publishing his book on religion.

1795   Publishes *On Perpetual Peace*; Schiller publishes *Letters on the Aesthetic Education of Man*.

1796   Gives his final lecture at the University of Königsberg.

1797   Publishes *The Metaphysics of Morals*.

1798   Elected member of the Siena Academy of Sciences; publishes *The Conflict of the Faculties* and *Anthropology from a Pragmatic Point of View*; death of Frederick William II.

1799   Publishes 'Open Declaration against Fichte', repudiating the latter's interpretation of the Critical Philosophy; third edition of the *Critique of Judgement*; Napoleon becomes First Consul.

1801   Schiller publishes his essay *On the Sublime*.

1803   Kant falls seriously ill in October; death of Herder; Beethoven completes his third symphony (the 'Eroica').

1804   Kant dies on 12 February and is interred on 28 February; Napoleon crowned Emperor of France.

ANALYTICAL TABLE OF CONTENTS

Critique of Judgement

Preface   3

Introduction   7
  I. The division of philosophy   7
 II. The realm of philosophy in general   10
III. The critique of judgement as a means of connecting
     the two parts of philosophy in a whole   12
 IV. Judgement as a faculty by which laws are
     prescribed *a priori*   15
  V. The principle of the formal purposiveness of nature
     is a transcendental principle of judgement   16
 VI. The association of the feeling of pleasure with the
     concept of the purposiveness of nature   21
VII. The aesthetic representation of the purposiveness
     of nature   23
VIII. The logical representation of the purposiveness
     of nature   27
 IX. The connecting of the legislations of understanding
     and reason by means of judgement   29

PART I. CRITIQUE OF AESTHETIC JUDGEMENT

FIRST SECTION *Analytic of aesthetic judgement*

First book. Analytic of the beautiful

  First moment of the judgement of taste: moment of quality

    § 1. The judgement of taste is aesthetic   35
    § 2. The delight which determines the judgement of
         taste is independent of all interest   36
    § 3. Delight in the agreeable is coupled with interest   37
    § 4. Delight in the good is coupled with interest   39
    § 5. Comparison of the three specifically different
         kinds of delight   41

  Second moment of the judgement of taste: moment of quantity

    § 6. The beautiful is that which, apart from concepts, is
         represented as the object of a universal delight   42

§ 7. Comparison of the beautiful with the agreeable
and the good by means of the above characteristic   43
§ 8. In a judgement of taste the universality of delight
is only represented as subjective   45
§ 9. Investigation of the question whether in a judgement
of taste the feeling of pleasure precedes the judging
of the object or the latter precedes the former   49

Third moment of judgements of taste: moment of the relation
of the ends brought under review in such judgements

§ 10. Purposiveness in general   51
§ 11. The sole foundation of the judgement of taste is
the form of purposiveness of an object (or mode
of representing it)   52
§ 12. The judgement of taste rests upon *a priori* grounds   53
§ 13. The pure judgement of taste is independent of
charm and emotion   54
§ 14. Elucidation by means of examples   54
§ 15. The judgement of taste is entirely independent of
the concept of perfection   57
§ 16. A judgement of taste by which an object is
described as beautiful under the condition of a
determinate concept is not pure   60
§ 17. The ideal of beauty   62

Fourth moment of the judgement of taste: moment of the
modality of the delight in the object

§ 18. Character of the modality in a judgement of taste   67
§ 19. The subjective necessity attributed to a judgement
of taste is conditioned   68
§ 20. The condition of the necessity advanced by a
judgement of taste is the idea of a common sense   68
§ 21. Have we any ground for presupposing a
common sense?   69
§ 22. The necessity of the universal assent that is
thought in a judgement of taste, is a subjective
necessity which, under the presupposition of a
common sense, is represented as objective   70

General remark on the first section of the analytic   71

Second book. Analytic of the sublime

§ 23. Transition from the faculty of judging the
beautiful to that of judging the sublime 75
§ 24. On the division of an investigation of the feeling
of the sublime 77
A. The mathematically sublime
§ 25. Definition of the term 'sublime' 78
§ 26. The estimation of the magnitude of natural things
requisite for the idea of the sublime 81
§ 27. Quality of the delight in the judging of the sublime 87
B. The dynamically sublime in nature
§ 28. Nature as might 90
§ 29. Modality of the judgement on the sublime in nature 94

General remark upon the exposition of aesthetic
reflective judgements 96

Deduction of pure aesthetic judgements
§ 30. The deduction of aesthetic judgements upon
objects of nature must not be directed to what
we call sublime in nature, but only to the beautiful 109
§ 31. Of the method of the deduction of judgements
of taste 110
§ 32. First peculiarity of the judgement of taste 111
§ 33. Second peculiarity of the judgement of taste 113
§ 34. An objective principle of taste is not possible 115
§ 35. The principle of taste is the subjective principle
of the general power of judgement 116
§ 36. The problem of a deduction of judgements of taste 117
§ 37. What exactly it is, that is asserted *a priori* of
an object in a judgement of taste 119
§ 38. Deduction of judgements of taste 119

Remark 120

§ 39. The communicability of a sensation 121
§ 40. Taste as a kind of *sensus communis* 123
§ 41. The empirical interest in the beautiful 126
§ 42. The intellectual interest in the beautiful 127
§ 43. Art in general 132
§ 44. Fine art 134

§ 45. Fine art is an art, so far as it has at the same
       time the appearance of being nature   135
§ 46. Fine art is the art of genius   136
§ 47. Elucidation and confirmation of the above
       explanation of genius   137
§ 48. The relation of genius to taste   140
§ 49. The faculties of the mind which constitute genius   142
§ 50. The combination of taste and genius in products
       of fine art   148
§ 51. The division of the fine arts   149
§ 52. The combination of the fine arts in one and the
       same product   154
§ 53. Comparison of the aesthetic worth of the fine arts   155
§ 54. Remark   159

SECOND SECTION *Dialectic of aesthetic judgement*

§ 55.   165
§ 56. Representation of the antinomy of taste   165
§ 57. Solution of the antinomy of taste   166

Remark 1   169

Remark 2   172

§ 58. The idealism of the purposiveness of both nature and
       art, as the unique principle of aesthetic judgement   174
§ 59. Beauty as the symbol of morality   178
§ 60. Appendix. The methodology of taste   182

PART II. CRITIQUE OF TELEOLOGICAL JUDGEMENT

§ 61. The objective purposiveness of nature   187

FIRST DIVISION *Analytic of teleological judgement*

§ 62. Purely formal, as distinguished from material,
       objective purposiveness   190
§ 63. The relative, as distinguished from the intrinsic,
       purposiveness of nature   194
§ 64. The distinctive character of things considered as
       natural ends   197
§ 65. Things considered as natural ends are organisms   200
§ 66. The principle on which the intrinsic purposiveness
       in organisms is judged   204

§ 67. The principle on which nature in general
is judged teleologically as a system of ends   205
§ 68. The principle of teleology considered as an
inherent principle of natural science   209

SECOND DIVISION *Dialectic of teleological judgement*

§ 69. What is an antinomy of judgement?   213
§ 70. Exposition of this antinomy   214
§ 71. Introduction to the solution of the above antinomy   216
§ 72. The various kinds of systems dealing with the
purposiveness of nature   217
§ 73. None of the above systems does what it
professes to do   220
§ 74. The impossibility of treating the concept of a
technic of nature dogmatically springs from
the inexplicability of a natural end   223
§ 75. The concept of an objective purposiveness of
nature is a critical principle of reason for the use
of reflective judgement   225
§ 76. Remark   228
§ 77. The peculiarity of human understanding that makes
the concept of a natural end possible for us   232
§ 78. The union of the principle of the universal
mechanism of matter with the teleological principle
in the technic of nature   238

APPENDIX *Theory of the method of teleological judgement*

§ 79. Whether teleology must be treated as a branch of
natural science   245
§ 80. The necessary subordination of the principle of
mechanism to the teleological principle in the
explanation of a thing regarded as a natural end   246
§ 81. The association of mechanism with the teleological
principle which we apply to the explanation of
a natural end considered as a product of nature   250
§ 82. The teleological system in the extrinsic relations
of organisms   253
§ 83. The ultimate end of nature as a teleological system   258
§ 84. The final end of the existence of the world, that is,
of creation itself   263

§ 85. Physico-theology 265
§ 86. Ethico-theology 271

Remark 274

§ 87. The moral proof of the existence of God 276
§ 88. Limitation of the validity of the moral proof 281

Remark 287

§ 89. The use of the moral argument 288
§ 90. The type of assurance in a teleological proof
of the existence of God 290
§ 91. The type of assurance produced by a practical faith 295

General remark on teleology 304

APPENDIX. THE 'FIRST INTRODUCTION' TO
THE *CRITIQUE OF JUDGEMENT*

I. Philosophy as a system 315
II. The system of the higher cognitive faculties which
lies at the basis of philosophy 319
III. The system of all the faculties of the human mind 321
IV. Experience as a system for the power of judgement 323
V. The reflective power of judgement 325
VI. The purposiveness of natural forms as so many
particular systems 329
VII. The technic of the power of judgement as the ground
of the idea of a technic of nature 330
VIII. The aesthetic of the faculty of judging 332
IX. Teleological judging 340
X. The search for a principle of the technical power
of judgement 344
XI. The encyclopedic introduction of the critique of
judgement into the system of the critique of pure
reason 347
XII. The division of the critique of judgement 352

CRITIQUE OF JUDGEMENT

PREFACE

TO THE FIRST EDITION,* 1790

THE faculty of knowledge from *a priori* principles may be called *pure reason*, and the general investigation into its possibility and bounds the critique of pure reason. This is permissible although 'pure reason', as was the case with the same use of terms in our first work, is only intended to denote reason in its theoretical employment, and although there is no desire to bring under review its faculty as practical reason and its special principles as such. That critique is, then, an investigation addressed simply to our faculty of knowing things *a priori*. Hence it makes our *cognitive faculties* its sole concern, to the exclusion of the feeling of pleasure or displeasure and the faculty of desire; and among the cognitive faculties it confines its attention to the *understanding* and its *a priori* principles, to the exclusion of *judgement* and *reason*, (faculties that also belong to theoretical cognition,) because it turns out in the sequel that there is no cognitive faculty other than understanding capable of affording constitutive *a priori* principles of knowledge. Accordingly the critique which sifts these faculties one and all, so as to try the possible claims of each of the other faculties to a share in the clear possession of knowledge from roots of its own, retains nothing but what *understanding* prescribes *a priori* as a law for nature as the sum of phenomena—the form of these being similarly furnished *a priori*. All other pure concepts it relegates to the rank of ideas, which are beyond the reach of our faculty of theoretical cognition: though they are not without their use nor redundant, but discharge certain functions as regulative principles. For these concepts serve partly to restrain the officious pretensions of understanding, which, presuming on its ability to supply *a priori* the conditions of the possibility of all things which it is capable of knowing, behaves as if it had thus determined these bounds as those of the possibility of all things generally, and partly also to lead understanding, in its study of nature, according to a principle of completeness, unattainable as this remains for it, and so to promote the ultimate aim of all knowledge.

Properly, therefore, it was the *understanding*—which, so far as it contains constitutive *a priori* cognitive principles, has its special realm, and one, moreover, in our *faculty of knowledge*—that the critique, called in a general way that of pure reason, was intended to establish in secure but particular possession against all other competitors. In the same way *reason*, which contains constitutive *a priori* principles solely in respect of the *faculty of desire*, finds its possessions assigned to it by the critique of practical reason.

But now comes the *power of judgement*, which in the order of our cognitive faculties forms a middle term between understanding and reason. Has *it* also got independent *a priori* principles? If so, are they constitutive, or are they merely regulative, thus indicating no special realm? And do they give a rule *a priori* to the feeling of pleasure and displeasure, as the middle term between the faculties of cognition and desire, just as understanding prescribes laws *a priori* for the former and reason for the latter? This is the topic to which the present critique is devoted.

A critique of pure reason, i.e. of our faculty of judging on *a priori* principles, would be incomplete if the critical examination of judgement, which is a faculty of knowledge, and, as such, lays claim to independent principles, were not dealt with separately. Still, however, its principles cannot, in a system of pure philosophy, form a separate constituent part intermediate between the theoretical and practical divisions, but may when needful be annexed to one or other as occasion requires. For if such a system is some day worked out under the general name of metaphysics—and its full and complete execution is both possible and of the utmost importance for the employment of reason in all areas of its activity—the critical examination of the ground for this edifice must have been previously carried down to the very depths of the foundations of the faculty of principles independent of experience, lest in some quarter it might give way, and, sinking, inevitably bring with it the ruin of all.

169   We may readily gather, however, from the nature of the power of judgement (whose correct employment is so necessary and universally requisite that it is just this faculty that is intended when we speak of sound understanding) that the discovery of a peculiar principle belonging to it—and some such it must contain in itself *a priori*, for otherwise it would not be cognitive faculty the distinctive character of which is obvious to the most commonplace criticism—must be a task involving considerable difficulties. For this principle is one which must not be derived from *a priori* concepts, seeing that these are the property of understanding, and judgement is only directed to their application. It has, therefore, itself to furnish a concept, and one from which, properly, we get no cognition of a thing, but which it can itself employ as a

rule only—but not as an objective rule to which it can adapt its judgement, because, for that, another faculty of judgement would again be required to enable us to decide whether the case was one for the application of the rule or not.

It is chiefly in those acts of judgement that are called aesthetic, and which relate to the beautiful and sublime, whether of nature or art, that one meets with the above difficulty about a principle (whether it be subjective or objective). And yet the critical search for a principle of judgement in their case is the most important item in a critique of this faculty. For, although they do not of themselves contribute a whit to the knowledge of things, they still belong to the faculty of knowledge, and indicate an immediate bearing of this faculty upon the feeling of pleasure or displeasure according to some *a priori* principle, and do so without confusing this principle with what is capable of being a determining ground of the faculty of desire, for the latter has its principles *a priori* in concepts of reason.—The logical judging of nature, however, stands on a different footing. It deals with cases in which experience presents a conformity to law in things, which the understanding's general concept of the sensible is no longer adequate to render intelligible or explicable, and in which judgement may have recourse to itself for a principle of the reference of the natural thing to the unknowable supersensible and, indeed, must employ some such principle, though with a regard only to itself and the knowledge of nature. For in these cases the application of such an *a priori* principle for the *cognition* of what is in the world is both possible and necessary, and simultaneously opens out prospects which are profitable for practical reason. But here there is no immediate reference to the feeling of pleasure or displeasure. But this is precisely the enigma in the principle of judgement that necessitates a separate division for this faculty in the critique,—for there was nothing to prevent the 170 formation of logical judgements according to concepts (from which no immediate conclusion can ever be drawn to the feeling of pleasure or displeasure) having been treated, with a critical statement of its limitations, in an appendage to the theoretical part of philosophy.

The present investigation of taste, as a faculty of aesthetic judgement, not being undertaken with a view to the formation or culture of taste (which will pursue its course in the future, as in the past, independently of such inquiries) but being merely directed to its transcendental aspects, I feel assured of its indulgent criticism in respect of any shortcomings on that score. But in all that is relevant to the transcendental aspect it must be prepared to stand the test of the most rigorous examination. Yet even here I venture to hope that the difficulty of unravelling a problem so involved in its nature may serve as an excuse for a certain amount of hardly avoidable obscurity in its solution, provided that the accuracy of our statement of the principle is proved with all requisite clearness. I admit that the mode of deriving the phenomenon of the power of judgement from that principle has not all the lucidity that is rightly demanded elsewhere, where the subject is cognition by concepts, and that I believe I have in fact attained in the second part of this work.

With this, then, I bring my entire critical undertaking to a close. I shall hasten to the doctrinal part, in order, as far as possible, to snatch from my advancing years what time may yet be favourable to the task. It is obvious that no separate division of doctrine is reserved for the faculty of judgement, seeing that with judgement critique takes the place of theory; but, following the division of philosophy into theoretical and practical, and of pure philosophy in the same way, the whole ground will be covered by the metaphysics of nature and that of morals.*

INTRODUCTION

I

THE DIVISION OF PHILOSOPHY

PHILOSOPHY may be said to contain the principles of the rational cognition that concepts afford us of things (not merely, as with Logic, the principles of the form of thought in general irrespective of the objects), and, thus interpreted, the course, usually adopted, of dividing it into *theoretical* and *practical* is perfectly sound. But this makes imperative a specific distinction on the part of the concepts by which the principles of this rational cognition get their object assigned to them, for if the concepts are not distinct they fail to justify a division, which always presupposes that the principles belonging to the rational cognition of the several parts of the science in question are themselves mutually exclusive.

Now there are but two kinds of concepts, and these yield a corresponding number of distinct principles of the possibility of their objects. The concepts referred to are those *of nature* and that *of freedom*. By the first of these a *theoretical* cognition from *a priori* principles becomes possible. In respect of such cognition, however, the second, by its very concept, imports no more than a negative principle (that of simple antithesis), while for the determination of the will, on the other hand, it establishes fundamental principles which enlarge the scope of its activity, and which on that account are called *practical*. Hence the division of philosophy falls properly into two parts, quite distinct in their principles—a theoretical part, as *philosophy of nature*, and a practical part, as *philosophy of morals* (for this is what the practical legislation of reason by the concept of freedom is called). Hitherto, however, in the application of these expressions to the division of the different principles, and with them to the division of philosophy, a gross misuse of the terms has prevailed; for what is practical according to concepts of nature has been taken as identical with what is practical according to the concept of freedom, with the result that a division has been made under these heads of theoretical and practical, by which, in effect, there has been no division at all (seeing that both parts might have similar principles). 172

The will—for this is what is said—is the faculty of desire and, as such, is just one of the many natural causes in the world, the one, namely, which acts through concepts; and whatever is represented as possible (or necessary) through the efficacy of will is called practically possible (or necessary): the intention being to distinguish its possibility (or necessity) from the physical possibility or necessity of an effect the causality of whose cause is not determined in its production by concepts (but rather, as with lifeless matter, by mechanism, and, as with the lower animals, by instinct).—Now, the question in respect of the practical faculty: whether, that is to say, the concept, by which the causality of the will gets its rule, is a concept of nature or of freedom, is here left quite open.

The latter distinction, however, is essential. For, let the concept determining the causality be a concept of nature, and then the principles are *technically-practical;* but, let it be a concept of freedom, and they are *morally-practical.* Now, in the division of a rational science the difference between objects that require different principles for their cognition is the difference on which everything turns. Hence technically-practical principles belong to theoretical philosophy (the theory of nature), whereas those morally-practical alone form the second part, that is, practical philosophy (the theory of ethics).

All technically-practical rules (i.e. those of art and skill generally, or even of prudence, as a skill in exercising an influence over human beings and their wills) must, in so far as their principles rest upon concepts, be reckoned only as corollaries to theoretical philosophy. For they only touch the possibility of things according to concepts of nature, and this embraces, not only the means discoverable in nature for the purpose, but even the will itself (as a faculty of desire, and consequently a natural faculty), so far as it is determinable in accordance with these rules by natural motives. Still these practical rules are not called laws (like physical laws), but only precepts. This is due to the fact that the will does not stand simply under the natural concept, but also under the concept of freedom. In the latter connexion its principles are called laws, and these principles, with the addition of what follows from them, alone constitute the second or practical part of philosophy.

The solution of the problems of pure geometry is not allocated to a special part of that science, nor does the art of land-surveying merit the name of practical, in contradistinction to pure, as a second part of the general science of geometry, and with equally little, or perhaps less, right can the mechanical or chemical art of experiment or of observation be ranked as a practical part of the science of nature, or, in fine, domestic, agricultural, or political economy, the art of social intercourse, the principles of dietetics, or even general instruction as to the attainment of happiness, or as much as the control of the inclinations or the restraining of the affects with a view thereto, be denominated practical philosophy—not to mention forming these latter into a second part of philosophy in general. For, between them all, the above contain nothing more than rules of skill, which are thus only technically practical—the skill being directed to producing an effect which is possible according to natural concepts of causes and effects. As these concepts belong to theoretical philosophy they are subject to those precepts as mere corollaries of theoretical philosophy (i.e. as corollaries of natural science), and so cannot claim any place in any special philosophy called practical. On the other hand the morally practical precepts, which are founded entirely on the concept of freedom, to the complete exclusion of grounds taken from nature for the determination of the will, form quite a special kind of precepts. These, too, like the rules obeyed by nature, are, without qualification, called laws—though they do not, like the latter, rest on sensible conditions, but upon a supersensible principle—and they require a separate part of philosophy allotted to them as their own, corresponding to the theoretical part, and termed practical philosophy.

Hence it is evident that a sum of practical precepts furnished by philosophy does not form a special part of philosophy, co-ordinate with the theoretical, by reason of its precepts being practical—for that they might be, notwithstanding that their principles were derived wholly from the theoretical knowledge of nature (as technically-practical rules). But an adequate reason only exists where their principle, being in no way borrowed from the concept of nature, which is always sensibly conditioned, rests consequently on the supersensible, which the concept of freedom alone makes cognizable by means of its formal laws, and where, therefore, they are morally-practical, i.e. not merely precepts and rules in this or that interest, but laws independent of all antecedent reference to ends or aims.

II

THE REALM OF PHILOSOPHY IN GENERAL

THE employment of our faculty of cognition from principles, and with
it philosophy, is coextensive with the applicability of *a priori* concepts.

Now a division of the sum of all the objects to which those concepts
are referred for the purpose, where possible, of accomplishing knowledge of the former, may be made according to the varied competence
or incompetence of our faculty in that connexion.

Concepts, so far as they are referred to objects apart from the question of whether knowledge of them is possible or not, have their field,
which is determined simply by the relation in which their object
stands to our faculty of cognition in general.—The part of this field
in which knowledge is possible for us, is a territory (*territorium*) for these
concepts and the requisite cognitive faculty. The part of the territory
over which they exercise legislative authority is the realm (*ditio*) of these
concepts, and their appropriate cognitive faculty. Empirical concepts
have, therefore, their territory, doubtless, in nature as the complex of all
sensible objects, but they have no realm (only a dwelling-place, *domi-
cilium*), for, although they are formed according to law, they are not
themselves legislative, but the rules founded on them are empirical,
and consequently contingent.

Our entire faculty of cognition has two realms, that of natural concepts and that of the concept of freedom, for through both it prescribes
laws *a priori*. In accordance with this distinction, then, philosophy is
divisible into theoretical and practical. But the territory upon which its
realm is established, and over which it *exercises* its legislative authority,
is still always confined to the complex of the objects of all possible experience, taken as no more than mere phenomena, for otherwise legislation by the understanding in respect of them is unthinkable.

The function of prescribing laws by means of concepts of nature
is discharged by understanding, and is theoretical. That of prescribing
laws by means of the concept of freedom is discharged by reason and
is merely practical. It is only in the practical sphere that reason can
prescribe laws; in respect of theoretical knowledge (of nature) it can
175 only (as advised by the understanding with respect to laws) deduce
from given laws their logical consequences, which still always remain
restricted to nature. But we cannot reverse this and say that where

rules are practical, reason is then and there *legislative*, since the rules might be technically practical.

Understanding and reason, therefore, have two distinct jurisdictions over one and the same territory of experience. But neither can interfere with the other. For the concept of freedom just as little disturbs the legislation of nature, as the concept of nature influences legislation through the concept of freedom.—That it is possible for us at least to think without contradiction of both these jurisdictions, and their appropriate faculties, as coexisting in the same subject, was shown by the critique of pure reason, since it disposed of the objections on the other side by detecting their dialectical illusion.

Still, how does it happen that these two different realms do not form *one* realm, seeing that, while they do not limit each other in their legislation, they continually do so in their effects in the sensible world? The explanation lies in the fact that the concept of nature doubtless represents its objects in intuition, yet not as things in themselves, but as mere phenomena, whereas the concept of freedom represents in its object what is no doubt a thing in itself, but it does not make it intuitable, and further that neither the one nor the other is capable, therefore, of furnishing a theoretical cognition of its object (or even of the thinking subject) as a thing in itself, or, as this would be, of the supersensible—the idea of which has certainly to be introduced as the basis of the possibility of all those objects of experience, although it cannot itself ever be elevated or extended into a cognition.

Our entire cognitive faculty is, therefore, presented with an unbounded, but, also, inaccessible field—the field of the supersensible—in which we seek in vain for a territory, and on which, therefore, we can have no realm for theoretical cognition, be it for concepts of understanding or of reason. This field we must indeed occupy with ideas in the interest as well of the theoretical as the practical employment of reason, but in connexion with the laws arising from the concept of freedom we cannot procure for these ideas any but practical reality, which, accordingly, fails to advance our theoretical cognition one step towards the supersensible.

Albeit, then, between the realm of the natural concept, as the sensible, and the realm of the concept of freedom, as the supersensible, 176 there is a great gulf fixed, so that it is not possible to pass from the former to the latter (by means of the theoretical employment of reason), just as if they were so many separate worlds, the first of which is powerless to exercise influence on the second: still the latter is *meant* to influence the former—that is to say, the concept of freedom is meant to actualize in the sensible world the end proposed by its laws; and nature must consequently also be capable of being regarded in such a way that in the conformity to law of its form it at least harmonizes with the possibility of the ends to be effectuated in it according to the laws of freedom.—There must, therefore, be a ground of the *unity* of the supersensible that lies at the basis of nature, with what the concept of freedom contains in a practical way, and although the concept of this ground neither theoretically nor practically attains to a knowledge of it, and so has no peculiar realm of its own, still it renders possible the transition from the mode of thought according to the principles of the one to that according to the principles of the other.

III

THE CRITIQUE OF JUDGEMENT AS A MEANS OF CONNECTING THE TWO PARTS OF PHILOSOPHY IN A WHOLE

THE critique which deals with what our cognitive faculties are capable of yielding *a priori* has properly speaking no realm in respect of objects; for it is not a doctrine, its sole business being to investigate whether, having regard to the general bearings of our faculties, a doctrine is possible by their means, and if so, how. Its field extends to all their pretensions, with a view to confining them within their legitimate bounds. But what is shut out of the division of philosophy may still be admitted as a principal part into the general critique of our faculty of pure cognition, in the event, namely, of its containing principles which are not in themselves available either for theoretical or practical employment.

Concepts of nature contain the ground of all theoretical cognition *a priori* and rest, as we saw, upon the legislative authority of understanding.—The concept of freedom contains the ground of all sensuously unconditioned practical precepts *a priori*, and rests upon that of reason. Both faculties, therefore, besides their application in point of logical form to principles of whatever origin, have, in addition, their own peculiar jurisdiction in the matter of their content, and so,

there being no further (*a priori*) jurisdiction above them, the division 177
of philosophy into theoretical and practical is justified.

But there is still further in the family of our higher cognitive faculties
a middle term between understanding and reason. This is *judgement*, of
which we may reasonably presume by analogy that it may likewise contain, if not a special authority to prescribe laws, still a principle peculiar
to itself upon which laws are sought, although one merely subjective
a priori. This principle, even if it has no field of objects appropriate to
it as its realm, may still have some territory or other with a certain
character, for which just this very principle alone may be valid.

But in addition to the above considerations there is yet (to judge
by analogy) a further ground, upon which judgement may be brought
into line with another arrangement of our powers of representation,
and one that appears to be of even greater importance than that of its
kinship with the family of cognitive faculties. For all faculties of the
soul, or capacities, are reducible to three, which do not admit of any
further derivation from a common ground: the *faculty of knowledge*,
the *feeling of pleasure or displeasure*, and the *faculty of desire*.[1] For the 178

---

[1] Where one has reason to suppose that a relation subsists between concepts, that are
used as empirical principles, and the faculty of pure cognition *a priori*, it is worth while
attempting, in consideration of this connexion, to give them a transcendental definition—
a definition, that is, by pure categories, so far as these by themselves adequately indicate the
distinction of the concept in question from others. This course follows that of the mathematician, who leaves the empirical data of his problem indeterminate, and only brings their
relation in pure synthesis under the concepts of pure arithmetic, and thus generalizes his
solution.—I have been taken to task for adopting a similar procedure (*Critique of Practical
Reason*, Preface, p. 16) and fault has been found with my definition of the faculty of desire,
as *a faculty which by means of its representations is the cause of the actuality of the objects of those
representations*: for mere *wishes* would still be desires, and yet in their case every one is ready
to abandon all claim to being able by means of them alone to call their object into existence.—But this proves no more than the presence of desires in man by which he is in contradiction with himself. For in such a case he seeks the production of the object by means
of his representation alone, without any hope of its being effectual, since he is conscious that
his mechanical powers (if I may so call those which are not psychological), which would
have to be determined by that representation, are either unequal to the task of realizing the
object (by the intervention of means, therefore) or else are addressed to what is quite impossible, as, for example, to undo the past (*O mihi praeteritos*, etc.*) or, to be able to annihilate
the interval that, with intolerable delay, divides us from the wished-for moment.—Now,
conscious as we are in such fantastic desires of the inefficiency of our representations,
(or even of their futility,) as *causes* of their objects, there is still involved in every *wish* a
reference of the same as cause, and therefore the representation of its *causality*, and this is
especially discernible where the wish, as *longing*, is an affect. For such affects, since they
dilate the heart and render it inert and thus exhaust its powers, show that a strain is kept on
being exerted and re-exerted on these powers by the representations, but that the mind is

faculty of cognition understanding alone is legislative, if (as must be the case where it is considered on its own account free of confusion with the faculty of desire) this faculty, as that of *theoretical cognition*, is referred to nature, in respect of which alone (as phenomenon) it is possible for us to prescribe laws by means of *a priori* concepts of nature, which are properly pure concepts of understanding.—For the faculty of desire, as a higher faculty operating under the concept of freedom, only reason (in which alone this concept has a place) prescribes laws *a priori.*—Now between the faculties of knowledge and desire stands the feeling of pleasure, just as judgement is intermediate between understanding and reason. Hence we may, provisionally at least, assume that judgement likewise contains an *a priori* principle of its own, and that, since pleasure or displeasure is necessarily combined with the faculty of desire (be it antecedent to its principle, as with the lower desires, or, as with the higher, only supervening upon its determination by the moral law), it will effect a transition from the faculty of pure knowledge, i.e. from the realm of concepts of nature, to that of the concept of freedom, just as in its logical employment it makes possible the transition from understanding to reason.

Hence, despite the fact of philosophy being only divisible into two principal parts, the theoretical and the practical, and despite the fact of all that we may have to say of the special principles of judgement having to be assigned to its theoretical part, i.e. to rational cognition according to concepts of nature: still the critique of pure reason, which must settle this whole question before the above system is taken in hand, so as to substantiate its possibility, consists of three parts: the critique of pure understanding, of pure judgement, and of pure reason, which faculties are called pure on the ground of their being legislative *a priori.*

allowed continually to relapse and become languid upon recognition of the impossibility before it. Even prayers for the aversion of great, and, so far as we can see, inevitable evils, and many superstitious means for attaining ends impossible of attainment by natural means, prove the causal reference of representations to their objects—a causality which not even the consciousness of inefficiency for producing the effect can deter from straining towards it.—But why our nature should be furnished with a propensity to consciously vain desires is a teleological problem of anthropology. It would seem that were we not to be determined to the exertion of our power before we had assured ourselves of the efficiency of our faculty for producing an object, our power would remain to a large extent unused. For as a rule we only first learn to know our powers by making trial of them. This deceit of vain desires is therefore only the result of a beneficent disposition in our nature.

IV

JUDGEMENT AS A FACULTY BY WHICH LAWS ARE
PRESCRIBED *A PRIORI*

JUDGEMENT in general is the faculty of thinking the particular as contained under the universal. If the universal (the rule, principle, or law) is given, then the judgement which subsumes the particular under it is *determining*.* This is so even where such a judgement is transcendental and, as such, provides the conditions *a priori* in conformity with which alone subsumption under that universal can be effected. If, however, only the particular is given and the universal has to be found for it, then the judgement is simply *reflective*.*

Determining judgement determines under universal transcendental laws furnished by understanding and is subsumptive only; the law is marked out for it *a priori*, and it has no need to devise a law for its own guidance to enable it to subordinate the particular in nature to the universal.—But there are such manifold forms of nature, so many modifications, as it were, of the universal transcendental concepts of nature, left undetermined by the laws furnished by pure understanding *a priori* as above mentioned, and for the reason that these laws only touch the general possibility of a nature (as an object of the senses), that there must also be laws in this regard. These laws, being empirical, may be contingent as far as the light of *our* understanding goes, but still, if they are to be called laws (as the concept of a nature requires), they must be regarded as necessary on a principle, unknown though it be to us, of the unity of the manifold. Reflective judgement which is compelled to ascend from the particular in nature to the universal, stands, therefore, in need of a principle. This principle it cannot borrow from experience, because what it has to do is to establish just the unity of all empirical principles under higher, though likewise empirical, principles, and thence the possibility of the systematic subordination of higher and lower principles. Such a transcendental principle, therefore, reflective judgement can only give as a law from and to itself. It cannot derive it from any other quarter (as it would then be a case of determining judgement). Nor can it prescribe it to nature, for reflection on the laws of nature adjusts itself to nature, and not nature to the conditions according to which we strive to obtain a concept of it,—a concept that is quite contingent in respect of these conditions.

Now the principle sought can only be this: as universal laws of nature have their ground in our understanding, which prescribes them to nature (though only according to the universal concept of it as nature), particular empirical laws must be regarded, in respect of that which is left undetermined in them by these universal laws, according to a unity such as they would have if an understanding (though it be not ours) had supplied them for the benefit of our cognitive faculties, so as to render possible a system of experience according to particular natural laws. This is not to be taken as implying that such an understanding must be actually assumed (for it is only reflective judgement which avails itself of this idea as a principle for the purpose of reflection and not for determining anything); but this faculty rather gives by this means a law to itself alone and not to nature.

Now the concept of an object, so far as it contains at the same time the ground of the actuality of this object, is called its *end*, and the agreement of a thing with that constitution of things which is only possible according to ends, is called the *purposiveness* of its form.* Accordingly the principle of judgement, in respect of the form of the things of nature under empirical laws generally, is the *purposiveness of nature* in its multiplicity. In other words, by this concept nature is
181 represented as if an understanding contained the ground of the unity of the manifold of its empirical laws.

The purposiveness of nature is, therefore, a particular *a priori* concept, which has its origin solely in reflective judgement. For we cannot ascribe to the products of nature anything like a reference of nature in them to ends, but we can only make use of this concept to reflect upon them in respect of the nexus of phenomena in nature—a nexus given according to empirical laws. Furthermore, this concept is entirely different from practical purposiveness (in human art or even morals), though it is doubtless thought after this analogy.

V

THE PRINCIPLE OF THE FORMAL PURPOSIVENESS OF NATURE IS A TRANSCENDENTAL PRINCIPLE OF JUDGEMENT

A TRANSCENDENTAL principle is one through which we represent *a priori* the universal condition under which alone things can become objects of our cognition generally. A principle, on the other hand, is called metaphysical, where it represents *a priori* the condition under which alone objects whose concept has to be given empirically, may become further determined *a priori*. Thus the principle of the cognition of bodies as substances, and as changeable substances, is transcendental where the statement is that their change must have a cause: but it is metaphysical where it asserts that their change must have an *external* cause. For in the first case bodies need only be thought through ontological predicates (pure concepts of understanding), e.g. as substance, to enable the proposition to be cognized *a priori*; whereas, in the second case, the empirical concept of a body (as a movable thing in space) must be introduced to support the proposition, although, once this is done, it may be seen quite *a priori* that the latter predicate (movement only by means of an external cause) applies to bodies.—In this way, as I shall show presently, the principle of the purposiveness of nature (in the multiplicity of its empirical laws) is a transcendental principle. For the concept of objects, regarded as standing under this principle, is only the pure concept of objects of possible empirical cognition generally, and involves nothing empirical. On the other hand 182 the principle of practical purposiveness, implied in the idea of the *determination* of a free *will*, would be a metaphysical principle, because the concept of a faculty of desire, as will, has to be given empirically, i.e. is not included among transcendental predicates. But both these principles are, nonetheless, not empirical, but *a priori* principles; because no further experience is required for the synthesis of the predicate with the empirical concept of the subject of their judgements, but it may be apprehended quite *a priori*.

That the concept of a purposiveness of nature belongs to transcendental principles is abundantly evident from the maxims of judgement upon which we rely *a priori* in the investigation of nature, and which yet have to do with no more than the possibility of experience, and consequently of the knowledge of nature,—but of nature not merely in a general way, but as determined by a manifold of particular laws.—These maxims crop up frequently enough in the course of this science, though only in a scattered way. They are aphorisms of metaphysical wisdom, making their appearance in a number of rules the necessity of which cannot be demonstrated from concepts. 'Nature takes the shortest way (*lex parsimoniae*); yet it makes no leap, either in the sequence of its changes, or in the juxtaposition of specifically different forms (*lex continui in natura*); its vast variety in empirical laws is, for all that, unity under a few principles (*principia praeter necessitatem non sunt multiplicanda*)'; and so forth.

If we propose to assign the origin of these elementary rules, and attempt to do so on psychological lines, we are flying entirely in the face of their meaning. For they tell us, not what happens, i.e. according to what rule our powers of judgement actually discharge their functions, and how we judge, but how we ought to judge; and we cannot get this logical objective necessity where the principles are merely empirical. Hence the purposiveness of nature for our cognitive faculties and their employment, which manifestly radiates from them, is a transcendental principle of judgements, and so needs also a transcendental deduction, by means of which the ground for this mode of judging must be traced to the *a priori* sources of knowledge.

Now, looking at the grounds of the possibility of an experience, the
183 first thing, of course, that meets us is something necessary— namely, the universal laws apart from which nature in general (as an object of sense) cannot be thought. These rest on the categories, applied to the formal conditions of all intuition possible for us, so far as it is also given *a priori*. Under these laws judgement is determining; for it has nothing else to do than to subsume under given laws. For instance, understanding says: all change has its cause (universal law of nature); transcendental judgement has nothing further to do than to furnish *a priori* the condition of subsumption under the concept of understanding placed before it: this we get in the succession of the determinations of one and the same thing. Now for nature in general, as an object of possible experience, that law is cognized as absolutely necessary.—But besides this formal time-condition, the objects of empirical cognition are determined, or, so far as we can judge *a priori*, are determinable, in various ways, so that specifically differentiated natures, over and above what they have in common as things of nature in general, are further capable of being causes in an infinite variety of ways; and each of these modes must, on the concept of a cause in general, have its rule, which is a law, and, consequently, imports necessity: although owing to the constitution and limitations of our faculties of cognition we may entirely fail to see this necessity. Accordingly, in respect of nature's merely empirical laws, we must think in nature a possibility of an endless multiplicity of empirical laws, which yet are contingent so far as our insight goes, i.e. cannot be cognized *a priori*. In respect of these we judge the unity of nature according to empirical laws, and the possibility

of the unity of experience, as a system according to empirical laws, to be contingent. But, now, such a unity is one which must be necessarily presupposed and assumed, as otherwise we should not have a thorough-going connexion of empirical cognition in a whole of experience. For the universal laws of nature, while providing, certainly, for such a connexion among things generically, as things of nature in general, do not do so for them specifically as such particular things of nature. Hence judgement is compelled, for its own guidance, to adopt it as an *a priori* principle, that what is for human insight contingent in the particular (empirical) laws of nature contains nevertheless unity of law in the synthesis of its manifold in an intrinsically possible experience—unfathomable, though still thinkable, as such unity may, no 184 doubt, be for us. Consequently, as the unity of law in a synthesis, which is cognized by us in obedience to a necessary aim (a need of the understanding), though recognized at the same time as contingent, is represented as a purposiveness of objects (here of nature), so judgement, which, in respect of things under possible (yet to be discovered) empirical laws, is merely reflective, must regard nature in respect of the latter according to a *principle of purposiveness* for our cognitive faculty, which then finds expression in the above maxims of judgement. Now this transcendental concept of a purposiveness of nature is neither a concept of nature nor of freedom, since it attributes nothing at all to the object, i.e. to nature, but only represents the unique mode in which we must proceed in our reflection upon the objects of nature with a view to getting a thoroughly interconnected whole of experience, and so is a subjective principle, i.e. maxim, of judgement. For this reason, too, just as if it were a lucky chance that favoured us, we rejoice (or are properly speaking relieved of a want) where we meet with such systematic unity under merely empirical laws: although we must necessarily assume the presence of such a unity, apart from any ability on our part to apprehend or prove its existence.

In order to convince ourselves of the correctness of this deduction of the concept before us, and the necessity of assuming it as a transcendental principle of cognition, let us just remind ourselves of the magnitude of the task. We have to form a connected experience from given perceptions of a nature containing a maybe endless multiplicity of empirical laws, and this problem has its seat *a priori* in our understanding. This understanding is no doubt *a priori* in possession of universal laws of nature, apart from which nature would be incapable of being an object of experience at all. But over and above this it needs a certain order of nature in its particular rules which are only capable of being brought to its knowledge empirically, and which, so far as it is concerned, are contingent. These rules, without which we would have no means of advance from the universal analogy of a possible experience in general to a particular, must be regarded by understanding as laws, i.e. as necessary—for otherwise they would not form one order of nature—though it be unable to cognize or ever get an insight into their necessity. Albeit, then, it can determine nothing *a priori* in respect of these (objects), it must, in pursuit of such empirical so-called laws, lay at the basis of all reflection upon them an *a priori* principle, to the effect, namely, that a cognizable order of nature is possible according to them. A principle of this kind is expressed in the following propositions. There is in nature a subordination of genera and species comprehensible by us: Each of these genera again approximates to the others on a common principle, so that a transition may be possible from one to the other, and thereby to a higher genus: While it seems at the outset unavoidable for our understanding to assume for the specific variety of natural effects a like number of various kinds of causality, yet these may all be reduced to a small number of principles, the quest for which is our business; and so forth. This adaptation of nature to our cognitive faculties is presupposed *a priori* by judgement on behalf of its reflection upon it according to empirical laws. But understanding all the while recognizes it objectively as contingent, and it is merely judgement that attributes it to nature as transcendental purposiveness, i.e. a purposiveness in respect of the subject's faculty of cognition. For, were it not for this presupposition, we should have no order of nature in accordance with empirical laws, and, consequently, no guiding-thread for an experience that has to be brought to bear upon these in all their variety, or for an investigation of them.

For it is quite conceivable that, despite all the uniformity of the things of nature according to universal laws, without which we would not have the form of general empirical knowledge at all, the specific variety of the empirical laws of nature, with their effects, might still be so great as to make it impossible for our understanding to discover in nature an intelligible order, to divide its products into genera and species so as to avail ourselves of the principles of explanation and comprehension of one for explaining and interpreting another, and out of material coming to hand in such confusion (properly speaking only infinitely multiform and ill-adapted to our power of apprehension) to make a consistent context of experience.

Thus judgement, also, is equipped with an *a priori* principle for the possibility of nature, but only in a subjective respect. By means of this it prescribes a law, not to nature (as autonomy), but to itself (as heautonomy), to guide its reflection upon nature. This law may be called *the law of the specification of nature* in respect of its empirical laws. It is not one cognized *a priori* in nature, but judgement adopts it in the interests of a natural order, cognizable by our understanding, in the division which it makes of nature's universal laws when it seeks to subordinate to them a variety of particular laws. So when it is said that nature specifies its universal laws on a principle of purposiveness for our cognitive faculties, i.e. of suitability for the human understanding and its necessary function of finding the universal for the particular presented to it by perception, and again for varieties (which are, of course, common for each species) connexion in the unity of principle, we do not thereby either prescribe a law to nature, or learn one from it by observation—although the principle in question may be confirmed by this means. For it is not a principle of determining but merely of reflective judgement. All that is intended is that, no matter what is the order and disposition of nature in respect of its universal laws, we must investigate its empirical laws throughout on that principle and the maxims based on it, because only so far as that principle applies can we make any headway in the employment of our understanding in experience, or gain knowledge.

186

VI

The Association of the Feeling of Pleasure with the Concept of the Purposiveness of Nature

THE conceived harmony of nature in the manifold of its particular laws with our need of finding universality of principles for it must, so far as our insight goes, be deemed contingent, but nonetheless indispensable for the requirements of our understanding, and, consequently, a purposiveness by which nature is in accord with our aim, but only so far as this is directed to knowledge.—The universal laws of understanding, which are equally laws of nature, are, although arising from spontaneity, just as necessary for nature as the laws of motion applicable

to matter. Their origin does not presuppose any regard to our cognitive faculties, seeing that it is only by their means that we first come by any conception of the meaning of a knowledge of things (of nature), and they
187 of necessity apply to nature as object of our cognition in general. But it is contingent, so far as we can see, that the order of nature in its particular laws, with their wealth of at least possible variety and heterogeneity transcending all our powers of comprehension, should still in actual fact be commensurate with these powers. To find out this order is an undertaking on the part of our understanding, which pursues it with a regard to a necessary end of its own, that, namely, of introducing into nature unity of principle. This end must, then, be attributed to nature by judgement, since no law can be here prescribed to it by understanding.

The attainment of every aim is coupled with a feeling of pleasure. Now where such attainment has for its condition a representation *a priori*—as here a principle for reflective judgement in general—the feeling of pleasure also is determined by a ground which is *a priori* and valid for all human beings: and that, too, merely by virtue of the reference of the object to our faculty of cognition. As the concept of purposiveness here takes no cognizance whatever of the faculty of desire, it differs entirely from all practical purposiveness of nature.

As a matter of fact, we do not, and cannot, find in ourselves the slightest effect on the feeling of pleasure from the coincidence of perceptions with the laws in accordance with the universal concepts of nature (the categories), since in their case the understanding necessarily follows the bent of its own nature without ulterior aim. But, while this is so, the discovery, on the other hand, that two or more empirical heterogeneous laws of nature are allied under one principle that embraces them both, is the ground of a very appreciable pleasure, often even of admiration, and such, too, as does not wear off even though we are already familiar enough with its object. It is true that we no longer notice any decided pleasure in the comprehensibility of nature, or in the unity of its divisions into genera and species, without which the empirical concepts, that afford us our knowledge of nature in its particular laws, would not be possible. Still it is certain that the pleasure appeared in due course, and only by reason of the most ordinary experience being impossible without it, has it become gradually fused with simple cognition, and no longer arrests particular attention.—Something, then, that makes us attentive in our judging of nature to its purposiveness for our understanding—an endeavour to bring, where possible, its heterogeneous laws under higher, though still always empirical, laws—is required, in order that, on meeting with success, pleasure may be felt in this their accord with our cognitive faculty, an accord which is regarded by us as purely contingent. As against this a representation of nature would be altogether displeasing to us, if it forewarned us that, on the least investigation carried beyond the commonest experience, we should come in contact with such a heterogeneity of its laws as would make the union of its particular laws under universal empirical laws impossible for our understanding. For this would conflict with the principle of the subjectively purposive specification of nature in its genera, and with our own reflective judgement in respect of the latter.

Yet this presupposition of judgement is so indeterminate on the question of the extent of the prevalence of that ideal purposiveness of nature for our cognitive faculties, that if we are told that a more searching or enlarged knowledge of nature, derived from observation, must eventually bring us into contact with a multiplicity of laws that no human understanding could reduce to a principle, we can reconcile ourselves to the thought. But still we listen more gladly to others who hold out to us the hope that the more intimately we come to know the recesses of nature, or the better we are able to compare it with further aspects as yet unknown to us, the more simple shall we find it in its principles, and the further our experience advances the more harmonious shall we find it in the apparent heterogeneity of its empirical laws. For our judgement calls on us to proceed on the principle of the conformity of nature to our faculty of cognition, so far as that principle extends, without deciding—for the rule is not given to us by determining judgement—whether bounds are anywhere set to it or not. For while in respect of the rational employment of our cognitive faculty bounds may be definitely determined, in the empirical field no such determination of bounds is possible.

VII

THE AESTHETIC REPRESENTATION OF THE PURPOSIVENESS OF NATURE

THAT which is purely subjective in the representation of an object, i.e. what constitutes its reference to the subject, not to the object, is its

aesthetic character. On the other hand, that which in such a representation serves, or is available, for the determination of the object
189 (for the purpose of knowledge), is its logical validity. In the cognition of an object of the senses both sides are presented conjointly. In the sensuous representation of external things the quality of space in which we intuit them is the merely subjective side of my representation of them (by which what the things might be in themselves as objects is left quite open), and it is on account of that reference that the object in being intuited in space is also thought merely as a phenomenon. But despite its purely subjective quality, space is still a constituent of the knowledge of things as phenomena. *Sensation* (here external) also agrees in expressing a merely subjective side of our representations of external things, but one which is properly their matter (through which we are given something with real existence), just as space is the mere *a priori* form of the possibility of their intuition; and so sensation is, nonetheless, also employed in the cognition of external objects.

But that subjective side of a representation *which is incapable of becoming an element of cognition*, is the *pleasure* or *displeasure* connected with it; for through it I cognize nothing in the object of the representation, although it may easily be the result of the operation of some cognition or other. Now the purposiveness of a thing, so far as it is represented in our perception of it, is in no way a character of the object itself (for a character of this kind is not one that can be perceived), although it may be inferred from a cognition of things. In the purposiveness, therefore, which is prior to the cognition of an object, and which, even apart from any desire to make use of the representation of it for the purpose of a cognition, is yet immediately connected with it, we have the subjective character belonging to it that is incapable of becoming a constituent of knowledge. Hence we only apply the term 'purposive' to the object on account of its representation being immediately coupled with the feeling of pleasure: and this representation itself is an aesthetic representation of the purposiveness.—The only question is whether such a representation of purposiveness exists at all.

If pleasure is connected with the mere apprehension (*apprehensio*) of the form of an object of intuition, apart from any reference it may have to a concept for the purpose of a determinate cognition, this does not make the representation referable to the object, but solely to the subject. In such a case the pleasure can express nothing but the conformity of the object to the cognitive faculties brought into play

in reflective judgement, and so far as they are in play, and hence merely 190
a subjective formal purposiveness of the object. For that apprehension
of forms in the imagination can never take place without reflective
judgement, even when it has no intention of so doing, comparing them
at least with its faculty of referring intuitions to concepts. If, now, in
this comparison, imagination (as the faculty of intuitions *a priori*) is
undesignedly brought into accord with understanding (as the faculty
of concepts) by means of a given representation, and a feeling of
pleasure is thereby aroused, then the object must be regarded as purposive for reflective judgement. A judgement of this kind is an aesthetic
judgement upon the purposiveness of the object, which does not
depend upon any available concept of the object, and does not provide
one. When the form of an object (as opposed to the matter of its representation, as sensation) is, in the mere act of reflecting upon it, without
regard to any concept to be obtained from it, judged as the ground of
a pleasure in the representation of such an object, then this pleasure
is also judged to be combined necessarily with the representation of it,
and so not merely for the subject apprehending this form, but for all in
general who pass judgement. The object is then called beautiful; and
the faculty of judging by means of such a pleasure (and so also with universal validity) is called taste. For since the ground of the pleasure is
made to reside merely in the form of the object for reflection generally,
consequently not in any sensation of the object, and without any reference, either, to any concept that might have something or other in view,
it is with the conformity to law in the empirical employment of judgement generally (unity of imagination and understanding) in the subject,
and with this alone, that the representation of the object in reflection,
the conditions of which are universally valid *a priori*, accords. And, as
this accordance of the object with the faculties of the subject is contingent, it gives rise to a representation of a finality on the part of the object
in respect of the cognitive faculties of the subject.

Here, now, is a pleasure which—as is the case with all pleasure or
displeasure that is not brought about through the agency of the concept
of freedom (i.e. through the antecedent determination of the higher faculty of desire by means of pure reason)—no concepts could ever enable
us to regard as necessarily connected with the representation of an
object. It must always be only through reflective perception that it is 191
cognized as conjoined with this representation. As with all empirical
judgements, it is, consequently, unable to announce objective necessity

or lay claim to *a priori* validity. But, then, the judgement of taste in fact only lays claim, like every other empirical judgement, to be valid for everyone, and, despite its inner contingency this is always possible. The only point that is strange or out of the way about it, is that it is not an empirical concept, but a feeling of pleasure (and so not a concept at all), that is yet demanded from everyone by the judgement of taste, just as if it were a predicate united to the cognition of the object, and that is meant to be conjoined with its representation.

A singular empirical judgement, as, for example, the judgement of one who perceives a movable drop of water in a rock-crystal, rightly expects everyone to find the fact as stated, since the judgement has been formed according to the universal conditions of determining judgement under the laws of a possible experience in general. In the same way one who feels pleasure in simple reflection on the form of an object, without having any concept in mind, rightly lays claim to the agreement of everyone, although this judgement is empirical and a singular judgement. For the ground of this pleasure is found in the universal, though subjective, condition of reflective judgements, namely the purposive harmony of an object (whether it be a product of nature or of art) with the mutual relation of the faculties of cognition (imagination and understanding) which are requisite for every empirical cognition. The pleasure in judgements of taste is, therefore, dependent doubtless on an empirical representation, and cannot be united *a priori* to any concept (one cannot determine *a priori* what object will be in accordance with taste or not—one must find out the object that is so); but then it is only made the determining ground of this judgement by virtue of our consciousness of its resting simply upon reflection and the universal, though only subjective, conditions of the harmony of that reflection with the knowledge of objects in general, for which the form of the object is purposive.

This is why judgements of taste are subjected to a critique in respect of their possibility. For their possibility presupposes an *a priori* principle, although that principle is neither a cognitive principle for understanding nor a practical principle for the will, and is 192 thus in no way determining *a priori*.

Susceptibility to pleasure arising from reflection on the forms of things (whether of nature or of art) betokens, however, not only a purposiveness on the part of objects in their relation to reflective judgement in the subject, in accordance with the concept of nature, but also, conversely, a purposiveness on the part of the subject, answering to the concept of freedom, in respect of the form, or even formlessness, of objects. The result is that the aesthetic judgement refers not merely, as a judgement of taste, to the beautiful, but also, as springing from a higher intellectual feeling, to the *sublime*. Hence the above-mentioned critique of aesthetic judgement must be divided on these lines into two main parts.

VIII

THE LOGICAL REPRESENTATION OF THE PURPOSIVENESS OF NATURE

THERE are two ways in which purposiveness may be represented in an object given in experience. It may be made to turn on what is purely subjective. In this case the object is considered in respect of its form as present in *apprehension* (*apprehensio*) prior to any concept; and the harmony of this form with the cognitive faculties, promoting the combination of the intuition with concepts for cognition generally, is represented as a purposiveness of the form of the object. Or, on the other hand, the representation of purposiveness may be made to turn on what is objective, in which case it is represented as the harmony of the form of the object with the possibility of the thing itself according to an antecedent concept of it containing the ground of this form. We have seen that the representation of the former kind of purposiveness rests on the pleasure immediately felt in mere reflection on the form of the object. But that of the latter kind of purposiveness, as it refers the form of the object, not to the subject's cognitive faculties engaged in its apprehension, but to a definite cognition of the object under a given concept, has nothing to do with a feeling of pleasure in things, but only with understanding and its judging of them. Where the concept of an object is given, the function of judgement, in its employment of that concept for cognition, consists in *presentation* (*exhibitio*), i.e. in placing beside the concept an intuition corresponding to it. Here it may be that our own imagination is the agent employed, as in the case of art, where we realize a preconceived concept of an object which we set before ourselves as an end. Or the agent may be nature in its technic (as in the case of organic bodies) when we read into it our own concept of an end to assist our judging of its product. In this case what is represented is not a mere *purposiveness* of nature in the form of the thing, but this very product as a *natural end.*—Although our concept that nature, in its empirical laws, is subjectively purposive in its forms is in no way a concept of the object, but only a principle of judgement for providing itself with concepts in the vast multiplicity of nature, so that it may be able to take its bearings, yet, on the analogy of an end, as it were a regard to our cognitive faculties is here attributed to nature. *Natural beauty* may, therefore, be looked on as the *presentation* of the concept of formal, i.e. merely subjective, purposiveness and *natural ends* as the presentation of the concept of a real, i.e. objective, purposiveness. The former of these we judge by taste (aesthetically by means of the feeling of pleasure), the latter by understanding and reason (logically according to concepts).

On these considerations is based the division of the critique of judgement into that of the *aesthetic* and the *teleological* power of judgement. By the first is meant the faculty of judging formal purposiveness (otherwise called subjective) by the feeling of pleasure or displeasure, by the second the faculty of judging the real purposiveness (objective) of nature by the understanding and reason.

In a critique of judgement the part dealing with aesthetic judgement is essentially relevant, as it alone contains a principle introduced by judgement completely *a priori* as the basis of its reflection upon nature. This is the principle of nature's formal purposiveness for our cognitive faculties in its particular (empirical) laws—a principle without which understanding could not find itself in nature: whereas no reason is assignable *a priori*, nor is so much as the possibility of one apparent from the concept of nature as an object of experience, whether in its universal or in its particular aspects, why there should be objective ends of nature, i.e. things only possible as natural ends. But it is only judgement that, without being itself possessed *a priori* of a principle in that regard, in actually occurring cases (of certain products) contains the rule for employing the concept of ends in the interest of reason, once 194 the above transcendental principle has already prepared understanding to apply to nature the concept of an end (at least in respect of its form).

But the transcendental principle by which a purposiveness of nature, in its subjective reference to our cognitive faculties, is represented in the form of a thing as a principle of its judging, leaves quite undetermined the question of where and in what cases we have to judge the object as a product according to a principle of purposiveness, instead of simply according to universal laws of nature. It assigns to the *aesthetic* judgement the task of deciding the conformity of this product (in its form) to our cognitive faculties as a question of taste (a matter which the aesthetic judgement decides, not by any harmony with concepts, but by feeling). On the other hand judgement as teleologically employed assigns the determinate conditions under which something (e.g. an organized body) is to be judged in accordance with the idea of an end of nature. But it can adduce no principle from the concept of nature, as an object of experience, to give it its authority to ascribe *a priori* to nature a reference to ends, or even only indeterminately to assume them from actual experience in the case of such products. The reason for this is that in order to be able merely empirically to cognize objective purposiveness in a certain object, many particular experiences must be collected and reviewed under the unity of their principle.— Aesthetic judgement is, therefore, a special faculty of judging according to a rule, but not according to concepts. Teleological judgement is not a special faculty, but merely general reflective judgement proceeding, as it always does in theoretical cognition, according to concepts, but in respect of certain objects of nature, following special principles—those, namely, of a judgement that is merely reflective and does not determine objects. Hence, as regards its application, it belongs to the theoretical part of philosophy, and on account of its special principles, which are not determining, as principles belonging to doctrine have to be, it must also form a special part of the critique. On the other hand the aesthetic judgement contributes nothing to the cognition of its objects. Hence it must *only* be allocated to the critique of the judging subject and of its faculties of knowledge so far as these are capable of possessing *a priori* principles, whatever their use (theoretical or practical) may otherwise be—a critique which is the propaedeutic of all philosophy.

IX

The connecting of the Legislations of Understanding and Reason by means of Judgement

UNDERSTANDING prescribes laws *a priori* for nature as an object of the senses, so that we may have a theoretical knowledge of it in a possible experience. Reason prescribes laws *a priori* for freedom and its peculiar causality as the supersensible in the subject, so that we may have a purely practical knowledge. The realm of the concept of nature under the one legislation, and that of the concept of freedom under the other, are completely cut off from all reciprocal influence, that they might severally (each according to its own principles) exert upon the other, by the broad gulf that divides the supersensible from phenomena. The concept of freedom determines nothing in respect of the theoretical cognition of nature; and the concept of nature likewise nothing in respect of the practical laws of freedom. To that extent, then, it is not possible to throw a bridge from the one realm to the other.—Yet although the determining grounds of causality according to the concept of freedom (and the practical rule that this contains) have no place in nature, and the sensible cannot determine the supersensible in the subject; still the converse is possible (not, it is true, in respect of the knowledge of nature, but of the consequences arising from the supersensible and bearing on the sensible). So much indeed is implied in the concept of a causality by freedom, the *agency* of which, in conformity with the formal laws of freedom, is to take effect in the world. The word *cause*, however, in its application to the supersensible only signifies the *ground* that determines the causality of things of nature to an effect in conformity with their appropriate natural laws, but at the same time also in unison with the formal principle of the laws of reason—a ground which, while its possibility is impenetrable, may still be completely cleared of the charge of contradiction that it is alleged to involve.[2] The effect

196 in accordance with the concept of freedom is the final end which (or the manifestation of which in the sensible world) is to exist, and this presupposes the condition of the possibility of that end in nature (i.e. in the nature of the subject as a being of the sensible world, namely,

---

[2] One of the various supposed contradictions in this complete distinction of the causality of nature from that through freedom, is expressed in the objection that when I speak of *hindrances* opposed by nature to causality according to laws of freedom (moral laws) or of *assistance* lent to it by nature, I am all the time admitting an *influence* of the former upon the latter. But the misinterpretation is easily avoided, if attention is only paid to the meaning of the statement. The resistance or furtherance is not between nature and freedom, but between the former as phenomenon and *the effects* of the latter as phenomena in the world of sense. Even the causality of freedom (of pure and practical reason) is the causality of a natural cause subordinated to freedom (a causality of the subject regarded as a human being, and consequently as a phenomenon), and one, the ground of whose determination is contained in the intelligible, that is thought under freedom, in a manner that is not further or otherwise explicable (just as in the case of that intelligible that forms the supersensible substrate of nature).

as a human being). It is so presupposed *a priori*, and without regard to the practical, by judgement. This faculty, with its concept of a *purposiveness* of nature, provides us with the mediating concept between concepts of nature and the concept of freedom—a concept that makes possible the transition from the purely theoretical to the purely practical and from conformity to law in accordance with the former to final ends in accordance with the latter. For through that concept we cognize the possibility of the final end that can only be actualized in nature and in harmony with its laws.

Understanding, by the possibility of its supplying *a priori* laws for nature, furnishes a proof of the fact that nature is cognized by us only as phenomenon, and in so doing points to its having a supersensible substrate; but this substrate it leaves quite *undetermined*. Judgement by the *a priori* principle of its judging of nature according to its possible particular laws provides this supersensible substrate (within as well as without us) with *determinability through the intellectual faculty*. But reason gives *determination* to the same *a priori* by its practical law. Thus judgement makes possible the transition from the realm of the concept of nature to that of the concept of freedom.

In respect of the faculties of the soul generally, regarded as higher faculties, i.e. as faculties involving an autonomy, understanding is the one that contains the *constitutive a priori* principles for the *faculty of cognition* (the theoretical knowledge of nature). The *feeling of pleasure and displeasure* is provided for by the judgement in its independence from concepts and from sensations that refer to the determination of the faculty of desire and would thus be capable of being immediately 197 practical. For the *faculty of desire* there is reason, which is practical without mediation of any pleasure of whatsoever origin, and which determines for it, as a higher faculty, the final end that is attended at the same time with pure intellectual delight in the object.—Judgement's concept of a purposiveness of nature falls, besides, under the head of natural concepts, but only as a regulative principle of the cognitive faculties—although the aesthetic judgement on certain objects (of nature or of art) which occasions that concept, is a constitutive principle in respect of the feeling of pleasure or displeasure. The spontaneity in the play of the cognitive faculties whose harmonious accord contains the ground of this pleasure, makes the concept in question, in its consequences, a suitable mediating link connecting the realm of the concept of nature with that of the concept of freedom, as this accord at the same time promotes the receptivity of the mind for moral feeling. The following table may facilitate the review of all the above faculties in their systematic unity.[3]

All the Faculties of the Mind	Cognitive Faculties
Cognitive faculties	Understanding
Feeling of pleasure and displeasure	Judgement
Faculty of desire	Reason
A priori Principles	*Application*
Conformity to law	Nature
Purposiveness	Art
Final End	Freedom

---

[3] It has been thought somewhat suspicious that my divisions in pure philosophy should almost always turn out to be threefold. But it is due to the nature of the case. If a division is to be *a priori* it must be either analytic, according to the law of contradiction—and then it is always twofold (*quodlibet ens est aut A aut non A**)—or else it is *synthetic*. If it is to be derived in the latter case from *a priori* concepts (not, as in mathematics, from the *a priori* intuition corresponding to the concept,) then, to meet the requirements of synthetic unity in general, namely (1) a condition, (2) a conditioned, (3) the concept arising from the union of the conditioned with its condition, the division must of necessity be trichotomous.

PART I
CRITIQUE OF
AESTHETIC JUDGEMENT

FIRST SECTION
Analytic of Aesthetic Judgement

FIRST BOOK
ANALYTIC OF THE BEAUTIFUL

FIRST MOMENT
OF THE JUDGEMENT OF TASTE:[1] MOMENT OF QUALITY

§ 1

The judgement of taste is aesthetic

IF we wish to discern whether anything is beautiful or not, we do not refer the representation of it to the object by means of the understanding with a view to cognition, but by means of the imagination (acting perhaps in conjunction with the understanding) we refer the representation to the subject and its feeling of pleasure or displeasure. The judgement of taste, therefore, is not a cognitive judgement, and so not logical, but is aesthetic—which means that it is one whose determining ground *cannot be other than subjective.* Every reference of representations is capable of being objective, even that of sensations (in which case it signifies the real in an empirical representation). The one exception to this is the feeling of pleasure or displeasure. This denotes nothing in the object, but is a feeling which the subject has of itself and of the manner in which it is affected by the representation.

To apprehend a regular and appropriate building with one's cognitive faculties, whether the mode of representation be clear or confused, is quite a different thing from being conscious of this

204

---

[1] The definition of taste here relied upon is that it is the faculty of judging the beautiful. But the discovery of what is required for calling an object beautiful must be reserved for the analysis of judgements of taste. In my search for the moments* to which attention is paid by this judgement in its reflection, I have followed the guidance of the logical functions of judging (for a judgement of taste always involves a reference to understanding). I have brought the moment of quality first under review, because this is what the aesthetic judgement on the beautiful looks to in the first instance.

representation with an accompanying sensation of delight.* Here the representation is referred wholly to the subject, and what is more to its feeling of life—under the name of the feeling of pleasure or displeasure—and this forms the basis of a quite separate faculty of discriminating and judging, that contributes nothing to knowledge. All it does is to compare the given representation in the subject with the entire faculty of representations of which the mind is conscious in the feeling of its state. Given representations in a judgement may be empirical, and so aesthetic; but the judgement which is pronounced by their means is logical, provided it refers them to the object. Conversely, even if the given representations be rational, but are referred in a judgement solely to the subject (to its feeling), they are always to that extent aesthetic.

§ 2

*The delight which determines the judgement of taste is
independent of all interest*

THE delight which we connect with the representation of the existence of an object is called interest. Such a delight, therefore, always involves a reference to the faculty of desire, either as its determining ground, or else as necessarily implicated with its determining ground. Now, where the question is whether something is beautiful, we do not want to know, whether we, or anyone else, are, or even could be, concerned with the existence of the thing, but rather how we judge it on the basis of mere contemplation (intuition or reflection). If anyone asks me whether I consider that the palace I see before me is beautiful, I may, perhaps, reply that I do not care for things of that sort that are merely made to be gaped at. Or I may reply in the same strain as that Iroquois *sachem** who said that nothing in Paris pleased him better than the eating-houses. I may even go a step further and inveigh with the vigour of a *Rousseau** against the vanity of the great who spend the sweat of the people on such superfluous things. Or, in fine, I may quite easily persuade myself that if I found myself on an uninhabited island, without hope of ever again encountering human beings, and could conjure such a splendid edifice into existence by a mere wish, I should still not trouble to do so, so long as I had a hut there that was comfortable enough for me. All this may be admitted and approved; only it is not the point now at issue.

All one wants to know is whether the mere representation of the object is to my liking, no matter how indifferent I may be to the existence of the object of this representation. It is quite plain that in order to say that the object *is beautiful*, and to show that I have taste, everything turns on what I make of this representation within myself, and not on any factor which makes me dependent on the existence of the object. Everyone must allow that a judgement on the beautiful which is tinged with the slightest interest, is very partial and not a pure judgement of taste. One must not be in the least prepossessed in favour of the existence of the thing, but must preserve complete indifference in this respect, in order to play the part of judge in matters of taste.

This proposition, which is of the utmost importance, cannot be better explained than by contrasting the pure disinterested[2] delight which appears in the judgement of taste with that which is allied to an interest—especially if we can also assure ourselves that there are no other kinds of interest beyond those presently to be mentioned.

§ 3

Delight IN THE AGREEABLE *is coupled with interest*

That is AGREEABLE *which the senses find pleasing in sensation.* This at once affords a convenient opportunity for condemning and directing particular attention to a prevalent confusion of the double meaning of which the word 'sensation' is capable. All delight (so it is said or thought) is itself sensation (of a pleasure). Consequently everything that pleases, and for the very reason that it pleases, is agreeable—and according to its different degrees, or its relations to other agreeable sensations, is *attractive, charming, delicious, enjoyable*, etc. But if this is conceded, then impressions of the senses, which determine inclination, or principles of reason, which determine the will, or mere contemplated forms of intuition, which determine judgement, are all on a par in everything relevant to their effect upon the feeling of pleasure, for this would be agreeableness in the sensation of one's state; and since, 206

---

[2] A judgement upon an object of our delight may be wholly *disinterested* but nonetheless very *interesting*, i.e. it relies on no interest, but it produces one. Of this kind are all pure moral judgements. But, of themselves, judgements of taste do not even set up any interest whatsoever. Only in society is it *interesting* to have taste—a point which will be explained in the sequel.

in the last resort, all the elaborate work of our faculties must issue in and unite in the practical as its goal, we could credit our faculties with no other appreciation of things and the worth of things, than that consisting in the gratification which they promise. How this is attained is in the end immaterial; and, as the choice of the means is here the only thing that can make a difference, people might indeed blame one another for folly or imprudence, but never for baseness or wickedness; for they are all, each according to his own way of looking at things, pursuing one goal, which for each is the gratification in question.

When a modification of the feeling of pleasure or displeasure is termed sensation, this expression is given quite a different meaning to that which it bears when I call the representation of a thing (through the senses as a receptivity pertaining to the faculty of knowledge) sensation. For in the latter case the representation is referred to the object, but in the former it is referred solely to the subject and is not available for any cognition, not even for that by which the subject *cognizes* itself.

Now in the above definition the word sensation is used to denote an objective representation of the senses; and, to avoid continually running the risk of misinterpretation, we shall call that which must always remain purely subjective, and is absolutely incapable of forming a representation of an object, by the familiar name of feeling. The green colour of the meadows belongs to *objective* sensation, as the perception of an object of the senses; but its agreeableness belongs to *subjective* sensation, by which no object is represented: i.e. to feeling, through which the object is regarded as an object of delight (which involves no cognition of the object).

207   Now, that a judgement on an object by which its agreeableness is affirmed, expresses an interest in it, is evident from the fact that through sensation it provokes a desire for similar objects, consequently the delight presupposes, not the simple judgement about it, but the bearing its existence has upon my state so far as it is affected by such an object. Hence we do not merely say of the agreeable that it *pleases*, but that it *gratifies*. I do not accord it a simple approval, but inclination is aroused by it, and where agreeableness is of the liveliest type a judgement on the character of the object is so entirely out of place, that those who are always intent only on enjoyment (for that is the word used to denote intensity of gratification) would gladly dispense with all judgement.

§ 4

Delight IN THE GOOD *is coupled with interest*

THAT is *good* which by means of reason commends itself by its mere concept. We call that *good for something* (useful) which only pleases as a means; but that which pleases on its own account we call *good in itself*. In both cases the concept of an end is implied, and consequently the relation of reason to (at least possible) willing, and thus a delight in the *existence* of an object or action, i.e. some interest or other.

To deem something good, I must always know what sort of a thing the object is intended to be, i.e. I must have a concept of it. That is not necessary to enable me to see beauty in something. Flowers, free patterns, lines aimlessly intertwining—technically termed foliage,—have no signification, depend upon no determinate concept, and yet please. Delight in the beautiful must depend upon the reflection on an object leading towards some concept or other (whatever it may be). It is thus also differentiated from the agreeable, which rests entirely upon sensation.

In many cases, no doubt, the agreeable and the good seem convertible terms. Thus it is commonly said that all (especially lasting) gratification is of itself good; which is almost equivalent to saying that to be permanently agreeable and to be good are identical. But it is readily apparent that this is merely a mistaken confusion of words, for the concepts appropriate to these expressions are far from 208 interchangeable. The agreeable, which, as such, represents the object solely in relation to the senses, must first be brought under principles of reason through the concept of an end, to be, as an object of will, called good. But that the reference to delight is wholly different where what gratifies is at the same time called *good*, is evident from the fact that with the good the question always is whether it is mediately or immediately good, i.e. useful or good in itself; whereas with the agreeable this point can never arise, since the word always means what pleases immediately—and it is just the same with what I call beautiful.

Even in everyday speech a distinction is drawn between the agreeable and the good. We do not scruple to say of a dish that stimulates the sense of taste with spices and other condiments that it is agreeable—confessing all the while that it is not good: because, while it immediately *satisfies* the senses, it is mediately displeasing, i.e. to reason that looks ahead to the consequences. Even in our judgement of health this same distinction may be traced. To all that possess it, it is immediately agreeable—at least negatively, i.e. as absence of all bodily pains. But, if we are to say that it is good, we must further apply to reason to direct it to ends, that is, we must regard it as a state that puts us in a congenial mood for all we have to do. Finally, in respect of happiness everyone believes that the greatest aggregate of the pleasures of life, taking duration as well as number into account, merits the name of a true, indeed even of the highest, good. But reason sets its face against this too. Agreeableness is enjoyment. But if this is all that we are bent on, it would be foolish to be scrupulous about the means that procure it for us—whether it be obtained passively by the bounty of nature or actively and by our own efforts. But that there is any intrinsic worth in the existence of one who merely lives for *enjoyment*, however busy he may be in this respect, even when in so doing he serves others—all equally with himself intent only on enjoyment—as an excellent means to that one end, and does so, moreover, because through sympathy he shares all their gratifications,—this is a view to which reason will never let itself be brought round. Only by what one does heedless of enjoyment, in complete freedom and independently of what nature could passively 209 procure for him, does he give to his life, as the existence of a person, an absolute worth. Happiness, with all its plethora of pleasures, is far from being an unconditioned good.[3]

But, despite all this difference between the agreeable and the good, they both agree in being invariably coupled with an interest in their object. This is true, not only of the agreeable, § 3, and of the mediately good, i.e. the useful, which pleases as a means to some pleasure, but also of that which is good absolutely and from every point of view, namely the moral good which carries with it the highest interest. For the good is the object of will, i.e. of a rationally determined faculty of desire). But to will something, and to take a delight in its existence, i.e. to take an interest in it, are identical.

---

[3] An obligation to enjoyment is a patent absurdity. And the same, then, must also be said of a supposed obligation to actions that have merely enjoyment for their aim, no matter how spiritually this enjoyment may be refined in thought (or embellished), and even if it be a mystical, so-called heavenly, enjoyment.

§ 5

Comparison of the three specifically different kinds of delight

BOTH the agreeable and the good involve a reference to the faculty of desire, and are thus attended, the former with a delight pathologically conditioned (by stimuli), the latter with a pure practical delight. Such delight is determined not merely by the representation of the object, but also by the represented bond of connexion between the subject and the existence of the object. It is not merely the object, but also its existence, that pleases. On the other hand the judgement of taste is simply *contemplative*, i.e. it is a judgement which is indifferent as to the existence of an object, and only decides how its character stands with the feeling of pleasure and displeasure. But not even is this contemplation itself directed to concepts; for the judgement of taste is not a cognitive judgement (neither a theoretical one nor a practical), and hence, also, is not *grounded* on concepts, nor yet *intentionally directed* to them.

The agreeable, the beautiful, and the good thus denote three different relations of representations to the feeling of pleasure and displeasure, as a feeling in respect of which we distinguish different 210 objects or modes of representation. Also, the corresponding expressions which indicate our satisfaction in them are different. The *agreeable* is what GRATIFIES us; the *beautiful* what simply PLEASES us; the *good* what is ESTEEMED (*approved*), i.e. that on which we set an objective worth. Agreeableness is a significant factor even with animals devoid of reason; beauty has purport and significance only for human beings, i.e. for beings at once animal and rational (but not merely for them as rational beings—as spirits for example—but only for them as both animal and rational); whereas the good is good for every rational being in general;—a proposition which can only receive its complete justification and explanation in what follows. Of all these three kinds of delight, that of taste in the beautiful may be said to be the one and only disinterested and *free* delight; for, with it, no interest, whether of sense or reason, extorts approval. And so we may say that delight, in the three cases mentioned, is related to *inclination*, to *favour*, or to *respect*. FOR FAVOUR is the only free liking. An object of inclination, and one which a law of reason imposes upon our desire, leaves us no freedom to turn anything into an object of pleasure.

All interest presupposes a need, or calls one forth; and, being a ground determining approval, deprives the judgement on the object of its freedom.

So far as the interest of inclination in the case of the agreeable goes, everyone says: Hunger is the best sauce; and people with a healthy appetite relish everything, so long as it is something they can eat. Such delight, consequently, gives no indication of taste having anything to do with choice. Only when people's needs have been satisfied can we tell who among the crowd has taste or not. Similarly there may be correct habits (conduct) without virtue, politeness without good-will, propriety without honour, etc. For where the moral law speaks, there is, objectively, no room left for free choice as to what one has to do; and to show taste in the way one carries out its dictates, or in judging the way others do so, is a totally different matter from displaying the moral frame of one's mind. For the latter involves a command and produces a need of something, whereas moral taste only plays with the objects of delight without committing itself to any.

211   DEFINITION OF THE BEAUTIFUL DERIVED FROM
                         THE FIRST MOMENT

Taste is the faculty of judging an object or a mode of representation by means of a delight or aversion *apart from any interest*. The object of such a delight is called *beautiful*.

                        SECOND MOMENT

        OF THE JUDGEMENT OF TASTE: MOMENT OF QUANTITY

                            § 6

The beautiful is that which, apart from concepts, is represented as
        the object of a UNIVERSAL *delight*

THIS definition of the beautiful is derivable from the foregoing definition of it as an object of delight apart from any interest. For where anyone is conscious that his delight in an object is with him independent of interest, it is inevitable that he should judge the object as one containing a ground of delight for all human beings. For, since the delight is not based on any inclination of the subject (or on any other deliberate interest), but the judging subject feels himself completely *free* in respect of the liking which he accords to the object, he can find as reason for his delight no personal conditions to which his own subjective self might alone be party. Hence he must regard it as resting on what he may also presuppose in every other person; and therefore he must believe that he has reason for expecting a similar delight from everyone. Accordingly he will speak of the beautiful as if beauty were a feature of the object and the judgement were logical (forming a cognition of the object by concepts of it); although it is only aesthetic, and contains merely a reference of the representation of the object to the subject;—because it still bears this resemblance to the logical judgement, that it may be presupposed to be valid for everyone. But this universality cannot spring from concepts. For from concepts there is no transition to the feeling of pleasure or displeasure (save in the case of pure practical laws, which, however, carry an interest with them; and such an interest does not attach to the pure judgement of taste). The result is that the judgement of taste, with its attendant consciousness of detachment from all interest, must involve a claim to validity for everyone, and must do so apart from a universality directed to objects, i.e. there must be coupled with it a claim to subjective universality. 212

§ 7

Comparison of the beautiful with the agreeable and the good by means of the above characteristic

As regards the *agreeable* everyone concedes that his judgement, which he bases on a private feeling, and in which he declares that an object pleases him, is restricted merely to himself personally. Thus he does not take it amiss if, when he says that Canary-wine is agreeable, another corrects the expression and reminds him that he ought to say: It is agreeable *to me*. This applies not only to the taste of the tongue, the palate, and the throat, but to what may with anyone be agreeable to eye or ear. A violet colour is to one soft and lovely, but to another dull and faded. One person likes the tone of wind instruments, another prefers that of string instruments. To quarrel over such points with the idea of condemning another's judgement as incorrect when it differs from our own, as if the opposition between the two judgements were logical, would be folly. With the agreeable, therefore, the principle holds good: *Everyone has his own taste* (that of the senses).

The beautiful stands on quite a different footing. It would, on the contrary, be ridiculous if anyone who plumed himself on his taste were to think of justifying himself by saying: This object (the building we see, the dress that person has on, the concert we hear, the poem submitted to our judgement) is beautiful *for me*. For if it merely pleases *him*, he must not call it *beautiful*. Many things may for him possess charm and agreeableness—no one cares about that; but when he declares something to be beautiful, he expects the same delight from others. He judges not merely for himself, but for everyone, and then speaks of beauty as if it were a property of things. Thus he says the *thing* is beautiful; and it is not as if he counted on others agreeing in his judgement of liking owing to his having found them in such agreement on a number of occasions, but he *demands* this agreement of them. He blames them if they judge differently, and denies them taste, which he still requires of them as something they ought to have; and to this extent it is not open to us to say: Everyone has his own taste. This would be equivalent to saying that there is no such thing at all as taste, i.e. no aesthetic judgement capable of making a rightful claim upon the assent of everyone.

Yet even in the case of the agreeable we find that the judgements people form do betray a prevalent agreement among them, which leads to our crediting some with taste and denying it to others, and that, too, not as an organic sense but as a faculty of judging in respect of the agreeable generally. So of one who knows how to entertain his guests with pleasures (of enjoyment through all the senses) in such a way that one and all are pleased, we say that he has taste. But the universality here is only understood in a comparative sense; and the rules that apply are, like all empirical rules, *general* only, not *universal*,—the latter being what the judgement of taste upon the beautiful deals or claims to deal in. It is a judgement in respect of sociability in so far as it rests on empirical rules. In respect of the good it is true that judgements also rightly assert a claim to validity for everyone; but the good is only represented as an object of universal delight *by means of a concept*, which is the case neither with the agreeable nor the beautiful.

§ 8

In a judgement of taste the universality of delight is only represented as subjective

THIS particular form of the universality of an aesthetic judgement, which is to be met with in a judgement of taste, is a remarkable feature, not for the logician certainly, but for the transcendental philosopher. It calls for no small effort on his part to discover its origin, but in return it brings to light a property of our cognitive faculty which, without this analysis, would have remained unknown.

First, one must get firmly into one's mind that by the judgement of taste (upon the beautiful) the delight in an object is imputed to 214 *everyone*, yet without being grounded on a concept (for then it would be the good), and that this claim to universality is such an essential factor of a judgement by which we describe anything as *beautiful*, that were it not for its being present to the mind it would never enter into anyone's head to use this expression, but everything that pleased without a concept would be ranked as agreeable. For in respect of the agreeable everyone is allowed to have his own opinion, and no one insists upon others agreeing with his judgement of taste, which is what is invariably done in the judgement of taste about beauty. The first of these I may call the taste of the senses, the second, the taste of reflection: the first laying down judgements merely private, the second, on the other hand, judgements ostensibly of general (public) validity, but both alike being aesthetic (not practical) judgements about an object merely in respect of the bearings of its representation on the feeling of pleasure or displeasure. Now it does seem strange that while with the taste of the senses experience not only shows that its judgement (of pleasure or displeasure in something) is not universally valid, but everyone willingly refrains from imputing this agreement to others (despite the frequent actual prevalence of a considerable consensus of general opinion even in these judgements), the taste of reflection, which, as experience teaches, has often enough to put up with a dismissal of its claims to the universal validity of its judgement (upon the beautiful), can (as it actually does) find it possible for all that, to formulate judgements capable of demanding this agreement in its universality. Such agreement it does in fact require from everyone for each of its judgements of taste—the persons who pass these judgements not quarrelling over the possibility of such a claim, but only failing in particular cases to come to terms as to the correct application of this faculty.

First of all we have here to note that a universality which does not rest upon concepts of the object (even though these are only empirical) is in no way logical, but aesthetic, i.e. does not involve any objective quantity of the judgement, but only one that is subjective. For this universality I use the expression *universal validity*, which denotes the validity of the reference of a representation, not to the cognitive faculties, but to the feeling of pleasure or displeasure for every subject. (The same expression, however, may also be employed for the logical quantity of the judgement, provided we add *objective* universal validity, to distinguish it from the merely subjective universal validity which is always aesthetic.)

Now a judgement that has *objective universal validity* has always got the subjective also, i.e. if the judgement is valid for everything which is contained under a given concept, it is valid also for all who represent an object by means of this concept. But from a *subjective universal validity*, i.e. the aesthetic, that does not rest on any concept, no conclusion can be drawn to the logical; because judgements of that kind have no bearing upon the object. But for this very reason the aesthetic universality attributed to a judgement must also be of a special kind, seeing that it does not join the predicate of beauty to the concept of the object taken in its entire logical sphere, and yet does extend this predicate over the whole sphere of *judging subjects*.

In their logical quantity all judgements of taste are *singular* judgements. For, since I must present the object immediately to my feeling of pleasure or displeasure, and that, too, without the aid of concepts, such judgements cannot have the quantity of judgements with objective universal validity. Yet by taking the singular representation of the object of the judgement of taste, and by comparison converting it into a concept according to the conditions determining that judgement, we can arrive at a logically universal judgement. For instance, by a judgement of taste I describe the rose at which I am looking as beautiful. The judgement, on the other hand, resulting from the comparison of a number of singular representations: Roses in general are beautiful, is no longer pronounced as a purely aesthetic judgement, but as a logical judgement grounded on one that is aesthetic.

Now the judgement, 'The rose is agreeable' (to smell) is also, no doubt, an aesthetic and singular judgement, but then it is not one of taste but of the senses. For it has this point of difference from a judgement of taste, that the latter imports an *aesthetic quantity* of universality, i.e. of validity for everyone which is not to be met with in a judgement upon the agreeable. It is only judgements upon the good which, while they also determine the delight in an object, possess logical and not mere aesthetic universality; for it is as involving a cognition of the object that they are valid of it, and on that account valid for everyone.

When we judge objects merely on the basis of concepts, all representation of beauty goes by the board. There can, therefore, be no rule according to which anyone is to be compelled to recognize anything 216 as beautiful. Whether a dress, a house, or a flower is beautiful is a matter upon which one declines to allow one's judgement to be swayed by any reasons or principles. We want to get a look at the object with our own eyes, just as if our delight depended on sensation. And yet, if upon so doing, we call the object beautiful, we believe ourselves to be speaking with a universal voice, and lay claim to the concurrence of everyone, whereas no private sensation would be decisive except for the observer alone and his own liking.

Here, now, we may perceive that nothing is postulated in the judgement of taste but such a *universal voice* in respect of delight that is not mediated by concepts; consequently, only the *possibility* of an aesthetic judgement capable of being at the same time deemed valid for everyone. The judgement of taste itself does not *postulate* the agreement of everyone (for it is only competent for a logically universal judgement to do this, in that it is able to bring forward reasons); it only *imputes* this agreement to everyone, as an instance of the rule in respect of which it looks for confirmation, not from concepts, but from the concurrence of others. The universal voice is, therefore, only an idea—resting upon grounds the investigation of which is here postponed. It may be a matter of uncertainty whether a person who thinks he is laying down a judgement of taste is, in fact, judging in conformity with that idea; but that this idea is what is contemplated in his judgement, and that, consequently, it is meant to be a judgement of taste, is proclaimed by his use of the expression 'beauty'. For himself he can be certain on the point from his mere consciousness of the separation of everything belonging to the agreeable and the good from the delight remaining to him; and this is all for which he promises himself the agreement of everyone—a claim which, under these conditions, he would also be warranted in making, were it not that he frequently violated them, and thus passed an erroneous judgement of taste.

§ 9

Investigation of the question of whether in a judgement of taste the feeling of pleasure precedes the judging of the object or the latter precedes the former

THE solution of this problem is the key to the critique of taste, and so is worthy of all attention.

217   If the pleasure in a given object came first and if the universal communicability of this pleasure were all that the judgement of taste is meant to allow to the representation of the object, this approach would be self-contradictory. For a pleasure of that kind would be nothing but the feeling of mere agreeableness to the senses, and so, from its very nature, would possess no more than private validity, seeing that it would be immediately dependent on the representation through which the object *is given*.

Hence it is the universal capacity for being communicated incident to the state of the mind in the given representation which, as the subjective condition of the judgement of taste, must underlie the latter, with the pleasure in the object as its consequence. Nothing, however, is capable of being universally communicated but cognition and representation in so far as it pertains to cognition. For it is only as thus pertaining that the representation is objective, and it is this alone that gives it a universal point of reference with which the power of representation of everyone is obliged to harmonize. If, then, the determining ground of the judgement as to this universal communicability of the representation is to be merely subjective, that is to say, is to be conceived independently of any concept of the object, it can be nothing else than the state of the mind that presents itself in the mutual relation of the powers of representation so far as they refer a given representation *to cognition in general*.

The cognitive powers brought into play by this representation are here engaged in a free play, since no determinate concept restricts them to a particular rule of cognition. Hence the state of the mind in this representation must be one of a feeling of the free play of the powers of representation in a given representation for a cognition in general. Now a representation, whereby an object is given, involves, in order that it may become a source of cognition at all, *imagination* for bringing together the manifold of intuition, and *understanding* for the unity of the concept uniting the representations. This state of *free play* of the cognitive faculties attending a representation by which an object is given must admit of universal communication: because cognition, as a definition of the object with which given representations (in any subject whatever) are to accord, is the one and only representation which is valid for everyone.

As the subjective universal communicability of the mode of representation in a judgement of taste is to obtain apart from the presupposition of any determinate concept, it can be nothing else than the state of the mind involved in the free play of imagination and understanding (so far as these are in mutual accord, as is requisite for *cognition in general*): for we are conscious that this subjective relation suitable for a cognition in general must be just as valid for everyone, and consequently as universally communicable, as is any determinate cognition, which always rests upon that relation as its subjective condition. 218

Now this purely subjective (aesthetic) judging of the object, or of the representation through which it is given, is antecedent to the pleasure in it, and is the basis of this pleasure in the harmony of the cognitive faculties. Again, the above-described universality of the subjective conditions of judging objects forms the sole foundation of this universal subjective validity of the delight which we connect with the representation of the object that we call beautiful.

That an ability to communicate one's state of mind, even though it be only in respect of our cognitive faculties, is attended with a pleasure, is a fact which might easily be demonstrated from the natural propensity of mankind to social life, i.e. empirically and psychologically. But what we have here in view calls for something more than this. In a judgement of taste the pleasure felt by us is expected from everyone else as necessary, just as if, when we call something beautiful, beauty was to be regarded as a quality of the object forming part of its inherent determination according to concepts; although beauty is for itself, apart from any reference to the feeling of the subject, nothing. But the discussion of this question must be reserved until we have answered the further one of whether, and how, aesthetic judgements are possible *a priori*.

At present we are exercised with the lesser question of the way in which we become conscious, in a judgement of taste, of a reciprocal subjective common accord of the powers of cognition. Is it aesthetically by sensation and our mere inner sense? Or is it intellectually by consciousness of our intentional activity in bringing these powers into play?

Now if the given representation occasioning the judgement of taste were a concept which united understanding and imagination in the judgement of the object so as to give a cognition of the object, the consciousness of this relation would be intellectual (as in the objective schematism of judgement dealt with in the *Critique*). But, then, in that case the judgement would not be laid down with respect to

219 pleasure and displeasure, and so would not be a judgement of taste. But, now, the judgement of taste determines the object, independently of concepts, in respect of delight and of the predicate of beauty. There is, therefore, no other way for the subjective unity of the relation in question to make itself known than by sensation. The enlivening of both faculties (imagination and understanding) to an indeterminate, but yet, thanks to the given representation, harmonious activity, such as belongs to cognition generally, is the sensation whose universal communicability is postulated by the judgement of taste. An objective relation can, of course, only be thought, yet in so far as, in respect of its conditions, it is subjective, it may be felt in its effect upon the mind, and, in the case of a relation (like that of the powers of representation to a faculty of cognition generally) which does not rest on any concept, no other consciousness of it is possible beyond that through the sensation of its effect upon the mind— an effect consisting in the more lightened play of both mental powers (imagination and understanding) as enlivened by their mutual accord. A representation which is singular and independent of comparison with other representations, and, being such, yet accords with the conditions of the universality that is the general concern of understanding, is one that brings the cognitive faculties into that proportionate accord which we require for all cognition and which we therefore deem valid for everyone who is so constituted as to judge by means of understanding and the senses in combination (i.e. for everyone).

DEFINITION OF THE BEAUTIFUL DRAWN FROM
THE SECOND MOMENT

The *beautiful* is that which, apart from a concept, pleases universally.

THIRD MOMENT

OF JUDGEMENTS OF TASTE: MOMENT OF
THE *RELATION* OF THE ENDS BROUGHT UNDER
REVIEW IN SUCH JUDGEMENTS

§ 10

Purposiveness in general

LET us define the meaning of 'an end' in transcendental terms (i.e.
without presupposing anything empirical, such as the feeling of
pleasure). An end is the object of a concept so far as this concept is 220
regarded as the cause of the object (the real ground of its possibility);
and the causality of a *concept* in respect of its *object* is purposiveness
(*forma finalis*). Where, then, not the cognition of an object merely,
but the object itself (its form or real existence) as an effect, is thought
to be possible only through a concept of it, there we imagine an end.
The representation of the effect is here the determining ground of
its cause and precedes the latter. The consciousness of the causality
of a representation in respect of the state of the subject as one tending *to preserve a continuance* of that state, may here be said to denote
in a general way what is called pleasure; whereas displeasure is that
representation which contains the ground for converting the state of
the representations into their opposite (for hindering or removing
them).

The faculty of desire, so far as it is determinable only through
concepts, i.e. so as to act in conformity with the representation of an
end, would be the will. But an object, or state of mind, or even an
action may, although its possibility does not necessarily presuppose
the representation of an end, be called purposive simply on account of
its possibility being only explicable and intelligible for us by virtue
of an assumption on our part of a fundamental causality according
to ends, i.e. a will that would have so ordained it according to a

certain represented rule. Purposiveness, therefore, may exist apart
from a purpose, in so far as we do not locate the causes of this form
in a will, but yet are able to render the explanation of its possibility
intelligible to ourselves only by deriving it from a will. Now we are
not always obliged to look with the eye of reason into what we observe
(i.e. to consider it in its possibility). So we may at least observe a
purposiveness with respect to form, and trace it in objects—though
by reflection only—without resting it on an end (as the material of
the *nexus finalis*).

221   § 11

The sole foundation of the judgement of taste is the FORM OF
PURPOSIVENESS *of an object (or mode of representing it)*

WHENEVER an end is regarded as a source of delight it always imports
an interest as determining ground of the judgement on the object of
pleasure. Hence the judgement of taste cannot rest on any subjective
end as its ground. But neither can any representation of an objective
end, i.e. of the possibility of the object itself on principles of purposive connexion, determine the judgement of taste, and, consequently,
neither can any concept of the good. For the judgement of taste is an
aesthetic and not a cognitive judgement, and so does not deal with
any *concept* of the character or of the internal or external possibility,
by this or that cause, of the object, but simply with the relation of the
powers of representation to one another in so far as they are determined by a representation.

Now this relation, present when an object is characterized as beautiful, is coupled with the feeling of pleasure. This pleasure is by the
judgement of taste pronounced valid for everyone; hence an agreeableness attending the representation is just as incapable of containing the determining ground of the judgement as the representation
of the perfection of the object or the concept of the good. We are thus
left with the subjective purposiveness in the representation of an
object, exclusive of any end (objective or subjective)—consequently
the bare form of purposiveness in the representation whereby an
object is *given* to us, so far as we are conscious of it—as that which
is alone capable of constituting the delight which, apart from any
concept, we judge as universally communicable, and so of forming
the determining ground of the judgement of taste.

§ 12

The judgement of taste rests upon a priori *grounds*

To determine *a priori* the connexion of the feeling of pleasure or displeasure as an effect, with some representation or other (sensation or
concept) as its cause, is utterly impossible; for that would be a causal
relation which (with objects of experience) is always one that can
only be cognized *a posteriori* and with the help of experience. True,   222
in the *Critique of Practical Reason* we did actually derive *a priori* from
universal moral concepts the feeling of respect (as a particular and
peculiar modification of this feeling which does not strictly answer
either to the pleasure or displeasure which we receive from empirical objects). But there we were further able to pass beyond the limits
of experience and call in aid a causality resting on a supersensible
attribute of the subject, namely that of freedom. But even there it
was not this *feeling* exactly that we deduced from the idea of the
moral as cause, but from this was derived simply the determination
of the will. But the mental state of a will determined by anything
whatsoever is already in itself a feeling of pleasure and identical with
it, and so does not issue from the latter as an effect. Such an effect
must only be assumed where the concept of the moral as a good precedes the determination of the will by the law; for in that case it
would be futile to derive the pleasure combined with the concept
from this concept as a mere cognition.

Now the pleasure in aesthetic judgements stands on a similar
footing: only that here it is merely contemplative and does not bring
about an interest in the object; whereas in the moral judgement it is
practical. The consciousness of mere formal purposiveness in the
play of the cognitive faculties of the subject attending a representation whereby an object is given, is the pleasure itself, because it
involves a determining ground of the subject's activity in respect of
the enlivening of its cognitive powers, and thus an internal causality
(which is purposive) in respect of cognition generally, but without
being limited to any determinate cognition, and consequently a mere
form of the subjective purposiveness of a representation in an aesthetic judgement. This pleasure is also in no way practical, neither
resembling that from the pathological ground of agreeableness nor
that from the intellectual ground of the represented good. But still it

involves an inherent causality, that, namely, of *preserving a continuance* of the state of the representation itself and the active engagement of the cognitive powers without ulterior aim. We *dwell* on the contemplation of the beautiful because this contemplation strengthens and reproduces itself. The case is analogous (but analogous only) to the way we dwell upon a charm in the representation of an object which keeps arresting the attention, the mind all the while remaining passive.

§ 13

The pure judgement of taste is independent of charm and emotion

EVERY interest vitiates the judgement of taste and robs it of its impartiality. This is especially so where instead of, like the interest of reason, allowing purposiveness to precede the feeling of pleasure, it grounds it upon this feeling—which is what always happens in aesthetic judgements upon anything so far as it gratifies or pains. Hence judgements so influenced can either lay no claim at all to a universally valid delight, or else must diminish their claim in proportion as sensations of the kind in question enter into the determining grounds of taste. Taste that requires an added element of *charm* and *emotion* for its delight, not to speak of adopting this as the measure of its approval, has not yet emerged from barbarism.

And yet charms are frequently not only ranked with beauty (which ought properly to be a question merely of the form) as contributory to the aesthetic universal delight, but they have been accredited as beauties in themselves, and consequently the matter of delight passed off for the form. This is a misconception which, like many others that have still an underlying element of truth, may be removed by a careful definition of these concepts.

A judgement of taste which is uninfluenced by charm or emotion, (though these may be associated with the delight in the beautiful), and whose determining ground, therefore, is simply purposiveness of form, is *a pure judgement of taste*.

§ 14

Elucidation by means of examples

AESTHETIC, just like theoretical (logical) judgements, are divisible into empirical and pure. The first are those by which agreeableness or disagreeableness, the second those by which beauty, is predicated of an object or its mode of representation. The former are judgements of the senses (material aesthetic judgements), the latter (as formal) alone judgements of taste proper.

A judgement of taste, therefore, is only pure so far as its determining 224 ground is commingled with no merely empirical delight. But this always transpires where charm or emotion have a share in the judgement by which something is to be described as beautiful.

Here now there is a recrudescence of a number of specious objections that go so far as to claim that charm is not merely a necessary ingredient of beauty, but is even of itself sufficient to merit the name of beautiful. A mere colour, such as the green of a plot of grass, or a mere tone (as distinguished from sound or noise), like that of a violin, is described by most people as in itself beautiful, notwithstanding the fact that both seem to depend merely on the matter of the representations—in other words, simply on sensation, which only entitles them to be called agreeable. But it will at the same time be observed that sensations of colour as well as of tone are only entitled to be immediately regarded as beautiful where, in either case, they are *pure*. This is a determination which directly concerns their form, and it is the only one which these representations possess that admits with certainty of being universally communicated. For it is not to be assumed that even the quality of the sensations agrees in all subjects, and we can hardly take it for granted that the agreeableness of a colour, or of the tone of a musical instrument, which we judge to be preferable to that of another, will be similarly judged by everyone.

Assuming with *Euler** that colours are isochronous vibrations (*pulsus*) of the aether, as tones are of the air set in vibration by sound, and, what is most important, that the mind not only perceives by the senses their effect in stimulating the organs, but also, by reflection, the regular play of the impressions (and consequently the form in which different representations are united)—which I, still, in no way doubt—then colour and tone would not be mere sensations. They would be nothing short of formal determinations of the unity of a manifold of sensations, and in that case could even be ranked as beauties in their own right.

But the purity of a simple mode of sensation means that its uniformity is not disturbed or broken by any foreign sensation. It belongs merely to the form; for abstraction may there be made from the

quality of the mode of such sensation (what colour or tone, if any, it
represents). For this reason all simple colours are regarded as beautiful in so far as they are pure. Composite colours do not possess this
225   advantage because, not being simple, there is no standard for judging whether they should be called pure or impure.

But as for the beauty ascribed to the object on account of its
form, and the supposition that it is capable of being enhanced by
charm, this is a common error and one very prejudicial to genuine,
uncorrupted, sincere taste. Nevertheless charms may be added to
beauty to lend to the mind, beyond a bare delight, a further interest
in the representation of the object, and thus to advocate taste and
its cultivation. This applies especially where taste is as yet crude
and untrained. But they are positively subversive of the judgement
of taste, if allowed to obtrude themselves as grounds of judging
beauty. For so far are they from contributing to beauty, that it is only
where taste is still weak and untrained, that, like aliens, they are
admitted as a favour, and only on terms that they do not disturb that
beautiful form.

In painting, sculpture, and in fact in all the formative arts, in
architecture and horticulture, in so far as they are fine arts, the *design*
is what is essential. Here it is not what gratifies in sensation but
merely what pleases by its form, that is the fundamental prerequisite
for taste. The colours which give brilliancy to the sketch are part of
the charm. They may no doubt, in their own way, enliven the object
for sensation, but make it really worth looking at and beautiful they
cannot. Indeed, more often than not the requirements of the beautiful form restrict them to a very narrow compass, and, even where
charm is admitted, it is only this form that serves to ennoble them.

All form of objects of the senses (both of outer and also, mediately,
of inner sense) is either *figure* or *play*. In the latter case it is either
play of figures (in space: mime and dance), or mere play of sensations
(in time). The *charm* of colours, or of the agreeable tones of instruments, may be added: but the *design* in the former and the *composition*
in the latter constitute the proper object of the pure judgement of
taste. To say that the purity alike of colours and of tones, or their variety and contrast, seem to contribute to beauty, is by no means to imply
that, because in themselves agreeable, they therefore yield an addition
to the delight in the form and one on a par with it. The real meaning
226   rather is that they make this form more clearly, definitely, and

completely perceptible, and besides enliven the representation by their charm, as they excite and sustain the attention directed to the object itself.

Even what is called *ornamentation* (*parerga*), i.e. what is only an adjunct, and not an intrinsic constituent in the complete representation of the object, in augmenting the delight of taste does so only by means of its form. Thus it is with the frames of pictures or the drapery on statues, or the colonnades of palaces. But if the ornamentation does not itself enter into the composition of the beautiful form—if it is introduced like a gold frame merely to win approval for the picture by means of its charm—it is then called *finery* and takes away from the genuine beauty.

Emotion—a sensation where an agreeable feeling is produced merely by means of a momentary check followed by a more powerful outpouring of the vital force—is quite foreign to beauty. Sublimity (with which the feeling of emotion is connected) requires, however, a different standard of judging from that which underlies taste. A pure judgement of taste has, then, for its determining ground neither charm nor emotion, in a word, no sensation as matter of the aesthetic judgement.

§ 15

The judgement of taste is entirely independent of the concept of perfection

Objective purposiveness can only be cognized by means of a reference of the manifold to a determinate end, and hence only through a concept. This alone makes it clear that the beautiful, which is judged on the ground of a mere formal purposiveness, i.e. a purposiveness without a purpose, is wholly independent of the representation of the good. For the latter presupposes an objective purposiveness, i.e. the reference of the object to a determinate end.

Objective purposiveness is either external, i.e. the *utility*, or internal, i.e. the *perfection*, of the object. That the delight in an object on account of which we call it beautiful is incapable of resting on the representation of its utility, is abundantly evident from the two preceding moments; for in that case, it would not be an immediate delight in the object, 227 which latter is the essential condition of the judgement upon beauty. But in an objective, internal purposiveness, i.e. perfection, we have what is more akin to the predicate of beauty, and so this has been held even by philosophers of reputation to be convertible with beauty, though subject to the qualification: *where it is thought in a confused way*. In a critique of taste it is of the utmost importance to decide whether beauty is really reducible to the concept of perfection.

For judging objective purposiveness we always require the concept of an end, and, where such purposiveness has to be, not an external one (utility), but an internal one, the concept of an internal end containing the ground of the internal possibility of the object. Now an end is in general that, the *concept* of which may be regarded as the ground of the possibility of the object itself. So in order to represent an objective purposiveness in a thing we must first have a concept of *what sort of a thing it is to be*. The agreement of the manifold in a thing with this concept (which supplies the rule of its synthesis) is the *qualitative perfection* of the thing. *Quantitative* perfection is entirely distinct from this. It consists in the completeness of anything after its kind, and is a mere concept of quantity (of totality). In its case the question of *what the thing is to be* is regarded as definitely disposed of, and we only ask whether it is possessed of *all* the requisites that go to make it such. What is formal in the representation of a thing, i.e. the agreement of its manifold with a unity (i.e. irrespective of what it is to be) does not, of itself, afford us any cognition whatsoever of objective purposiveness. For since abstraction is made from this unity as *end* (what the thing is to be) nothing is left but the subjective purposiveness of the representations in the mind of the subject intuiting. This gives a certain purposiveness of the representing state of the subject, in which the subject feels itself quite at home in its effort to grasp a given form in the imagination, but no perfection of any object, the latter not being here thought through any concept of an end. For instance, if in a forest I light upon a plot of grass, round which trees stand in a circle, and if I do not then form any representation of an end, such as that it is meant to be used, say, for country dances, then not the least hint of a concept of perfection is given by the mere form. To suppose a formal *objective* purposiveness that is yet devoid of any purpose, i.e. the mere form of a *perfection* (apart from any matter or *concept* of that with which it is to agree, even though there was the mere general idea of a conformity to law) is a veritable contradiction.

Now the judgement of taste is an aesthetic judgement, i.e. one resting on subjective grounds. No concept can be its determining ground, and hence not one of a determinate end. Beauty, therefore, as a formal subjective purposiveness, involves no thought whatsoever of a perfection of the object, as a would-be formal purposiveness which yet, for all that, is objective: and the distinction between the concepts of the beautiful and the good, which represents both as differing only in their logical form, the first being merely a confused, the second a clearly defined, concept of perfection, while otherwise alike in content and origin, all goes for nothing: for then there would be no *specific* difference between them, but the judgement of taste would be just as much a cognitive judgement as one by which something is described as good—just as the man in the street, when he says that deceit is wrong, bases his judgement on confused, but the philosopher on clear grounds, while both appeal in reality to the same principles of reason. But I have already stated that an aesthetic judgement is quite unique, and affords absolutely no (not even a confused) knowledge of the object. It is only through a logical judgement that we get knowledge. The aesthetic judgement, on the other hand, refers the representation, by which an object is given, solely to the subject, and brings to our notice no character of the object, but only the purposive form in the determination of the powers of representation engaged upon it. The judgement is called aesthetic for the very reason that its determining ground cannot be a concept, but is rather the feeling (of inner sense) of the concerted play of the mental powers as something only capable of being felt. If, on the other hand, confused concepts, and the objective judgement based on them, are going to be called aesthetic, we shall find ourselves with an understanding judging by sense, or a sense representing its objects by concepts—a mere choice of contradictions. The faculty of concepts, whether they be confused or clear, is understanding; and although understanding has (as in all judgements) its rôle in the judgement of taste, as an aesthetic judgement, its rôle there is not that of a faculty for cognizing an object, but of 229 a faculty for determining that judgement and its representation (without a concept) according to its relation to the subject and its inner feeling, and for doing so in so far as that judgement is possible according to a universal rule.

§ 16

A judgement of taste by which an object is described as beautiful under the condition of a determinate concept is not pure

THERE are two kinds of beauty: free beauty (*pulchritudo vaga*), or beauty which is merely dependent (*pulchritudo adhaerens*). The first presupposes no concept of what the object should be; the second does presuppose such a concept and, with it, an answering perfection of the object. Those of the first kind are said to be (self-subsisting) beauties of this thing or that thing; the other kind of beauty, being attached to a concept (conditioned beauty), is ascribed to objects which come under the concept of a particular end.

Flowers are free beauties of nature. Hardly anyone but a botanist knows the true nature of a flower, and even he, while recognizing in the flower the reproductive organ of the plant, pays no attention to this natural end when using his taste to judge of its beauty. Hence no perfection of any kind—no internal purposiveness, as something to which the arrangement of the manifold is related—underlies this judgement. Many birds (the parrot, the humming-bird, the bird of paradise), and a number of marine crustacea, are self-subsisting beauties which have nothing to do with any object defined with respect to its end, but please freely and on their own account. So designs *à la grecque*,* foliage for framework or on wall-papers, etc., have no intrinsic meaning; they represent nothing—no object under a determinate concept—and are free beauties. We may also rank in the same class what in music are called fantasias (without a theme), and, indeed, all music that is not set to words.

In the judgement of a free beauty (according to mere form) we have the pure judgement of taste. No concept is here presupposed of any end for which the manifold should serve the given object, and which the latter, therefore, should represent—an incumbrance which would only restrict the freedom of the imagination that, as it were, is at play in the contemplation of the outward form.

But the beauty of man (including under this head that of a man, woman, or child), the beauty of a horse, or of a building (such as a church, palace, arsenal, or summer-house), presupposes a concept of the end that defines what the thing has to be, and consequently a concept of its perfection; and is therefore merely adherent beauty. Now, just as it hinders the purity of the judgement of taste to have the agreeable (of sensation) joined with beauty to which properly only the form is relevant, so to combine the good with beauty (the good, namely, of the manifold to the thing itself according to its end) mars its purity.

Much might be added to a building that would immediately please the eye, were it not intended for a church. A figure might be beautified with all manner of flourishes and light but regular lines, as is done by the New Zealanders with their tattooing, were we dealing with anything but the figure of a human being. And here is one whose rugged features might be softened and given a more pleasing countenance, only he has got to be a man, or is, perhaps, a warrior that has to have a warlike appearance.

Now the delight in the manifold of a thing, in reference to the internal end that determines its possibility, is a delight based on a concept, whereas delight in the beautiful is such as does not presuppose any concept, but is immediately coupled with the representation through which the object is given (not through which it is thought). If, now, the judgement of taste in respect of the latter delight is made dependent upon the end involved in the former delight as a judgement of reason, and is thus placed under a restriction, then it is no longer a free and pure judgement of taste.

Taste, it is true, stands to gain by this combination of intellectual delight with the aesthetic. For it becomes fixed, and, while not universal, it enables rules to be prescribed for it in respect of certain purposively determined objects. But these rules are then not rules of taste, but merely rules for establishing a union of taste with reason, i.e. of the beautiful with the good—rules by which the former becomes available as an intentional instrument in respect of the latter, for the purpose of bringing that temper of the mind which is self-sustaining and of subjective universal validity to the support and maintenance 231 of that mode of thought which, while possessing objective universal validity, can only be preserved by a resolute effort. But, strictly speaking, perfection neither gains by beauty, nor beauty by perfection. The truth is rather this, when we compare the representation through which an object is given to us with the object (in respect of what it is meant to be) by means of a concept, we cannot help reviewing it also in respect of the sensation in the subject. Hence there results a gain to the *entire faculty* of our power of representation when harmony prevails between both states of mind.

In respect of an object with a determinate internal end, a judgement of taste would only be pure where the person judging either has no concept of this end, or else makes abstraction from it in his judgement. But in cases like this, although such a person should lay down a correct judgement of taste, since he would be judging the object as a free beauty, he would still be censured by another who saw nothing in its beauty but a dependent quality (i.e. who looked to the end of the object) and would be accused by him of false taste, though both would, in their own way, be judging correctly: the one according to what he had present to his senses, the other according to what was present in his thoughts. This distinction enables us to settle many disputes about beauty on the part of critics; for we may show them how one side is dealing with free beauty, and the other with that which is dependent: the former making a pure judgement of taste, the latter an applied judgement taste.

§ 17
The ideal of beauty

THERE can be no objective rule of taste by which what is beautiful may be defined by means of concepts. For every judgement from that source is aesthetic, i.e. its determining ground is the feeling of the subject, and not any concept of an object. It is merely wasted labour to look for a principle of taste that affords a universal criterion of the beautiful by determinate concepts; because what is sought is something impossible and inherently contradictory. But in the universal communicability of the sensation (of delight or aversion)—a communicability, too, that exists apart from any concept—in the accord, so far as possible, of all ages and nations as to this feeling in the representation of certain objects, we have the empirical criterion, weak indeed and scarce sufficient to raise a presumption, of the derivation of a taste, thus confirmed by examples, from a deep-seated ground, one shared alike by all human beings, underlying their agreement in judging the forms under which objects are given to them.

For this reason some products of taste are looked on as *exemplary*—not meaning thereby that by imitating others taste may be acquired. For taste must be an intrinsically original faculty; whereas one who imitates a model, while showing skill commensurate with his success, only displays taste in so far as he judges this model himself.[4] Hence it follows that the highest model, the arche-type of taste, is a mere idea, which each person must produce in his own consciousness, and according to which he must form his judge-ment of everything that is an object of taste, or that is an example of critical taste, and even of universal taste itself. Properly speaking, an *idea* signifies a concept of reason, and an *ideal* the representation of an individual existence as adequate to an idea. Hence this archetype of taste—which rests, indeed, upon reason's indeterminate idea of a maximum, but is not, however, capable of being represented by means of concepts, but only in an individual presentation—may more appropriately be called the ideal of the beautiful. While not having this ideal in our possession, we still strive to produce it within us. But it is bound to be merely an ideal of the imagination, seeing that it rests, not upon concepts, but upon the presentation—the faculty of presentation being the imagination.—Now, how do we arrive at such an ideal of beauty? Is it *a priori* or empirically? Further, what species of the beautiful admits of an ideal?

First of all, we do well to observe that the beauty for which an ideal has to be sought cannot be a beauty that is *free and at large*, but must be one *fixed* by a concept of objective purposiveness. Hence it cannot belong to the object of an altogether pure judgement of taste, but must attach to one that is partly intellectual. In other words, what-ever kind of grounds there may be for judging an ideal, there must be some underlying idea of reason according to determinate con-cepts, by which the end underlying the internal possibility of the object is determined *a priori*. An ideal of beautiful flowers, of a beau-tiful suite of furniture, or of a beautiful view, is unthinkable. But, it may also be impossible to represent an ideal of a beauty dependent on determinate ends, e.g. a beautiful residence, a beautiful tree, a beautiful garden, etc., presumably because their ends are not sufficiently defined and fixed by their concept, with the result that their purposiveness is nearly as free as with beauty that is quite *at large*. Only what has in itself the end of its existence—only the *human being* that is able himself to determine his ends by reason, or,

233

---

[4] Models of taste with respect to the arts of speech must be composed in a dead and learned language; the first, to prevent their having to suffer the changes that inevitably over-take living ones, making dignified expressions become degraded, common ones antiquated, and ones newly created after a short period of time obsolete; the second to ensure its having a grammar that is not subject to the caprices of fashion, but has fixed rules of its own.

where he has to derive them from external perception, can still compare them with essential and universal ends, and then further pronounce aesthetically upon their accord with such ends, only this, among all objects in the world, admits, therefore, of an ideal of *beauty*, just as humanity in his person, as intelligence, alone admits of the ideal of *perfection*.

Two factors are here involved. *First*, there is the aesthetic *normal idea*, which is an individual intuition (of the imagination). This represents the norm by which we judge a human being as a member of a particular animal species. *Secondly*, there is the *rational idea*. This deals with the ends of humanity so far as they are incapable of sensuous representation, and converts them into a principle for judging his outward form, through which these ends are revealed in their phenomenal effect. The normal idea must draw from experience the constituents which it requires for the form of an animal of a particular kind. But the greatest purposiveness in the construction of this form—that which would serve as a universal norm for the aesthetic judging of each individual of the species in question—the image that, as it were, forms an intentional basis underlying the technic of nature, to which no separate individual, but only the species as a whole, is adequate, has its seat merely in the idea of the judging subject. Yet it is, with all its proportions, an aesthetic idea, and, as such, capable of being fully presented *in concreto* in a model image. Now, how is this effected? In order to render the process to some extent intelligible (for who can wrest nature's whole secret from her?), let us attempt a psychological explanation.

234 It is of note that the imagination, in a manner quite incomprehensible to us, is able on occasion, even after a long lapse of time, not only to recall the signs for concepts, but also to reproduce the image and shape of an object out of a countless number of others of a different, or even of the very same, kind. And, further, if the mind is engaged upon comparisons, we may well suppose that it can in actual fact, though the process is partly unconscious, superimpose as it were one image upon another, and from the coincidence of a number of the same kind arrive at a mean contour which serves as a common standard for all. Say, for instance, a person has seen a thousand full-grown men. Now if he wishes to judge normal size determined upon a comparative estimate, then imagination (to my mind) allows

a great number of these images (perhaps the whole thousand) to fall one upon the other, and, if I may be allowed to extend to the case the analogy of optical presentation, in the space where they come most preponderantly together, and within the contour where the place is illuminated by the greatest concentration of colour, one gets a perception of the *average size*, which alike in height and breadth is equally removed from the extreme limits of the greatest and smallest statures; and this is the stature of a beautiful man. (The same result could be obtained in a mechanical way, by taking the measures of all the thousand, and adding together their heights, and their breadths (and thicknesses), and dividing the sum in each case by a thousand.) But the power of imagination does all this by means of a dynamical effect upon the organ of inner sense, arising from the frequent apprehension of such forms. If, again, for our average man we seek on similar lines for the average head, and for this the average nose, and so on, then we get the figure that underlies the normal idea of a beautiful man in the country where the comparison is instituted. For this reason a black man must necessarily (under these empirical conditions) have a different normal idea of the beauty of forms from what a white man has, and the Chinese person one different from the European. And the process would be just the same with the *model* of a beautiful horse or dog (of a particular breed).—This *normal idea* is not derived from proportions taken from experience *as determinate rules*: rather it is according to this idea that rules for judging first become possible. It is something intermediate between all singular intuitions of individuals, with their manifold variations—a floating image for the whole genus, which nature has set as an archetype underlying those of her products that belong to the same species, but which in no single case she seems to have completely attained. But the normal idea is far from giving the complete *archetype* of *beauty* in the genus. It only gives the form that constitutes the indispensable condition of all beauty, and, consequently, only *correctness* in the presentation of the genus. It is, as the famous *Doryphorus* of *Polycletus* was called, the *rule* (and *Myron's* Cow* might be similarly employed for its kind). It cannot, for that very reason, contain anything specifically characteristic; for otherwise it would not be the *normal idea* for the genus. Further, it is not by beauty that its presentation pleases, but merely because it does not contradict any of the conditions

235

under which alone a thing belonging to this genus can be beautiful. The presentation is merely academically correct.[5]

But the *ideal* of the beautiful is still something different from its *normal idea*. For reasons already stated it is only to be sought in the *human figure*. Here the ideal consists in the expression of the *moral*, apart from which the object would not please at once universally and positively (not merely negatively in a presentation that is academically correct). The visible expression of moral ideas that govern the human being inwardly can, of course, only be drawn from experience; but their combination with all that our reason connects with the morally good in the idea of the highest purposiveness—benevolence, purity, strength, or equanimity, etc.—may be made, as it were, visible in bodily manifestation (as effect of what is internal), and this embodiment involves a union of pure ideas of reason and great imaginative power, in one who would even form a judgement of it, not to speak of being the author of its presentation. The correctness of such an ideal of beauty is evidenced by its not permitting any sensuous charm to mingle with the delight in its object, in which it still allows us to take a great interest. This fact in turn shows that judging according to such a standard can never be purely aesthetic, and that judging according to an ideal of beauty cannot be a simple judgement of taste.

DEFINITION OF THE BEAUTIFUL DERIVED FROM THIS THIRD MOMENT

Beauty is the form of *purposiveness* in an object, so far as this is perceived in it *apart from the representation of an end*.[6]

[5] It will be found that a perfectly regular face—one that a painter might fix his eye on for a model—ordinarily conveys nothing. This is because it is devoid of anything characteristic, and so the idea of the species is expressed in it rather than the specific qualities of a person. The exaggeration of what is characteristic in this way, i.e. exaggeration violating the normal idea (the purposiveness of the species), is called *caricature*. Also experience shows that these quite regular faces indicate as a rule only an inwardly mediocre human being; presumably—if one may assume that nature in its external form expresses the proportions of the inner—because, where none of the mental qualities exceed the proportion requisite to constitute an individual free from faults, nothing can be expected in the way of what is called *genius*, in which nature seems to make a departure from its usual relations of the mental powers in favour of some special one.

[6] As telling against this explanation, the instance may be adduced, that there are things in which we see a form suggesting adaptation to an end, without any end being cognized in them—as, for example, the stone implements frequently obtained from

FOURTH MOMENT

OF THE JUDGEMENT OF TASTE: MOMENT OF THE MODALITY OF THE DELIGHT IN THE OBJECT

§ 18

Character of the modality in a judgement of taste

I MAY assert in the case of every representation that the connection of a pleasure with the representation (as a cognition) is at least *possible*. Of what I call *agreeable* I assert that it *actually* causes pleasure in me. But what we have in mind in the case of the *beautiful* is a *necessary* reference on its part to delight. However, this necessity is of a special kind. It is not a theoretical objective necessity—such as would let us cognize *a priori* that everyone *will feel* this delight in the object that is called beautiful by me. Nor yet is it a practical necessity, in which case, thanks to concepts of a pure rational will in which free agents are supplied with a rule, this delight is the necessary consequence of an objective law, and simply means that one ought absolutely (without ulterior aim) to act in a certain way. Rather, being such a necessity as is thought in an aesthetic judgement, it can only be termed *exemplary*. In other words it is a necessity of the assent of *all* to a judgement regarded as exemplifying a universal rule which cannot be formulated. Since an aesthetic judgement is not an objective or cognitive judgement, this necessity is not derivable from determinate concepts, and so is not apodictic. Much less is it inferable from the universality of experience (of a complete agreement of judgements about the beauty of a certain object). For, apart from the fact that experience would hardly furnish sufficient evidence for this purpose, empirical judgements do not afford any foundation for a concept of the necessity of these judgements.

237

---

sepulchral tumuli and supplied with a hole, as if designed for a handle; and although these by their shape manifestly indicate a purposiveness, the end of which is unknown, they are not on that account described as beautiful. But the very fact of their being regarded as artificial products involves an immediate recognition that their shape is attributed to some purpose or other and to a definite end. For this reason there is no immediate delight whatever in their contemplation. A flower, on the other hand, such as a tulip, is regarded as beautiful, because we meet with a certain purposiveness in its perception, which, in our judgement of it, is not referred to any end whatever.

§ 19

The subjective necessity attributed to a judgement of taste is conditioned

THE judgement of taste expects agreement from everyone; and a person who describes something as beautiful insists that everyone *ought* to give the object in question his approval and follow suit in describing it as beautiful. The *ought* in aesthetic judgements, therefore, despite an accordance with all the requisite data for passing judgement, is still only pronounced conditionally. We are suitors for agreement from everyone else, because we are fortified with a ground common to all. Further, we would be able to count on this agreement, provided we were always assured of the correct subsumption of the case under that ground as the rule of approval.

§ 20

The condition of the necessity advanced by a judgement of taste is the idea of a common sense

IF judgements of taste (like cognitive judgements) were in possession
238 of a definite objective principle, then one who in his judgement followed such a principle would claim unconditioned necessity for it. Again, if they were devoid of any principle, as are those of the mere taste of the senses, then no thought of any necessity on their part would enter one's head. Therefore they must have a subjective principle, and one which determines what pleases or displeases, by means of feeling only and not through concepts, but yet with universal validity. Such a principle, however, could only be regarded as a *common sense*. This differs essentially from common understanding, which is also sometimes called common sense (*sensus communis*): for the judgement of the latter is not one by feeling, but always one by concepts, though usually only in the shape of obscurely represented principles.

The judgement of taste, therefore, depends on our presupposing the existence of a common sense. (But this is not to be taken to mean some external sense, but the effect arising from the free play of our powers of cognition.) Only under the presupposition, I repeat, of such a common sense, are we able to lay down a judgement of taste.

§ 21

Have we any ground for presupposing a common sense?

COGNITIONS and judgements must, together with their attendant conviction, admit of being universally communicated; for otherwise no correspondence with the object could be ascribed to them. They would all amount to nothing but a mere subjective play of the powers of representation, just as scepticism would have it. But if cognitions are to admit of communication, then our state of mind, i.e. the way the cognitive powers are attuned for cognition generally, and, in fact, the relative proportion suitable for a representation (by which an object is given to us) from which cognition is to result, must also admit of being universally communicated, since, without this, which is the subjective condition of the act of knowing, knowledge, as an effect, would not arise. And this is always what actually happens where a given object, through the intervention of the senses, sets the imagination to work in combining the manifold, and the imagination, in turn, sets the understanding to work in unifying the manifold under concepts. But this disposition of the cognitive powers has a relative proportion differing with the diversity of the objects that are given. However, there must be one in which this internal ratio suitable for enlivening (one faculty by the other) is best adapted for both mental powers in respect of cognition (of given objects) generally; and this disposition can only be determined through feeling (and not 239 by concepts). Since, now, this disposition itself must admit of being universally communicated, and hence also the feeling of it (in the case of a given representation), while again, the universal communicability of a feeling presupposes a common sense: it follows that our assumption of it is well founded. And here, too, we do not have to take our stand on psychological observations, but we assume a common sense as the necessary condition of the universal communicability of our knowledge, which is presupposed in every logic and every principle of knowledge that is not one of scepticism.

§ 22

The necessity of the universal assent that is thought in a judgement of taste, is a subjective necessity which, under the presupposition of a common sense, is represented as objective

IN all judgements by which we describe anything as beautiful we tolerate no one else being of a different opinion, and yet we do not rest our judgement upon concepts, but only on our feeling. Accordingly we introduce this underlying feeling not as a private feeling, but as a common one. Now, for this purpose, experience cannot be made the ground of this common sense, for the latter is invoked to justify judgements containing an 'ought'. The assertion is not that everyone *will* fall in with our judgement, but rather that everyone *ought* to agree with it. Here I put forward my judgement of taste as an example of the judgement of common sense, and attribute to it on that account *exemplary* validity. Hence common sense is a mere ideal norm. With this as presupposition, a judgement that acccords with it, as well as the delight in an object expressed in that judgement, is rightly converted into a rule for everyone. For the principle, while it is only subjective, being yet assumed as subjectively universal (a necessary idea for everyone), could, in what concerns the consensus of different judging subjects, demand universal assent like an objective principle, provided we were assured of our subsumption under it being correct.

This indeterminate norm of a common sense is, as a matter of fact, presupposed by us; as is shown by our presuming to lay down judgements of taste. But does such a common sense in fact exist as a constitutive principle of the possibility of experience, or is it formed for us as a regulative principle by a still higher principle of reason, that for higher ends first seeks to produce in us a common sense? Is taste, in other words, a natural and original faculty, or is it only the idea of one that is artificial and to be acquired by us, so that a judgement of taste, with its expectation of universal assent, is but a demand of reason for generating such unanimity in this sensing, and does the 'ought', i.e. the objective necessity of the coincidence of the feeling of all with the particular feeling of each, only betoken the possibility of arriving at some sort of agreement in these matters, and the judgement of taste only adduce an example of the application of this principle? These are questions which as yet we are neither willing nor in a position to investigate. For the present we have only to resolve the faculty of taste into its elements, and to unite these ultimately in the idea of a common sense.

DEFINITION OF THE BEAUTIFUL DRAWN FROM THE FOURTH MOMENT

The beautiful is that which, apart from a concept, is cognized as object of a *necessary* delight.

GENERAL REMARK ON THE FIRST SECTION OF THE ANALYTIC*

The result to be extracted from the foregoing analysis is in effect this: that everything comes down to the concept of taste as a faculty for judging an object in reference to the *free conformity to law* of the imagination. If, now, imagination must in the judgement of taste be regarded in its freedom, then, to begin with, it is not taken as reproductive, as in its subjection to the laws of association, but as productive and active in its own right (as originator of arbitrary forms of possible intuitions). And although in the apprehension of a given object of the senses it is tied down to a determinate form of this object and, to that extent, does not enjoy free play (as it does in poetry), still it is easy to conceive that the object may supply ready-made to the imagination just such a form of the arrangement of the manifold, as 241 the imagination, if it were left to itself, would freely project in harmony with the general *conformity to law of the understanding*. But that the *imagination* should be both *free* and *of itself conformable to law*, i.e. carry autonomy with it, is a contradiction. The understanding alone gives the law. Where, however, the imagination is compelled to follow a course laid down by a determinate law, then what the form of the product is to be is determined by concepts; but, in that case, as already shown, the delight is not delight in the beautiful, but in the good, (in perfection, though it be no more than formal perfection), and the judgement is not one due to taste. Hence it is only a conformity to law without a law, and a subjective harmonizing of the imagination and the understanding without an objective one—which latter would mean that the representation was referred to a determinate concept of the object—that is consistent with the free conformity to law of the understanding (which has also been called purposiveness without a purpose) and with the specific character of a judgement of taste.

Now geometrically regular figures, a circle, a square, a cube, and the like, are commonly brought forward by critics of taste as the most simple and unquestionable examples of beauty. And yet the very reason why they are called regular, is because the only way of representing them is by looking on them as mere presentations of a determinate concept by which the figure has its rule (according to which alone it is possible) prescribed for it. One or other of these two views must, therefore, be wrong: either the verdict of the critics that attributes beauty to such figures, or else our own, which makes purposiveness apart from any concept necessary for beauty.

One would scarce think it necessary for a person with taste to take more delight in a circle than in a scrawled outline, in an equilateral and equiangular quadrilateral than in one that is all lob-sided, and, as it were, deformed. The requirements of common understanding ensure such a preference without the least demand upon taste. Where some purpose is perceived, as, for instance, that of judging the area of a plot of land, or rendering intelligible the relation of divided parts to one another and to the whole, then regular figures, and those of the simplest kind, are needed; and the delight does not rest immediately upon the way the figure strikes the eye, but upon its
242 serviceability for all manner of possible purposes. A room with the walls making oblique angles, a plot laid out in a garden in a similar way, even any violation of symmetry, as well in the figure of animals (e.g. being one-eyed) as in that of buildings, or of flower-beds, is displeasing because of its counter-purposive form, not only in a practical way in respect of some definite use to which the thing may be put, but for a judgement that looks to all manner of possible purposes. With the judgement of taste the case is different. For, when it is pure, it combines delight or aversion immediately with the bare *contemplation* of the object irrespective of its use or of any end.

The regularity that conduces to the concept of an object is, in fact, the indispensable condition (*conditio sine qua non*) of grasping the object as a single representation and giving to the manifold its determinate form. This determination is an end in respect of knowledge; and in this connexion it is invariably coupled with delight (such as attends the accomplishment of any, even problematical, purpose). Here, however, we have merely the value set upon the solution that satisfies the problem, and not a free and indeterminately purposive entertainment of the powers of the mind with what is called beautiful.

In the latter case understanding is at the service of imagination, in the former this relation is reversed.

With a thing that owes its possibility to a purpose, a building, or even an animal, its regularity, which consists in symmetry, must express the unity of the intuition accompanying the concept of its end, and belongs with it to cognition. But where all that is intended is the maintenance of a free play of the powers of representation (subject, however, to the condition that there is to be nothing for understanding to take exception to), in ornamental gardens, in the decoration of rooms, in all kinds of tasteful implements etc., regularity that betrays constraint is to be avoided as far as possible. Thus English taste in gardens, and baroque taste in furniture, push the freedom of imagination to the verge of what is grotesque—the idea being that in this divorce from all constraint of rules the precise instance is being afforded where taste can exhibit its perfection in projects of the imagination to the fullest extent.

All stiff regularity (such as that which borders on mathematical regularity) is inherently repugnant to taste, in that the contemplation of it affords us no lasting entertainment. Indeed, where it has neither cognition nor some determinate practical end expressly in view, we 243 get heartily tired of it. On the other hand, anything that gives the imagination scope for unstudied and purposive play is always fresh to us. We do not grow weary of the very sight of it. *Marsden* in his description of Sumatra* observes that the free beauties of nature so surround the beholder on all sides that they cease to have much attraction for him. On the other hand he found a pepper garden full of charm, on coming across it in mid-forest with its rows of parallel stakes on which the plant twines itself. From all this he infers that wild, and in its appearance quite irregular beauty, is only pleasing as a change to one whose eyes have become surfeited with regular beauty. But he need only have made the experiment of passing one day in his pepper garden to realize that once the regularity has enabled the understanding to put itself in accord with the order that is its constant requirement, instead of the object diverting him any longer, it imposes an irksome constraint upon the imagination: whereas nature subject to no constraint of artificial rules, and lavish, as it there is, in its luxuriant variety can supply constant nourishment for his taste.— Even a bird's song, which we can reduce to no musical rule, seems to have more freedom in it, and thus to offer more for taste, than the human voice singing in accordance with all the rules that the art of music prescribes; for we grow tired much sooner of frequent and lengthy repetitions of the latter. Yet here most likely our sympathy with the joy of a dear little creature is confused with the beauty of its song, for if exactly imitated by a human being (as has been sometimes done with the notes of the nightingale) it would strike our ear as wholly destitute of taste.

Further, beautiful objects have to be distinguished from beautiful views of objects (where the distance often prevents a clear perception). In the latter case taste appears to fasten, not so much on what the imagination *grasps* in this field, as on the encouragement it receives in the way of *invention*, i.e. in the peculiar fantasies with which the mind entertains itself as it is being continually stirred by the variety that strikes the eye. It is just as when we watch the changing shapes of the fire in the hearth or of a rippling brook: neither of
244 which are things of beauty, but nonetheless convey a charm to the imagination, because they sustain its free play.

SECOND BOOK

ANALYTIC OF THE SUBLIME

§ 23

Transition from the faculty of judging the beautiful
to that of judging the sublime

THE beautiful and the sublime agree on the point of pleasing on their own account. Further they agree in not presupposing either a judgement of the senses or a logically determining judgement, but one of reflection. Hence it follows that the delight does not depend upon a sensation, as with the agreeable, nor upon a definite concept, as does the delight in the good, although it has, for all that, an indeterminate reference to concepts. Consequently the delight is connected with the mere presentation or faculty of presentation, and is thus taken to express the accord, in a given intuition, of the faculty of presentation, or the imagination, with the *faculty of concepts* that belongs to understanding or reason, in the sense of the former faculty assisting the latter. Hence both kinds of judgements are *singular*, and yet such as profess to be universally valid in respect of every subject, despite the fact that their claims are directed merely to the feeling of pleasure and not to any knowledge of the object.

There are, however, also important and striking differences between the two. The beautiful in nature is a question of the form of the object, and this consists in limitation, whereas the sublime is to be found in an object even devoid of form, so far as it immediately involves, or else by its presence provokes, a representation of *limitlessness*, yet with a super-added thought of its totality. Accordingly the beautiful seems to be regarded as a presentation of an indeterminate concept of the understanding, the sublime as a presentation of an indeterminate concept of reason. Hence the delight is in the former case coupled with the representation of *quality*, but in this case with that of *quantity*. Moreover, the former delight is very different from the latter in kind. For the beautiful is directly attended with a feeling of the furtherance of life, and is thus compatible with charms and a playful imagination. On the other hand, the feeling of the sublime is a pleasure that only arises indirectly, being brought about by the feeling of a 245

momentary check to the vital forces followed at once by a discharge all
the more powerful, and so it is an emotion that seems to be no play, but
a serious matter in the exercise of the imagination. Hence charms are
also incompatible with it; and, since the mind is not simply attracted by
the object, but is also alternately repelled thereby, the delight in the
sublime does not so much involve positive pleasure as admiration or
respect, i.e. merits the name of a negative pleasure.

But the most important and vital distinction between the sublime
and the beautiful is certainly this: that if, as is allowable, we here
confine our attention in the first instance to the sublime in objects of
nature (that of art being always restricted by the conditions of an
agreement with nature), we observe that whereas natural beauty
(such as is self-subsisting) conveys a purposiveness in its form making
the object appear, as it were, already adapted to our power of judgement, so that it thus forms of itself an object of our delight, that
which, without our indulging in any refinements of thought, but,
simply in our apprehension of it, excites the feeling of the sublime,
may appear, indeed, in point of form to contravene the ends of our
power of judgement, to be ill-adapted to our faculty of presentation,
and to do violence, as it were, to the imagination, and yet it is judged
all the more sublime on that account.

From this it may be seen at once that we express ourselves on the
whole inaccurately if we term any *object of nature* sublime, although
we may with perfect propriety call many such objects beautiful. For
how can that which is apprehended as inherently counter-purposive
be noted with an expression of approval? All that we can say is that
the object lends itself to the presentation of a sublimity discoverable in
the mind. For the sublime, in the strict sense of the word, cannot be
contained in any sensuous form, but rather concerns ideas of reason,
which, although no adequate presentation of them is possible, may be
aroused and called to mind by that very inadequacy itself which does
admit of sensuous presentation. Thus the broad ocean agitated by
246 storms cannot be called sublime. The sight of it is horrible, and one
must have stored one's mind in advance with a wealth of ideas, if
such an intuition is to attune it to a feeling which is itself sublime—
sublime because the mind has been incited to abandon sensibility,
and employ itself upon ideas involving a higher purposiveness.

Self-subsisting natural beauty reveals to us a technic of nature
which shows it in the light of a system ordered in accordance with

laws the principle of which is not to be found within the range of our entire faculty of understanding. This principle is that of a purposiveness relative to the employment of judgement in respect of phenomena which have thus to be assigned, not merely to nature regarded as aimless mechanism, but also to nature regarded after the analogy of art. Hence it gives a veritable extension, not, of course, to our knowledge of objects of nature, but to our conception of nature itself— nature as mere mechanism being enlarged to the conception of nature as art—an extension inviting profound inquiries as to the possibility of such a form. But in what we are wont to call sublime in nature there is such an absence of anything leading to particular objective principles and corresponding forms of nature, that it is rather in its chaos, or in its wildest and most irregular disorder and desolation, provided it gives signs of magnitude and power, that nature chiefly excites the ideas of the sublime. Hence we see that the concept of the sublime in nature is far less important and rich in consequences than that of its beauty. It gives on the whole no indication of anything purposive in nature itself, but only in the possible *employment* of our intuitions of it in inducing a feeling in our own selves of a purposiveness quite independent of nature. For the beautiful in nature we must seek a ground external to ourselves, but for the sublime one merely in ourselves and the attitude of mind that introduces sublimity into the representation of nature. This is a very needful preliminary remark. It entirely separates the ideas of the sublime from that of a purposiveness of *nature*, and makes the theory of the sublime a mere appendage to the aesthetic judgement of the purposiveness of nature, because it does not give a representation of any particular form in nature, but involves no more than the development of a purposive employment by the imagination of its own representation.

§ 24

On the division of an investigation of the feeling of the sublime

In the division of the moments of an aesthetic estimate of objects in respect of the feeling of the sublime, the course of the analytic will be able to follow the same principle as in the analysis of judgements of taste. For, the judgement being one of the aesthetic reflective judgement, the delight in the sublime, just like that in the beautiful, must in its *quantity* be shown to be universally valid, in its *quality* independent of interest, in its *relation* subjective purposiveness, and the latter, in its *modality*, necessary. Hence the method here will not depart from the lines followed in the preceding section: unless something is made of the point that there, where the aesthetic judgement bore on the form of the object, we began with the investigation of its quality, whereas here, considering the formlessness that may belong to what we call sublime, we begin with that of its quantity, as first moment of the aesthetic judgement on the sublime—a divergence of method the reason for which is evident from § 23.

But the analysis of the sublime demands a division not required by that of the beautiful, namely one into the *mathematically* and the *dynamically* sublime.

For the feeling of the sublime involves as its characteristic feature a *movement* of the mind combined with the judging of the object, whereas taste in respect of the beautiful presupposes that the mind is in *restful* contemplation, and preserves it in this state. But this movement has to be judged as subjectively purposive (since the sublime pleases). Hence it is referred through the imagination either to the *faculty of cognition* or to that of *desire*; but to whichever faculty the reference is made the finality of the given representation is judged only in respect of these faculties (apart from end or interest). Accordingly the first is attributed to the object as a *mathematical*, the second as a *dynamical*, attunement of the imagination. Hence we arrive at the above mentioned twofold mode of representing an object as sublime.

248   A. THE MATHEMATICALLY SUBLIME

§ 25

Definition of the term 'sublime'

Sublime is the name given to what is *absolutely great*. But to be great and to be a magnitude are entirely different concepts (*magnitudo* and *quantitas*). In the same way to *assert without qualification* (*simpliciter*) that something is great, is quite a different thing from saying that it is *absolutely great* (*absolute, non comparative magnum*). The latter is *what is beyond all comparison great*.—What, then, is the meaning of the assertion that anything is great, or small, or of medium size? What is indicated is not a pure concept of understanding, still less an intuition of the senses; and just as little is it a concept of reason, for it does not import any principle of cognition. It must, therefore, be a concept of judgement, or have its source in one, and must introduce as basis of the judgement a subjective purposiveness of the representation with reference to the power of judgement. Given a multiplicity of the homogeneous together constituting one thing, and we may at once cognize from the thing itself that it is a *magnitude* (*quantum*). No comparison with other things is required. But to determine *how great* it is always requires something else, which itself has magnitude, for its measure. Now, since in the judging of magnitude we have to take into account not merely the multiplicity (number of units) but also the magnitude of the unit (the measure), and since the magnitude of this unit in turn always requires something else as its measure and as the standard of its comparison, and so on, we see that the computation of the magnitude of phenomena is, in all cases, utterly incapable of affording us any absolute concept of a magnitude, and can, instead, only afford one that is always based on comparison.

If, now, I assert without qualification that anything is great, it would seem that I have nothing in the way of a comparison present to my mind, or at least nothing involving an objective measure, for no attempt is thus made to determine how great the object is. But, despite the standard of comparison being merely subjective, the claim of the judgement is nonetheless one to universal agreement; the judgements: 'That man is beautiful' and 'He is tall' do not purport to speak only for the judging subject, but, like theoretical judgements, they demand the assent of everyone.

Now in a judgement that without qualification describes anything 249 as great, it is not merely meant that the object has a magnitude, but greatness is ascribed to it pre-eminently among many other objects of a like kind, yet without the extent of this pre-eminence being determined. Hence a standard is certainly laid at the basis of the judgement, which standard is presupposed to be one that can be taken as the same for everyone, but which is available only for an aesthetic judging of the greatness, and not for one that is logical (mathematically determined), for the standard is a merely subjective one underlying the reflective judgement upon the greatness. Furthermore, this standard may be empirical, as, let us say, the average size of the men known to us, of animals of a certain kind, of trees, of houses, of mountains, and so forth. Or it may be a standard given *a priori*, which by reason of the imperfections of the judging subject is restricted to subjective conditions of presentation *in concreto*: as, in the practical sphere, the greatness of a particular virtue, or of public liberty and justice in a country; or, in the theoretical sphere, the greatness of the accuracy or inaccuracy of an experiment or measurement, etc.

Here, now, it is noteworthy that, although we have no interest whatever in the object, i.e. its real existence may be a matter of no concern to us, still its mere greatness, regarded even as devoid of form, is able to convey a universally communicable delight and so involve the consciousness of a subjective purposiveness in the employment of our cognitive faculties, but not, be it remembered, a delight in the object, for the latter may be formless, but, in contradistinction to what is the case with the beautiful, where the reflective judgement finds itself set to a key that is final in respect of cognition generally, a delight in an extension affecting the imagination itself.

If (under the aforementioned restriction) we say of an object, without qualification, that it is great, this is not a mathematically determining, but a mere reflective judgement upon its representation, which is subjectively purposive for a particular employment of our cognitive faculties in the judging of magnitude, and we then always couple with the representation a kind of respect, just as we couple a kind of contempt with what we call absolutely small. Moreover, the judging of things as great or small extends to everything, even to all their qualities. Thus we call even their beauty great or small. The reason for this is to be found in the fact that we have only got to present a thing in intuition, as the faculty of judgement directs (consequently to represent it aesthetically), for it to be in its entirety a phenomenon, and hence a quantum.

250

If, however, we call anything not merely great, but, without qualification, absolutely, and in every respect (beyond all comparison) great, that is to say, sublime, we soon perceive that for this it is not permissible to seek an appropriate standard outside itself, but merely in itself. It is a greatness comparable to itself alone. Hence it comes that the sublime is not to be looked for in the things of nature, but only in our own ideas. But it must be left to the deduction to show in which of them it resides.

The above definition may also be expressed in this way: *that is sublime in comparison with which all else is small*. Here we readily see that nothing can be given in nature, no matter how great we may judge it

to be, which, regarded in some other relation, may not be degraded
to the level of the infinitely little, and nothing so small which in comparison with some still smaller standard may not for our imagination
be enlarged to the greatness of a world. Telescopes have put within
our reach an abundance of material to go upon in making the first
observation, and microscopes the same in making the second.
Nothing, therefore, which can be an object of the senses is to be
termed sublime when treated on this footing. But precisely because
there is a striving in our imagination towards progress *ad infinitum*,
while reason demands absolute totality, as a real idea that same
inability on the part of our faculty for the estimation of the magnitude of things of the world of the senses to attain to the idea, is the
awakening of a feeling of a supersensible faculty within us; and it is
the use to which judgement naturally puts particular objects on
behalf of this latter feeling, and not the object of the senses, that is
absolutely great, and every other contrasted employment small.
Consequently it is the attunement of the spirit evoked by a particular representation engaging the attention of reflective judgement, and
not the object, that is to be called sublime.

The foregoing formulae defining the sublime may, therefore, be
supplemented by yet another: *The sublime is that, the mere capacity of
thinking which evidences a faculty of mind transcending every standard
of the senses.*

§ 26

*The estimation of the magnitude of natural things requisite
for the idea of the sublime*

THE estimation of magnitude by means of concepts of number (or
their signs in algebra) is mathematical, but that in mere intuition (by
the eye) is aesthetic. Now we can only get definite concepts of *how
great* anything is by having recourse to numbers (or, at any rate, by
getting approximate measurements by means of numerical series
progressing *ad infinitum*), the unit being the measure; and to this
extent all logical estimation of magnitude is mathematical. But, as the
magnitude of the measure has to be assumed as a known quantity, if,
to form an estimate of this, we must again have recourse to numbers
involving another standard for their unit, and consequently must again
proceed mathematically, we can never arrive at a first or fundamental

measure, and so cannot get any definite concept of a given magnitude. The estimation of the magnitude of the fundamental measure must, therefore, consist merely in the immediate grasp which we can get of it in intuition, and the use to which our imagination can put this in presenting the numerical concepts: i.e. all estimation of the magnitude of objects of nature is in the last resort aesthetic (i.e. subjectively and not objectively determined).

Now for the mathematical estimation of magnitude there is, of course, no greatest possible magnitude (for the power of numbers extends to infinity), but for the aesthetic estimation there certainly is, and of it I say that where it is considered an absolute measure beyond which no greater is possible subjectively (i.e. for the judging subject), it then conveys the idea of the sublime, and calls forth that emotion which no mathematical estimation of magnitudes by numbers can evoke (except in so far as the fundamental aesthetic measure is vividly preserved for the imagination): because the latter presents only the relative magnitude due to comparison with others of a like kind, whereas the former presents magnitude absolutely, so far as the mind can grasp it in an intuition.

To take in a quantum intuitively in the imagination so as to be able to use it as a measure, or unit for estimating magnitude by numbers, involves two operations of this faculty: *apprehension* (*apprehensio*) and *comprehension* (*comprehensio aesthetica*). Apprehension presents no difficulty: for this process can be carried on *ad infinitum*; but with the

252 advance of apprehension comprehension becomes more difficult at every step and soon attains its maximum, and this is the aesthetically greatest fundamental measure for the estimation of magnitude. For if the apprehension has reached a point beyond which the representations of sensuous intuition in the case of the parts first apprehended begin to disappear from the imagination as this advances to the apprehension of yet others, as much, then, is lost at one end as is gained at the other, and for comprehension we get a maximum which the imagination cannot exceed.

This explains Savary's observations in his account of Egypt,* that in order to get the full emotional effect of the size of the pyramids we must avoid coming too near just as much as remaining too far away. For in the latter case the representation of the apprehended parts (the tiers of stones) is merely obscure, and produces no effect upon the aesthetic judgement of the subject. In the former, however, it takes the eye some time to complete the apprehension from the base to the summit; but in this interval the first tiers always in part disappear before the imagination has taken in the last, and so the comprehension is never complete.—The same explanation may also sufficiently account for the bewilderment, or sort of perplexity, which, as is said, seizes the visitor on first entering St. Peter's in Rome. For here a feeling comes home to him of the inadequacy of his imagination for presenting the idea of a whole within which that imagination attains its maximum, and, in its fruitless efforts to extend this limit, recoils upon itself, but in so doing succumbs to an emotional delight.

At present I am not disposed to deal with the ground of this delight, connected, as it is, with a representation in which we would least of all look for it—a representation, namely, that lets us see its own inadequacy, and consequently its subjective lack of purposiveness for our judgement in the estimation of magnitude—but confine myself to the remark that if the aesthetic judgement is to be *pure* (*unmixed with any teleological judgement* which, as such, belongs to reason), and if we are to give a suitable example of it for the critique of *aesthetic* judgement, we must not point to the sublime in works of art, e.g. buildings, statues and the like, where a human end determines the form as well as the magnitude, nor yet in things of nature, *that in their very concept import a determinate end*, e.g. animals of a recognized natural order, but in raw nature merely as involving magnitude (and only in this so far as it does not convey any charm or any emotion arising from actual danger). For in a representation of this kind nature contains nothing monstrous (nor what is either magnificent or horrible)—the magnitude apprehended may be increased to any extent provided imagination is able to grasp it all in one whole. An object is *monstrous* where by its size it defeats the end that forms its concept. The *colossal* is the mere presentation of a concept which is almost too great for presentation, i.e. borders on the relatively monstrous; for the end to be attained by the presentation of a concept is made harder to realize by the intuition of the object being almost too great for our faculty of apprehension.—A pure judgement upon the sublime must, however, have no end belonging to the object as its determining ground, if it is to be aesthetic and not to be tainted with any judgement of understanding or reason.

253

Since whatever is to be a source of pleasure, apart from interest, to the merely reflective judgement must involve in its representation subjective, and, as such, universally valid purposiveness—though here, however, no purposiveness of the *form* of the object underlies our judging (as it does in the case of the beautiful)—the question arises: What is this subjective purposiveness, and what enables it to be prescribed as a norm so as to yield a ground for universally valid delight in the mere estimation of magnitude, and that, too, in a case where it is pushed to the point at which our faculty of imagination breaks down in presenting the concept of a magnitude, and proves unequal to its task?

In the successive aggregation of units requisite for the representation of magnitudes the imagination of itself advances *ad infinitum* without let or hindrance—understanding, however, conducting it by means of concepts of number for which the former must supply the schema. This procedure belongs to the logical estimation of magnitude, and, as such, is doubtless something objectively purposive according to the concept of an end (as all measurement is), but it is not anything which for the aesthetic judgement is purposive or pleasing. 254 Further, in this intentional purposiveness there is nothing compelling us to tax the utmost powers of the imagination, and drive it as far as ever it can reach in its presentations, so as to enlarge the size of the measure, and thus make the single intuition holding the many in one (the *comprehension*) as great as possible. For in the estimation of magnitude by the understanding (arithmetic) we get just as far, whether the comprehension of the units is pushed to the number 10 (as in the decadic system) or only to 4 (as in the tetradic); the further production of magnitude being earned out by the successive aggregation of units, or, if the quantum is given in intuition, by apprehension, merely progressively (not comprehensively), according to an adopted principle of progression. In this mathematical estimation of magnitude understanding is as well served and as satisfied whether imagination selects for the unit a magnitude which one can take in at a glance, e.g. a foot, or a perch, or else a German mile, or even the earth's diameter, the apprehension of which is indeed possible, but not its comprehension in an intuition of the imagination (i.e. it is not possible by means of a *comprehensio aesthetica*, though quite so by means of a *comprehensio logica* in a numerical concept). In each case the logical estimation of magnitude advances *ad infinitum* with nothing to stop it.

The mind, however, hearkens now to the voice of reason within itself, which for all given magnitudes—even for those which can never be completely apprehended, though (in sensuous representation) judged as completely given—requires totality, and consequently comprehension in *one* intuition, and which calls for a *presentation* answering to all the above members of a progressively increasing numerical series, and does not exempt even the infinite (space and time past) from this requirement, but rather renders it inevitable for us to regard this infinite (in the judgement of common reason) as *completely given* (i.e. given in its totality).

But the infinite is absolutely (not merely comparatively) great. In comparison with this all else (in the way of magnitudes of the same order) is small. But the point of capital importance is that the mere ability even to think it as *a whole* indicates a faculty of mind transcending every standard of the senses. For the latter would entail a comprehension yielding as unit a standard bearing to the infinite a definite ratio expressible in numbers, which is impossible. Still the *mere ability even to think* the given infinite without contradiction, is something that requires the presence in the human mind of a faculty that is itself supersensible. For it is only through this faculty and its idea of a noumenon, which latter, while not itself admitting of any intuition, is yet introduced as substrate underlying the intuition of the world as mere phenomenon, that the infinite of the sensible world, in the pure intellectual estimation of magnitude, is *completely* comprehended *under* a concept, although in the mathematical estimation *by means of numerical concepts* it can never be completely thought. Even a faculty enabling the infinite of supersensible intuition to be regarded as given (in its intelligible substrate), transcends every standard of sensibility, and is great beyond all comparison even with the faculty of mathematical estimation: not, of course, from a theoretical point of view that looks to the interests of our faculty of knowledge, but as a broadening of the mind that from another (the practical) point of view feels itself empowered to pass beyond the narrow confines of sensibility.

Nature, therefore, is sublime in such of its phenomena as in their intuition convey the idea of their infinity. But this can only occur through the inadequacy of even the greatest effort of our imagination

255

in the estimation of the magnitude of an object. But, now, in the case of the mathematical estimation of magnitude imagination is quite competent to supply a measure equal to the requirements of any object. For the numerical concepts of the understanding can by progressive synthesis make any measure adequate to any given magnitude. Hence it must be the *aesthetic* estimation of magnitude in which we get at once a feeling of the effort towards a comprehension that exceeds the faculty of imagination for mentally grasping the progressive apprehension in a whole of intuition, and, with it, a perception of the inadequacy of this faculty, which has no bounds to its progress, for taking in and using for the estimation of magnitude a fundamental measure that understanding could turn to account without the least trouble. Now the proper unchangeable fundamental measure of nature is its absolute whole, which, with it, regarded as a phenomenon, means infinity comprehended. But, since this fundamental measure is a self-contradictory concept (owing to the impossibility of the absolute totality of an endless progression), it follows that where the size of a natural object is such that the imagination spends its whole faculty of comprehension upon it in vain, it must carry our concept of nature to a supersensible substrate (underlying both nature and our faculty of thought) which is great beyond every standard of the senses. Thus, instead of the object, it is rather the disposition of the mind in estimating it that we have to judge as *sublime*.

256

Therefore, just as the aesthetic judgement in its judgement of the beautiful refers the imagination in its free play to the *understanding*, to bring out its agreement with the *concepts* of the latter in general (apart from their determination): so in its judging of a thing as sublime it refers that faculty to *reason* to bring out its subjective accord with *ideas* of reason (indeterminately indicated), i.e. to induce a disposition of the mind conformable to that which the influence of definite (practical) ideas would produce upon feeling, and in common accord with it.

This makes it evident that true sublimity must be sought only in the mind of the judging subject, and not in the object of nature that occasions this disposition by the judgement formed of it. Who would apply the term 'sublime' even to shapeless mountain masses towering one above the other in wild disorder, with their pyramids of ice, or to the dark tempestuous ocean, or such like things? But in the contemplation of them, without any regard to their form, the mind abandons itself to the imagination and to a reason placed, though quite apart from any definite end, in conjunction therewith, and merely broadening its view, and it feels itself elevated in its own judgement of itself on finding all the might of imagination still unequal to its ideas.

We get examples of the mathematically sublime of nature in mere intuition in all those instances where our imagination is afforded, not so much a greater numerical concept as a large unit as measure (for shortening the numerical series). A tree judged by the height of a human being gives, at all events, a standard for a mountain; and, supposing this is, say, a mile high, it can serve as unit for the number expressing the earth's diameter, so as to make it intuitable; similarly the earth's diameter for the known planetary system; this again for the system of the Milky Way; and the immeasurable host of such systems, which go by the name of nebulae, and most likely in turn themselves form such a system, holds out no prospect of a limit. Now in the aesthetic judging of such an immeasurable whole, the sublime does not lie so much in the greatness of the number, as in the fact that in our onward advance we always arrive at proportionately greater units. The systematic division of the cosmos conduces to this result. For it represents all that is great in nature as in turn becoming 257 little; or, to be more exact, it represents our imagination in all its boundlessness, and with it nature, as sinking into insignificance before the ideas of reason, once their adequate presentation is attempted.

§ 27
Quality of the delight in the judging of the sublime

THE feeling of our incapacity to attain to an idea *that is a law for us*, is RESPECT. Now the idea of the comprehension of any phenomenon whatever, that may be given us, in a whole of intuition, is an idea imposed upon us by a law of reason, which recognizes no definite, universally valid and unchangeable measure except the absolute whole. But our imagination, even when taxing itself to the uttermost on the score of this required comprehension of a given object in a whole of intuition (and so with a view to the presentation of the idea of reason), betrays its limits and its inadequacy, but still, at the same time, its proper vocation of making itself adequate to the same as a law. Therefore the feeling of the sublime in nature is respect for our own vocation, which we attribute to an object of nature by a certain subreption (substitution of a respect for the object in place of one for the idea of humanity in our own self—the subject); and this feeling renders, as it were, intuitable the supremacy of our cognitive faculties on the rational side over the greatest faculty of sensibility.

The feeling of the sublime is, therefore, at once a feeling of displeasure, arising from the inadequacy of imagination in the aesthetic estimation of magnitude to attain to its estimation by reason, and a simultaneously awakened pleasure, arising from this very judgement of the inadequacy of the greatest faculty of sense being in accord with ideas of reason, so far as the effort to attain to these is for us a law. It is, in other words, for us a law (of reason), which belongs to our vocation, that we should esteem as small in comparison with ideas of reason everything which for us is great in nature as an object of the senses; and that which makes us alive to the feeling of this supersensible side of our being harmonizes with that law. Now the greatest effort of the imagination in the presentation of the unit for the estimation of magnitude involves in itself a reference to something *absolutely great*, consequently a reference also to the law of reason that this alone is to be adopted as the supreme measure of what is great. Therefore the inner perception of the inadequacy of every standard of sense to serve for the rational estimation of magnitude is a coming into accord with reason's laws, and a displeasure that arouses the feeling of our own supersensible vocation, according to which it is purposive, and consequently a pleasure, to find every standard of sensibility falling short of the ideas of reason.

The mind feels itself *set in motion* in the representation of the sublime in nature; whereas in the aesthetic judgement upon what is beautiful therein it is in *restful* contemplation. This movement, especially in its inception, may be compared with a shaking, i.e. with a rapidly alternating repulsion and attraction produced by one and the same object. This excess for the imagination (towards which it is driven in the apprehension of the intuition) is like an abyss in which it fears to lose itself; yet again for the rational idea of the supersensible it is not excessive, but conformable to law, and directed to eliciting such an effort on the part of the imagination: and so in turn as much a source of attraction as it was repellent to mere sensibility. But the judgement itself all the while steadfastly preserves its aesthetic character, because it represents, without being grounded on any determinate concept of the object, merely the subjective play of the mental powers (imagination and reason) as harmonious by virtue of their very contrast. For just as in the judging of the beautiful imagination and *understanding* by their concord generate a subjective purposiveness of the mental faculties, so imagination and *reason* do so here by their conflict—that is to say they induce a feeling of our possessing a pure and self-sufficient reason, or a faculty for the estimation of magnitude, whose pre-eminence can only be made intuitively evident by the inadequacy of that faculty which in the presentation of magnitudes (of objects of the senses) is itself unbounded.

Measurement of a space (as apprehension) is at the same time a description of it, and so an objective movement in the imagination and a progression. On the other hand the comprehension of the manifold in the unity, not of thought, but of intuition, and consequently the comprehension of the successively apprehended parts at one glance, is a retrogression that removes the time-condition in the progression 259 of the imagination, and renders *co-existence* intuitable. Therefore, since the time-series is a condition of inner sense and of an intuition, it is a subjective movement of the imagination by which it does violence to inner sense—a violence which must be proportionately more striking the greater the quantum which the imagination comprehends in one intuition. The effort, therefore, to receive in a single intuition a measure for magnitudes which it takes an appreciable time to apprehend, is a mode of representation which, subjectively considered, is counter-purposive, but, objectively, is requisite for the estimation of magnitude, and is consequently purposive. Here the very same violence that is wrought on the subject through the imagination is judged as purposive *with respect to the entire vocation* of the mind.

The *quality* of the feeling of the sublime consists in its being, in respect of the faculty of aesthetic judging, a feeling of displeasure at an object, which yet, at the same time, is represented as purposive— a representation which derives its possibility from the fact that the subject's very incapacity betrays the consciousness of an unlimited capacity of the same subject, and that the mind can aesthetically judge the latter only through the former.

In the case of the logical estimation of magnitude the impossibility of ever arriving at absolute totality by the progressive measurement of things of the sensible world in time and space was cognized as an objective impossibility, i.e. one of *thinking* the infinite as given, and not as simply subjective, i.e. an incapacity for *grasping* it; for nothing turns there on the amount of the comprehension in one intuition, as measure, but everything depends on a numerical concept. But in an aesthetic estimation of magnitude the numerical concept must drop away or undergo a change. The only thing that is purposive for such estimation is the comprehension on the part of imagination in respect of the unit of measure (the concept of a law of the successive production of the concept of magnitude being consequently avoided).—If, now, a magnitude begins to tax the utmost stretch of our faculty of comprehension in an intuition, and numerical magnitudes—in respect of which we are conscious of the boundlessness of our faculty—still call upon the imagination for aesthetic comprehension in a greater unit, the mind then gets a feeling of being aesthetically confined within bounds. Nevertheless, with a view to the extension of imagination necessary for adequacy with what is unbounded in our faculty of reason, namely the idea of the absolute whole, the attendant displeasure, and, consequently, the lack of purposiveness in our faculty of imagination is still represented as purposive for ideas of reason and their arousal. But in this very way the aesthetic judgement itself is subjectively purposive for reason as source of ideas, i.e. of such an intellectual comprehension as makes all aesthetic comprehension small, and the object is received as sublime with a pleasure that is only possible by means of a displeasure.

B. THE DYNAMICALLY SUBLIME IN NATURE

§ 28

Nature as Might

Might is a power which is superior to great hindrances. It is termed *dominion* if it is also superior to the resistance of that which itself possesses might. Nature considered in an aesthetic judgement as might that has no dominion over us, is *dynamically sublime*.

If we are to judge nature as dynamically sublime, it must be represented as a source of fear (though the converse, that every object that is a source of fear is, in our aesthetic judgement, sublime, does not hold). For in forming an aesthetic judgement (no concept being present) the superiority to hindrances can only be judged according to the greatness of the resistance. Now that which we strive to resist is an evil, and, if we do not find our powers commensurate to the task, an object of fear. Hence the aesthetic judgement can only deem nature a might, and so dynamically sublime, in so far as it is looked upon as an object of fear.

But we may look upon an object as *fearful*, and yet not be afraid *of* it, if, that is, our judgement takes the form of our simply *picturing to ourselves* the case of our wishing to offer some resistance to it, and recognizing that all such resistance would be quite futile. So the righteous man fears God without being afraid of him, because he regards the case of his wishing to resist God and his commandments as one which need cause *him* no anxiety. But in every such case, 261 regarded by him as not intrinsically impossible, he cognizes him as one to be feared.

One who is in a state of fear can no more play the part of a judge of the sublime of nature than one captivated by inclination and appetite can of the beautiful. He flees from the sight of an object filling him with dread; and it is impossible to take delight in terror that is seriously entertained. Hence the agreeableness arising from the cessation of an uneasiness is *a state of joy*. But this, depending upon deliverance from a danger, is a rejoicing accompanied with a resolve never again to put oneself in the way of the danger: in fact we do not like bringing back to mind how we felt on that occasion—not to speak of going in search of an opportunity for experiencing it again.

Bold, overhanging, and, as it were, threatening rocks, thunder-clouds piled up the vault of heaven, borne along with flashes and peals, volcanoes in all their violence of destruction, hurricanes leaving desolation in their track, the boundless ocean rising with rebellious force, the high waterfall of some mighty river, and the like, make our power of resistance of trifling moment in comparison with their might. But, provided our own position is secure, their aspect is all the more attractive for its fearfulness; and we readily call these objects sublime, because they raise the forces of the soul above the height of vulgar commonplace, and discover within us a power of resistance of quite another kind, which gives us courage to be able to measure ourselves against the seeming omnipotence of nature.

In the immeasurableness of nature and the inadequacy of our faculty for adopting a standard proportionate to the aesthetic estimation of the magnitude of its *realm*, we found our own limitation. But with this we also found in our rational faculty another non-sensuous standard, one which has that infinity itself under it as unit, and in comparison with which everything in nature is small, and so found in our minds a pre-eminence over nature even in its immeasurability. Now in just the same way the irresistibility of the might of nature forces upon us the recognition of our physical helplessness as beings of nature, but at the same time reveals a faculty of judging ourselves as independent of nature, and discovers a pre-eminence above nature that is the foundation of a self-preservation of quite another kind from that

262 which may be assailed and brought into danger by external nature. This saves humanity in our own person from humiliation, even though as human beings we would have to submit to external violence. In this way external nature is not aesthetically judged as sublime in so far as it arouses fear, but rather because it summons our power (one not of nature) to regard as small those things of which we are inclined to be solicitous (worldly goods, health, and life), and hence to regard its might (to which in these matters we are no doubt subjected) as exercising over us and our personality no such rude dominion that we should bow down before it, once the question becomes one of our highest principles and of our asserting or forsaking them. Therefore nature is here called sublime merely because it elevates the imagination to a presentation of those cases in which the mind can come to feel the sublimity of its own vocation even over nature.

This self-esteem loses nothing by the fact that we must see ourselves safe in order to feel this soul-stirring delight—a fact from which it might seemingly be argued that, as there is no seriousness in the danger, so there is just as little seriousness in the sublimity of our spiritual faculty. For here the delight only concerns the *vocation* of our faculty disclosed in such a case, in so far as this faculty has its root in our nature although its development and exercise is left to ourselves and remains our responsibility. Here indeed there is truth—no matter how conscious we may be, when we stretch our reflection so far, of our actual present helplessness.

This principle has, doubtless, the appearance of being too far-fetched and subtle, and so of lying beyond the reach of an aesthetic judgement. But observation of human beings proves the reverse, and that it may be the foundation of the commonest judgements, although one is not always conscious of its presence. For what is it that, even to the savage, is the object of the greatest admiration? It is someone who is undaunted, who knows no fear, and who, therefore, does not give way to danger, but sets vigorously to work with full deliberation. Even where civilization has reached a high pitch there remains this special reverence for the soldier; only that there is then further required of him that he should also exhibit all the virtues of peace— gentleness, sympathy and even proper care for his own person; and for the reason that in this we recognize that his mind is above the threats of danger. And so, comparing the statesman and the general, men may argue as they please as to the pre-eminent respect which is 263 due to either above the other; but the verdict of the aesthetic judgement is for the latter. War itself, provided it is conducted with order and a sacred respect for the rights of civilians, has something sublime about it, and gives nations that carry it on in such a manner a stamp of mind only the more sublime the more numerous the dangers to which they are exposed, and which they are able to meet with fortitude. On the other hand, a prolonged peace favours the predominance of a mere commercial spirit, and with it a debasing self-interest, cowardice, and weakness, and tends to degrade the character of the people.

So far as sublimity is predicated of might, this solution of the concept of it appears at variance with the fact that we tend to represent God in the tempest, the storm, the earthquake, and the like, as presenting himself in his wrath, but at the same time also in his sublimity, and yet here it would be alike folly and presumption to imagine a pre-eminence of our minds over the operations and, as it appears, even over the direction of such might. Here, instead of a feeling of the sublimity of our own nature, submission, prostration, and a feeling of utter helplessness seem more to constitute the attitude of mind befitting the manifestation of such an object, and to be that also more customarily associated with the idea of it on the occasion of a natural phenomenon of this kind. In religion, as a rule, prostration, adoration with bowed head, coupled with contrite, timorous posture and voice, seems to be the only becoming demeanour in presence of the Divinity, and accordingly most peoples have assumed and still observe it. Yet this cast of mind is far from being intrinsically and necessarily involved in the idea of the *sublimity* of a religion and of its object. The individual that is actually in a state of fear, finding in himself good reason to be so, because he is conscious of offending with his evil disposition against a might directed by a will at once irresistible and just, is far from being in the frame of mind for admiring divine greatness, for which a mood of calm reflection and a quite free judgement are required. Only when he becomes conscious of having a disposition that is upright and acceptable to God, do those operations of might serve to stir within him the idea of the sublimity of this being, so far as he recognizes the existence in himself of a sublimity of disposition consonant with the divine will, and is thus raised above the dread of such operations of nature, in which he no longer sees God pouring forth his wrath. Even humility, taking the form of an uncompromising judgement upon his shortcomings, which, with the consciousness of good intentions, might readily be glossed over on the ground of the frailty of human nature, is a sublime temper of the mind voluntarily to undergo the pain of remorse as a means of more and more effectually eradicating its cause. In this way religion is intrinsically distinguished from superstition, which latter rears in the mind, not reverence for the sublime, but dread and apprehension of the all-powerful being to whose will terror-stricken man sees himself subjected, yet without according him due honour. From this nothing can arise but grace-begging and vain adulation, instead of a religion consisting in a good life.

Sublimity, therefore, does not reside in any of the things of nature, but only in our own mind, in so far as we may become conscious of our superiority over nature within, and thus also over nature without us (as exerting influence upon us). Everything that provokes this feeling in us, including the *might* of nature which challenges our strength, is then, though improperly, called sublime, and it is only under presupposition of this idea within us, and in relation to it, that we are capable of attaining to the idea of the sublimity of that being which inspires deep respect in us, not by the mere display of its might in nature, but more by the faculty which is harboured in us of judging that might without fear, and of regarding our vocation as sublimely exalted above it.

§ 29

Modality of the judgement on the sublime in nature

BEAUTIFUL nature contains countless things as to which we at once take everyone as in their judgement concurring with our own, and as to which we may further expect this concurrence without going very far wrong. But in respect of our judgement upon the sublime in nature we cannot so easily vouch for its ready acceptance by others. For a far higher degree of culture, not merely of the aesthetic judgement, but also of the faculties of cognition which lie at its basis, seems to be requisite to enable us to lay down a judgement upon this high distinction of natural objects.

The mental mood appropriate for a feeling of the sublime requires 265 the mind's susceptibility for ideas, since it is precisely in the failure of nature to attain to these—and consequently only under presupposition of this susceptibility and of the straining of the imagination to use nature as a schema for ideas—that there is something forbidding to sensibility, but which, for all that, has an attraction for us, arising from the fact of its being a dominion which reason exercises over sensibility with a view to extending it to the requirements of its own realm (the practical) and letting it look out beyond itself into the infinite, which for it is an abyss. In fact, without the development of moral ideas, that which, thanks to preparatory culture, we call sublime, merely strikes the untutored individual as terrifying. He will see in the evidences which the ravages of nature give of her dominion, and in the vast scale of her might, compared with which his own is diminished to insignificance, only the misery, peril, and distress that would encompass those who were thrown to its mercy. So the simple-minded, and, for the most part, intelligent Savoyard peasant (as Herr von Saussure relates)* unhesitatingly called all lovers of snow-mountains fools. And who can tell whether he would have been so wide of the mark, if that student of nature had taken the risk of the dangers to which he exposed himself merely, as most travellers do, for a fad, or so as some day to be able to give a moving account of his adventures? But the mind of Saussure was bent on the instruction of mankind, and soul-stirring sensations that excellent man indeed enjoyed, and the reader of his travels got them thrown into the bargain.

But the fact that culture is requisite for the judgement upon the sublime in nature (more than for that upon the beautiful) does not involve its being an original product of culture and something introduced in a more or less conventional way into society. Rather is it in human nature that its foundations are laid, and, in fact, in that which, at once with common understanding, we may expect everyone to possess and may require of them, namely, a native capacity for the feeling for (practical) ideas, i.e. for moral feeling.

This, now, is the foundation of the necessity of that agreement between other people's judgements upon the sublime and our own, which we make our own imply. For just as we taunt a person who is quite inappreciative when judging an object of nature in which we see beauty, with lack *of taste*, so we say of a person who remains unaffected in the presence of what we consider sublime, that he has no *feeling*. But we demand both taste and feeling of everyone, and, granted some degree of culture, we give them credit for both. Still, we do so with this difference: that, in the case of the former, since judgement there refers the imagination merely to the understanding, as the faculty of concepts, we make the requirement as a matter of course, whereas in the case of the latter, since here the judgement refers the imagination to reason, as a faculty of ideas, we do so only under a subjective presupposition (which, however, we believe we are warranted in making), namely that of the moral feeling in human beings. And, on this assumption, we attribute necessity to the latter aesthetic judgement also.

In this modality of aesthetic judgements, namely their assumed necessity, lies what is for the critique of judgement a moment of capital importance. For this is exactly what makes an *a priori* principle apparent in their case, and lifts them out of the sphere of empirical psychology, in which otherwise they would remain buried amid the feelings of gratification and pain (only with the senseless epithet of *finer* feeling), so as to place them, and, thanks to them, to place the faculty of judgement itself, in the class of judgements of which the basis of an *a priori* principle is the distinguishing feature, and, thus distinguished, to introduce them into transcendental philosophy.

GENERAL REMARK UPON THE EXPOSITION OF AESTHETIC REFLECTIVE JUDGEMENTS

In relation to the feeling of pleasure an object is to be counted either as *agreeable*, or *beautiful*, or *sublime*, or *good* (absolutely), (*iucundum, pulchrum, sublime, honestum*).

As the motive of desires the *agreeable* is invariably of one and the same kind, no matter what its source or how specifically different the representation (of sense and sensation objectively considered). Hence in judging its influence upon the mind the multitude of its charms (simultaneous or successive) is alone relevant, and so only, as it were, the mass of the agreeable sensation, and it is only by its *quantity*, therefore, that this can be made intelligible. Further it in no way conduces to our culture, but belongs only to mere enjoyment.—The *beautiful*, on the other hand, requires the representation of a certain *quality* of the object, that permits also of being understood and reduced to concepts, (although in the aesthetic judgement it is not so reduced), and it cultivates, as it instructs us to attend to purposiveness in the feeling of pleasure.—The *sublime* consists merely in the *relation* exhibited by the judgement of the serviceability of the sensible in the representation of nature for a possible supersensible employment.— The *absolutely good*, judged subjectively according to the feeling it inspires, (the object of the moral feeling,) as the determinability of the powers of the subject by means of the representation of an *absolutely necessitating* law, is principally distinguished by the *modality* of a necessity resting upon concepts *a priori*, and involving not a mere *claim*, but a *command* upon everyone to assent, and belongs intrinsically not to the aesthetic, but to the pure intellectual judgement. Further, it is not ascribed to nature but to freedom, and that in a determining and not a merely reflective judgement. But the *determinability of the subject* by means of this idea, and, what is more, that of a subject which can be sensible, in the way of a *modification of its state*, to *hindrances* on the part of sensibility, while, at the same time, it can by surmounting them feel superiority over them—a determinability, in other words, as moral feeling—is still so allied to aesthetic judgement and its *formal conditions* as to be capable of being pressed into the service of the aesthetic representation of the conformity to law of action from duty, i.e. of the representation of this as sublime, or even as beautiful, without forfeiting its purity—an impossible result were one to make it naturally bound up with the feeling of the agreeable.

The effective result to be extracted from the exposition so far given of both kinds of aesthetic judgements may be summed up in the following brief definitions:

The *beautiful* is what pleases in the mere judging of it (consequently not by intervention of any feeling of sense in accordance with a concept of the understanding). From this it follows at once that it must please apart from all interest.

The *sublime* is what pleases immediately through its resistance to the interest of the senses.

267

Both, as definitions of aesthetic universally valid judging, have reference to subjective grounds. In the one case the reference is to grounds of sensibility, in so far as these are purposive on behalf of the contemplative understanding, in the other case in so far as, in their opposition to sensibility, they are, on the contrary, purposive in reference to the ends of practical reason. Both, however, as united in the same subject, are purposive in reference to the moral feeling. The beautiful prepares us to love something, even nature, apart from any interest: the sublime to esteem something highly even in opposition to our (sensuous) interest.

268   The sublime may be described in this way: It is an object (of nature) the *representation of which determines the mind to regard the elevation of nature beyond our reach as equivalent to a presentation of ideas.*

In a literal sense and according to their logical import, ideas cannot be presented. But if we enlarge our empirical faculty of representation (mathematical or dynamical) with a view to the intuition of nature, reason inevitably steps forward, as the faculty concerned with the independence of the absolute totality, and calls forth the effort of the mind, unavailing though it be, to make the representation of sense adequate to this totality. This effort, and the feeling of the unattainability of the idea by means of imagination, is itself a presentation of the subjective purposiveness of our mind in the employment of the imagination in the interests of the mind's supersensible vocation, and compels us subjectively to *think* nature itself in its totality as a presentation of something supersensible, without our being able to produce this presentation *objectively*.

For we readily see that nature in space and time falls entirely short of the unconditioned, consequently also of the absolutely great, which still the commonest reason demands. And by this we are also reminded that we have only to do with nature as phenomenon, and that this itself must be regarded as the mere presentation of a nature in itself (which exists in the idea of reason). But this idea of the supersensible, which no doubt we cannot further determine—so that we cannot *cognize* nature as its presentation, but only *think* it as such—is awakened in us by an object the aesthetic judging of which strains the imagination to its utmost, whether in respect of its extension (mathematical), or of its might over the mind (dynamical). For it is founded upon the feeling of a sphere of the mind which altogether exceeds the realm of nature (i.e. upon the moral feeling), with regard to which the representation of the object is judged as subjectively purposive.

As a matter of fact, a feeling for the sublime in nature is hardly thinkable unless in association with a disposition of mind resembling the moral. And though, like that feeling, the immediate pleasure in the beautiful in nature presupposes and cultivates a certain *liberality* of thought, i.e. makes our delight independent of any mere enjoyment of sense, still it represents freedom rather as in *play* than as exercising a law-governed *activity*, which is the genuine characteristic of human morality, where reason has to impose its dominion upon sensibility. There is, however, this qualification, that in the aesthetic judgement upon the sublime this dominion is represented as exercised through the imagination itself as an instrument of reason. 269

Thus, too, delight in the sublime in nature is only *negative* (whereas that in the beautiful is *positive*): that is to say it is a feeling of imagination by its own act depriving itself of its freedom by receiving a purposive determination in accordance with a law other than that of its empirical employment. In this way it gains an extension and a might greater than that which it sacrifices. But the ground of this is hidden from it, and in its place it *feels* the sacrifice or deprivation, as well as its cause, to which it is subjected. The *astonishment* amounting almost to terror, the horror and sacred awe, that seizes us when gazing upon the prospect of mountains ascending to heaven, deep ravines and torrents raging there, deep-shadowed solitudes that invite to brooding melancholy, and the like—all this, when we are assured of our own safety, is not actual fear. Rather is it an attempt to gain access to it through imagination, for the purpose of feeling the might of this faculty in combining the movement of the mind thereby aroused with its serenity, and of thus being superior to internal and, therefore, to external, nature, so far as the latter can have any bearing upon our feeling of well-being. For the imagination, in accordance with laws of association, makes our state of contentment dependent upon physical conditions. But acting in accordance with principles of the schematism of judgement (consequently so far as it is subordinated to freedom) it is at the same time an instrument of reason and its ideas. But in this capacity it is a might enabling us to assert our independence as against the influences of nature, to degrade what is great in respect of the latter to the level of what is little, and thus to locate the absolutely great only in the proper vocation of the subject.

This reflection of aesthetic judgement by which it raises itself to the point of adequacy with reason, though without any determinate concept of reason, is still a representation of the object as subjectively purposive, by virtue even of the objective inadequacy of the imagination in its greatest extension for meeting the demands of reason (as the faculty of ideas).

Here we have to attend generally to what has been already adverted to, that in the transcendental aesthetic of judgement there must be no question of anything but pure aesthetic judgements. Consequently examples are not to be selected from such beautiful or sublime objects as presuppose the concept of an end. For then the purposiveness would be either teleological, or based upon mere sensations of an object (gratification or pain) and so, in the first case, not aesthetic, and, in the second, not merely formal. So, if we call the sight of the starry heaven *sublime*, we must not found our judgement of it upon any concepts of worlds inhabited by rational beings, with the bright spots, which we see filling the space above us, as their suns moving in orbits prescribed for them with the wisest regard to ends. But we must take it, just as it strikes the eye, as a broad and all-embracing canopy: and it is merely under such a representation that we may posit the sublimity which the pure aesthetic judgement attributes to this object. Similarly, as to the prospect of the ocean, we are not to regard it as we, with our minds stored with knowledge on a variety of matters (which, however, is not contained in the immediate intuition), are accustomed to represent it in *thought*, as, let us say, a spacious realm of aquatic creatures, or as the mighty reservoirs from which are drawn the vapours that fill the air with clouds of moisture for the good of the land, or yet as an element which no doubt divides continent from continent, but at the same time affords the means of the greatest commercial intercourse between them—for in this way we get nothing beyond teleological judgements. Instead of this we must be able to see sublimity in the ocean, regarding it, as the poets do, according to what the impression upon the eye reveals, as, let us say, in its calm, a clear mirror of water bounded only by the heavens, or, be it disturbed, as threatening to overwhelm and engulf everything. The same is to be said of the sublime and beautiful in the human form. Here, for determining grounds of the judgement, we must not have recourse to concepts of ends *subserved* by all its limbs and members, or allow their accordance with these ends to *influence* our aesthetic judgement (in such case no longer pure), although it is certainly also a necessary condition of aesthetic delight that they should not conflict with these ends. Aesthetic purposiveness is the conformity to law of judgement in its *freedom*. The delight in the object depends upon the reference which we seek to give to the imagination, namely that it is to entertain the mind in a free activity. If, on the other hand, something else,—be it sensation or concept of the understanding— determines the judgement, it is then conformable to law, no doubt, 271 but not an act of *free* judgement.

Hence to speak of intellectual beauty or sublimity is to use expressions which, in the *first* place, are not quite correct. For these are aesthetic modes of representation which would be entirely foreign to us were we merely pure intelligences (or if we even put ourselves in thought in the position of such). *Secondly*, although both, as objects of an intellectual (moral) delight, are compatible with aesthetic delight to the extent of not *resting* upon any interest, still, on the other hand, there is a difficulty in the way of their alliance with such delight, since their function is to *produce* an interest, and, on the assumption that the presentation has to accord with delight in the aesthetic judging, this interest could only be effected by means of an interest of the senses combined with it in the presentation. But in this way the intellectual purposiveness would be violated and rendered impure.

The object of a pure and unconditioned intellectual delight is the moral law in the might which it exerts in us over all *antecedent* motives of the mind. Now, since it is only through sacrifices that this might makes itself known to us aesthetically, (and this involves a deprivation of something—though in the interests of inner freedom—whilst in turn it reveals in us an unfathomable depth of this supersensible faculty, the consequences of which extend beyond our visible reach), it follows that the delight, looked at from the aesthetic side (in reference to sensibility) is negative, i.e. opposed to this interest, but from the intellectual side, positive and bound up with an interest. Hence it follows that the intellectual and intrinsically purposive (moral) good, estimated aesthetically, instead of being represented as beautiful, must rather be represented as sublime, with the result that it arouses more a feeling of respect (which disdains charm) than of love or of the heart being drawn towards it—for human nature does not of its own proper motion accord with the good, but only by virtue of the dominion which reason exercises over sensibility. Conversely, that, too, which we call sublime in external nature, or even internal nature (e.g. certain affects) is only represented as a might of the mind enabling it to overcome this or that hindrance of sensibility by means of moral principles, and it is from this that it derives its interest.

I must dwell a while on the latter point. The idea of the good 272 connected with affect is *enthusiasm*. This state of mind appears to be sublime: so much so that there is a common saying that nothing great can be achieved without it. But now every affect[7] is blind either as to the choice of its end, or, supposing this has been furnished by reason, in the way it is effected—for it is that movement of the mind whereby the exercise of free deliberation upon fundamental principles, with a view to determining oneself accordingly, is rendered impossible. On this account it cannot merit any delight on the part of reason. Yet, from an aesthetic point of view, enthusiasm is sublime, because it is an effort of one's powers called forth by ideas which give to the mind an impetus of far stronger and more enduring efficacy than the stimulus afforded by sensible representations. But (as seems strange) even *freedom from affect* (*apatheia, phlegma in significatu bono*) in a mind that strenuously follows its unswerving principles is sublime, and that, too, in a manner vastly superior, because it has at the same time the delight of pure reason on its side. Such a stamp of mind is alone called noble. This expression, however, comes in time to be applied to things—such as buildings, a garment, literary style, a person's bearing, and the like—provided they do not so much excite *astonishment* (the affect attending the representation of novelty exceeding expectation) as *admiration* (an astonishment which does not cease when the novelty wears off)—and this obtains where ideas undesignedly and artlessly accord in their presentation with aesthetic delight.

Every affect of the STRENUOUS TYPE (such, that is, as excites the consciousness of our power of overcoming every resistance (*animi strenui*)) is *aesthetically sublime*, e.g. anger, even desperation (the *rage of forlorn hope* but not *faint-hearted* despair). On the other hand,

---

[7] There is a specific distinction between *affects* and *passions*. Affects are related merely to feeling; passions belong to the faculty of desire, and are inclinations that hinder or render impossible all determinability of the power of choice through principles. Affects are impetuous and irresponsible: passions are abiding and deliberate. Thus resentment, in the form of anger, is an affect: but in the form of hatred (vindictiveness) it is a passion. Under no circumstances can the latter be called sublime; for, while the freedom of the mind is, no doubt, *impeded* in the case of affects, in passion it is abrogated.

affect of the LANGUID TYPE (which converts the very effort of resistance into an object of displeasure (*animum languidum*)) has nothing 273
noble about it, though it may take its rank as possessing beauty of the
sensuous order. Hence the *emotions* capable of attaining the strength
of an affect are very diverse. We have *spirited*, and we have *tender*
emotions. When the strength of the latter reaches that of an affect
they can be turned to no account. The propensity to indulge in them
is *sentimentality*. A sympathetic grief that refuses to be consoled, or
one that has to do with imaginary misfortune to which we deliberately give way so far as to allow our fantasy to delude us into thinking it actual fact, indicates and goes to make a tender, but at the same
time weak, soul, which shows a beautiful side, and may no doubt be
called fanciful, but never enthusiastic. Romances, maudlin dramas,
shallow homilies, which trifle with so-called (though falsely so) noble
sentiments, but in fact make the heart enervated, insensitive to the
stern precepts of duty, and incapable of respect for the worth of
humanity in our own person and the rights of human beings (which
is something quite other than their happiness), and in general incapable of all firm principles; even a religious discourse which recom-
mends a cringing and abject grace-begging and favour-seeking,
abandoning all reliance on our own ability to resist the evil within us,
in place of the vigorous resolution to try to get the better of our inclinations by means of those powers which, frail though we may be, are
still left to us; that false humility by which self-abasement, whining
hypocritical repentance and a merely passive frame of mind are set
down as the method by which alone we can become acceptable to
the Supreme Being—these have nothing to do with what may be
reckoned to belong to beauty, not to speak of the sublimity of mental
temperament.

  But even impetuous movements of the mind—whether they be
allied under the name of edification with ideas of religion, or, as
pertaining merely to culture, with ideas involving a social interest—
no matter how much they strain the imagination, can in no way lay
claim to the honour of a *sublime* presentation, if they do not leave
behind them a temper of mind which, though it be only indirectly,
has an influence upon the consciousness of the mind's strength and
resoluteness in respect of that which carries with it pure intellectual
purposiveness (the supersensible). For, in the absence of this, all
these emotions belong only to *motion*, which we welcome in the

interests of good health. The agreeable lassitude that follows upon
274 being stirred up in that way by the play of the affects, is a fruition of
the state of well-being arising from the restoration of the equilibrium
of the various vital forces within us. This, in the last resort, comes to
no more than what the Eastern voluptuaries find so soothing when
they get their bodies massaged, and all their muscles and joints softly
pressed and bent; only that in the first case the principle that occasions the movement is chiefly internal, whereas here it is entirely
external. Thus, many an individual believes himself edified by a
sermon in which there is no establishment of anything (no system of
good maxims); or thinks himself improved by a tragedy, when he is
merely glad at having relieved himself of boredom. Thus the sublime
must in every case have reference to our *way of thinking*, i.e. to maxims
directed to giving to the intellectual side of our nature and to the
ideas of reason supremacy over sensibility.

We have no reason to fear that the feeling of the sublime will suffer
from an abstract mode of presentation like this, which is altogether
negative with regard to the sensuous. For though the imagination, no
doubt, finds nothing beyond the sensible world on which it can lay
hold, still this thrusting aside of the sensible barriers gives it a feeling
of being unbounded; and that removal is thus a presentation of
the infinite. As such it can never be anything more than a negative
presentation—but still it expands the soul. Perhaps there is no more
sublime passage in the Jewish Law than the commandment: Thou
shalt not make unto thee any graven image, or any likeness of any
thing that is in heaven or on earth, or under the earth, etc. This commandment can alone explain the enthusiasm which the Jewish
people, in their moral period, felt for their religion when comparing
themselves with others, or the pride inspired by Mohammedanism.
The very same holds good of our representation of the moral law and
of our intrinsic capacity for morality. The fear that, if we divest this
representation of everything that can commend it to the senses, it
will thereupon be attended only with a cold and lifeless approbation
and not with any moving force or emotion, is wholly unwarranted. The
very reverse is the truth. For when nothing any longer presents itself
to the senses, and the unmistakable and ineffaceable idea of morality
is all that now remains, there would be need rather of tempering the
ardour of an unbounded imagination to prevent it rising to enthusiasm,
than of seeking to lend these ideas the aid of images and childish

devices for fear of their lack of power. For this reason governments 275
have gladly let religion be fully equipped with these accessories, seeking in this way to relieve their subjects of the exertion, but to deprive
them, at the same time, of the ability, required for expanding their
spiritual powers beyond the limits arbitrarily laid down for them,
and this makes it all the easier to treat them as though they were
merely passive.

This pure, elevating, merely negative presentation of morality
involves, on the other hand, no fear of *fanaticism*, which is a *delusion*
that would *will some* VISION *beyond all the bounds of sensibility*; i.e.
would dream according to principles (rational raving). The safeguard
is the purely negative character of the presentation. For *the inscrutability of the idea of freedom* precludes all positive presentation. The moral
law, however, is a sufficient and original source of determination
within us: so it does not for a moment permit us to cast about for a
ground of determination external to itself. If enthusiasm is comparable
to *delirium*, fanaticism may be compared to *mania*. Of these the latter
is least of all compatible with the sublime, for it is *profoundly* ridiculous. In enthusiasm, as an affect, the imagination is unbridled; in
fanaticism, as a deep-seated, brooding passion, it is ungoverned. The
first is a transitory state to which the healthiest understanding is liable
to become at times the victim; the second is an undermining disease.

Simplicity (artless purposiveness) is, as it were, the style adopted
by nature in the sublime. It is also that of morality. The latter is a
second (supersensible) nature, whose laws alone we know, without
being able to attain to an intuition of the supersensible faculty within
us—that which contains the ground of this legislation.

One further remark. The delight in the sublime, no less than in
the beautiful, by reason of its universal *communicability* is not only
plainly distinguished from other aesthetic judgements, but also from
this same property acquires an interest in society (in which it admits
of such communication). Yet, despite this, we have to note the fact
that *isolation from all society* is looked upon as something sublime,
provided it rests upon ideas which disregard all sensible interest. To
be self-sufficing, and so not to stand in need of society, yet without
being unsociable, i.e. without shunning it, is something approaching
the sublime—a remark applicable to all superiority over needs. On
the other hand, to shun our fellow human beings from *misanthropy*, 276
because of enmity towards them, or from *anthropophobia*, because we

imagine the hand of everyone is against us, is partly odious, partly contemptible. There is, however, a misanthropy, (most improperly so called,) the tendency towards which is to be found with advancing years in many right-minded people, that, as far as *good will* goes, is, no doubt, philanthropic enough, but as the result of long and sad experience, is widely removed from *delight* in mankind. We see evidences of this in the propensity to reclusiveness, in the fanciful desire for a retired country seat, or else (with the young) in the dream of the happiness of being able to spend one's life with a little family on an island unknown to the rest of the world—material of which novelists or writers of Robinsonades know how to make such good use. Falsehood, ingratitude, injustice, the puerility of the ends which we ourselves look upon as great and momentous, and to attain which we inflict upon our fellow human beings all imaginable evils—these all so contradict the idea of what people might be if they only would, and are so at variance with our active wish to see them better, that, to avoid hating where we cannot love, it seems but a slight sacrifice to forgo all the joys of fellowship with our kind. This sadness which is not directed to the evils which fate brings down upon others (a sadness which springs from sympathy), but to those which they inflict upon themselves (one which is based on antipathy in questions of principle), is sublime because it is founded on ideas, whereas that springing from sympathy can only be accounted beautiful.—*Saussure*, who was no less ingenious than profound, in the description of his Alpine travels remarks of *Bonhomme*, one of the Savoy mountains, 'There reigns there a certain *insipid sadness*.' He recognized, therefore, that, besides this, there is an *interesting* sadness, such as is inspired by the sight of some desolate place into which men might gladly withdraw themselves so as to hear no more of the world without, and be no longer versed in its affairs, a place, however, which must yet not be so altogether inhospitable as only to afford a most miserable retreat for a human being.— I only make this observation as a reminder that even sorrow (but not dispirited sadness) may take its place among the *vigorous* affects, provided it has its root in moral ideas. If, however, it is grounded upon sympathy, and, as such, is lovable, it belongs only to the *languid* affections. And this serves to call attention to the mental temperament which in the first case alone is *sublime*.

The transcendental exposition of aesthetic judgements now 277 brought to a close may be compared with the physiological one, as worked out by *Burke* and many acute men among us, so that we may see where a merely empirical exposition of the sublime and beautiful would bring us. *Burke*,[8] who deserves to be called the foremost author* in this method of treatment, deduces, on these lines, 'that the feeling of the sublime is grounded on the impulse towards self-preservation and on *fear*, i.e. on a pain, which, since it does not go the length of disordering the bodily parts, calls forth movements which, as they clear the vessels, whether fine or gross, of a dangerous and troublesome encumbrance, are capable of producing delight; not pleasure but a sort of delightful horror, a sort of tranquillity tinged with terror.' The beautiful, which he grounds on love (from which, still, he would have desire kept separate), he reduces to 'the relaxing, slackening, and enervating of the fibres of the body, and consequently a softening, a dissolving, a languor, and a fainting, dying, and melting away for pleasure'. And this explanation he supports, not alone by instances in which the feeling of the beautiful as well as of the sublime is capable of being excited in us by the imagination in conjunction with the understanding, but even by instances when it is in conjunction with sensations.—As psychological observations these analyses of our mental phenomena are extremely fine, and supply a wealth of material for the favourite investigations of empirical anthropology. But, besides that, there is no denying the fact that all representations within us, no matter whether they are objectively merely sensible or wholly intellectual, are still subjectively associable with gratification or pain, however imperceptible either of these may be. (For these representations one and all affect the feeling of life, and none of them, so far as it is a modification of the subject, can be indifferent.) We must even admit that, as Epicurus maintained, *gratification* and *pain* though proceeding from the imagination or even from representations of the understanding, are always in the last resort corporeal, since apart from any feeling of the bodily organ 278 life would be merely a consciousness of one's existence, and could not include any feeling of well-being or the reverse, i.e. of the furtherance or hindrance of the vital forces. For, of itself alone, the

---

[8] See p. 223 of the German translation of his work: *Philosophische Untersuchungen über den Ursprung unserer Begriffe vom Schönen und Erhabenen*. Riga, published by Hartknock, 1773.

mind is all life (the life-principle itself), and hindrance or furtherance has to be sought outside it, and yet in the human being himself, consequently in the connexion with his body.

But if we attribute the delight in the object wholly and entirely to the gratification which it affords through charm or emotion, then we must not expect from *anyone else* agreement with the aesthetic judgement passed by *us*. For in such matters each person rightly consults his own personal feeling alone. But in that case there is an end of all censure in matters of taste—unless the example afforded by others as the result of a contingent coincidence of their judgements is to be held over us as *commanding* our assent. But this principle we would presumably resent, and appeal to our natural right of submitting a judgement to our own sense, where it rests upon the immediate feeling of personal well-being, instead of submitting it to that of others.

Hence if the import of the judgement of taste, where we appraise it as a judgement entitled to require the concurrence of everyone, cannot be *egoistic*, but must necessarily, from its inner nature, be allowed a *pluralistic* validity, i.e. on account of what taste itself is, and not on account of the examples which others give of their taste, then it must found upon some *a priori* principle (whether it be subjective or objective), and no amount of prying into the empirical laws of the changes that go on within the mind can succeed in establishing such a principle. For these laws only yield a knowledge of how we do judge, but they do not give us a command as to how we ought to judge, and, what is more, such a command as is *unconditioned*—and commands of this kind are presupposed by judgements of taste, inasmuch as they require delight to be taken as *immediately* connected with a representation. Accordingly, though the empirical exposition of aesthetic judgements may be a first step towards accumulating the material for a higher investigation, yet a transcendental examination of this faculty is possible, and forms an essential part of the critique of taste. For, if taste were not in possession of *a priori* principles, it could not possibly sit in judgement upon the judgements of others, and pass sentence of commendation or condemnation upon them, with even the least semblance of authority.

The remaining part of the Analytic of aesthetic judgement contains first of all the:—

§ 30

The deduction of aesthetic judgements* upon objects of nature
must not be directed to what we call sublime in nature,
but only to the beautiful

THE claim of an aesthetic judgement to universal validity for every subject, being a judgement which must rely on some *a priori* principle, stands in need of a deduction (i.e. a derivation of its title). Further, where the delight or aversion turns on the *form of the object* this has to be something over and above the exposition of the judgement. Such is the case with judgements of taste upon the beautiful in nature. For there the purposiveness has its foundation in the object and its outward form—although it does not signify the reference of this to other objects according to concepts (for the purpose of cognitive judgements), but is merely concerned in general with the apprehension of this form so far as it proves accordant in the mind with the *faculty* of concepts as well as with that of their presentation (which is identical with that of apprehension). With regard to the beautiful in nature, therefore, we may start a number of questions touching the cause of this purposiveness of their forms: e.g. How we are to explain why nature has scattered beauty abroad with so lavish a hand, even in the depth of the ocean where it can but seldom be glimpsed by the human eye—for which alone it is purposive.

But the sublime in nature—if we pass upon it a pure aesthetic judgement unmixed with concepts of perfection, as objective purposiveness, which would make the judgement teleological—may be regarded as completely lacking in form or figure, and nonetheless be looked upon as an object of pure delight, and indicate a subjective purposiveness of the given representation. So, now, the question suggests itself, whether in addition to the exposition of what is thought in an aesthetic judgement of this kind, we may be called upon to give a deduction of its claim to some (subjective) *a priori* principle.

This we may meet with the reply that the sublime in nature is 280 improperly so called, and that sublimity should, in strictness, be attributed merely to the attitude of thought, or, rather, to that which serves as the basis for this in human nature. The apprehension of an object otherwise formless and in conflict with ends supplies the mere occasion for our coming to a consciousness of this basis; and the object is in this way put to a subjectively purposive *use*, but it is not judged as subjectively-purposive *on its own account* and because of its form. (It is, as it were, a *species finalis accepta, non data*.) Consequently the exposition we gave of judgements upon the sublime in nature was at the same time their deduction. For in our analysis of the reflection on the part of judgement in this case we found that in such judgements there is a purposive relation of the cognitive faculties, which has to be laid *a priori* at the basis of the faculty of ends (the will), and which is therefore itself *a priori* purposive. This, then, at once involves the deduction, i.e. the justification of the claim of such a judgement to universally-necessary validity.

Hence we may confine our search to one for the deduction of judgements of taste, i.e. of judgements upon the beauty of things of nature, and this will satisfactorily dispose of the problem for the entire aesthetic faculty of judgement.

§ 31

Of the method of the deduction of judgements of taste

THE obligation to furnish a deduction, i.e. a guarantee of the legitimacy of judgements of a particular kind, only arises where the judgement lays claim to necessity. This is the case even where it requires subjective universality, i.e. the agreement of everyone, even though the judgement is not a cognitive judgement, but only one of pleasure or displeasure in a given object, i.e. an assumption of a subjective purposiveness that has a thorough-going validity for everyone, and which, since the judgement is one of taste, is not to be grounded upon any concept of the thing.

Now, in the latter case, we are not dealing with a judgement of cognition—neither with a theoretical one based on the concept of a *nature* in general, supplied by the understanding, nor with a (pure) practical one based on the idea of *freedom*, as given *a priori* by reason—and so we are not called upon to justify *a priori* the validity of a judgement which represents either what a thing is, or that there is something which I ought to do in order to produce it. Consequently, if for
281 judgement generally we demonstrate the *universal validity* of a *singular* judgement expressing the subjective purposiveness of an empirical

representation of the form of an object, we shall do all that is needed to explain how it is possible that something can please in the mere judging of it (without sensation or concept), and how, just as the judging of an object for the sake of a *cognition* generally has universal rules, the delight of any one person may be pronounced as a rule for every other.

Now if this universal validity is not to be based on a collection of votes and interrogation of others as to what sort of sensations they experience, but is to rest, as it were, upon an autonomy of the subject passing judgement on the feeling of pleasure (in the given representation), i.e. upon his own taste, and yet is also not to be derived from concepts; then it follows that such a judgement—and such the judgement of taste in fact is—has a double and also logical peculiarity. For, *first*, it has universal validity *a priori*, yet without having a logical universality according to concepts, but only the universality of a singular judgement. *Secondly*, it has a necessity (which must invariably rest upon *a priori* grounds) but one which depends upon no *a priori* proofs by the representation of which it would be competent to enforce the assent which the judgement of taste demands of everyone.

The solution of these logical peculiarities, which distinguish a judgement of taste from all cognitive judgements, will of itself suffice for a deduction of this strange faculty, provided we abstract at the outset from all content of the judgement, namely from the feeling of pleasure, and merely compare the aesthetic form with the form of objective judgements as prescribed by logic. We shall first try, with the help of examples, to illustrate and bring out these characteristic properties of taste.

§ 32

First peculiarity of the judgement of taste

THE judgement of taste determines its object in respect of delight (as a thing of beauty) with a claim to the agreement of *everyone*, just as if it were objective.

To say: This flower is beautiful, is tantamount to repeating its own proper claim to the delight of everyone. The agreeableness of its smell gives it no claim at all. One person revels in it, but it gives another a headache. Now what else are we to suppose from this than that its beauty is to be taken for a property of the flower itself which 282 does not adapt itself to the diversity of heads and the individual senses of the multitude, but to which they must adapt themselves, if they are going to pass judgement upon it. And yet this is not the way the matter stands. For the judgement of taste consists precisely in a thing being called beautiful solely in respect of that quality in which it adapts itself to our mode of receiving it.

Besides, every judgement which is to show the taste of the individual, is required to be an independent judgement of the individual in question. There must be no need of groping about among other people's judgements and getting previous instruction from their delight in or aversion to the same object. Consequently his judgement should be given out *a priori*, and not as an imitation relying on the general pleasure a thing gives as a matter of fact. One would think, however, that a judgement *a priori* must involve a concept of the object for the cognition of which it contains the principle. But the judgement of taste is not grounded on concepts, and is in no way a cognition, but only an aesthetic judgement.

Hence it is that a youthful poet refuses to allow himself to be dissuaded from the conviction that his poem is beautiful, either by the judgement of the public or of his friends. And even if he lends them an ear, he does so, not because he has now come to a different judgement, but because, though the whole public, at least so far as his work is concerned, should have false taste, he still, in his desire for recognition, finds good reason to accommodate himself to the popular error (even against his own judgement). It is only later, when his judgement has been sharpened by exercise, that of his own free will and accord he deserts his former judgements—behaving in just the same way as with those of his judgements which depend wholly upon reason. Taste lays claim simply to autonomy. To make the judgements of others the determining ground of one's own would be heteronomy.

The fact that we recommend the works of the ancients as models, and rightly too, and call their authors classical, as constituting a sort of nobility among writers that leads the way and thereby gives laws to the people, seems to indicate *a posteriori* sources of taste, and to contradict the autonomy of taste in each individual. But we might just as well say that the ancient mathematicians, who, to this day, are looked upon as the almost indispensable models of perfect thoroughness and elegance in synthetic methods, prove that reason also is on our part only imitative, and that it is incompetent with the deepest intuition to produce of itself rigorous proofs by means of the construction of concepts. There is no employment of our powers, no matter how free, not even of reason itself (that must draw all its judgements from the common *a priori* source), which, if each individual had always to start afresh with the crude equipment of his natural state, would not get itself involved in blundering attempts, if those of others did not lie before it as a warning. Not that predecessors make those who follow in their steps mere imitators, but by their methods they set others upon the track of seeking in themselves for the principles, and so of adopting their own, often better, course. Even in religion—where undoubtedly everyone has to derive his rule of conduct from himself, seeing that he himself remains responsible for it, and, when he goes wrong, cannot shift the blame upon others as teachers or leaders—general precepts learned at the feet either of priests or philosophers, or even drawn from one's own resources, are never so efficacious as an example of virtue or holiness, which, historically portrayed, does not dispense with the autonomy of virtue drawn from the spontaneous and original idea of morality (*a priori*), or convert this into a mechanical process of imitation. *Following* which has reference to a precedent, and not imitation, is the proper expression for all influence which the products of an exemplary *author* may exert upon others—and this means no more than going to the same sources for a creative work as those to which he went for his creations, and learning from one's predecessor no more than the mode of availing oneself of such sources. Taste, just because its judgement cannot be determined by concepts or precepts, is among all faculties and talents the very one that stands most in need of examples of what has in the course of culture maintained itself longest in esteem. Thus it avoids an early lapse into crudity, and a return to the rudeness of its earliest efforts.

§ 33

Second peculiarity of the judgement of taste

PROOFS are of no avail whatever for determining the judgement of taste, and in this connexion matters stand just as they would were that judgement simply *subjective*.

If anyone does not think a building, view, or poem beautiful, then, *in the first place* he refuses, so far as his inmost conviction goes, to allow approval to be wrung from him by a hundred voices all lauding it to the skies. Of course he may affect to be pleased with it, so as not to be considered as wanting in taste. He may even begin to harbour doubts as to whether he has formed his taste upon an acquaintance with a sufficient number of objects of a particular kind (just as one who in the distance recognizes, as he believes, something as a wood, which everyone else regards as a town, becomes doubtful of the judgement of his own eyesight). But, for all that, he clearly perceives that the approval of others affords no valid proof, available for the judging of beauty. He recognizes that others, perchance, may see and observe for him, and that, what many have seen in one and the same way may, for the purpose of a theoretical, and therefore logical judgement, serve as an adequate ground of proof for him, albeit he believes he saw otherwise, but that what has pleased others can never serve him as the ground of an aesthetic judgement. The judgement of others, where unfavourable to ours, may, no doubt, rightly make us suspicious in respect of our own, but convince us that it is wrong it never can. Hence there is no empirical *ground of proof* that can coerce anyone's judgement of taste.

In the second place, a proof *a priori* according to definite rules is still less capable of determining the judgement as to beauty. If anyone reads me his poem, or brings me to a play, which, all said and done, fails to commend itself to my taste, then let him adduce *Batteux* or *Lessing,** or still older and more famous critics of taste, with all the host of rules laid down by them, as a proof of the beauty of his poem; let certain passages particularly displeasing to me accord completely with the rules of beauty, (as set out by these critics and universally recognized): I stop my ears: I do not want to hear any reasons or any arguing about the matter. I would prefer to suppose that those rules of the critics were at fault, or at least have no application, than to allow my judgement to be determined by *a priori* proofs. I take my stand on the ground that my judgement is to be one of taste, and not one of understanding or reason.

This would appear to be one of the chief reasons why this faculty of aesthetic judgement has been given the name of taste. For someone may recount to me all the ingredients of a dish, and observe of each and everyone of them that it is just what I like, and, in addition, rightly commend the wholesomeness of the food; yet I am deaf to all these arguments. I try the dish with *my own* tongue and palate, and I pass judgement according to their verdict (not according to universal principles).

As a matter of fact the judgement of taste is invariably laid down as a singular judgement upon the object. The understanding can, from the comparison of the object, in point of delight, with the judgements of others, form a universal judgement, e.g. 'All tulips are beautiful'. But that judgement is then not one of taste, but is a logical judgement which converts the reference of an object to our taste into a predicate belonging to things of a certain kind. But it is only the judgement whereby I regard an individual given tulip as beautiful, i.e. regard my delight in it as of universal validity, that is a judgement of taste. Its peculiarity, however, consists in the fact that, although it has merely subjective validity, still it extends its claims to *all* subjects, as unreservedly as it would if it were an object-ive judgement, resting on grounds of cognition and capable of being proved by demonstration.

§ 34
An objective principle of taste is not possible

A PRINCIPLE of taste would mean a fundamental premiss under the condition of which one might subsume the concept of an object, and then, by a syllogism, draw the inference that it is beautiful. That, however, is absolutely impossible. For I must feel the pleasure immediately in the representation of the object, and I cannot be talked into it by any grounds of proof. Thus although critics, as *Hume* says,* are able to reason more plausibly than cooks, they must still share the same fate. For the determining ground of their judgement they are not able to look to the force of demonstrations, but only to the reflection of the subject upon his own state (of pleasure or displeasure), to the 286 exclusion of precepts and rules.

There is, however, a matter upon which it is competent for critics to exercise their subtlety, and upon which they ought to do so, so long as it tends to the rectification and extension of our judgements of taste. But that matter is not one of exhibiting the determining ground of aesthetic judgements of this kind in a universally applic-able formula—which is impossible. Rather it is the investigation of the faculties of cognition and their function in these judgements, and the illustration, by the analysis of examples, of their mutual subjective purposiveness, the form of which in a given representation has been shown above to constitute the beauty of their object. Hence with regard to the representation whereby an object is given, the critique of taste itself is only subjective; viz. it is the art or science of reducing the mutual relation of the understanding and the imagination in the given representation (without reference to antecedent sensation or concept), consequently their accordance or discordance, to rules, and of determining them with regard to their conditions. It is *art* if it only illustrates this by examples; it is *science* if it deduces the possibility of such judging from the nature of these faculties as faculties of knowledge in general. It is only with the latter, as transcendental critique, that we have here any concern. Its proper scope is the development and justification of the subjective principle of taste, as an *a priori* principle of judgement. As an art, critique merely looks to the physiological (here psychological), and, consequently, empirical rules, according to which in actual fact taste proceeds (passing by the question of their possibility), and seeks to apply them in judging its objects. The latter critique criticizes the products of fine art, just as the former does the faculty of judging them.

§ 35

The principle of taste is the subjective principle of the general power of judgement

THE judgement of taste is differentiated from logical judgement by the fact that, whereas the latter subsumes a representation under a concept of the object, the judgement of taste does not subsume under a concept at all—for, if it did, necessary and universal approval would be capable of being enforced by proofs. And yet it does bear this resemblance to the logical judgement, that it asserts a universality and 287 necessity, not, however, according to concepts of the object, but a universality and necessity that are, consequently, merely subjective. Now the concepts in a judgement constitute its content (what belongs to the cognition of the object). But the judgement of taste is not determinable by means of concepts. Hence it can only have its ground in the subjective formal condition of a judgement in general. The subjective condition of all judgements is the judging faculty itself, or the power of judgement. Employed in respect of a representation whereby an object is given, this requires the harmonious accordance of two powers of representation. These are, the imagination (for the intuition and the arrangement of the manifold of intuition), and the understanding (for the concept as a representation of the unity of this arrangement). Now, since no concept of the object underlies the judgement here, it can consist only in the subsumption of the imagination itself (in the case of a representation whereby an object is given) under the conditions enabling the understanding in general to advance from the intuition to concepts. That is to say, since the freedom of the imagination consists precisely in the fact that it schematizes without a concept, the judgement of taste must found upon a mere sensation of the mutually enlivening activity of the imagination in its *freedom*, and of the understanding with its *conformity to law*. It must therefore rest upon a feeling that allows the object to be estimated by the purposiveness of the representation (by which an object is given) for the furtherance of the cognitive faculties in their free play. Taste, then, as a subjective power of judgement, contains a principle of subsumption, not of intuitions under *concepts*, but of the *faculty* of intuitions or presentations, i.e. of the imagination, under the *faculty* of concepts, i.e. the understanding, so far as the former *in its freedom* accords with the latter *in its conformity to law*.

For the discovery of this title by means of a deduction of judgements of taste, we can only avail ourselves of the guidance of the formal peculiarities of judgements of this kind, and consequently the mere consideration of their logical form.

§ 36
The problem of a deduction of judgements of taste

To form a cognitive judgement we may immediately connect with the perception of an object the concept of an object in general, the 288 empirical predicates of which are contained in that perception. In this way a judgement of experience is produced. Now this judgement rests on the foundation of *a priori* concepts of the synthetic unity of the manifold of intuition enabling it to be thought as the determination of an object. These concepts (the categories) call for a deduction, and such was supplied in the *Critique of Pure Reason*. That deduction enabled us to solve the problem, How are synthetic *a priori* cognitive judgements possible? This problem had, accordingly, to do with the *a priori* principles of pure understanding and its theoretical judgements.

But we may also immediately connect with a perception a feeling of pleasure (or displeasure) and a delight attending the representation of the object and serving it instead of a predicate. In this way there arises a judgement which is aesthetic and not cognitive. Now, if such a judgement is not merely one of sensation, but a formal judgement of reflection that demands this delight from everyone as necessary, something must lie at its basis as its *a priori* principle. This principle may, indeed, be a mere subjective one (supposing an objective one should be impossible for judgements of this kind), but, even as such, it requires a deduction to make it intelligible how an aesthetic judgement can lay claim to necessity. That, now, is what lies at the bottom of the problem upon which we are at present engaged, i.e. How are judgements of taste possible? This problem, therefore, is concerned with the *a priori* principles of pure judgement in *aesthetic* judgements, i.e. not those in which (as in theoretical judgements) it has merely to subsume under objective concepts of understanding, and in which it comes under a law, but rather those in which it is itself, subjectively, object as well as law.

We may also put the problem in this way: How is a judgement possible which, going merely upon the individual's *own* feeling of pleasure in an object independent of the concept of it, judges this as a pleasure attached to the representation of the same object *in every other individual*, and does so *a priori*, i.e. without being allowed to wait and see if other people will be of the same mind?

It is easy to see that judgements of taste are synthetic, for they go beyond the concept and even the intuition of the object, and join as predicate to that intuition something which is not even a cognition at all, namely, the feeling of pleasure (or displeasure). But, although the predicate (the *personal* pleasure that is connected with the representation) is empirical, still we need not go further than what is involved in the expressions of their claim to see that, so far as concerns the agreement required of *everyone*, they are *a priori* judgements, or mean to pass for such. This problem of the critique of the power of judgement, therefore, is part of the general problem of transcendental philosophy: How are synthetic *a priori* judgements possible?

§ 37

What exactly it is, that is asserted a priori *of an object in a judgement of taste*

THE immediate connection of the representation of an object with pleasure can only be a matter of internal perception, and, if nothing more than this were at issue, would only yield a mere empirical judgement. For with no representation can I *a priori* connect a determinate feeling (of pleasure or displeasure) except where I rely upon the basis of an *a priori* principle in reason determining the will. The truth is that the pleasure (in the moral feeling) is the consequence of the determination of the will by the principle. It cannot, therefore, be compared with the pleasure in taste. For it requires a determinate concept of a law: whereas the pleasure in taste has to be connected immediately with the mere judging prior to any concept. For the same reason, also, all judgements of taste are singular judgements, for they unite their predicate of delight, not to a concept, but to a given singular empirical representation.

Hence, in a judgement of taste, what is represented *a priori* as a universal rule for the judgement and as valid for everyone, is not the pleasure but the *universal validity* of this pleasure perceived, as it is, to be combined in the mind with the mere judging of an object. A judgement to the effect that it is with pleasure that I perceive and judge some object is an empirical judgement. But if it asserts that I think the object beautiful, i.e. that I may attribute that delight to everyone as necessary, it is then an *a priori* judgement.

§ 38

Deduction of judgements of taste

ADMITTING that in a pure judgement of taste the delight in the object is connected with the mere judging of its form, then what we feel to be associated in the mind with the representation of the object 290 is nothing else than its subjective purposiveness for judgement. Since, now, in respect of the formal rules of judging, apart from all matter (whether sensation or concept), judgement can only be directed to the subjective conditions of its employment in general (which is not restricted to the particular mode of the senses nor to a particular concept of the understanding) and so can only be directed to that subjective factor which we may presuppose in all human beings (as requisite for a possible experience generally), it follows that the accordance of a representation with these conditions of the judgement must admit of being assumed valid *a priori* for everyone. In other words, we are warranted in expecting from everyone the pleasure or subjective purposiveness of the representation in respect of the relation of the cognitive faculties engaged in the judging of a sensible object in general.[9]

Remark

What makes this deduction so easy is that it is spared the necessity of having to justify the objective reality of a concept. For beauty is not a concept of the object, and the judgement of taste is not a cognitive judgement. The latter simply claims that we are justified in presupposing that the same subjective conditions of judgement which we find in ourselves are universally present in everyone, and further that we have rightly subsumed the given object under these conditions. The latter, no doubt, has to face unavoidable difficulties which do not affect the logical judgement. (For there the subsumption is under concepts; whereas in the aesthetic judgement it is under a mere sensible relation of the imagination and understanding mutually harmonizing with one another in the represented form of the object, in which case the subsumption may easily prove fallacious.) But this in no way detracts from the legitimacy of the claim of the judgement to count upon universal agreement—a claim which amounts to no more than this: the correctness of the principle of judging validly for everyone upon subjective grounds. For as to the difficulty and uncertainty concerning the correctness of the subsumption under that principle, it no more casts a doubt upon the legitimacy of the claim to this validity on

---

[9] In order to be justified in claiming universal agreement for an aesthetic judgement merely resting on subjective grounds it is sufficient to assume: (1) that the subjective conditions of this faculty of aesthetic judgement are identical in all human beings in what concerns the relation of the cognitive faculties, there brought into action, with a view to a cognition in general. This must be true, as otherwise human beings would be incapable of communicating their representations or even their knowledge; (2) that the judgement has paid regard merely to this relation (consequently merely to the *formal condition* of the faculty of judgement), and is pure, i.e. is free from confusion either with concepts of the object or sensations as determining grounds. If any mistake is made in this latter point this only touches the incorrect application to a particular case of the right which a law gives us, and does not do away with the right generally.

the part of an aesthetic judgement generally, or, therefore, upon the principle itself, than the mistakes (though not so often or easily incurred) to which the subsumption of the logical judgement under its principle is similarly liable, can render the latter principle, which is objective, open to doubt. But if the question were: How is it possible to assume *a priori* that nature is a sum of objects of taste? the problem would then have reference to teleology, because it would have to be regarded as an end of nature belonging essentially to its concept that it should exhibit forms that are purposive for our judgement. But the correctness of this assumption may still be seriously questioned, while the actual existence of beauties of nature is clear to experience.

§ 39
The communicability of a sensation

SENSATION, as the real in perception, where referred to knowledge, is called bodily sensation and its specific quality may be represented as completely communicable to others in a like mode, provided we assume that everyone has a like sense to our own. This, however, is an absolutely inadmissible presupposition in the case of a bodily sensation. Thus a person who is without a sense of smell cannot have a sensation of this kind communicated to him, and, even if he does not suffer from this deficiency, we still cannot be certain that he gets precisely the same sensation from a flower that we get from it. But still more divergent must we consider individuals to be in respect of the *agreeableness* or *disagreeableness* derived from the sensation of one and the same object of the senses, and it is absolutely out of the question to require that pleasure in such objects should be acknowledged by everyone. Pleasure of this kind, since it enters into the mind 292 through the senses—our rôle, therefore, being a passive one—may be called the pleasure of *enjoyment*.

On the other hand delight in an action on the score of its moral character is not a pleasure of enjoyment, but one of self-activity and its correspondence with the idea of what it is meant to be. But this feeling, which is called the moral feeling, requires concepts, and is the presentation of a purposiveness, not free, but according to law. It, therefore, admits of communication only by means of reason and, if the pleasure is to be of the same kind for everyone, by means of very determinate practical concepts of reason.

The pleasure in the sublime in nature, as one of contemplation subtly involving reason, lays claim also to universal participation, but still it presupposes another feeling, that, namely, of our super-sensible vocation, which feeling, however obscure it may be, has a moral foundation. But there is absolutely no authority for my pre-supposing that others will pay attention to this, and take a delight in beholding the uncouth dimensions of nature (one that in truth cannot be ascribed to the sight of it, which is terrifying rather than otherwise). Nevertheless, having regard to the fact that attention ought to be paid upon every appropriate occasion to this moral predisposition, we may still demand that delight from everyone; but we can do so only through the moral law, which, in its turn, rests upon concepts of reason.

The pleasure in the beautiful is, on the other hand, neither a plea-sure of enjoyment nor of an activity according to law, nor yet one of a contemplation involving subtle reasoning in accordance with ideas, but rather of mere reflection. Without any guiding-line of end or principle this pleasure attends the ordinary apprehension of an object by means of the imagination, as the faculty of intuition, but with a reference to the understanding as faculty of concepts, and through the operation of a process of judgement which has also to be invoked in order to obtain the commonest experience. In the latter case, however, its functions are directed to perceiving an empirical objective concept, whereas in the former (in the aesthetic mode of judging) merely to perceiving the adequacy of the representation for engaging both faculties of knowledge in their freedom in an harmo-nious (subjectively-purposive) employment, i.e. to feeling with pleasure the subjective bearings of the representation. This pleasure must of necessity depend for everyone upon the same conditions, seeing that they are the subjective conditions of the possibility of a cognition in general, and the proportion of these cognitive faculties, 293 which is requisite for taste is requisite also for ordinary sound under-standing, the presence of which we are entitled to presuppose in everyone. And, for this reason also, one who judges with taste (provided he does not make a mistake as to this consciousness, and does not take the matter for the form, or charm for beauty), can impute the subjective purposiveness, i.e. his delight in the object, to everyone else, and suppose his feeling universally communicable, and that, too, without the mediation of concepts.

§ 40
Taste as a kind of sensus communis

THE name of 'sense' is often given to judgement where what attracts attention is not so much its reflective act as merely its result. So we speak of a sense of truth, of a sense of propriety, or of justice, and so forth. And yet, of course, we know, or at least ought well enough to know, that an empirical sense cannot be the true abode of these concepts, not to speak of its being competent, even in the slightest degree, to pronounce universal rules. On the contrary, we recognize that a representation of this kind, whether it be of truth, propriety, beauty, or justice, could never enter our thoughts were we not able to raise ourselves above the level of the senses to that of higher faculties of cognition. *Common human understanding* which, as mere sound (not yet cultivated) understanding, is looked upon as the least we can expect from anyone claiming the name of a human being, has therefore the doubtful honour of having the name of common sense (*sensus communis*) bestowed upon it; and bestowed, too, in an acceptation of the word *common* (not merely in our own language, where it actually has a double meaning, but also in many others) which makes it amount to what is *vulgar*—what is everywhere to be met with—a quality which by no means confers credit or distinction upon its possessor.

However, by the name *sensus communis* is to be understood the idea of a *public* sense, i.e. a faculty of judging which in its reflective act takes account (*a priori*) of the mode of representation of everyone else, in order, *as it were*, to weigh its judgement with the collective reason of mankind, and thereby avoid the illusion arising from subjective and personal conditions which could readily be taken for objective, an illusion that would exert a prejudicial influence upon its judgement. 294 This is accomplished by weighing the judgement, not so much with actual, as rather with the merely possible, judgements of others, and by putting ourselves in the position of everyone else, as the result of a mere abstraction from the limitations which contingently affect our own judging. This, in turn, is effected by so far as possible leaving out the element of matter, i.e. sensation, in our general state of representational activity, and confining attention to the formal peculiarities of our representation or general state of representational activity.

Now it may seem that this operation of reflection is too artificial to be attributed to the faculty which we call *common* sense. But this is an appearance due only to its expression in abstract formulae. In itself nothing is more natural than to abstract from charm and emotion where one is looking for a judgement intended to serve as a universal rule.

While the following maxims of common human understanding do not properly come in here as constituent parts of the critique of taste, they may still serve to elucidate its fundamental propositions. They are these: (1) to think for oneself; (2) to think from the standpoint of everyone else; (3) always to think consistently. The first is the maxim of *unprejudiced* thought, the second that of *broadened* thought, the third that of *consistent* thought. The first is the maxim of a never-*passive* reason. To be given to such passivity, consequently to heteronomy of reason, is called *prejudice*; and the greatest of all prejudices is that of fancying nature not to be subject to rules which the understanding by virtue of its own essential law lays at its basis, i.e. *superstition*. Emancipation from superstition is called *enlightenment*;[10] for although this term applies also to emancipation from prejudices generally, still superstition deserves pre-eminently (*in sensu eminenti*) to be called a prejudice. For the condition of blindness into which superstition places us, and which it even demands from us as an obligation, makes the need of being led by others, and consequently the passive state of the reason, all too evident. As to the second maxim belonging to our habits of thought, we have become accustomed to calling a man narrow (*narrow*, as opposed to being of *broadened mind*) whose talents fall short of what is required for employment upon work of any magnitude (especially that involving intensity). But the question here is not one of the faculty of cognition, but of the *mental habit* of making a purposive use of it. This, however small the range and degree to which a person's natural endowments extend, still indicates an individual of *broadened mind*: if he detaches himself from the subjective personal conditions of his judgement, which cramp the minds of so

295

---

[10] We readily see that enlightenment, while easy, no doubt, *in thesi*, *in hypothesi* is difficult and slow of realization. For not to be passive with one's reason, but always to be self-legislative is doubtless quite an easy matter for one who only desires to live up to his essential end, and does not seek to know what is beyond his understanding. But as the tendency in the latter direction is hardly avoidable, and others are always coming and promising with full assurance that they are able to satisfy one's curiosity, it must be very difficult to preserve or restore in the mind (and particularly in the public mind) that merely negative attitude (which constitutes enlightenment proper).

many others, and reflects upon his own judgement from a *universal standpoint* (which he can only determine by shifting his ground to the standpoint of others). The third maxim—that, namely, of *consistent* thought—is the hardest of attainment, and is only attainable by the union of both the former, and after constant attention to them has made one at home in their observance. We may say: the first of these is the maxim of understanding, the second that of judgement, the third that of reason.

I resume the thread of the discussion interrupted by the above digression, and I say that taste can with more justice be called a *sensus communis* than can sound understanding; and that the aesthetic, rather than the intellectual, judgement can bear the name of a public sense,[11] i.e. taking it that we are prepared to use the word 'sense' of an effect that mere reflection has upon the mind; for then by sense we mean the feeling of pleasure. We might even define taste as the faculty of judging what makes our feeling in a given representation *universally communicable* without the mediation of a concept.

The aptitude of human beings for communicating their thoughts requires, also, a relation between the imagination and the understanding, in order to connect intuitions with concepts, and concepts, in turn, with intuitions, which both unite in cognition. But there the agreement of both mental powers is *according to law*, and under the constraint of determinate concepts. Only when the imagination in its freedom stirs the understanding, and the understanding apart from concepts sets the imagination into regular play, does the representation communicate itself not as thought, but as an internal feeling of a purposive state of the mind.

Taste is, therefore, the faculty of judging *a priori* the communicability of the feelings that, without the mediation of a concept, are connected with a given representation.

Supposing, now, that we could assume that the mere universal communicability of our feeling must of itself carry with it an interest for us (an assumption, however, which we are not entitled to draw as a conclusion from the character of a merely reflective judgement), we should then be in a position to explain how the feeling in the judgement of taste comes to be expected from everyone as a sort of duty.

296

[11] Taste may be designated a *sensus communis aestheticus*, common human understanding a *sensus communis logicus*.

§ 41

The empirical interest in the beautiful

ABUNDANT proof has been given above to show that the judgement of taste by which something is declared beautiful must have no interest *as its determining ground*. But it does not follow from this that after it has once been posited as a pure aesthetic judgement, an interest cannot then enter into combination with it. This combination, however, can never be anything but indirect. Taste must, that is to say, first of all be represented in conjunction with something else, if the delight attending the mere reflection upon an object is to admit of any further connection with *a pleasure in the existence* of the object (as that wherein all interest consists). For the saying, *a posse ad esse non valet consequentia*,* which is applied to cognitive judgements, holds good here in the case of aesthetic judgements. Now this 'something else' may be something empirical, such as an inclination proper to the nature of human beings, or it may be something intellectual, as a property of the will whereby it admits of rational determination *a priori*. Both of these involve a delight in the existence of the object, and so can lay the foundation for an interest in what has already pleased of itself and without regard to any interest whatsoever.

The empirical interest in the beautiful exists only in *society*. And if we admit that the impulse to society is natural to mankind, and that
297 the suitability for and the propensity towards it, i.e. *sociability*, is a property essential to the requirements of human beings as creatures intended for society, and one, therefore, that belongs to *humanity*, it is inevitable that we should also look upon taste in the light of a faculty for judging whatever enables us to communicate even our *feeling* to everyone else, and hence as a means of promoting that upon which the natural inclination of everyone is set.

With no one to take into account but himself, an individual abandoned on a desert island would not adorn either himself or his hut, nor would he look for flowers, and still less plant them, with the object of providing himself with personal adornments. Only in society does it occur to him to be not merely a human being, but a human being refined in his own way (the beginning of civilization)—for that is how we judge of one who has the bent and turn for communicating his pleasure to others, and who is not quite satisfied with an object unless his feeling of delight in it can be shared in communion with others.

Further, a regard to universal communicability is a thing which everyone expects and requires from everyone else, just as if it were part of an original contract dictated by humanity itself. And thus, no doubt, at first only charms, e.g. colours for painting oneself (roucou among the Caribs and cinnabar among the Iroquois), or flowers, sea-shells, beautifully coloured feathers, then, in the course of time, also beautiful forms (as in canoes, apparel, etc.) which convey no gratification, i.e. delight of enjoyment, become of moment in society and attract a considerable interest. Eventually, when civilization has reached its height it makes this work of communication almost the main business of refined inclination, and the entire value of sensations is placed in the degree to which they permit of universal communication. At this stage, then, even where the pleasure which each one has in an object is but insignificant and possesses of itself no conspicuous interest, still the idea of its universal communicability almost indefinitely augments its value.

This interest, indirectly attached to the beautiful by the inclination towards society, and, consequently, empirical, is, however, of no importance for us here. For that to which we have alone to look is what can have a bearing *a priori*, even though indirect, upon the judgement of taste. For, if even in this form an associated interest should betray itself, taste would then reveal a transition on the part of our faculty of judging from the enjoyment of sense to the moral feeling. This would not merely mean that we should be supplied with a more effectual guide for the final employment of taste, but taste would further be presented as a link in the chain of the human faculties *a priori* upon which all legislation must depend. This much may certainly be said of the empirical interest in objects of taste, and in taste itself, that as taste thus pays homage to inclination, however refined, such interest will nevertheless readily fuse also with all inclinations and passions, which in society attain to their greatest variety and highest degree, and the interest in the beautiful, if this is made its ground, can but afford a very ambiguous transition from the agreeable to the good. We have reason, however, to inquire whether this transition may not still in some way be furthered by means of taste when taken in its purity.

§ 42

The intellectual interest in the beautiful

IT has been with the best intentions that those who love to see in the ultimate end of humanity, namely the morally good, the goal of all activities to which human beings are impelled by the inner bent of their nature, have regarded it as a mark of a good moral character to take an interest in the beautiful generally. But they have, not without reason, been contradicted by others who appeal to the fact of experience, that *virtuosi* in matters of taste, being not only often, but one might say as a general rule, vain, capricious, and addicted to injurious passions, could perhaps more rarely than others lay claim to any pre-eminent attachment to moral principles. And so it would seem, not only that the feeling for the beautiful is specifically different from the moral feeling (which as a matter of fact is the case), but also that the interest which we may combine with it, will hardly consort with the moral, and certainly not on grounds of inner affinity.

Now I willingly admit that the interest in the *beautiful of art* (including under this heading the artificial use of natural beauties for personal adornment, and so from vanity) gives no evidence at all of a habit of mind attached to the morally good, or even inclined that way. But, on the other hand, I do maintain that to take an *immediate interest* in the beauty of *nature* (not merely to have taste in judging it) is always a mark of a good soul; and that, where this interest is habitual, it is at least indicative of a temper of mind favourable to the moral feeling that it should readily associate itself with the *contemplation of nature*. It must, however, be borne in mind that I mean to refer strictly to the beautiful *forms* of nature, and to put to one side the *charms* which she is wont so lavishly to combine with them; because, though the interest in these is no doubt immediate, it is nevertheless empirical.

One who alone (and without any intention of communicating his observations to others) regards the beautiful form of a wild flower, a bird, an insect, or the like, out of admiration and love of them, and being loath to let them escape him in nature, even at the risk of some misadventure to himself—so far from there being any prospect of advantage to him—such a one takes an immediate, and in fact intellectual, interest in the beauty of nature. This means that he is not merely pleased with nature's product in respect of its form, but is also pleased at its existence, and is so without any charm of sense having a share in the matter, or without his associating with it any end whatsoever.

In this connexion, however, it is of note that were we to play a trick on our lover of the beautiful, and plant in the ground artificial flowers (which can be made so as to look just like natural ones), and perch artfully carved birds on the branches of trees, and he were to find out how he had been deceived, the immediate interest which these things previously had for him would at once vanish—though, perhaps, a different interest might intervene in its stead, that, namely, of vanity in decorating his room with them for the eyes of others. The fact is that our intuition and reflection must have as their concomitant the thought that the beauty in question is nature's handiwork; and this is the sole basis of the immediate interest that is taken in it. Failing this we are either left with a bare judgement of taste devoid of all interest whatever, or else only with one that is combined with an interest that is mediate, involving, namely, a reference to society; and this latter affords no reliable indication of morally good habits of thought.

The advantage which natural beauty enjoys over that of art, even where it is excelled by the latter in point of form, in yet being alone able to awaken an immediate interest, accords with the refined and well-grounded habits of thought of all those who have cultivated their moral feeling. If a person with taste enough to judge of works of fine art with the greatest correctness and refinement readily quits the room in which he meets with those beauties that minister to 300 vanity or, at least, social joys, and betakes himself to the beautiful in nature, so that he may there find as it were a feast for his spirit in a train of thought which he can never completely evolve, we will then regard this his choice even with veneration, and give him credit for a beautiful soul, to which no connoisseur or art collector can lay claim on the score of the interest which his objects have for him.—Here, now, are two kinds of objects which in the judgement of mere taste could scarcely contend with one another for a superiority. What then, is the distinction that makes us hold them in such different esteem?

We have a faculty of judgement which is merely aesthetic—a faculty of judging of forms without the aid of concepts, and of finding, in the mere judging of them, a delight that we at the same time make into a rule for everyone, without this judgement being founded on an interest, or yet producing one.—On the other hand we have also a faculty of intellectual judgement for the mere forms of practical maxims (so far as they are of themselves qualified for universal legislation)—a faculty of determining an *a priori* delight, which we make into a law for everyone, without our judgement being founded on any interest, *though here it produces one*. The pleasure or displeasure in the former judgement is called that of taste; the latter is called that of the moral feeling.

But, now, reason is further interested in ideas (for which in our moral feeling it brings about an immediate interest) having also objective reality. That is to say, it is of interest to reason that nature should at least show a trace or give a hint that it contains in itself some ground or other for assuming a uniform accordance of its products with our wholly disinterested delight (a delight which we cognize *a priori* as a law for everyone without being able to ground it upon proofs). That being so, reason must take an interest in every manifestation on the part of nature of some such accordance. Hence the mind cannot reflect on the beauty of *nature* without at the same time finding its interest engaged. But this interest is akin to the moral. One, then, who takes such an interest in the beautiful in nature can only do so in so far as he has previously set his interest deep in the foundations of the morally good. On these grounds we have reason for presuming the presence of at least the germ of a good moral disposition in the case of someone to whom the beauty of nature is a matter of immediate interest.

It will be said that this interpretation of aesthetic judgements on the basis of kinship with our moral feeling has far too studied an appearance to be accepted as the true reading of the cypher in which nature speaks to us figuratively through its beautiful forms. But, first of all, this immediate interest in the beauty of nature is not in fact common. It is peculiar to those whose habits of thought are already trained to the good or else are eminently susceptible of such training; and under these circumstances the analogy in which the pure judgement of taste that, without relying upon any interest, gives us a feeling of delight, and at the same time represents it *a priori* as proper to humanity in general, stands to the moral judgement that does just the same from concepts, is one which, without any clear, subtle, and deliberate reflection, conduces to a like immediate interest being taken in the objects of the former judgement as in those of the latter—with this one difference, that the interest in the first case is free, while in the latter it is one founded on objective laws. In addition to this there is our admiration of nature which in her beautiful products displays herself as art, not as mere matter of chance, but, as it were, designedly, according to a law-directed arrangement, and as purposiveness apart from any purpose. As we never meet with such an end outside ourselves, we naturally look for it in ourselves, and, in fact, in that which constitutes the ultimate end of our existence—namely in our moral vocation. (The inquiry into the ground of the possibility of such a natural purposiveness will, however, first come under discussion in the analysis of teleology.)

The fact that the delight in beautiful art does not, in the pure judgement of taste, involve an immediate interest, as does that in beautiful nature, may be readily explained. For the former is either such an imitation of the latter as goes the length of deceiving us, in which case it acts upon us in the character of a natural beauty, which we take it to be; or else it is an intentional art obviously directed to our delight. In the latter case, however, the delight in the product would, it is true, be brought about immediately by taste, but there would be nothing but a mediate interest in the cause that lay beneath—an interest, namely, in an art only capable of interesting by its end, and never in itself. It will, perhaps, be said that this is also the case where an object of nature only interests by its beauty so far as a moral idea is brought into partnership therewith. But it is not the object that is of immediate interest, but rather the inherent character of the beauty qualifying it for such a partnership—a character, therefore, that inwardly belongs to the character of beauty. 302

The charms in natural beauty, which are to be found blended, as it were, so frequently with beauty of form, belong either to the modifications of light (in colouring) or of sound (in tones). For these are the only sensations which permit not merely of a feeling of the senses, but also of reflection upon the form of these modifications of the senses, and so embody as it were a language in which nature addresses us and which seems to possess a higher meaning. Thus the white colour of the lily seems to dispose the mind to ideas of innocence, and the other seven colours, following the series from the red to the violet, similarly to ideas of (1) sublimity, (2) courage, (3) candour, (4) amiability, (5) modesty, (6) constancy, (7) tenderness. The bird's song tells of joyousness and contentment with its existence. At least so we interpret nature—whether such be its purpose or not. But it is the indispensable requisite of the interest which we here take in beauty, that the beauty should be that of nature, and it vanishes completely as soon as we are conscious of having been deceived, and that it is only the work of art—so completely that even taste can then no longer find in it anything beautiful nor sight anything attractive.

What do poets set more store on than the nightingale's bewitching and beautiful note, in a lonely thicket on a still summer evening by the soft light of the moon? And yet we have instances of how, where no such songster was to be found, a jovial host has played a trick on the guests with him on a visit to enjoy the country air, and has done so to their huge satisfaction, by hiding in a thicket a rogue of a youth who (with a reed or rush in his mouth) knew how to reproduce this note so as to hit off nature to perfection. But the instant one realizes that it is all a fraud no one will long endure listening to this song that before was regarded as so attractive. And it is just the same with the song of any other bird. It must be nature, or be mistaken by us for nature, to enable us to take an immediate *interest* in the beautiful as such; and this is all the more so if we may even call upon others to take a similar interest. And such a demand we do in fact make, since we regard as coarse and low the habits of thought of those who have no *feeling* for beautiful nature (for this is the word we use for susceptibility to an interest in the contemplation of beautiful nature), and who devote themselves to the merely sensuous enjoyments found in eating and drinking.

§ 43
Art in general

(1) *Art* is distinguished from *nature* as making (*facere*) is from acting or *operating* in general (*agere*), and the product or the result of the former is distinguished from that of the latter as *work* (*opus*) from effect (*effectus*).

By right it is only production through freedom, i.e. through an act of will that places reason at the basis of its action, that should be termed art.* For, although we are pleased to call what bees produce (their regularly constructed cells) a work of art, we only do so on the strength of an analogy with art; that is to say, as soon as we call to mind that no rational deliberation forms the basis of their labour, we say at once that it is a product of their nature (of instinct), and it is only to their creator that we ascribe it as art.

If, as sometimes happens, in a search through a bog, we light on a piece of hewn wood, we do not say it is a product of nature but of art. Its producing cause had an end in view to which the object owes its form. Apart from such cases, we recognize an art in everything formed in such a way that its actuality must have been preceded by a representation of the thing in its cause (as even in the case of the bees), although the effect could not have been *thought* by the cause. But where anything is called absolutely a work of art, to distinguish it from a natural product, then some work of man is always understood.

(2) *Art*, as human skill, is distinguished also from *science* (as *ability* from *knowledge*), as a practical from a theoretical faculty, as technic from theory (as the art of surveying from geometry). For this reason, also, what one *can* do the moment one only *knows* what is to be done, hence without anything more than sufficient knowledge of the desired result, is not called art. To art that alone belongs for which the possession of the most complete knowledge does not involve one's having then and there the skill to do it. *Camper* describes 304 very exactly* how the best shoe must be made, but he, doubtless, was not able to turn one out himself.[12]

(3) *Art* is further distinguished from *handicraft*. The first is called *free*, the other may be called *renumerative art*. We look on the former as something which could only prove purposive (be a success) as play, i.e. an occupation which is agreeable on its own account; but on the second as labour, i.e. a business, which on its own account is disagreeable (drudgery), and is only attractive by means of what it results in (e.g. the pay), and which is consequently capable of being a compulsory imposition. Whether in the list of arts and crafts we are to rank watchmakers as artists, and smiths on the contrary as craftsmen, requires a standpoint different from that here adopted—one, that is to say, taking account of the proportion of the talents which the business undertaken in either case must necessarily involve. Whether, also, among the so-called seven free arts some may not have been included which should be reckoned as sciences, and many, too, that resemble handicraft, is a matter I will not discuss here. It is not amiss, however, to remind the reader of this: that in all free arts something of a compulsory character is still required, or, as it is called, a *mechanism*, without which the *spirit*, which in art must be *free*, and which alone gives life to the work, would be bodyless and

---

[12] In my part of the country, if you set the common man a problem like that of Columbus and his egg, he says, 'There is no art in that, it is only science': i.e. you *can* do it if you know *how*; and he says just the same of all the would-be arts of jugglers. To that of the tight-rope dancer, on the other hand, he has not the least compunction in giving the name of art.

evanescent (e.g. in the poetic art there must be correctness and wealth
of language, likewise prosody and metre). For not a few leaders of a
newer school believe that the best way to promote a free art is to
sweep away all restraint, and convert it from labour into mere play.

§ 44
Fine art

THERE is no science of the beautiful, but only a critique. Nor, again,
is there such a thing as beautiful science, but only beautiful art.*
For a science of the beautiful would have to determine scientifically,
305 i.e. by means of proofs, whether a thing was to be considered beautiful or not; and the judgement upon beauty, consequently, would, if
belonging to science, fail to be a judgement of taste. As for a beautiful
science—a science which, as such, is to be beautiful, is a nonsense.
For if, treating it as a science, we were to ask for reasons and proofs,
we would be put off with elegant phrases (*bons mots*). What has given
rise to the current expression *beautiful sciences* is, doubtless, no more
than this, that common observation has, quite accurately, noted the
fact that for fine art, in the fulness of its perfection, a large store of
knowledge is required, as, for example, knowledge of ancient languages, acquaintance with classical authors, history, antiquarian
learning, and so forth. Hence these historical sciences, owing to the
fact that they form the necessary preparation and groundwork for
fine art, and partly also owing to the fact that they are taken to comprise even the knowledge of the products of fine art (rhetoric and
poetry), have by a confusion of words, actually acquired the name of
beautiful sciences.

Where art, merely seeking to actualize a possible object to the
cognition of which it is adequate, performs whatever acts are required
for that purpose, then it is *mechanical*. But should the feeling of
pleasure be what it has immediately in view it is then termed *aesthetic*
art. As such it may be either *agreeable* or *fine* art. The description
'agreeable art' applies where the end of the art is that the pleasure
should accompany the representations considered as mere *sensations*,
the description 'fine art' where it is to accompany them considered as
modes of cognition.

Agreeable arts are those which have mere enjoyment for their object.
Such are all the charms that can gratify a dinner party: entertaining

narrative, the art of engaging the whole table in unrestrained and sprightly conversation, or with jest and laughter inducing a certain air of gaiety. Here, as the saying goes, there may be much chattering over the glasses, without a person wishing to be brought to book for all he utters, because it is only given out for the entertainment of the moment, and not as a lasting matter to be made the subject of reflection or repetition. (Of the same sort is also the art of arranging the table for enjoyment, or, at large banquets, the music of the orchestra—a quaint idea intended to act on the mind merely as an agreeable noise fostering a genial spirit, which, without anyone paying the smallest attention to the composition, promotes the free flow 306 of conversation between guest and guest.) In addition must be included play of every kind which is attended with no further interest than that of making the time pass by unheeded.

Fine art, on the other hand, is a mode of representation which is intrinsically purposive, and which, although devoid of an end, has the effect of advancing the culture of the mental powers in the interests of social communication.

The universal communicability of a pleasure involves in its very concept that the pleasure is not one of enjoyment arising out of mere sensation, but must be one of reflection. Hence aesthetic art, as art which is beautiful, is one having for its standard the reflective judgement and not bodily sensation.

§ 45
Fine art is an art, so far as it has at the same time the appearance of being nature

A PRODUCT of fine art must be recognized to be art and not nature. Nevertheless the purposiveness in its form must appear just as free from the constraint of arbitrary rules as if it were a product of mere nature. Upon this feeling of freedom in the play of our cognitive faculties—which play has at the same time to be purposive—rests that pleasure which alone is universally communicable without being based on concepts. Nature proved beautiful when it wore the appearance of art; and art can only be termed beautiful, where we are conscious of its being art, while yet it has the appearance of nature.

For, whether we are dealing with beauty of nature or beauty of art, we may make the universal statement: *that is beautiful which pleases in the mere judging of it* (not in sensation or by means of a concept). Now art has always got a definite intention of producing something. Were this 'something', however, to be mere sensation (something merely subjective), intended to be accompanied with pleasure, then such product would, in our judging of it, only please through the agency of the feeling of the senses. On the other hand, if the intention were one directed to the production of a definite object, then, supposing this were attained by art, the object would only please by means of a concept. But in both cases the art would please, not in *the mere judging of it*, i.e. not as fine art, but rather as mechanical art.

307   Hence the purposiveness in the product of fine art, intentional though it be, must not have the appearance of being intentional; i.e. we must be able to *look upon* fine art as nature, although we recognize it to be art. But the way in which a product of art seems like nature, is by the presence of perfect *exactness* in the agreement with rules prescribing how alone the product can be what it is intended to be, but with an absence of *laboured effect* (without academic form betraying itself), i.e. without a trace appearing of the artist having always had the rule present to him and of its having fettered his mental powers.

§ 46
Fine art is the art of genius

Genius is the talent (natural endowment) which gives the rule to art. Since talent, as an innate productive faculty of the artist, belongs itself to nature, we may put it this way: *Genius* is the innate mental aptitude (*ingenium*) *through which* nature gives the rule to art.

Whatever may be the merits of this definition, and whether it is merely arbitrary, or whether it is adequate or not to the concept usually associated with the word *genius* (a point which the following sections have to clear up), it may still be shown at the outset that, according to this acceptation of the word, fine arts must necessarily be regarded as arts of *genius*.

For every art presupposes rules which are laid down as the foundation which first enables a product, if it is to be called one of art, to be represented as possible. The concept of fine art, however, does not permit of the judgement upon the beauty of its product being derived from any rule that has a *concept* for its determining ground, and that depends, consequently, on a concept of the way in which the product is possible. Consequently fine art cannot of its own self excogitate the rule according to which it is to realize its product. But since, for all that, a product can never be called art unless there is a preceding rule, it follows that nature in the individual (and by virtue of the harmony of his faculties) must give the rule to art, i.e. fine art is only possible as a product of genius.

From this it may be seen that genius (1) is a *talent* for producing that for which no definite rule can be given: and not an aptitude in the way of cleverness for what can be learned according to some rule; and that consequently *originality* must be its primary property. (2) Since there may also be original nonsense, its products must at the same time be models, i.e. be *exemplary*; and, consequently, though not themselves derived from imitation, they must serve that purpose for others, i.e. as a standard or rule of judging. (3) It cannot indicate scientifically how it brings about its product, but rather gives the rule as *nature*. Hence, where an author owes a product to his genius, he does not himself know how the *ideas* for it have entered into his head, nor has he it in his power to invent the like at pleasure, or methodically, and communicate the same to others in such precepts as would enable them to produce similar products. (Hence, presumably, our word *Genie* is derived from *genius*, as the peculiar guardian and guiding spirit bestowed upon a human being at birth, by the inspiration of which those original ideas were obtained.) (4) Nature prescribes the rule through genius not to science but to art, and this also only in so far as it is to be fine art.

§ 47
Elucidation and confirmation of the above explanation of genius

EVERYONE is agreed on the point of the complete opposition between genius and the *spirit of imitation*. Now since learning is nothing but imitation, the greatest ability, or aptness as a pupil (capacity), is still, as such, not equivalent to genius. Even if someone weaves his own thoughts or fancies, instead of merely taking in what others have thought, and even though he go so far as to bring fresh gains to art and science, this does not afford a valid reason for calling such an intelligent, and often very intelligent, individual, a *genius*, in contradistinction to one who goes by the name of a *block-head*, because he can never do more than merely learn and follow a lead. For what is accomplished in this way is something that *could* have been learned. Hence it all lies in the natural path of investigation and reflection according to rules, and so is not specifically distinguishable from what may be acquired as the result of diligence backed up by imitation. So all that *Newton* has set forth in his immortal work* on the Principles of Natural Philosophy may well be learned, however great a mind it took to find it all out, but we cannot learn to write in a true poetic vein, no matter how complete all the precepts of the poetic art may be, or however excellent its models. The reason is that all the steps that Newton had to take from the first elements of geometry to his greatest and most profound discoveries were such as he could make intuitively evident and plain to follow, not only for himself but for everyone else. On the other hand no *Homer* or *Wieland** can show how his ideas, so rich at once in fantasy and in thought, enter and assemble themselves in his brain, for the good reason that he does not himself know, and so cannot teach others. In matters of science, therefore, the greatest inventor differs only in degree from the most laborious imitator and apprentice, whereas he differs specifically from one endowed by nature for fine art. No disparagement, however, of those great men, to whom the human race is so deeply indebted, is involved in this comparison of them with those who on the score of their talent for fine art are so favoured by nature. The talent for science is formed for the continued advances of greater perfection in knowledge, with all its dependent practical advantages, as also for imparting the same to others. Hence scientists can boast a considerable advantage over those who merit the honour of being called geniuses, since genius reaches a point at which art must come to a halt, as there is a limit imposed upon it which it cannot transcend. This limit has in all probability been long since attained. In addition, such skill cannot be communicated, but requires to be bestowed directly from the hand of nature upon each individual, and so with him it dies, awaiting the day when nature once again endows another in the same way—one who needs no more than an example to set the talent of which he is conscious at work on similar lines.

Seeing, then, that the natural endowment of art (as fine art) must furnish the rule, what kind of rule must this be? It cannot be one set down in a formula and serving as a precept—for then the judgement upon the beautiful would be determinable according to concepts.

309

Rather must the rule be gathered from the execution, i.e. from the product, which others may use to put their own talent to the test, so as to let it serve as a model, not for *imitation*, but for *following*. The possibility of this is difficult to explain. The artist's ideas arouse comparable ideas on the part of his pupil, presuming nature to have endowed him with a comparable proportion of the mental powers. For this reason the models of fine art are the only means of handing down this art to posterity. This is something which cannot be done 310 by mere descriptions (especially not in the field of the arts of speech), and in these arts, furthermore, only those models can become classical of which the ancient, dead languages, preserved as learned, are the medium.

Despite the marked difference that distinguishes mechanical art, as an art merely depending upon diligence and learning, from fine art, as that of genius, there is still no fine art in which something mechanical, capable of being at once comprehended and followed in obedience to rules, and consequently something *academic* does not constitute the essential condition of the art. For the thought of something as end must be present, or else its product would not be ascribed to an art at all, but would be a mere product of chance. But the realization of an end necessitates determinate rules which we cannot venture to dispense with. Now, seeing that originality of talent is one (though not the sole) essential factor that goes to make up the character of genius, shallow minds fancy that the best evidence they can give of their being full-blown geniuses is by emancipating themselves from all academic constraint of rules, in the belief that one cuts a finer figure on the back of an ill-tempered than of a trained horse. Genius can do no more than furnish rich *material* for products of fine art; its elaboration and its *form* require a talent academically trained, so that it may be employed in such a way as to stand the test of judgement. But, for a person to hold forth and pass sentence like a genius in matters that fall to the province of the most patient rational investigation, is ridiculous in the extreme. One is at a loss to know whether to laugh more at the impostor who envelops himself in such a cloud—in which we are given fuller scope to our imagination at the expense of all use of our judgement,—or at the simple-minded public which imagines that its inability clearly to cognize and comprehend this masterpiece of penetration is due to its being confronted by new truths *en masse*, in comparison with which,

detail, due to carefully weighed exposition and an academic examination of fundamental principles, seems to it only the work of a tyro.

311   § 48
                    The relation of genius to taste

FOR *judging* beautiful objects, as such, what is required is *taste*; but
for fine art, i.e. the *production* of such objects, one needs *genius*.

If we consider genius as the talent for fine art (which the proper
signification of the word imports), and if we would analyse it from
this point of view into the faculties which must concur to constitute
such a talent, it is imperative at the outset accurately to determine the
difference between beauty of nature, which it only requires taste to
judge, and beauty of art, which requires genius for its possibility (a
possibility to which regard must also be paid in judging such an object).

A beauty of nature is a *beautiful thing*; beauty of art is a *beautiful
representation* of a thing.

To enable me to judge a beauty of nature, as such, I do not need
to be previously possessed of a concept of what sort of a thing the
object is intended to be, i.e. I am not obliged to know its material
purposiveness (the end), but, rather, in judging it apart from any
knowledge of the end, the mere form pleases on its own account. If,
however, the object is presented as a product of art, and is as such to
be declared beautiful, then, seeing that art always presupposes an
end in the cause (and its causality), a concept of what the thing is
intended to be must already be provided. And, since the agreement
of the manifold in a thing with an inner character belonging to
it as its end constitutes the perfection of the thing, it follows that in
judging beauty of art the perfection of the thing must be also taken
into account—a matter which in judging a beauty of nature, as beautiful, is quite irrelevant.—It is true that in forming a judgement,
especially of animate objects of nature, e.g. of a human being or a
horse, objective purposiveness is also commonly taken into account
with a view to judgement upon their beauty; but then the judgement
also ceases to be purely aesthetic, i.e. a mere judgement of taste.
Nature is no longer judged as it appears like art, but rather in so far
as it actually *is* art, though superhuman art; and the teleological
312 judgement serves as basis and condition of the aesthetic, and one

which the latter must regard. In such a case, where one says, for example, 'that is a beautiful woman,' what one in fact thinks is only this, that in her form nature excellently portrays the ends present in the female figure. For one has to extend one's view beyond the mere form to a concept, to enable the object to be thought in such manner by means of an aesthetic judgement that is logically conditioned.

Where fine art manifests its superiority is in the beautiful descriptions it gives of things that in nature would be ugly or displeasing.* The Furies, diseases, devastations of war, and the like, can (as evils) be very beautifully described, and even represented in pictures. One kind of ugliness alone is incapable of being represented conformably to nature without destroying all aesthetic delight, and consequently artistic beauty, namely, that which excites *disgust*. For, as in this strange sensation, which depends purely on the imagination, the object is represented as insisting, as it were, upon our enjoying it, while we violently resist it, the artificial representation of the object is no longer distinguishable from the nature of the object itself in our sensation, and so it cannot possibly be regarded as beautiful. The art of sculpture, again, since in its products art is almost confused with nature, has excluded from its creations the direct representation of ugly objects, and, instead, only sanctions, for example, the representation of death (in a beautiful *genius*), or of the warlike spirit (in Mars), by means of an allegory, or attributes which wear a pleasant guise, and so only indirectly, through an interpretation on the part of reason, and not for the pure aesthetic judgement.

So much for the beautiful representation of an object, which is properly only the form of the presentation of a concept, and the means by which the latter is universally communicated. To give this form, however, to the product of fine art, taste merely is required. By this the artist, having practised and corrected his taste by a variety of examples from nature or art, guides his work and, after many, and often laborious, attempts to satisfy taste, finds the form which commends itself to him. Hence this form is not, as it were, a matter of inspiration, or of a free swinging of the powers of the mind, but rather of a slow and even painful process of improvement, directed to making the form adequate to his thought without prejudice to the 313 freedom in the play of those powers.

Taste is, however, merely a faculty of judging, rather than a productive one; and what conforms to it is not, merely on that account, a work of fine art. It may belong to useful and mechanical art, or even to science, as a product following definite rules which are capable of being learned and which must be closely followed. But the pleasing form imparted to the work is only the vehicle of communication and a mode, as it were, of execution, in respect of which one remains to a certain extent free, notwithstanding being otherwise tied down to a definite end. So we demand that tableware, or even a moral dissertation, and, indeed, a sermon, must bear this form of fine art, yet without its appearing *studied*. But one would not call them on this account works of fine art. A poem, a musical composition, a picture-gallery, and so forth, would, however, be placed under this head; and so in a would-be work of fine art we may frequently recognize genius without taste, and in another taste without genius.

§ 49

The faculties of the mind which constitute genius

OF certain products which are expected, partly at least, to stand on the footing of fine art, we say they are devoid of *spirit*; and this, although we find nothing to censure in them as far as taste goes. A poem may be very pretty and elegant, but is devoid of spirit. A narrative has precision and method, but is devoid of spirit. A speech on some festive occasion may be good in substance and ornate withal, but may be devoid of spirit. Conversation frequently is not devoid of entertainment, but yet devoid of spirit. Even of a woman we may well say, she is pretty, affable, and refined, but devoid of spirit. Now what do we mean here by 'spirit'?

'*Spirit*' in an aesthetic sense, signifies the animating principle in the mind. But that whereby this principle animates the soul—the material which it employs for that purpose—is that which sets the mental powers into a swing that is purposive, i.e. into a play which is self-maintaining and which strengthens those powers for such activity.

Now my proposition is that this principle is nothing else than the faculty of presenting *aesthetic ideas*. But, by an aesthetic idea I mean that representation of the imagination which evokes much thought, yet without the possibility of any definite thought whatever, i.e. *concept*, being adequate to it, and which language, consequently, can never quite fully capture or render completely intelligible.—It is

easily seen, that an aesthetic idea is the counterpart (pendant) of a
rational idea, which, conversely, is a concept, to which no *intuition*
(representation of the imagination) can be adequate.

The imagination (as a productive faculty of cognition) is a powerful agent for creating, as it were, a second nature out of the material
supplied to it by actual nature. It affords us entertainment where
experience proves too commonplace; and we even use it to refashion
experience, always following, no doubt, laws that are based on analogy, but still also following principles which have a higher seat in
reason (and which are every whit as natural to us as those followed
by the understanding in laying hold of empirical nature). By this
means we come to feel our freedom from the law of association
(which attaches to the empirical employment of the imagination),
with the result that the material can be borrowed by us from nature
in accordance with that law, but be worked up by us into something
else—namely, what surpasses nature.

Such representations of the imagination may be termed *ideas*. This
is partly because they at least strain after something lying out beyond
the confines of experience, and so seek to approximate to a presentation of rational concepts (i.e. intellectual ideas), thus giving to these
concepts the semblance of an objective reality. But, on the other hand,
there is this most important reason, that no concept can be wholly
adequate to them as internal intuitions. The poet essays the task of
giving sensible form to the rational ideas of invisible beings, the kingdom of the blessed, hell, eternity, creation, and so forth. Or, again, as
to things of which examples occur in experience, e.g. death, envy,
and all vices, as also love, fame, and the like, transgressing the limits
of experience he attempts with the aid of an imagination, which in
reaching for a maximum emulates the precedent of reason, to present
them for the senses with a completeness of which nature affords no
parallel; and it is in fact precisely in the poetic art that the faculty of
aesthetic ideas can show itself to full advantage. This faculty, however, regarded solely on its own account, is properly no more than a
talent (of the imagination).

If, now, we attach to a concept a representation of the imagination
belonging to its presentation, but evoking solely on its own account   315
such a wealth of thought as would never admit of comprehension in
a definite concept, and, as a consequence, giving aesthetically an
unbounded expansion to the concept itself, then the imagination here

displays a creative activity, and it sets the faculty of intellectual ideas (reason) into movement—a movement, occasioned by a representation, towards an extension of thought, that, while germane, no doubt, to the concept of the object, exceeds what can be grasped in that representation or clearly expressed.

Those forms which do not constitute the presentation of a given concept itself, but which, as further representations of the imagination, express the implications connected with it, and its kinship with other concepts, are called (aesthetic) *attributes* of an object, the concept of which, as an idea of reason, cannot be adequately presented. In this way Jupiter's eagle, with the lightning in its claws, is an attribute of the mighty king of heaven, and the peacock of its stately queen. They do not, like *logical attributes*, represent what lies in our concepts of the sublimity and majesty of creation, but rather something else—something that encourages the imagination to spread its flight over a whole host of kindred representations that provoke more thought than admits of expression in a concept determined by words. They furnish an *aesthetic idea*, which serves the above rational idea as a substitute for logical presentation, but with the proper task, however, of animating the mind by opening out for it a prospect into a field of kindred representations stretching beyond its ken. But it is not only in the arts of painting or sculpture, where the name of attribute is customarily employed, that fine art acts in this way; poetry and rhetoric also derive the spirit that animates their works wholly from the aesthetic attributes of the objects—attributes which go hand in hand with the logical, and give the imagination an impetus to bring more thought into play in the matter, though in an undeveloped manner, than allows of being brought within the embrace of a concept, or, therefore, of being definitely formulated in language.—For the sake of brevity I must confine myself to a few examples only. When the great king expresses himself in one of his poems* by saying:

'Let us depart this life untroubled and without regrets, leaving the world replete with our good deeds. Thus does the sun, his daily path completed, still shed a gentle light across the sky. The last rays it sends forth through the air, are its last sighs for the well-being of the world', he enlivens in this way his rational idea of a cosmopolitan sentiment even at the close of life, with the help of an attribute which the imagination (in remembering all the pleasures of a beautiful summer's day that is over and gone—a memory of which pleasures is suggested by

316

a serene evening) allies with that representation, and which stirs up a host of sensations and further representations for which no expression can be found. On the other hand, even an intellectual concept may serve, conversely, as attribute for a representation of the senses, and so enliven the latter with the idea of the supersensible; but only by the aesthetic aspect subjectively attaching to the consciousness of the supersensible being employed for the purpose. So, for example, a certain poet says* in his description of a beautiful morning: 'The sun arose, as out of virtue rises peace.' The consciousness of virtue, even where we put ourselves only in thought in the position of a virtuous man, diffuses in the mind a multitude of sublime and comforting feelings, and gives a boundless out-look into a happy future, such as no expression within the compass of a definite concept completely attains.[13]

In a word, the aesthetic idea is a representation of the imagination, allied with a given concept, with which, in the free employment of imagination, such a multiplicity of partial representations are bound up, that no expression indicating a definite concept can be found for it—one which on that account allows a concept to be supplemented in thought by much that is indefinable in words, and the feeling of which enlivens the cognitive faculties, and with language, as a mere thing of the letter, combines spirit.

The mental powers whose union in a certain relation constitutes *genius* are imagination and understanding. Now, since the imagination, in its employment on behalf of cognition, is subjected to the constraint of the understanding and the restriction of having to be conformable to the concept belonging thereto, whereas aesthetically it is free to furnish 317 of its own accord, over and above that agreement with the concept, a wealth of undeveloped material for the understanding, to which the latter paid no regard in its concept, but which it can make use of, not so much objectively for cognition, as subjectively for enlivening the cog-nitive faculties, and hence also indirectly for cognitions, it may be seen that genius properly consists in the happy relation, which science cannot teach nor diligence learn, enabling one to seek out ideas for a

---

[13] Perhaps there has never been a more sublime utterance, or a thought more sub-limely expressed, than the well-known inscription upon the Temple of *Isis* (Mother *Nature*): 'I am all that is, and that was, and that shall be, and no mortal hath raised the veil from before my face.' *Segner* made use of this idea* in a suggestive vignette on the frontispiece of his Natural Philosophy, in order to inspire his pupil at the threshold of that temple into which he was about to lead him, with such a holy awe as would dispose his mind to rapt attention

given concept, and, besides, to hit upon the *expression* for them—the expression by means of which the subjective condition of the mind aroused by the ideas as the concomitant of a concept may be communicated to others. This latter talent is properly that which is termed spirit. For to get an expression for what is indefinable in the mental state accompanying a particular representation and to make it universally communicable—whether the expression be in language or painting or statuary—is a thing requiring a faculty for laying hold of the rapid and transient play of the imagination, and for unifying it in a concept (which for that very reason is original, and reveals a new rule which could not have been inferred from any preceding principles or examples) that admits of communication without any constraint of rules.

———————————

If, after this analysis, we cast a glance back upon the above definition of what is called *genius*, we find: *First*, that it is a talent for art—not one for science, in which clearly known rules must take the lead and determine the procedure. *Secondly*, being a talent in the line of art, it presupposes a definite concept of the product—as its end. Hence it presupposes understanding, but, in addition, a representation, indeterminate though it be, of the material, i.e. of the intuition, required for the presentation of that concept, and so a relation of the imagination to the understanding. *Thirdly*, it displays itself, not so much in the working out of the projected end in the presentation of a definite *concept*, as rather in the portrayal, or expression of *aesthetic ideas* containing a wealth of material for effecting that intention. Consequently the imagination is represented by it in its freedom from all guidance of rules, but still as purposive for the presentation of the given con-
318 cept. *Fourthly*, and lastly, the unsought and undesigned subjective purposiveness in the free harmonizing of the imagination with the understanding's conformity to law presupposes a proportion and accord between these faculties such as cannot be brought about by any observance of rules, whether of science or mechanical imitation, but can only be produced by the nature of the subject.

Genius, according to these presuppositions, is the exemplary originality of the natural endowments of a subject in the *free* employment of his cognitive faculties. On this showing, the product of a genius (in respect of so much in this product as is attributable to genius, and not to possible learning or academic instruction) is an example, not to be imitated (for that would mean the loss of the element of genius, and just the very spirit of the work), but to be followed by another genius—one whom it arouses to a sense of his own originality in putting freedom from the constraint of rules so into force in his art, that for art itself a new rule is won—which is what shows a talent to be exemplary. Yet, since the genius is one who is favoured by nature—something which must be regarded as but a rare phenomenon—for other clever minds his example gives rise to a school, that is to say a methodical instruction according to rules, collected, so far as the circumstances admit, from such products of genius and their peculiarities. And, to that extent, fine art is for such persons a matter of imitation, for which nature, through the medium of a genius, gave the rule.

But this imitation becomes *aping* when the pupil *copies* everything down to the deformities which the genius only of necessity suffered to remain, because they could hardly be removed without loss of force to the idea. This courage has merit only in the case of a genius. A certain *boldness* of expression, and, in general, many a deviation from the common rule becomes him well, but in no sense is it a thing worthy of imitation. On the contrary it remains all through intrinsically a blemish, which one is bound to try to remove, but for which the genius is, as it were, allowed to plead a privilege, on the ground that a scrupulous carefulness would spoil what is inimitable in the impetuous ardour of his spirit. *Mannerism* is another kind of aping—an aping of *peculiarity* (originality) in general, for the sake of distancing oneself as far as possible from imitators, while the talent requisite to enable one to be at the same time *exemplary* is absent.—There are, in fact, two modes (*modi*) in general of arranging one's thoughts for utterance. The one is called a *manner* (*modus aestheticus*), the other a *method* (*modus logicus*). The distinction between them is this: the former possesses no 319 standard other than the *feeling* of unity in the presentation, whereas the latter here follows definite *principles*. As a consequence the former is alone admissible for fine art. It is only, however, where the manner of carrying the idea into execution in a product of art is *aimed at* singularity instead of being made appropriate to the idea, that *mannerism* is properly ascribed to such a product. The ostentatious (precious), forced, and affected styles, intended to mark one out from the crowd (though spirit is wanting), resemble the behaviour of a man who, as we say, hears himself speaking, or who stands and moves about as if he were on a stage to be gaped at—action which invariably betrays a tyro.

§ 50
The combination of taste and genius in products of fine art

To ask whether more stress should be laid in matters of fine art upon the presence of genius or upon that of taste, is equivalent to asking whether more turns upon imagination or upon judgement. Now, imagination rather entitles an art to be called an *inspired* than a *fine* art. It is only in respect of judgement that the name of fine art is deserved. Hence it follows that judgement, being the indispensable condition (*conditio sine qua non*), is at least what one must regard as of capital importance in forming a judgement of art as fine art. So far as beauty is concerned, to be fertile and original in ideas is not such an imperative requirement as it is that the imagination in its freedom should be in accordance with the understanding's conformity to law. For in lawless freedom imagination, with all its wealth, produces nothing but nonsense; the power of judgement, on the other hand, is the faculty that makes it consonant with understanding.

Taste, like judgement in general, is the discipline (or corrective) of genius. It severely clips its wings, and makes it seemly or polished; but at the same time it gives it guidance, directing and controlling its flight, so that it may preserve its purposive character. It introduces a clearness and order into the plenitude of thought, and in so doing gives stability to the ideas, and qualifies them at once for permanent and universal approval, for being followed by others, and for a continually progressive culture. And so, where the interests of both these qualities clash in a product, and there has to be a sacrifice of something, then it should rather be on the side of genius; and judgement, which in matters of fine art bases its decision on its own proper principles, will more readily endure an infringement of the freedom and wealth of the imagination, than that the understanding should be compromised.

The requisites for fine art are, therefore, *imagination, understanding, spirit*, and *taste*.[14]

---

[14] The first three faculties are first *brought into union* by means of the fourth. *Hume*, in his history, informs the English* that although they are second in their works to no other people in the world in respect of the evidence they afford of the three first qualities *separately* considered, still in what unites them they must yield to their neighbours, the French.

§ 51
The division of the fine arts

BEAUTY (whether it be of nature or of art) may in general be termed the *expression* of aesthetic ideas. But the proviso must be added that with beauty in art this idea must be occasioned through a concept of the object, whereas with beauty of nature the bare reflection upon a given intuition, apart from any concept of what the object is intended to be, is sufficient for awakening and communicating the idea of which that object is regarded as the *expression*.

Accordingly, if we wish to make a division of the fine arts, we can choose for that purpose, tentatively at least, no more convenient principle than the analogy which art bears to the mode of expression of which individuals avail themselves in speech, with a view to communicating themselves to one another as completely as possible, i.e. not merely in respect of their concepts but also in respect of their sensations.[15]—Such expression consists in *word*, *gesture*, and *tone* (articulation, gesticulation, and modulation). It is the combination of these three modes of expression which alone constitutes a complete communication of the speaker. For thought, intuition, and sensation are in this way conveyed to others simultaneously and in conjunction.

Hence there are only three kinds of fine art: the art of *speech*, *formative* art, and the art of the *play of sensations* (as external sense impressions). This division might also be arranged as a dichotomy, so that fine art would be divided into that of the expression of thoughts or intuitions, the latter being subdivided according to the distinction between the form and the matter (sensation). It would, however, in that case appear too abstract, and less in line with popular conceptions.

(1) The arts of SPEECH are *rhetoric* and *poetry*. *Rhetoric* is the art of engaging a serious business of the understanding as if it were a free play of the imagination; *poetry* that of conducting a free play of the imagination as if it were a serious business of the understanding.

Thus the *orator* announces a serious business, and for the purpose of entertaining his audience conducts it as if it were a mere *play* with ideas. The *poet* promises merely an entertaining *play* with ideas, and

---

[15] The reader is not to consider this scheme for a possible division of the fine arts as a deliberate theory. It is only one of the various attempts that can and ought to be made.

yet for the understanding there ensues as much as if the promotion of its business had been his one intention. The combination and harmony of the two faculties of cognition, those of sensibility and understanding, which, though, doubtless, indispensable to one another, do not readily permit of being united without compulsion and reciprocal infringement, must have the appearance of being undersigned and a spontaneous occurrence—otherwise it is not *fine* art. For this reason what is studied and laboured must here be avoided. For fine art must be free art in a double sense: i.e. not only in a sense opposed to remunerated work, as not being a work the magnitude of which may be judged, exacted, or paid for according to a definite standard, but free also in the sense that, while the mind, no doubt, occupies itself, still it does so without ulterior regard to any other end, and yet with a feeling of satisfaction and stimulation (independent of reward).

The orator, therefore, gives something which he does not promise, viz. an entertaining play of the imagination. On the other hand, there is something in which he fails to come up to his promise, and a thing, too, which is his avowed business, namely, the engagement of the understanding to some end. The poet's promise, on the contrary, is a modest one, and a mere play with ideas is all he holds out to us, but he accomplishes something worthy of being made a serious business, namely, the using of play to provide food for the understanding, and the giving of life to its concepts by means of the imagination. Hence the orator in reality performs less than he promises, the poet more.

(2) The FORMATIVE arts* or those for the expression of ideas in *sensuous intuition* (not by means of representations of mere imagination that are excited by words) are arts either of *sensuous truth* or of *sensuous semblance*. The first is called *plastic* art, the second *painting*. Both use figures in space for the expression of ideas: the former makes figures discernible to two senses, sight and touch (though, so far as the latter sense is concerned, without regard to beauty), the latter makes them discernible to the former sense alone. The aesthetic idea (archetype, original) is the fundamental basis of both in the imagination; but the figure which constitutes its expression (the ectype, the copy) is given either in its bodily extension (the way the object itself exists) or else in accordance with the image which it produces in the eye (according to its appearance when projected on a flat surface). Or, whatever the archetype is, either the reference to an actual end or only the semblance of one may be imposed upon reflection as its condition.

322

To *plastic* art, as the first kind of formative fine art, belong *sculpture* and *architecture*. The first is that which presents concepts of things corporeally, as they *might exist in nature* (though as fine art it directs its attention to aesthetic purposiveness). The *second* is the art of presenting concepts of things which are possible *only through art*, and the determining ground of whose form is not nature but an arbitrary end—and of presenting them both with a view to this purpose and yet, at the same time, with aesthetic purposiveness. In architecture the chief point is a certain *use* of the artistic object to which, as the condition, the aesthetic ideas are limited. In sculpture the mere *expression* of aesthetic ideas is the main intention. Thus statues of men, gods, animals, and so forth, belong to sculpture; but temples, splendid buildings for public concourse, or even dwelling-houses, triumphal arches, columns, mausoleums, and the like, erected as monuments, belong to architecture, and in fact all household furniture (the work of cabinet-makers, and so forth—things meant to be used) may be added to the list, on the ground that adaptation of the product to a particular use is the essential element in a *work of architecture*. On the other hand, a *mere piece of sculpture*, made simply to be looked at, and intended to please on its own account, is, as a corporeal presentation, a mere imitation of nature, though one in which regard is paid to aesthetic ideas, and in which, therefore, *sensuous truth* should not go the length of losing the appearance of being an art and a product of the power of choice.

Painting, as the second kind of formative art, which presents the *sensuous semblance* in artful combination with ideas, I would divide into 323 that of the beautiful *depiction of nature*, and that of the beautiful *arrangement* of its *products*. The first is *painting proper*, the second *landscape gardening*. For the first gives only the semblance of bodily extension; whereas the second, while giving the latter, according to its truth, gives only the semblance of utility and employment for ends other than the play of the imagination in the contemplation of its forms.[16]

---

[16] It seems strange that landscape gardening may be regarded as a kind of painting, notwithstanding that it presents its forms corporeally. But, as it takes its forms bodily from nature (the trees, shrubs, grasses, and flowers taken, originally at least, from wood and field) it is to that extent not an art such as, let us say, plastic art. Further, the arrangement which it makes is not conditioned by any concept of the object or of its end (as is the case in sculpture), but by the mere free play of the imagination in the act of contemplation. Hence it bears a degree of resemblance to simple aesthetic painting that

The latter consists in no more than decking out the ground with the
same manifold variety (grasses, flowers, shrubs, and trees, and even
water, hills, and dales) as that with which nature presents it to our
view, only arranged differently and in obedience to certain ideas. The
beautiful arrangement of corporeal things, however, is also a thing for
the eye only, just like painting—the sense of touch can form no intuitable representation of such a form. In addition I would place under
the head of painting, in the wide sense, the decoration of rooms by
means of hangings, ornamental accessories, and all beautiful furniture
the sole function of which is *to be looked at*; and in the same way the
art of tasteful dressing (with rings, snuff-boxes, etc.). For a *parterre* of
various flowers, a room with a variety of ornaments (including even
the ladies' attire), go to make at a festive gathering a sort of picture
which, like pictures in the true sense of the word (those which are not
intended *to teach* history or natural science), has no business beyond
appealing to the eye, in order to entertain the imagination in free play
with ideas, and to engage actively the aesthetic power of judgement
independently of any definite end. No matter how heterogeneous, on
324 the mechanical side, may be the craft involved in all this decoration,
and no matter what a variety of artists may be required, still the judgement of taste, so far as it is one upon what is beautiful in this art, is
determined in one and the same way: namely, as a judgement only
upon the forms (without regard to any end) as they present themselves to the eye, singly or in combination, according to their effect
upon the imagination.—The justification, however, of bringing
formative art (by analogy) under a common head with gesture in a
speech, lies in the fact that through these figures the spirit of the
artist furnishes a bodily expression for the substance and character of
his thought, and makes the thing itself speak, as it were, in mimic
language—a very common play of our fantasy that attributes to lifeless things a spirit suitable to their form, and that uses them as its
mouthpiece.

(3) The art of the BEAUTIFUL PLAY OF SENSATIONS (sensations
that arise from external stimulation) which is a play of sensations that

has no definite theme (but by means of light and shade makes a pleasing composition of
atmosphere, land, and water).—Throughout, the reader is to weigh the above only as an
effort to connect the fine arts under a principle, which, in the present instance, is
intended to be that of the expression of aesthetic ideas (following the analogy of a language), and not as a positive and deliberate derivation of the connexion.

has nevertheless to permit of universal communication, can only be concerned with the proportion of the different degrees of attunement (tension) in the sense to which the sensation belongs, i.e. with its tone. In this comprehensive sense of the word it may be divided into the artistic play of sensations of hearing and of sight, consequently into *music* and the *art of colour*.—It is remarkable that these two senses, over and above that receptivity for impressions as is required to obtain concepts of external objects by means of these impressions, also admit of a peculiar associated sensation of which we cannot easily determine whether it is based on sensibility or reflection; and that this affectability may at times be lacking, although the sense, in other respects, and in what concerns its employment for the cognition of objects, is by no means deficient but particularly keen. In other words, we cannot confidently assert whether a colour or a tone (sound) is merely an agreeable sensation, or whether they are in themselves a beautiful play of sensations, and in being judged aesthetically, convey, as such, a delight in their form. If we consider the velocity of the vibrations of light, or, in the second case, of the air, which in all probability far outstrips any capacity on our part for forming an immediate judgement in perception of the time-interval between them, we should be led to believe that it is only the *effect* of those vibrating movements upon the elastic parts of our body, that can be evident to the senses, but that the *time-interval* between them is not noticed nor involved in our judgement, and that, consequently, all 325 that enters into combination with colours and tones is the agreeableness, and not the beauty, of their composition. But, let us consider, on the other hand, *first*, the mathematical character both of the proportion of those vibrations in music, and of our judgement upon it, and, as is reasonable, form an estimate of colour contrasts on the analogy of the latter. *Secondly*, let us consult the instances, albeit rare, of individuals who, with the best of sight, have failed to distinguish colours, and, with the sharpest hearing, to distinguish tones, while for those who have this ability the perception of an altered quality (not merely of the degree of the sensation) in the case of the different intensities in the scale of colours or tones is definite, as is also the number of those which may be *intelligibly* distinguished. Bearing all this in mind we may feel compelled to look upon the sensations afforded by both, not as mere sense-impressions, but as the effect of a judging of form in the play of a number of sensations. The difference which the one opinion or the other occasions in judging of the basis of music would, however, only give rise to this much change in its definition, that either it is to be interpreted, as we have done, as the *beautiful* play of sensations (through hearing), or else as one of *agreeable* sensations. According to the former interpretation, alone, would music be represented out and out as a *fine* art, whereas according to the latter it would be represented as (in part at least) an *agreeable* art.

§ 52

The combination of the fine arts in one and the same product

RHETORIC may in a *drama* be combined with a pictorial presentation of its subjects as well as its objects; as may poetry with music in a *song*; and this again with a pictorial (theatrical) presentation in an *opera*; and so may the play of sensations in a piece of music with the play of figures in a *dance*, and so on. Even the presentation of the sublime, so far as it belongs to fine art, may be brought into union with beauty in a *tragedy in verse*, a *didactic poem* or an *oratorio*, and in this combination fine art is even more artistic. Whether it is also more beautiful (having regard to the multiplicity of different kinds of delight which 326 intersect with one another) may in some of these instances be doubted. Still in all fine art the essential element consists in the form which is purposive for observation and for judgement. Here the pleasure is at the same time culture, and disposes the spirit to ideas, making it thus susceptible to such pleasure and entertainment in greater abundance. The matter of sensation (charm or emotion) is not essential. Here the aim is merely enjoyment, which leaves nothing behind it with regard to the idea, and renders the spirit dull, the object in the course of time distasteful, and the mind dissatisfied with itself and ill-humoured, owing to a consciousness that in the judgement of reason its mood is contrary to purpose.

Where fine arts are not, either closely or remotely, brought into combination with moral ideas, which alone are attended with a self-sufficing delight, the above is the fate that ultimately awaits them. They then only serve for a diversion, of which one continually feels an increasing need in proportion as one has availed oneself of it as a means of dispelling one's discontented mind, with the result that one makes oneself ever more and more unprofitable and dissatisfied with oneself. With a view to the purpose first named the beauties of nature are in general the most beneficial, if one is early habituated to observe, judge, and admire them.

§ 53
Comparison of the aesthetic worth of the fine arts

Poetry (which owes its origin almost entirely to genius and is least willing to be led by precepts or example) holds the first rank among all the arts. It expands the mind by giving freedom to the imagination and by offering, from among the boundless multiplicity of possible forms accordant with a given concept, to whose bounds it is restricted, that one which couples with the presentation of the concept a wealth of thought to which no verbal expression is completely adequate, and by thus rising aesthetically to ideas. It invigorates the mind by letting it feel its faculty—free, spontaneous, and independent of determination by nature—of regarding and judging nature as phenomenon in the light of aspects which nature of itself does not afford us in experience, either for the senses or the understanding, and of employing it accordingly on behalf of, and as a sort of schema 327 for, the supersensible. It plays with semblance, which it produces at will, but not as an instrument of deception; for its avowed pursuit is merely one of play, which, however, understanding may turn to good account and employ for its own purpose.—Rhetoric, so far as this is taken to mean the art of persuasion, i.e. the art of deluding by means of such beautiful semblance (as *ars oratoria*), and not merely excellence of speech (eloquence and style), is a dialectic, which borrows from poetry only so much as is necessary to win over people's minds to the side of the speaker before they have weighed the matter, and to rob their verdict of its freedom. Hence it can be recommended neither for the bar nor the pulpit. For where civil laws, the right of individual persons, or the permanent instruction and determination of people's minds to a correct knowledge and a conscientious observance of their duty is at stake, then it is below the dignity of an undertaking of such import to exhibit even a trace of the exuberance of wit and imagination, and, still more, of the art of talking people round and prejudicing them in favour of anyone. For although such art is capable of being at times directed to ends intrinsically legitimate and praiseworthy, still it becomes reprehensible on account of the subjective injury done in this way to maxims and dispositions, even where objectively the action may be lawful. For it is not enough to do what is right, but we should practise it solely on the ground of its being right. Further, the simple lucid concept of human concerns of this kind, backed up with lively illustrations of it, exerts of itself, in the absence of any offence against the rules of euphony of speech or of propriety in the expression of ideas of reason (all which together make up excellence of speech), a sufficient influence upon human minds to obviate the necessity of having recourse here to the machinery of persuasion, which, being equally available for the purpose of putting a fine gloss or a cloak upon vice and error, fails to rid one completely of the lurking suspicion that one is being artfully hoodwinked. In poetry everything is straight and above board. It shows its hand: it desires to carry on a mere entertaining play with the imagination, and one consonant, in respect of form, with the laws of understanding; and it does not seek to steal upon and ensnare the understanding with a sensuous presentation.[17]

328   After poetry, *if we take charm and the capacity to move the mind into account*, I would give the next place to that art which comes nearer to it than to any other art of speech, and admits of very natural union with it, namely the art of *tone*. For though it speaks by means of mere sensations without concepts, and so does not, like poetry, leave behind it any food for thought, still it moves the mind more diversely, and, although with transient, still with intenser effect. It is certainly, however, more a matter of enjoyment than of culture—the play of thought incidentally excited by it being merely the effect of a more or less mechanical association—and it possesses less worth in

[17] I must confess to the pure delight which I have always been afforded by a beautiful poem; whereas the reading of the best speech of a Roman forensic orator, a modern parliamentary debater, or a preacher, has invariably been mingled with an unpleasant sense of disapproval of an insidious art that knows how, in matters of importance, to move people like machines to a judgement that must lose all its weight with them upon calm reflection. Force and elegance of speech (which together constitute rhetoric) belong to fine art; but oratory (*ars oratoria*), being the art of playing for one's own purpose upon the weaknesses of others (let this purpose be ever so good in intention or even in fact) merits no *respect* whatever. Besides, both at Athens and at Rome, it only attained its greatest height at a time when the state was hastening to its decay, and genuine patriotic sentiment was a thing of the past. One who sees the issue clearly, and who has a command of language in its wealth and its purity, and who is possessed of an imagination that is fertile and effective in presenting his ideas, and whose heart, withal, turns with lively sympathy to what is truly good—he is the *vir bonus dicendi peritus*,* the orator without art, but of great impressiveness, as *Cicero* would have him, though he may not himself always have remained faithful to this ideal.

the judgement of reason than any other of the fine arts. Hence, like all enjoyment, it calls for constant change, and does not stand frequent repetition without inducing weariness. Its charm, which admits of such universal communication, appears to rest on the following facts. Every expression in language has an associated tone suited to its sense. This tone indicates, more or less, a mode in which the speaker is affected, and in turn evokes it in the hearer also, in whom conversely it then also excites the idea which in language is expressed with such a tone. Further, just as modulation is, as it were, a universal language of sensations intelligible to every human being, so the art of tone wields the full force of this language wholly on its own account, namely, as a language of the affects, and in this way, according to the law of association, universally communicates the aesthetic ideas that are naturally combined therewith. But, further, inasmuch as those aesthetic ideas are not concepts or determinate thoughts, the form of the arrangement of these sensations (harmony and melody), taking the place of the form of a language, only serves the purpose of giving an expression to the aesthetic idea of an integral whole of an unutterable wealth of thought in accordance with a certain theme forming the dominant *affect* in the piece. This purpose is produced by means of a proportion in the accord of the sensations (an accord which may be brought mathematically under certain rules, since it rests, in the case of tones, upon the numerical relation of the vibrations of the air in the same time, so far as there is a combination of the tones simultaneously or in succession). Although this mathematical form is not represented by means of determinate concepts, to it alone belongs the delight which the mere reflection upon such a number of concomitant or consecutive sensations couples with this their play, as the universally valid condition of its beauty, and it is with reference to it alone that taste can lay claim to a right to anticipate the judgement of every human being.

But mathematics, certainly, plays not the slightest part in the charm and movement of the mind produced by music. Rather is it only the indispensable condition (*conditio sine qua non*) of that proportion of the combining as well as changing impressions which makes it possible to grasp them all in one and prevent them from destroying one another, and to let them, rather, conspire towards the production of a continuous movement and enlivening of the mind by affects that are in unison with it, and thus towards a contented self-enjoyment.

If, on the other hand, we measure the worth of the fine arts by the culture they supply to the mind, and adopt for our standard the expansion of the faculties whose confluence, in judgement, is necessary for cognition, music, then, since it plays merely with sensations, has the lowest place among the fine arts (just as it has perhaps the highest among those valued at the same time for their agreeableness). Looked at in this light it is far excelled by the formative arts. For, in putting the imagination into a play which is at once free and adapted to the understanding, they all the while carry on a serious business, since they execute a product which serves the concepts of understanding as a vehicle, permanent and appealing to us on its own account, for effecting their union with sensibility, and thus for promoting, as it 330 were, the urbanity of the higher powers of cognition. The two kinds of art pursue completely different courses. Music advances from sensations to indeterminate ideas: formative art from determinate ideas to sensations. The latter gives a *lasting* impression, the former one that is only *fleeting*. The former sensations imagination can recall and agreeably entertain itself with, while the latter either vanish entirely, or else, if involuntarily repeated by the imagination, are more oppressive to us than agreeable. Over and above all this, music has a certain lack of urbanity about it. For owing chiefly to the character of its instruments, it scatters its influence abroad to an uncalled-for extent (through the neighbourhood), and thus, as it were, becomes obtrusive and deprives others, outside the musical circle, of their freedom. This is a thing that the arts that address themselves to the eye do not do, for if one is not disposed to give admittance to their impressions, one has only to look the other way. The case is almost on a par with the practice of regaling oneself with a perfume that exhales its odours far and wide. The man who pulls his perfumed handkerchief from his pocket treats all around to it whether they like it or not, and compels them, if they want to breathe at all, to be parties to the enjoyment, and so the habit has gone out of fashion.[18]

Among the formative arts I would give the palm to *painting*: partly because it is the art of design, and, as such, the groundwork of all the other formative arts; partly because it can penetrate much further

[18] Those who have recommended the singing of hymns at family prayers have forgotten the amount of annoyance which they give to the general public by such *noisy* (and, as a rule, for that very reason, pharisaical) worship, for they compel their neighbours either to join in the singing or else abandon their meditations.

into the region of ideas, and in conformity with them give a greater
extension to the field of intuition than it is open to the others to do.

§ 54

Remark

As we have often shown, there is essential distinction between what
pleases simply in the judging of it and what *gratifies* (pleases in sensation). The latter is something which, unlike the former, we cannot
demand from everyone. Gratification (no matter whether its cause 331
has its seat even in ideas) appears always to consist in a feeling of
the furtherance of the entire life of human beings and, hence, also of
their bodily well-being, i.e. their health. And so, perhaps, Epicurus was
not wide of the mark* when he said that at bottom all gratification is
bodily sensation, and only misunderstood himself in ranking intellectual and even practical delight under the head of gratification.
Bearing in mind the latter distinction, it is readily explicable how
even the gratification a person feels is capable of displeasing him (like
the joy of a needy but good-natured individual on being made the
heir of an affectionate but penurious father), or how deep pain
may still give pleasure to the sufferer (as the sorrow of a widow over
the death of her deserving husband), or how there may be pleasure
over and above gratification (as in scientific pursuits), or how a pain
(as, for example, hatred, envy, and desire for revenge) may in addition be a source of displeasure. Here the delight or aversion depends
upon reason, and is one with *approval* or *disapproval*. Gratification
and pain, on the other hand, can only depend upon feeling, or upon
the prospect of a possible *well-being* or the *reverse* (irrespective of
its source).

The changing free play of sensations (which do not follow any
preconceived plan) is always a source of gratification, because it
promotes the feeling of health; and it is immaterial whether or not we
experience delight in the object of this play or even in the gratification itself when judged in the light of reason. Also this gratification
may amount to an affect, although we take no interest in the object
itself, or none, at least, proportionate to the degree of the affect. We
may divide the aforementioned play into that of *games of chance, harmony*, and *wit*. The *first* stands in need of an *interest*, whether it be of
vanity or self-seeking, but one which falls far short of that centred in

the way in which we seek to procure it. All that the *second* requires is
the change of *sensations*, each of which has its bearing on affect,
though without attaining to the degree of an affect, and excites aesthetic ideas. The *third* springs merely from the change of the representations in the power of judgement, which, while unproductive of
any thought conveying an interest, yet enlivens the mind.

What a fund of gratification must be afforded by play, without our
having to fall back upon any consideration of interest, is a matter to
which all our evening parties bear witness—for without play they
hardly ever escape falling flat. But the affects of hope, fear, joy, anger,
and derision here engage in play, as every moment they change their
parts, and are so lively that, as by an internal motion, the whole vital
function of the body seems to be furthered by the process—as is
proved by a vivacity of the mind produced—although no one comes
by anything in the way of profit or instruction. But as the play of
chance is not one that is beautiful, we will here lay it aside. Music, on
the contrary, and what provokes laughter are two kinds of play with
aesthetic ideas, or even with representations of the understanding, by
which, all said and done, nothing is thought. By mere force of change
they yet are able to afford lively gratification. This furnishes pretty
clear evidence that the enlivening effect of both is physical, despite
its being excited by ideas of the mind, and that the feeling of health,
arising from a movement of the viscera answering to that play, makes
up that entire gratification of an animated gathering upon the spirit
and refinement of which we set such store. Not any estimate of harmony in tones or flashes of wit, which, with its beauty, serves only as
a necessary vehicle, but rather the stimulated vital functions of the
body, the affect stirring the viscera and the diaphragm, and, in a
word, the feeling of health (of which we are only aware upon some
such occasion) are what constitute the gratification we experience at
being able to reach the body even through the soul and use the latter
as the physician of the former.

In music the course of this play is from bodily sensation to aesthetic
ideas (which are the objects for the affects), and then from these back
again, but with gathered strength, to the body. In jest (which just as
much as the former deserves to be ranked rather as an agreeable than
a fine art) the play arises from thoughts which collectively, so far as
seeking sensuous expression, engage the activity of the body. In this
presentation the understanding, missing what it expected, suddenly

lets go its hold, with the result that the effect of this slackening is felt in the body by the oscillation of the organs. This favours the restoration of the equilibrium of the latter, and exerts a beneficial influence upon the health.

Something absurd (something in which, therefore, the understanding can of itself find no delight) must be present in whatever is to raise a hearty convulsive laugh. *Laughter is an affect arising from a strained expectation being suddenly reduced to nothing.* This very reduction, at which certainly understanding cannot rejoice, is still indirectly a source of very lively enjoyment for a moment. Its cause must consequently lie in the influence of the representation upon the body, and the reciprocal effect of this upon the mind. This, moreover, cannot depend upon the representation being objectively an object of gratification, (for how can we derive gratification from a disappointment?) but must rest solely upon the fact that the reduction is a mere play of representations, and, as such, produces an equilibrium of the vital forces of the body.

Suppose that someone tells the following story: An Indian at an Englishman's table in Surat saw a bottle of ale opened, and all the beer turned into froth and flowing out. The repeated exclamations of the Indian showed his great astonishment. 'Well, what is so wonderful in that?' asked the Englishman. 'Oh, I'm not surprised myself,' said the Indian, 'at its getting out, but at how you ever managed to get it all in.' At this we laugh, and it gives us hearty pleasure. This is not because we believe ourselves, maybe, more quick-witted than this ignorant Indian, or because our understanding here brings to our notice any other ground of delight. It is rather that the bubble of our expectation was extended to the full and suddenly burst into nothing. Or, again, take the case of the heir of a wealthy relative being minded to make preparations for having the funeral obsequies on a most imposing scale, but complaining that things would not go right for him, because (as he said) 'the more money I give my mourners to look sad, the merrier they look'. At this we laugh outright, and the reason lies in the fact that we had an expectation which is suddenly reduced to nothing. We must be careful to observe that the reduction is not one into the positive contrary of an expected object—for that is always something, and may frequently pain us—but must be a reduction to nothing. For where a person arouses great expectation by recounting some tale, and at the close its untruth becomes at once

333

apparent to us, we are displeased at it. So it is, for instance, with the tale of people whose hair from excess of grief is said to have turned white in a single night. On the other hand, if a wag, wishing to cap the story, tells with the utmost elaboration of a merchant's grief, who, on his return journey from India to Europe with all his wealth in merchandise, was obliged by stress of storm to throw everything overboard, and grieved to such an extent that in the selfsame night his *wig* turned grey, we laugh and enjoy the tale. This is because we keep for a time playing on our own mistake about an object otherwise indifferent to us, or rather on the idea we ourselves were following out, and, beating it to and fro, just as if it were a ball eluding our grasp, when all we intend to do is just to get it into our hands and 334 hold it tight. Here our gratification is not excited by a knave or a fool getting a rebuff: for, even on its own account, the latter tale told with an air of seriousness would of itself be enough to set a whole table into roars of laughter; and the other matter would ordinarily not be worth a moment's thought.

It is noteworthy that in all such cases the joke must have something in it capable of momentarily deceiving us. Hence, when the semblance vanishes into nothing, the mind looks back in order to try it over again, and thus by a rapidly succeeding tension and relaxation it is thrown to and fro and put in oscillation. Since the snapping of what was, as it were, tightening up the string takes place suddenly (not by a gradual loosening), the oscillation must bring about a mental movement and a sympathetic internal movement of the body. This continues involuntarily and produces fatigue, but in so doing it also affords recreation (the effects of a commotion conducive to health).

For supposing we assume that some movement in the bodily organs is associated sympathetically with all our thoughts, it is readily intelligible how the sudden act above referred to, of shifting the mind now to one standpoint and now to the other, to enable it to contemplate its object, may involve a corresponding and reciprocal straining and slackening of the elastic parts of our viscera, which communicates itself to the diaphragm (and resembles that felt by ticklish people), in the course of which the lungs expel the air with rapidly succeeding interruptions, resulting in a movement beneficial to health. This alone, and not what goes on in the mind, is the proper cause of the gratification in a thought that at bottom represents nothing.—
Voltaire said that heaven has given us two things* to compensate us

for the many miseries of life, *hope* and *sleep*. He might have added *laughter* to the list—if only the means of exciting it in men of intelligence were as ready to hand, and the wit or originality of humour which it requires were not just as rare as the talent is common for inventing stuff *that breaks one's head*, as mystic speculators do, or *that breaks one's neck*, as the genius does, or that *breaks one's heart* as sentimental novelists do (and moralists of the same type for that matter).

We may, therefore, as I conceive, concede Epicurus the point that all gratification, even when occasioned by concepts that evoke aesthetic ideas, is *animal*, i.e. bodily sensation. For from this admission the *spiritual* feeling of respect for moral ideas, which is not one of gratification, but a self-esteem (an esteem for humanity within us) that raises us above the need of gratification, suffers not a whit—no nor even the less noble feeling of *taste*. 335

In *naïveté* we meet with a joint product of both the above. *Naïveté* is the breaking forth of the ingenuousness originally natural to humanity, in opposition to the art of disguising oneself that has become a second nature. We laugh at the simplicity that is as yet a stranger to dissimulation, but we rejoice the while over the simplicity of nature that thwarts that art. We await the commonplace manner of artificial utterance, carefully calculated as a beautiful illusion, and lo! nature stands before us in unsullied innocence—nature that we were quite unprepared to meet, and that he who laid it bare had also no intention of revealing. That the outward appearance, beautiful but false, that usually assumes such importance in our judgement, is here, at a stroke, turned to a nullity, that, as it were, the rogue in us is nakedly exposed, calls forth the movement of the mind, in two successive and opposite directions, agitating the body at the same time with wholesome motion. But that something infinitely better than any accepted code of manners, namely purity of mind (or at least the potential for such purity), has not become wholly extinct in human nature, infuses seriousness and reverence into this play of judgement. But since it is only a manifestation that obtrudes itself for a moment, and the veil of a dissembling art is soon drawn over it again, there enters into the above feelings a touch of pity. This is an emotion of tenderness, playful in its way, that thus readily admits of combination with this sort of genial laughter. And, in fact, this emotion is as a rule associated with it, and, at the same time, tends to make amends to the person who provides such food for our merriment for

his embarrassment at not being wise after the common manner.—
For that reason an art of being *naïf* is a contradiction. But it is quite
possible to give a representation of *naïveté* in a fictitious personage,
and, rare as the art is, it is a fine art. With this *naïveté* we must not
confuse open-hearted simplicity, which only avoids spoiling nature
by artificiality, because it has no notion of the art of social life.

336   The *humorous* manner may also be ranked as a thing which in its
enlivening influence is clearly allied to the gratification provoked by
laughter. It belongs to originality of spirit, though not to the talent
for fine art. *Humour*, in a good sense, means the talent for being able
to put oneself at will into a certain frame of mind in which everything
is judged on lines that do not follow the beaten track (quite the
reverse in fact) and yet on lines that follow certain principles, rational
in the case of such a mental temperament. A person with whom such
variations are not a matter of choice is said *to have humours*;* but if a
person can assume them voluntarily, and of set purpose (on behalf of
a lively presentation drawn from a ludicrous contrast), he and his
way of speaking are termed *humorous*. This manner belongs, however, to agreeable rather than to fine art, because the object of the
latter must always have an evident intrinsic worth about it, and thus
demands a certain seriousness in its presentation, as taste does in
judging it.

Dialectic of Aesthetic Judgement

---

§ 55

FOR a power of judgement to be dialectical it must first of all be rationalizing; that is to say, its judgements must lay claim to universality,[19] and do so *a priori*, for it is in the antithesis of such judgements that dialectic consists. Hence there is nothing dialectical in the irreconcilability of aesthetic judgements of the senses (concerning the agreeable and disagreeable). And in so far as each person appeals merely to his own private taste, even the conflict of judgements of taste does not form a dialectic of taste—for no one is proposing to make his own judgement into a universal rule. Hence the only concept left to us of a dialectic affecting taste is one of a dialectic of the *critique* of taste (not of taste itself) in respect of its *principles*: for, on the question of the ground of the possibility of judgements of taste in general, mutually conflicting concepts naturally and unavoidably make their appearance. The transcendental critique of taste will, therefore, only include a part capable of bearing the name of a dialectic of the aesthetic judgement if we find an antinomy of the principles of this faculty which throws doubt upon its conformity to law, and hence also upon its inner possibility.

§ 56

Representation of the antinomy of taste

THE first commonplace concerning taste is contained in the proposition under cover of which everyone devoid of taste thinks to shelter himself from reproach: *everyone has his own taste*. This is only another way of saying that the determining ground of this judgement is merely

---

[19] Any judgement which sets up to be universal may be termed a rationalizing judgement (*iudicium ratiocinans*); for in so far as it is universal it may serve as the major premiss of a syllogism. On the other hand, only a judgement which is thought as the conclusion of a syllogism, and, therefore, as having an *a priori* foundation, can be called rational (*iudicium ratiocinatum*).

subjective (gratification or pain), and that the judgement has no right to the necessary agreement of others.

Its second commonplace, to which even those resort who concede the right of the judgement of taste to pronounce with validity for everyone, is: *there is no disputing about taste*. This amounts to saying that even though the determining ground of a judgement of taste be objective, it is not reducible to definite concepts, so that in respect of the judgement itself no *decision* can be reached by proofs, although it is quite open to us to *contend* upon the matter, and to contend with right. For though *contention* and *dispute* have this point in common, that they aim at bringing judgements into accordance out of and by means of their mutual opposition; yet they differ in the latter hoping to effect this from definite concepts, as grounds of proof, and, consequently, adopting *objective concepts* as grounds of the judgement. But where this is considered impracticable, dispute is regarded as alike out of the question.

Between these two commonplaces an intermediate proposition is readily seen to be missing. It is one which has certainly not become proverbial, but yet it is at the back of everyone's mind. It is that *there may be contention about taste* (although not a dispute). This proposition, however, involves the contrary of the first one. For in a matter in which contention is to be allowed, there must be a hope of coming to terms. Hence one must be able to reckon on grounds of judgement that possess more than private validity and are thus not merely subjective. And yet the above principle, *everyone has his own taste*, is directly opposed to this.

The principle of taste, therefore, exhibits the following antinomy:

1. *Thesis*. The judgement of taste is not based upon concepts; for, if it were, it would be open to dispute (decision by means of proofs).

2. *Antithesis*. The judgement of taste is based on concepts; for otherwise, despite diversity of judgement, there could be no room even for contention in the matter (a claim to the necessary agreement of others with this judgement).

§ 57

Solution of the antinomy of taste

THERE is no possibility of removing the conflict of the above principles, which underlie every judgement of taste (and which are only the two peculiarities of the judgement of taste previously set out in the

Analytic) except by showing that the concept to which the object is referred in a judgement of this kind is not taken in the same sense in both maxims of the aesthetic judgement; that this double sense, or point of view, in our judging, is necessary for our power of transcendental judgement; and that nevertheless the false appearance arising from the confusion of one with the other is a natural illusion, and so unavoidable.

The judgement of taste must have reference to some concept or other, as otherwise it would be absolutely impossible for it to lay claim to necessary validity for everyone. Yet it need not on that account be provable from a concept. For a concept may be either determinable, or else at once intrinsically undetermined and indeterminable. A concept of the understanding, which is determinable by means of predicates borrowed from sensible intuition and capable of corresponding to it, is of the first kind. But of the second kind is the transcendental rational concept of the supersensible, which lies at the basis of all that sensible intuition and is, therefore, incapable of being further determined theoretically.

Now the judgement of taste applies to objects of the senses, but not so as to determine a *concept* of them for the understanding; for it is not a cognitive judgement. Hence it is a singular representation of intuition referable to the feeling of pleasure, and, as such, only a private judgement. And to that extent it would be limited in its validity to the individual judging: the object is *for me* an object of delight, for others it may be otherwise:—everyone to his taste.

For all that, the judgement of taste contains beyond doubt an enlarged reference on the part of the representation of the object (and at the same time on the part of the subject also), which lays the foundation of an extension of judgements of this kind to necessity for everyone. This must of necessity be founded upon some concept or other, but such a concept as does not admit of being determined by intuition, and affords no knowledge of anything. Hence, too, it is a concept *which does not afford any proof* of the judgement of taste. But the mere pure rational concept of the supersensible lying at the basis of the object (and of the judging subject for that matter) as object of the senses, and thus as phenomenon, is just such a concept. For unless such a point of view were adopted there would be no means of saving the claim of the judgement of taste to universal validity. And if the concept forming the required basis were a concept

340

of understanding, though a mere confused one, as, let us say, of perfection, answering to which the sensible intuition of the beautiful might
be adduced, then it would be at least intrinsically possible to ground the
judgement of taste upon proofs, which contradicts the thesis.

All contradiction disappears, however, if I say: The judgement of
taste does depend upon a concept (of a general ground of the subjective purposiveness of nature for the power of judgement), but one
from which nothing can be cognized in respect of the object, and
nothing proved, because it is in itself indeterminable and useless for
knowledge. Yet by means of this very concept it acquires at the same
time validity for everyone (but with each individual, no doubt, as a
singular judgement immediately accompanying his intuition):
because its determining ground lies, perhaps, in the concept of what
may be regarded as the supersensible substrate of humanity.

The solution of an antinomy turns solely on the possibility of two
apparently conflicting propositions not being in fact contradictory,
but rather being capable of consisting together, although the explanation of the possibility of their concept transcends our faculties of
cognition. That this illusion is also natural and for human reason
unavoidable, as well as why it is so, and remains so, although upon
the solution of the apparent contradiction it no longer misleads us,
may be made intelligible from the above considerations.

For the concept, which the universal validity of a judgement must
have for its basis, is taken in the same sense in both the conflicting
judgements, yet two opposite predicates are asserted of it. The thesis
should therefore read: The judgement of taste is not based on *determinate* concepts; but the antithesis: The judgement of taste does rest
upon a concept, although an *indeterminate* one, (that, namely, of the
341 supersensible substrate of phenomena); and then there would be no
conflict between them.

Beyond removing this conflict between the claims and counter-
claims of taste we can do nothing. To supply a determinate objective
principle of taste in accordance with which its judgements might be
derived, tested, and proved, is an absolute impossibility, for then it
would not be a judgement of taste. The subjective principle—that is
to say, the indeterminate idea of the supersensible within us—can
only be indicated as the unique key to the enigma of this faculty,
itself concealed from us in its sources; and there is no further means
of making it any more intelligible.

The antinomy here exhibited and resolved rests upon the proper concept of taste as a merely reflective aesthetic judgement, and the two seemingly conflicting principles are reconciled on the ground that *they may both be true*, and this is sufficient. If, on the other hand, owing to the fact that the representation lying at the basis of the judgement of taste is singular, the determining ground of taste is taken, as by some it is, to be *agreeableness*, or, as others, looking to its universal validity, would have it, the principle of *perfection*, and if the definition of taste is framed accordingly, the result is an antinomy which is absolutely irresolvable unless we show *the falsity of both propositions* as contraries (not as simple contradictories). This would force the conclusion that the concept upon which each is grounded is self-contradictory. Thus it is evident that the removal of the antinomy of the aesthetic judgement pursues a course similar to that followed by the critique in the solution of the antinomies of pure theoretical reason; and that the antinomies, both here and in the *Critique of Practical Reason*, compel us, whether we like it or not, to look beyond the horizon of the sensible, and to seek in the supersensible the point of union of all our faculties *a priori*: for we are left with no other course to bring reason into harmony with itself.

Remark 1

We find such frequent occasion in transcendental philosophy for distinguishing ideas from concepts of the understanding that it may be of use to introduce technical terms answering to the distinction 342 between them. I think that no objection will be raised to my proposing some.—Ideas, in the most comprehensive sense of the word, are representations referred to an object according to a certain principle (subjective or objective), in so far as they can still never become a cognition of it. They are either referred to an intuition, in accordance with a merely subjective principle of the harmony of the cognitive faculties (imagination and understanding), and are then called *aesthetic*; or else they are referred to a concept according to an objective principle and yet are incapable of ever furnishing a cognition of the object, and are called *rational ideas*. In the latter case the concept is a *transcendent* concept, and, as such, differs from a concept of understanding, for which an adequately answering experience may always be supplied, and which, on that account, is called *immanent*.

An *aesthetic idea* cannot become a cognition, because it is an *intuition* (of the imagination) for which an adequate concept can never be found. A *rational idea* can never become a cognition, because it involves a *concept* (of the supersensible), for which a commensurate intuition can never be given.

Now the aesthetic idea might, I think, be called an *inexponible* representation of the imagination, the rational idea, on the other hand, an *indemonstrable* concept of reason. The production of both is presupposed to be not altogether groundless, but rather (following the above explanation of an idea in general) to take place in obedience to certain principles of the cognitive faculties to which they belong (subjective principles in the case of the former and objective in that of the latter).

Concepts of the understanding must, as such, always be demonstrable (if, as in anatomy, demonstration is understood in the sense merely of *presentation*). In other words, the object answering to such concepts must always be capable of being given in intuition (pure or empirical); for only in this way can they become cognitions. The concept of *magnitude* may be given *a priori* in the intuition of space, e.g. of a straight line, etc.; the concept of *cause* in impenetrability, in the impact of bodies, etc. Consequently both may be verified by means of an empirical intuition, i.e. the thought of them may be indicated (demonstrated, exhibited) in an example; and this it must be possible to do: for otherwise there would be no certainty of the thought not being empty, i.e. having no object.

In logic the expressions demonstrable or indemonstrable are ordinarily employed only in respect of *propositions*. A better designation would be to call the former, propositions only mediately, and the latter, propositions *immediately*, *certain*. For pure philosophy, too, has propositions of both these kinds— meaning thereby true propositions which are in the one case capable, and in the other incapable, of proof. But, in its character of philosophy, while it can, no doubt, prove on *a priori* grounds, it cannot demonstrate—unless we wish entirely to ignore the meaning of the word which makes demonstrate (*ostendere*, *exhibere*) equivalent to giving an accompanying presentation of the concept in intuition (be it in a proof or in a definition). Where the intuition is *a priori* this is called its construction, but when even the intuition is empirical, we have still got the illustration of the object, by which means objective reality is assured to the concept.

Thus an anatomist is said to 'demonstrate' the human eye when he renders the concept, of which he has previously given a discursive exposition, intuitable by means of the dissection of that organ.

It follows from the above that the rational concept of the supersensible substrate of all phenomena generally, or even of that which must be laid at the basis of our power of choice in respect of moral laws, i.e. the rational concept of transcendental freedom, is at once specifically an indemonstrable concept, and a rational idea, whereas virtue is so as a matter of degree. For nothing can be given which in itself qualitatively answers in experience to the rational concept of the former, while in the case of virtue no empirical product of the above causality attains the degree that the rational idea prescribes as the rule.

Just as the *imagination*, in the case of a rational idea, fails with its intuitions to attain to the given concept, so *understanding*, in the case of an aesthetic idea, fails with its concepts ever to attain to the completeness of the internal intuition which imagination conjoins with a given representation. Now since the reduction of a representation of the imagination to concepts is equivalent to *expounding* it, the aesthetic idea may be called an *inexponible* representation of the imagination (in its free play). I shall have an opportunity hereafter of dealing more fully with ideas of this kind. At present I confine myself to the remark, that both kinds of ideas, aesthetic ideas as well as rational, are bound to have their principles, and that the seat of these principles must in both cases be reason——the latter depending upon the objective, the former upon the subjective, principles of its employment. 344

Consonantly with this, GENIUS may also be defined as the faculty of *aesthetic ideas*. This serves at the same time to point out the reason why it is nature (the nature of the subject) and not a set purpose, that in products of genius gives the rule to art (as the production of the beautiful). For the beautiful must not be judged according to concepts, but by the purposive manner in which the imagination is attuned so as to accord with the faculty of concepts generally; and so rule and precept are incapable of serving as the requisite subjective standard for that aesthetic and unconditioned purposiveness in fine art which has to make a warranted claim to being bound to please everyone. Rather must such a standard be sought in the element of mere nature in the subject, which cannot be comprehended under rules or concepts, that is to say, the supersensible substrate of all the subject's faculties (unattainable by any concept of understanding), and consequently in that which forms the point of reference for the harmonious accord of all our faculties of cognition—the production of which accord is the ultimate end set by the intelligible basis of our nature. Thus alone is it possible for a subjective and yet universally valid principle *a priori* to lie at the basis of that purposiveness for which no objective principle can be prescribed.

Remark 2

The following important observation here naturally presents itself: There are *three kinds of antinomies* of pure reason, which, however, all agree in forcing reason to abandon the otherwise very natural assumption which takes the objects of the senses for things in themselves, and to regard them, instead, merely as phenomena, and to lay at their basis an intelligible substrate (something supersensible, the concept of which is only an idea and affords no proper knowledge). Apart from some such antinomy reason could never bring itself to take such a step as to adopt a principle so severely restricting the field of its speculation, and to submit to sacrifices involving the complete dissolution of so many otherwise glittering hopes. For even now that it is recompensed for this loss by the prospect of a proportionately
345 wider scope of action from a practical point of view, it is not without a pang of regret that it appears to part company with those hopes, and to break away from the old ties.

The reason for there being three kinds of antinomies is to be found in the fact that there are three faculties of cognition, understanding, judgement, and reason, each of which, being a higher faculty of cognition, must have its *a priori* principles. For, so far as reason passes judgement upon these principles themselves and their employment, it inexorably requires the unconditioned for the given conditioned in respect of them all. This can never be found unless the sensible, instead of being regarded as inherently belonging to things in themselves, is treated as a mere phenomenon, and, as such, being made to rest upon something supersensible (the intelligible substrate of external and internal nature) as the thing in itself. There is then (1) *for the cognitive faculty* an antinomy of reason in respect of the theoretical employment of understanding carried to the point of the unconditioned; (2) for *the feeling of pleasure and displeasure* an antinomy of reason in respect of the aesthetic employment of judgement; (3) *for the faculty of desire* an antinomy in respect of the practical employment of self-legislative reason. For all these faculties have their fundamental *a priori* principles, and, following an imperative demand of reason, must be able to judge and to determine their object *unconditionally* in accordance with these principles.

As to two of the antinomies of these higher cognitive faculties, those, namely, of their theoretical and of their practical employment, we have already shown elsewhere both that they are *inevitable*, if no cognisance is taken in such judgements of a supersensible substrate of the given objects as phenomena, and, on the other hand, that they *can be solved* the moment this is done. Now, as to the antinomy incident to the employment of judgement in conformity with the demand of reason, and the solution of it here given, we may say that to avoid facing it there are but the following alternatives. It is open to us to deny that any *a priori* principle lies at the basis of the aesthetic judgement of taste, with the result that all claim to the necessity of a universal consensus of opinion is an idle and empty delusion, and that a judgement of taste only deserves to be considered to this extent correct, that *it so happens* that a number share the same opinion, and even this, not, in truth, because an *a priori* principle is *presumed* to lie behind this agreement, but rather (as with the taste of the palate) because of the contingently similar organization of the 346 individuals. *Or else*, as the alternative, we should have to suppose that the judgement of taste is in fact a disguised judgement of reason on the perfection discovered in a thing and the reference of the manifold in it to an end, and that it is consequently only called aesthetic on account of the confusion that here besets our reflection, although fundamentally it is teleological. In this latter case the solution of the antinomy with the assistance of transcendental ideas might be declared otiose and nugatory, and the above laws of taste thus reconciled with the objects of the senses, not as mere phenomena, but even as things in themselves. How unsatisfactory both of those alternatives alike are as a means of escape has been shown in several places in our exposition of judgements of taste.

If, however, our deduction is at least credited with having been worked out on correct lines, even though it may not have been sufficiently clear in all its details, three ideas then stand out in evidence. *Firstly*, there is the supersensible in general, without further determination, as substrate of nature; *secondly*, this same supersensible as principle of the subjective purposiveness of nature for our cognitive faculties; *thirdly*, the same supersensible again, as principle of the ends of freedom, and principle of the common accord of these ends with freedom in the moral sphere.

§ 58

The idealism of the purposiveness of both nature and art, as the unique principle of aesthetic judgement

THE principle of taste may, to begin with, be placed on either of two footings. For taste may be said invariably to judge on empirical grounds of determination and such, therefore, as are only given *a posteriori* through the senses, or else it may be allowed to judge on an *a priori* ground. The former would be the *empiricism* of the critique of taste, the latter its *rationalism*. The first would obliterate the distinction that marks off the object of our delight from the *agreeable*; the *second*, supposing the judgement rested upon determinate concepts, would obliterate its distinction from the *good*. In this way *beauty* would find itself utterly banished from the world, and nothing but the dignity of a separate name, betokening, maybe, a certain blend of both the above-named kinds of delight, would be left in its stead. But we have shown the existence of grounds of delight which are *a priori*, and which, therefore, can consist with the principle of rationalism, and which are yet incapable of being grasped by *determinate concepts*.

As against the above we may say that the rationalism of the principle of taste may take the form either of the *realism* of purposiveness or of its *idealism*. Now, as a judgement of taste is not a cognitive judgement, and as beauty is not a property of the object considered on its own account, the rationalism of the principle of taste can never be placed in the fact that the purposiveness in this judgement is regarded in thought as objective. In other words, the judgement is not directed theoretically, nor, therefore, logically (no matter if only in a confused estimate) to the perfection of the object, but only *aesthetically* to the harmonizing of its representation in the imagination with the essential principles of judgement generally in the subject. For this reason the judgement of taste, and the distinction between its realism and its idealism, can only, even on the principle of rationalism, depend upon its subjective purposiveness interpreted in one or other of two ways. Either such subjective purposiveness is, in the first case, a harmony with our judgement pursued as an actual (intentional) *end* of nature (or of art), or else, in the second case, it is only a supervening purposive harmony with the needs of our faculty of judgement in its relation to nature and the forms which nature produces in accordance with particular laws, and one that is independent of an end, or spontaneous and contingent.

The beautiful forms displayed in the organic world all plead eloquently on the side of the realism of the aesthetic purposiveness of nature in support of the plausible assumption that beneath the production of the beautiful there must lie an antecedent idea in the producing cause—that is to say an *end* acting in the interest of our imagination. Flowers, blossoms, even the shapes of plants as a whole, the elegance of animal formations of all kinds, unnecessary for the discharge of any function on their part, but chosen as it were with an eye to our taste; and, beyond all else, the variety and harmony in the array of colours (in the pheasant, in crustacea, in insects, down even to the meanest flowers), so pleasing and charming to the eyes, but which, inasmuch as they touch the bare surface, and do not even here in any way affect the structure, of these creatures—a matter which might have a necessary bearing on their internal ends—seem to be designed entirely with a view to outward appearance: all these lend 348 great weight to the mode of explanation which assumes actual ends of nature in favour of our aesthetic judgement.

On the other hand, not only does reason, with its maxims enjoining upon us in all cases to avoid, as far as possible, any unnecessary multiplication of principles, set itself against this assumption, but we have nature in its free formations displaying on all sides extensive mechanical proclivity to producing forms seemingly made, as it were, for the aesthetic employment of our judgement, without affording the least support to the supposition of a need for anything over and above its mechanism, as mere nature, to enable them to be purposive for our judgement without their being grounded upon any idea. The above expression, *'free formations'* of nature, is, however, here used to denote such as are originally set up in a *fluid at rest* where the evaporation or separation of some constituent (sometimes merely of caloric) leaves the residue on solidification to assume a definite shape or structure (figure or texture) which differs with specific differences of the matter, but for the same matter is invariable. Here, however, it is taken for granted that, as the true meaning of a fluid requires, the matter in the fluid is completely dissolved and not a mere admixture of solid particles simply held there in suspension.

The formation, then, takes place by a precipitation, i.e. by a sudden solidification—not by a gradual transition from the fluid to the solid state, but, as it were, by a leap. This transition is termed *crystallization*. Freezing water offers the most familiar instance of a formation of this kind. There the process begins by straight threads of ice forming. These unite at angles of sixty degrees, whilst others similarly attach themselves to them at every point until the whole has turned into ice. But while this is going on the water between the threads of ice does not keep getting gradually more viscous, but remains as thoroughly fluid as it would be at a much higher temperature, although it is perfectly ice-cold. The matter that frees itself—that makes its sudden escape at the moment of solidification—is a considerable quantum of caloric. As this was merely required to preserve fluidity, its disappearance leaves the exising ice not a whit colder than the water which but a moment before was there as fluid.

There are many salts and also stones of a crystalline figure which owe their origin in like manner to some earthy substance being dissolved in water under the influence of agencies little understood. The drusy configurations of many minerals, of the cubical sulphide of lead, of the red silver ore, etc., are presumably also similarly formed in water, and by the precipitation of their particles, on their being forced by some cause or other to relinquish this vehicle and to unite among themselves in definite external shapes.

But, further, all substances rendered fluid by heat, which have become solid as the result of cooling, give, when broken, internal evidence of a definite texture, thus suggesting the inference that only for the interference of their own weight or the disturbance of the air, the exterior would also have exhibited their proper specific shape. This has been observed in the case of some metals where the exterior of a molten mass has hardened, but the interior remained fluid, and then, owing to the withdrawal of the still fluid portion in the interior, there has been an undisturbed precipitation of the remaining parts on the inside. A number of such mineral crystallizations, such as *spars*, *hematite*, *aragonite*, frequently present extremely beautiful shapes such as it might take art all its time to devise; and the halo in the grotto of Antiparos* is merely the work of water percolating through strata of gypsum.

The fluid state is, to all appearance, on the whole older than the solid, and plants as well as animal bodies are built up out of fluid nutritive matter, which quietly takes on form—in the case of the latter, admittedly, in obedience, primarily, to a certain original predisposition according to ends (which, as will be shown in Part II, must not be judged aesthetically, but teleologically by the principle of realism); but still all the while, perhaps, also following the universal law of the affinity of substances in the way they precipitate and freely form themselves. In the same way, again, where an atmosphere, which is a composite of different kinds of gas, is charged with watery fluids, and these separate from it owing to a reduction of the temperature, they produce snow-figures of shapes differing with the actual composition of the atmosphere. These are frequently of very artistic appearance and of extreme beauty. So without at all derogating from the teleological principle by which an organization is judged, it is readily conceivable how with beauty of flowers, of the plumage of birds, of crustacea, both as to their shape and their colour, we have only what may be ascribed to nature and its capacity for originating in free activity aesthetically purposive forms, independently of any particular guiding ends, according to chemical laws, by means of the chemical integration of the substance requisite for the organization. 350

But what shows plainly that the principle of the *ideality* of the purposiveness in the beauty of nature is the one upon which we ourselves invariably take our stand in our aesthetic judgements, forbidding us to have recourse to any realism of a natural end in favour of our faculty of representation as a principle of explanation, is that in our general judging of beauty we seek its standard *a priori* in ourselves, and, that the aesthetic faculty is itself legislative in respect of the judgement whether anything is beautiful or not. This could not be so on the assumption of a realism of the purposiveness of nature; because in that case we should have to go to nature for instruction as to what we should deem beautiful, and the judgement of taste would be subject to empirical principles. For in such judging the question does not turn on what nature is, or even on what it is for us in the way of an end, but on how we receive it. For nature to have fashioned its forms for our delight would inevitably imply an objective purposiveness on the part of nature, instead of a subjective purposiveness resting on the play of imagination in its freedom, where it is we who receive nature with favour, and not nature that does us a favour.

That nature affords us an opportunity for perceiving the inner purposiveness in the relation of our mental powers engaged in the estimate of certain of its products, and, indeed, such a purposiveness as arising from a supersensible basis is to be pronounced necessary and of universal validity, is a property of nature which cannot belong to it as its end, or rather, cannot be judged by us to be such an end. For otherwise the judgement that would be determined by reference to such an end would be grounded upon heteronomy, instead of being grounded upon autonomy and being free, as befits a judgement of taste.

The principle of the ideality of purposiveness is still more clearly apparent in fine art. For the point that sensations do not enable us to adopt an aesthetic realism of purposiveness (which would make art merely agreeable instead of beautiful) is one which it enjoys in common with beautiful nature. But the further point that the delight arising from aesthetic ideas must not be made dependent upon the successful attainment of determinate ends (as an art mechanically directed to results), and that, consequently, even in the case of the rationalism of the principle, an ideality of the ends and not their reality is fundamental, is brought home to us by the fact that 351 fine art, as such, must not be regarded as a product of understanding and science, but of genius, and must, therefore, derive its rule from *aesthetic* ideas, which are essentially different from rational ideas of determinate ends.

Just as the *ideality* of objects of the senses as phenomena is the only way of explaining the possibility of their forms admitting of *a priori* determination, so, also, the *idealism* of the purposiveness in judging the beautiful in nature and in art is the only hypothesis upon which a critique can explain the possibility of a judgement of taste that demands *a priori* validity for everyone (yet without basing the purposiveness represented in the object upon concepts).

§ 59
Beauty as the symbol of morality

INTUITIONS are always required to verify the reality of our concepts. If the concepts are empirical the intuitions are called *examples*: if they are pure concepts of the understanding the intuitions go by the name of *schemata*. But to call for a verification of the objective reality of rational concepts, i.e. of ideas, and, what is more, on behalf of the theoretical cognition of such a reality, is to demand an impossibility, because absolutely no intuition adequate to them can be given.

All *hypotyposis* (presentation, *subiectio sub adspectum*)* a rendering in terms of sense, is twofold. Either it is *schematic*, as where the intuition corresponding to a concept comprehended by the understanding is given *a priori*, or else it is *symbolic*, as where the concept is one which only reason can think, and to which no sensuous intuition can be adequate. In the latter case the concept is supplied with an intuition such that the procedure of judgement in dealing with it is merely analogous to that which it observes in schematism. In other words, what agrees with the concept is merely the rule of this procedure, and not the intuition itself. Hence the agreement is merely in the form of reflection, and not in the content.

Notwithstanding the adoption of the word *symbolic* by modern logicians in a sense opposed to an *intuitive* mode of representation, it is a wrong use of the word and subversive of its true meaning; for the symbolic is only a *mode* of the intuitive. The intuitive mode of representation is, in fact, divisible into the *schematic* and the *symbolic*. Both are hypotyposes, i.e. presentations (*exhibitiones*) not mere *marks*. Marks are merely designations of concepts by the aid of accompanying sensuous signs devoid of any intrinsic connexion with the intuition of the object. Their sole function is to afford a means of reinvoking the concepts according to the imagination's law of association—a purely subjective rôle. Such marks are either words or visible (algebraic or even mimetic) signs, simply as *expressions* for concepts.[20]

All intuitions by which *a priori* concepts are given a foothold are, therefore, either *schemata* or *symbols*. Schemata contain direct, symbols indirect, presentations of the concept. Schemata effect this presentation demonstratively, symbols by the aid of an analogy (for which recourse is had even to empirical intuitions), in which analogy judgement performs a double function: first in applying the concept to the object of a sensuous intuition, and then, secondly, in applying the mere rule of its reflection upon that intuition to quite another object, of which the former is but the symbol. In this way a monarchical state is represented as a living body when it is governed by constitutional laws, but as a mere machine (like a hand-mill) when it is governed by

---

[20] The intuitive mode of knowledge must be contrasted with the discursive mode (not with the symbolic). The former is either *schematic*, by means of *demonstration*, or *symbolic*, as a representation following a mere *analogy*.

an individual absolute will; but in both cases the representation is merely *symbolic*. For there is certainly no likeness between a despotic state and a hand-mill, whereas there surely is between the rules of reflection upon both and their causality. Hitherto this function has been but little analysed, worthy as it is of a deeper study. Still this is not the place to dwell upon it. In language we have many such indirect presentations modelled upon an analogy enabling the expression in question to contain, not the proper schema for the concept, but merely a symbol for reflection. Thus the words *ground* (support, basis), *to depend* (to be held up from above), to *flow* from (instead of to follow), *substance* (as Locke puts it: the support of accidents), and numberless others, are not schematic, but rather symbolic hypotyposes, and express concepts without employing a direct intuition for the purpose, but only drawing upon an analogy with one, i.e.
353 transferring the reflection upon an object of intuition to quite a new concept, and one with which perhaps no intuition could ever directly correspond. Supposing the name of knowledge may be given to what only amounts to a mere mode of representation (which is quite permissible where this is not a principle of the theoretical determination of the object in respect of what it is in itself, but of the practical determination of what the idea of it ought to be for us and for its purposive employment), then all our knowledge of God is merely symbolic; and one who takes it, with the properties of understanding, will, and so forth, which only manifest their objective reality in beings of this world, to be schematic, falls into anthropomorphism, just as, if he abandons every intuitive element, he falls into Deism which furnishes no knowledge whatsoever—not even from a practical point of view.

Now, I say, the beautiful is the symbol of the morally good, and only in this light (a point of view natural to everyone, and one which everyone demands from others as a duty) does it give us pleasure with an attendant claim to the agreement of everyone else, whereupon the mind becomes conscious of a certain ennoblement and elevation above mere sensibility to pleasure from impressions of the senses, and also appraises the worth of others on the score of a like maxim of their judgement. This is the *intelligible* toward which taste looks, as we have indicated in the preceding paragraph. It is, that is to say, what brings even our higher cognitive faculties into common accord, and is that apart from which sheer contradiction would arise between their nature and the claims put forward by taste. In this faculty judgement does not find itself subjected to a heteronomy of laws of experience as it does in the empirical judging of things—in respect of the objects of such a pure delight it gives the law to itself, just as reason does in respect of the faculty of desire. Here, too, both on account of this inner possibility in the subject, and on account of the external possibility of a nature harmonizing therewith, it finds a reference in itself to something in the subject itself and outside it, and which is not nature, nor yet freedom, but still is connected with the ground of the latter, i.e. the supersensible—a something in which the theoretical faculty is combined with the practical in a shared and unknown manner. We shall bring out a few points of this analogy, while taking care, at the same time, not to let the points of difference escape us.

(1) The beautiful pleases *immediately* (but only in reflective intu- 354 ition, not, like morality, in its concept). (2) It pleases *apart from all interest* (pleasure in the morally good is no doubt necessarily bound up with an interest, but not with one of the kind that are antecedent to the judgement upon the delight, but with one that judgement itself for the first time calls into existence). (3) *The freedom* of the imagination (consequently of our faculty in respect of its sensibility) is, in judging the beautiful, represented as in accord with the understanding's conformity to law (in moral judgements the freedom of the will is thought as the harmony of the latter with itself according to universal laws of reason). (4) The subjective principle of the judging of the beautiful is represented as *universal*, i.e. valid for every human being but as incognizable by means of any universal concept (the objective principle of morality is set forth as also universal, i.e. for all individuals, and, at the same time, for all actions of the same individual, and, besides, as cognizable by means of a universal concept). For this reason the moral judgement not only admits of definite constitutive principles, but is *only* possible by adopting these principles and their universality as the ground of its maxims.

Even common understanding tends to pay regard to this analogy; and we frequently apply to beautiful objects of nature or of art names that seem to rely upon the basis of moral judgement. We call buildings or trees majestic and stately, or plains laughing and joyful; even colours are called innocent, modest, soft, because they excite sensations containing something analogous to the consciousness of the state of mind produced by moral judgements. Taste makes, as it were, the transition from the charm of sense to habitual moral interest possible without too violent a leap, for it represents the imagination, even in its freedom, as purposive with respect to the understanding, and teaches us to find, even in sensuous objects, a free delight apart from any charm of sense.

§ 60

APPENDIX

The methodology of taste

THE division of a critique into a doctrine of elements and a doctrine of method—a division which is introductory to science—is one 355 inapplicable to the critique of taste. For there neither is, nor can be, a science of the beautiful, and the judgement of taste is not determinable by principles. For, as to the element of science in every art— a matter which turns upon *truth* in the presentation of the object of the art—while this is, no doubt, the indispensable condition (*conditio sine qua non*) of fine art, it is not itself fine art. Fine art, therefore, has only got a *manner* (*modus*), and not a *method* of teaching (*methodus*). The master must illustrate what the pupil is to achieve, and how achievement is to be attained, and the proper function of the universal rules to which he ultimately reduces his treatment is rather that of supplying a convenient text for recalling its chief moments to the pupil's mind, than of prescribing them to him. Yet, in all this, due regard must be paid to a certain ideal which art must keep in view, even though complete success constantly eludes its happiest efforts. Only by exciting the pupil's imagination to conformity with a given concept, by pointing out how the expression falls short of the idea to which, as aesthetic, the concept itself fails to attain, and by means of severe criticism, is it possible to prevent his promptly looking upon the examples set before him as the prototypes of excellence, and as models for him to imitate, without submission to any higher standard or to his own critical judgement. This would result in genius being stifled, and, with it, also the freedom of the imagination in its very conformity to law—a freedom without which a fine art is not possible, nor even as much as a correct taste of one's own for judging it.

The propaedeutic to all fine art, so far as the highest degree of its perfection is what is in view, appears to lie, not in precepts, but in the culture of the mental powers produced by a sound preparatory education in what are called the *humaniora**—so called, presumably, because *humanity* signifies, on the one hand, the universal *feeling of sympathy*, and, on the other, the faculty of being able to *communicate* universally one's inmost self—properties constituting in conjunction the befitting *social character* of mankind,* in contradistinction to the narrowly constricted life of animals. The age and the peoples in which the vigorous drive towards a social life *regulated by laws*—that which converts a people into an enduring community—grappled with the huge difficulties presented by the trying problem of bringing freedom (and therefore equality also) into union with constraint (more that of respect and dutiful submission than of fear). And such must have been the age, and such the people, that first discovered the art of reciprocal communication of ideas between the more cultured and cruder sections of the community, and how to bridge the difference between the breadth and refinement of the former and the natural simplicity and originality of the latter—in this way hitting upon that mean between higher culture and self-sufficing nature, that forms for taste also, as a sense common to all mankind, that true standard which no universal rules can supply. [356]

Hardly will a later age dispense with those models. For nature will ever recede farther into the background, so that eventually, without enduring examples of it, a future age would scarcely be in a position to form a concept of the happy union, in one and the same people, of the law-directed constraint belonging to the highest culture, with the force and rightness of a free nature aware of its proper worth.

However, taste is, in the ultimate analysis, a faculty that judges of the rendering of moral ideas in terms of the senses (through the intervention of a certain analogy in our reflection on both); and it is this rendering also, and the increased receptivity, founded upon it, for the feeling which these ideas evoke (termed moral sense), that are the origin of that pleasure which taste declares valid for mankind in general and not merely for the private feeling of each individual. This makes it clear that the true propaedeutic for laying the foundations of taste is the development of moral ideas and the culture of the moral feeling. For only when sensibility is brought into harmony with moral feeling can genuine taste assume a definite unchangeable form.

PART II

CRITIQUE OF
TELEOLOGICAL JUDGEMENT

§ 61

The objective purposiveness of nature

WE do not need to look beyond transcendental principles to find ample 359
reason for assuming a subjective purposiveness on the part of nature in
its particular laws. This is a purposiveness relative to comprehensibility—with respect to the human power of judgement—and to the possibility of uniting particular experiences into a connected system of
nature. In this system, then, we may further anticipate the possible
existence of some among the many products of nature that, as if
designed with special regard to our power of judgement, are of a form
particularly adapted to that faculty. Forms of this kind are those which
by their combination of unity and heterogeneity serve as it were to
strengthen and entertain the mental powers that enter into play in the
exercise of the faculty of judgement, and to them the name of *beautiful
forms* is accordingly given.

But the universal idea of nature, as the sum of objects of the senses,
gives us no reason whatever for assuming that things of nature serve
one another as means to ends, or that their very possibility is only
made fully intelligible by a causality of this sort. For since, in the case
of the beautiful forms above mentioned, the representation of the
things is something in ourselves, it can quite readily be thought even
a priori as one well-adapted and suitable for disposing our cognitive
faculties to an internally purposive harmony. But where the ends are
not ends of our own, and do not belong even to nature (which we do
not take to be an intelligent being), there is no reason at all for presuming *a priori* that they may or ought nevertheless to constitute a
special kind of causality or at least a quite peculiar order of nature. 360
What is more, the actual existence of these ends cannot be proved by
experience—save on the assumption of an antecedent process of
mental jugglery that only reads the conception of an end into the
nature of the things, and that, not deriving this conception from the
objects and what it knows of them from experience, makes use of
it more for the purpose of rendering nature intelligible to us by an
analogy to a subjective ground upon which our representations are
brought into inner connexion, than for that of cognizing nature from
objective grounds.

Besides, objective purposiveness, as a principle upon which physical objects are possible, is so far from attaching *necessarily* to the conception of nature, that it is the stock example adduced to show the contingency of nature and its form. So where the structure of a bird, for instance, the hollow formation of its bones, the position of its wings for producing motion and of its tail for steering, are cited, we are told that all this is in the highest degree contingent if we simply look to the *nexus effectivus* in nature, and do not call in aid a special kind of causality, namely, that of ends (*nexus finalis*). This means that nature, regarded as mere mechanism, could have fashioned itself in a thousand other different ways without lighting precisely on the unity based on a principle like this, and that, accordingly, it is only outside the conception of nature, and not in it, that we may hope to find some shadow of ground *a priori* for that unity.

We are right, however, in drawing upon teleological judging, at least problematically, with regard to the investigation of nature; but only with a view to bringing it under principles of observation and research by *analogy* to the causality that looks to ends, while not pretending to *explain* it by this means. Thus this is an activity of reflective, not of determining, judgement. Yet the conception of combinations and forms in nature that are determined by ends is at least *one more principle* for reducing its phenomena to rules in cases where the 361 laws of its purely mechanical causality do not carry us sufficiently far. For we are bringing forward a teleological ground where we endow a concept of an object—as if that concept were to be found in nature instead of in ourselves—with causality in respect of the object, or rather where we represent to ourselves the possibility of the object on the analogy of a causality of this kind—a causality such as we experience in ourselves—and so regard nature as possessed of a capacity of its own for acting *technically*; whereas if we did not ascribe such a mode of operation to nature, its causality would have to be regarded as blind mechanism. But this is a different thing from crediting nature with causes acting *designedly*, to which it may be regarded as subjected in following its particular laws. The latter would mean that teleology is based, not merely on a *regulative* principle, directed to the simple *judging* of phenomena, but is actually based on a *constitutive* principle available for *deriving* natural products from their causes: with the result that the concept of a natural end would no longer belong to reflective, but to determining, judgement. But in that case the concept would not really be specially connected with the power of judgement, as is the concept of beauty as a formal subjective purposiveness. It would, on the contrary, be a concept of reason, and would introduce a new causality into science—one which we are borrowing all the time solely from ourselves and attributing to other beings, although we do not mean to assume that they and we are similarly constituted.

FIRST DIVISION
Analytic of Teleological Judgement

---

§ 62
Purely formal, as distinguished from material, objective purposiveness

ALL geometrical figures drawn on a principle display a manifold objective purposiveness which has often been admired. This purposiveness is one of convenience on the part of the figure for solving a number of problems by a single principle, and even for solving each one of the problems in an infinite variety of ways. Here the purposiveness is manifestly objective and intellectual, not simply subjective and aesthetic. For it expresses the way the figure lends itself to the production of many proposed figures, and it is cognized through reason. Yet this purposiveness does not make the conception of the object itself possible, that is to say, we do not regard the object as possible simply because it may be turned to such use.

In such a simple figure as the circle lies the key to the solution of a host of problems every one of which would separately require elaborate materials, and this solution follows, we might say, directly as one of the infinite number of excellent properties of that figure. For instance, suppose we have to construct a triangle, being given the base and vertical angle. The problem is indeterminate, i.e. it admits of solution in an endless variety of ways. But the circle embraces them all in one, as the geometrical locus of all triangles satisfying this condition. Or two lines have to intersect one another so that the rectangle under the two parts of the one shall be equal to the rectangle under the two parts of the other. The solution of the problem is apparently full of difficulty. But all lines intersecting within a circle whose circumference passes through their extremities are divided directly in this ratio. The remaining curves similarly suggest to us other useful solutions, never contemplated in the rule upon which they are constructed. All conic sections, taken separately or compared with one another, are, however simple their definition, fruitful in principles for solving a host of possible problems.—It is a real joy to see the ardour with which the older geometricians investigated these properties of such lines, without allowing themselves to be troubled by the question which shallow minds raise, as to the supposed use of such knowledge. Thus they investigated the properties of the parabola in ignorance of the law of terrestrial gravitation which would have shown them its application to the trajectory of heavy bodies (for the direction of their gravitation when in motion may be regarded as parallel to the curve of a parabola). So again they investigated the properties of the ellipse without a suspicion that a gravitation was also discoverable in the celestial bodies, and without knowing the law that governs it as the distance from the point of attraction varies, and that makes the bodies describe this curve in free motion. While in all these labours they were working unwittingly for those who were to come after them, they delighted themselves with a purposiveness which, although belonging to the nature of the things, they were able to present completely *a priori* as necessary. Plato, himself a master of this science,* was fired with the idea of an original constitution of things, for the discovery of which we could dispense with all experience, and of a power of the mind enabling it to derive the harmony of real things from their supersensible principle (and with these real things he classed the properties of numbers with which the mind plays in music). Thus inspired he transcended the conceptions of experience and rose to ideas that seemed only explicable to him on the assumption of a community of intellect with the original source of all real things. No wonder that he banished from his school the man that was ignorant of geometry, since he thought that from the pure intuition residing in the depths of the human soul he could derive all that Anaxagoras inferred* from the objects of experience and their purposive connexion. For it is the necessity of that which, while appearing to be an original attribute belonging to the essential nature of things regardless of service to us, is yet purposive, and formed as if deliberately designed for our use, that is the source of our great admiration of nature—a source not so much external to ourselves as seated in our reason. Surely we may pardon 364 this admiration if, as the result of a misapprehension, it is inclined to rise by degrees to extravagant heights.

This intellectual purposiveness is simply formal, not real. In other words it is a purposiveness which does not imply an underlying end, and which, therefore, does not stand in need of teleology. As such, and although it is objective, not subjective like aesthetic purposiveness, its possibility is readily comprehensible, though only in the abstract. The figure of a circle is an intuition which understanding has determined according to a principle. This principle, which is arbitrarily assumed and made a fundamental conception, is applied to space, a form of intuition which, similarly, is only found in ourselves, and found *a priori*, as a representation. It is the unity of this principle that explains the unity of the numerous rules resulting from the construction of that conception. These rules display purposiveness from many possible points of view, but we must not rest this purposiveness on an *end*, or resort to any explanation beyond the above. This is different from finding order and regularity in complexes of external *things* enclosed within definite bounds, as, for instance, order and regularity in the trees, flower-beds, and walks in a garden, which is one that I cannot hope to deduce *a priori* from any delimitation I may make of space according to some rule out of my own head. For these are things having real existence—things that to be cognized must be given empirically—and not a mere representation in myself defined *a priori* on a principle. Hence the latter (empirical) purposiveness is *real*, and, being real, is dependent on the conception of an end.

But we can also quite easily see the reason for the admiration, and, in fact, regard it as justified, even where the purposiveness admired is perceived in the essential nature of the things, they being things whose concepts are such as we can construct. The various rules whose unity, derived from a principle, excites this admiration are one and all synthetic and do not follow from any *concept* of the object, as, for instance, from the concept of a circle, but require to have this object given in intuition. This gives the unity the appearance of having an external source of its rules distinct from our faculty of representation, just as if it were empirical. Hence the way the object answers to the understanding's own peculiar need for rules appears 365 intrinsically contingent and, therefore, only possible by virtue of an end expressly directed to its production. Now since this harmony, despite all the purposiveness mentioned, is not cognized empirically, but *a priori*, it is just what should bring home to us the fact that space, by the limitation of which (by means of the imagination acting in accordance with a concept) the object was alone possible, is not a quality of the things outside me, but a mere mode of representation existing in myself. Hence, where I draw a figure *in accordance with a concept*, or, in other words, when I form my own representation of what is given to me externally, be its own intrinsic nature what it may, what really happens is that I *introduce the purposiveness* into that figure or representation. I derive no empirical instruction as to the purposiveness from what is given to me externally, and consequently the figure is not one for which I require any special end external to myself and residing in the object. But this reflection presupposes a critical use of reason, and, therefore, it cannot be involved then and there in the judging of the object and its properties. Hence all that this judging immediately suggests to me is a unification of hetero-geneous rules (united even in their intrinsic diversity) in a principle the truth of which I can cognize *a priori*, without requiring for that purpose some special explanation lying beyond my conception, or, to put it more generally, beyond my own *a priori* representation. Now *astonishment* is a shock that the mind receives from a representation and the rule given through it being incompatible with the principles already grounded in the mind, and that accordingly makes one doubt one's own eyes or question one's judgement; but *admiration* is an astonishment that keeps continually recurring despite the disappear-ance of this doubt. Admiration is consequently quite a natural effect of observing the above-mentioned purposiveness in the essence of things (as phenomena), and so far there is really nothing to be said against it. For the agreement of the above form of sensuous intuition, which is called space, with the faculty of concepts, namely under-standing, not only leaves it inexplicable why it is this particular form of agreement and not some other, but, in addition, produces an expansion of the mind in which it suspects, so to speak, the existence of something lying beyond the confines of such sensuous representa-tions, in which, perhaps, although unknown to us, the ultimate source of that accordance could be found. It is true that we have also no need to know this source where we are merely concerned with the formal purposiveness of our *a priori* representations; but even the mere fact that we are compelled to look out in that direction excites an accompanying admiration for the object which obliges us to do so.

The name of *beauty* is customarily given to the properties above referred to—both those of geometrical figures and also those of numbers—on account of a certain purposiveness which they possess for employment in all kinds of ways in the field of knowledge, a 366 purposiveness which the simplicity of their construction would not lead us to expect. Thus people speak of this or that *beautiful* property of the circle, brought to light in this or that manner. But it is not by means of any aesthetic appreciation that we consider such properties purposive. There is no judging apart from a concept, making us take note of a purely *subjective* purposiveness in the free play of our cognitive faculties. On the contrary it is an intellectual judging according to concepts, in which we clearly recognize an objective purposiveness, that is to say, adaptability for all sorts of ends, i.e. an infinite manifold of ends. Such properties should rather be termed a *relative perfection*, than a beauty, of the mathematical figure. We cannot even properly allow the expression *intellectual beauty* at all: since, if we do, the word beauty must lose all definite meaning, and the delight of the intellect all superiority over that of the senses. The term beautiful could be better applied to a *demonstration* of the properties in question; since here understanding, as the faculty of concepts, and imagination, as the faculty of presenting them *a priori*, get a feeling of invigoration (which, with the addition of the precision introduced by reason, is called the elegance of the demonstration): for in this case the delight, although grounded on concepts, is at least subjective, whereas perfection involves an objective delight.

§ 63

The relative, as distinguished from the intrinsic, purposiveness of nature

THERE is only one case in which experience leads our judgement to the concept of an objective and material purposiveness, that is to say, to the concept of an end of nature. This is where the relation in which some cause stands to its effect is under review,[1] and where we are only able to see uniformity in this relation on introducing into the causal principle the idea of the effect and making it the source of the causality and the underlying condition on which the effect is possible. Now this can be done in two ways. We may regard the effect as

---

[1] Pure mathematics can never deal with the real existence of things, but only with their possibility, that is to say, with the possibility of an intuition answering to the concepts of the things. Hence it cannot touch the question of cause and effect, and, consequently, all the purposiveness there observed must always be regarded simply as formal, and never as a natural end.

being, as it stands, an art-product, or we may only regard it as what other possible objects in nature may employ for the purposes of their art. We may, in other words, look upon the effect either as an end, or else as a means which other causes use in the pursuit of ends. The latter purposiveness is termed utility, where it concerns human beings, and advantageousness where it concerns any other creatures. It is a purely relative purposiveness. The former, on the contrary, is an intrinsic purposiveness belonging to the thing itself as a natural object.

For example, rivers in their course carry down earth of all kinds that is good for the growth of plants, and this they deposit sometimes inland, sometimes at their mouths. On some coasts the high-tide carries this alluvial mud inland, or deposits it along the sea-shore. Thus the fruitful soil is increased, especially where man helps to hinder the ebb tide carrying the detritus off again, and the vegetable kingdom takes root in the former abode of fish and crustaceans. Nature has in this way itself produced most accretions to the land, and is still, though slowly, continuing the process. — There now arises the question if this result is to be considered an end on the part of nature, since it is fraught with benefit to man. I say 'to man', for the benefit to the vegetable kingdom cannot be taken into account, inasmuch as against the gain to the land there is, in turn, also as much loss to sea-life.

Or we may give an example of the advantageousness of particular things of nature as means for other forms of life—setting out with the assumption that these latter are ends. Thus there is no healthier soil for pine trees than a sandy soil. Now before the primeval sea withdrew from the land it left numerous sand tracts behind it in our northern regions. The result was that upon this soil, generally so unfavourable for cultivation of any kind, extensive pine forests were able to spring up—forests which we frequently blame our ancestors for having wantonly destroyed. Now it may be asked if this primordial deposit of sand tracts was not an end that nature had in view for the benefit of the possible pine forests that might grow on them. This much is clear: that if the pine forests are assumed to be a natural end, then the sand must be admitted to be an end also—though only a relative end—and one for which, in turn, the primeval sea's beach and its withdrawal were means; for in the series of the mutually subordinated members of a connection of ends each intermediate member must be regarded as an end, though not a final end, to which its proximate cause stands as means. Similarly, if it is granted that cattle, sheep, horses, and the like, were to be in the world, then there had to be grass on the earth, while alkaline plants had to grow in the deserts if camels were to thrive. Again, these and other herbivora had to abound if wolves, tigers, and lions were to exist. Consequently objective purposiveness based on advantageousness is not an immanent objective purposiveness of things: as though the sand, as simple sand, could not be conceived as the effect of its cause, the sea; unless we made this cause look to an end, and treated the effect, namely the sand, as an art-product. It is a purely relative purposiveness, and merely contingent to the thing itself to which it is ascribed; and although among the examples cited, the various kinds of herbs or plants, considered in their own right, are to be judged as organized products of nature, and, therefore, as things of art, yet, in relation to the animals that feed on them, they are to be regarded as mere raw material.

Moreover the freedom of man's causality enables him to adapt natural things to the purposes he has in view. These purposes are frequently foolish—as when he uses the gay-coloured feathers of birds for adorning his clothes, and coloured earths or juices of plants for painting himself. Sometimes they are reasonable, as when he uses the horse for riding, and the ox or, as in Minorca, even the ass or pig for ploughing. But we cannot here assume even a relative end of nature—relative, that is, to such uses. For man's reason informs him how to adapt things to his own arbitrary whims—whims for which he was not himself at all predestined by nature. All we can say is that *if* we assume that it is intended that human beings should live on the earth, then at least, those means without which they could not exist as animals, and even, on however low a plane, as rational animals, must also not be absent. But in that case, those natural things that are indispensable for such existence must equally be regarded as natural ends.

From what has been said we can easily see that the only condition on which extrinsic purposiveness, that is, the advantageousness of a thing for other things, can be looked on as an extrinsic natural end, is that the existence of the thing for which it is proximately or remotely advantageous is itself, and in its own right, an end of nature. But this is a matter that can never be decided by any mere study of

369 nature. Hence it follows that relative purposiveness, although, on a certain supposition, it points to natural purposiveness, does not warrant any absolute teleological judgement.

In cold countries the snow protects the seeds from the frost. It facilitates communication between people—through the use of sleighs. The Laplander finds animals in these regions, namely reindeer, to bring about this communication. The latter find sufficient food to live on in a dry moss which they have to scrape out for themselves from under the snow, yet they submit to being tamed without difficulty, and readily allow themselves to be deprived of the freedom in which they could quite well have supported themselves. For other dwellers in these ice-bound lands the sea is rich in its supply of animals that afford them fuel for heating their huts; in addition to which there are the food and clothing that these animals provide and the wood which the sea itself, as it were, washes in for them as material for their homes. Now here we have a truly marvellous confluence of many relations of nature to an end—the end being the Greenlanders, Laplanders, Samoyedes, Jakutes, and the like. But we do not see why human beings should live in these places at all. To say, therefore, that the *facts* that vapour falls from the atmosphere in the form of snow, that the ocean has its currents that wash into these regions the wood grown in warmer lands, and that great sea creatures containing quantities of oil are to be found there, *are due* to the idea of some benefit to certain poor creatures underlying the cause that brings together all these natural products, would be a very hazardous and arbitrary assertion. For supposing that all this utility on the part of nature were absent, then the capacity of the natural causes to serve this order of existence would not be missed. On the contrary it would seem audacious and inconsiderate on our part even to ask for such a capacity, or demand such an end from nature—for nothing but the greatest incompatibility between human beings could have dispersed them into such inhospitable regions.

§ 64

The distinctive character of things considered as natural ends

A THING is possible only as an end where the causality to which it owes its origin must not be sought in the mechanism of nature, 370 but in a cause whose capacity of acting is determined by concepts. What is required in order that we may perceive that a thing is only possible in this way is that its form is not possible on purely natural laws—that is to say, such laws as we may cognize by means of unaided understanding applied to objects of the senses—but that, on the contrary, even to know it empirically in respect of its cause and effect presupposes concepts of reason. Here we have, as far as any empirical laws of nature go, a *contingency* of the form of the thing in relation to reason. Now reason in every case insists on cognizing the necessity of the form of a natural product, even where it only desires to perceive the conditions involved in its production. In the given form above mentioned, however, it cannot discover this necessity. Hence the contingency is itself a ground for making us look upon the origin of the thing as if, just because of that contingency, it could only be possible through reason. But the causality, so construed, becomes the faculty of acting according to ends—that is to say, a will; and the object, which is represented as only deriving its possibility from such a will, will be represented as possible only as an end.

Suppose a person was in a country that seemed to be uninhabited and was to see a geometrical figure, say a regular hexagon, traced on the sand. As he reflected, and tried to form a concept of the figure, his reason would make him conscious, though perhaps obscurely, that in the production of this concept there was unity of principle. His reason would then forbid him to consider the sand, the neighbouring sea, the winds, or even animals with their footprints, as causes familiar to him, or any other irrational cause, as the ground of the possibility of such a form. For the contingency of coincidence with a concept like this, which is only possible in reason, would appear to him so infinitely great that there might just as well be no law of nature at all in the case. Hence it would seem that the cause of the production of such an effect could not be contained in the mere mechanical operation of nature, but that, on the contrary, a concept of such an object, as a concept that only reason can give and compare the object with, must likewise be what alone contains that causality. On these grounds it would appear to him that this effect was one that might without reservation be regarded as an end, though not as a natural end. In other words he would regard it as a product of *art*— *vestigium hominis video.**

But where a thing is recognized to be a product of nature, then something more is required—unless, perhaps, our very judging involves a contradiction—if, despite its being such a product, we are yet to judge it as an end, and, consequently, as a *natural end*.

As a provisional statement I would say that a thing exists as a natural end *if it is* (though in a double sense) *both cause and effect of itself*. For 371
this involves a kind of causality that we cannot associate with the mere concept of a nature unless we make that nature rest on an underlying end, but which can then, though incomprehensible, be thought without contradiction. Before analysing the component factors of this idea of a natural end, let us first illustrate its meaning by an example.

A tree produces, in the first place, another tree, according to a familiar law of nature. But the tree which it produces is of the same genus. Hence, in its *genus*, it produces itself. In the genus, now as effect, now as cause, continually generated from itself and likewise generating itself, it preserves itself generically.

Secondly, a tree produces itself even as an *individual*. It is true that we only call this kind of effect growth; but growth is here to be understood in a sense that makes it entirely different from any increase according to mechanical laws, and renders it equivalent, though under another name, to generation. The plant first prepares the matter that it assimilates and bestows upon it a specifically distinctive quality which the mechanism of nature outside it cannot supply, and it develops itself by means of a material which, in its composite character, is its own product. For, although in respect of the constituents that it derives from nature outside, it must be regarded as only an educt, yet in the separation and recombination of this raw material we find an original capacity of selection and construction on the part of natural beings of this kind such as infinitely outdistances all the efforts of art, when the latter attempts to reconstitute those products of the vegetable kingdom out of the elements which it obtains through their analysis, or else out of the material which nature supplies for their nourishment.

Thirdly, a part of a tree also generates itself in such a way that the preservation of one part is reciprocally dependent on the preservation of the other parts. An eye taken from the leaf of one tree and grafted onto the branch of another produces in the alien stock a growth of its own species, and similarly a scion grafted on the body of a different tree. Hence even in the case of the same tree each branch or leaf may be regarded as engrafted or inoculated into it, and, consequently, as a tree with a separate existence of its own, and only attaching itself to another and living parasitically on it. At the same 372 time the leaves are certainly products of the tree, but they also maintain it in turn; for repeated defoliation would kill it, and its growth is dependent upon the action of the leaves on the trunk. The way nature comes, in these forms of life, to her own aid in the case of injury, where the lack of one part necessary for the maintenance of the neighbouring parts is made good by the rest; the miscarriages or malformations in growth, where, on account of some chance defect or obstacle, certain parts adopt a completely new formation, so as to preserve the existing growth, and thus produce an anomalous form: these are matters which I only desire to mention here in passing, although they are among the most wonderful properties of the forms of organic life.

§ 65

Things considered as natural ends are organisms

WHERE a thing is a product of nature and yet, so regarded, has to be cognized as possible only as a natural end, it must, from its character as set out in the preceding section, stand to itself reciprocally in the relation of cause and effect. This is, however, a somewhat inexact and indeterminate expression that needs derivation from a determinate concept.

In so far as the causal connexion is thought merely by means of understanding it is a nexus constituting a series, namely of causes and effects, that is invariably progressive. The things that as effects presuppose others as their causes cannot themselves in turn be also causes of the latter. This causal connexion is termed that of efficient causes (*nexus effectivus*). On the other hand, however, we are also able to think a causal connexion according to a rational concept, that of ends, which, if regarded as a series, would involve regressive as well as progressive dependency. It would be one in which the thing that for the moment is designated effect deserves none the less, if we take the series regressively, to be called the cause of the thing of which it was said to be the effect. In the domain of practical matters, namely in art, we readily find examples of a nexus of this kind. Thus a house is certainly the cause of the money that is received as rent, but yet, conversely, the representation of this possible income was the cause of the building of the house. A causal nexus of this kind is termed that of final causes (*nexus finalis*). The former might, perhaps, more appropriately be called the nexus of real, and the latter the nexus of ideal causes, because with this use of terms it would be understood at once that there cannot be more than these two kinds of causality.

Now the *first* requisite of a thing, considered as a natural end, is that its parts, both as to their existence and form, are only possible by their relation to the whole. For the thing is itself an end, and is, therefore, grasped under a concept or an idea that must determine *a priori* all that is to be contained in it. But so far as the possibility of a thing is only thought in this way, it is simply a work of art. It is the product, in other words, of an intelligent cause, distinct from the matter, or parts, of the thing, and of one whose causality, in bringing together and combining the parts, is determined by its idea of a whole made possible through that idea, and consequently, not by external nature.

But if a thing is a product of nature, and in this character is notwithstanding to contain intrinsically and in its inner possibility a relation to ends, in other words, is to be possible only as a natural end and independently of the causality of the concepts of external rational agents, then this *second* requisite is involved, namely, that the parts of the thing combine of themselves into the unity of a whole by being reciprocally cause and effect of their form. For this is the only way in which it is possible that the idea of the whole may conversely, or reciprocally, determine in its turn the form and combination of all the parts, not as cause—for that would make it an art-product—but as the ground for the cognition of the systematic unity of the form and combination of all the manifold contained in the given matter for the person judging it.

What we require, therefore, in the case of a body which in its intrinsic nature and inner possibility has to be judged as a natural end, is as follows. Its parts must in their collective unity reciprocally produce one another alike as to form and combination, and thus by their own causality produce a whole, the concept of which, con-versely,—in a being possessing the causality according to concepts that is adequate for such a product—could in turn be the cause of the whole according to a principle, so that, consequently, the nexus of *efficient causes* might be no less judged as an *effect brought about by final* causes.

In such a natural product as this every part is thought as *owing* its presence to the *agency* of all the remaining parts, and also as existing

373

374 *for the sake of the others* and of the whole, that is as an instrument, or organ. But this is not enough—for it might be an instrument of art, and thus have no more than its general possibility referred to an end. On the contrary the part must be an organ *producing* the other parts—each, consequently, reciprocally producing the others. No instrument of art can answer to this description, but only the instrument of that nature from whose resources the materials of every instrument are drawn—even the materials for instruments of art. Only under these conditions and upon these terms can such a product be an *organized* and *self-organized being*, and, as such, be called a *natural end*.

In a watch one part is the instrument by which the movement of the others is effected, but one wheel is not the efficient cause of the production of the other. One part is certainly present for the sake of another, but it does not owe its presence to the agency of that other. For this reason, also, the producing cause of the watch and its form is not contained in the nature of this material, but lies outside the watch in a being that can act according to ideas of a whole which its causality makes possible. Hence one wheel in the watch does not produce the other, and, still less, does one watch produce other watches, by utilizing, or organizing, foreign material; hence it does not of itself replace parts of which it has been deprived, nor, if these are absent in the original construction, does it make good the deficiency by the addition of new parts; nor does it, so to speak, repair its own defects. But these are all things which we are justified in expecting from organized nature.—An organized being is, therefore, not a mere machine. For a machine has solely *motive power*, whereas an organized being possesses inherent *formative* power, and such, moreover, as it can impart to material devoid of it—material which it organizes. This, therefore, is a self-propagating formative power, which cannot be explained by the capacity of movement alone, that is to say, by mechanism.

We do not say half enough of nature and her capacity in organized products when we speak of this capacity as being the *analogue of art*. For what that suggests to our minds is an artist—a rational being—working from without. But nature, on the contrary, organizes itself, and does so in each species of its organized products—following a single pattern, certainly, as to general features, but nevertheless admitting deviations calculated to secure self-preservation under particular circumstances. We might perhaps come nearer to the description of this unfathomable property if we were to call it an *analogue of life*. But then either we should have to endow matter as mere matter with a property (hylozoism) that contradicts its essential nature; or else we should have to associate with it a foreign principle *standing in community* with it (a soul). But, if such a product is to be a natural product, then we have to adopt one or other of two courses in order to bring in a soul. Either we must presuppose organized matter as the instrument of such a soul, which makes organized matter no whit more intelligible, or else we must make the soul the artificer of this structure, in which case we must exclude the product from (corporeal) nature. Strictly speaking, therefore, the organization of nature has nothing analogous to any causality known to us.[2] Natural beauty may justly be termed the analogue of art, for it is only ascribed to the objects in respect of reflection upon the *outer* intuition of them and, therefore, only on account of their external form. But *intrinsic natural perfection*, as possessed by things that are only possible as *natural ends*, and that are therefore called organisms, is unthinkable and inexplicable on any analogy to any known physical, or natural, agency, not even excepting—since we ourselves are part of nature in the widest sense—the suggestion of any strictly apt analogy to human art.

The concept of a thing as intrinsically a natural end is, therefore, not a constitutive concept either of understanding or of reason, but yet it may be used by reflective judgement as a regulative concept for guiding our investigation of objects of this kind by a remote analogy with our own causality according to ends generally, and as a basis of reflection upon their supreme source. But in the latter connexion it cannot be used to promote our knowledge either of nature or of such original source of those objects, but must on the contrary be confined to the service of just the same practical faculty of reason in analogy with which we considered the cause of the purposiveness in question.

[2] We may, on the other hand, make use of an analogy to the above mentioned immediate physical ends to throw light on a certain union, which, however, is to be found more often in idea than in fact. Thus in the case of a complete transformation, recently undertaken, of a great people* into a state, the word *organization* has frequently, and with much propriety, been used for the constitution of the legal authorities and even of the entire body politic. For in a whole of this kind certainly no member should be a mere means, but should also be an end, and, seeing that he contributes to the possibility of the entire body, should have his position and function in turn defined by the idea of the whole.

Organisms are, therefore, the only beings in nature that, considered in their individual existence and apart from any relation to other
376 things, cannot be thought possible except as ends of nature. It is
they, then, that first afford objective reality to the concept of an *end*
that is an end *of nature* and not a practical end. Thus they supply natural science with the basis for a teleology, or, in other words, a way
of judging its objects on a special principle that it would otherwise be
absolutely unjustifiable to introduce into that science—seeing that
we are quite unable to perceive *a priori* the possibility of such a kind
of causality.

§ 66

*The principle on which the intrinsic purposiveness
in organisms is judged*

THIS principle, the statement of which serves to define what is meant
by organisms, is as follows: *an organized natural product is one in
which every part is reciprocally both end and means.* In such a product
nothing is in vain, without an end, or to be ascribed to a blind mechanism of nature.

It is true that the occasion for adopting this principle must be
derived from experience—from such experience, namely, as is
methodically pursued and is called observation. But owing to the
universality and necessity which that principle predicates of such
purposiveness, it cannot rest merely on empirical grounds, but must
have some underlying *a priori* principle. This principle, however,
may be one that is merely regulative, and it may be that the ends in
question only reside in the idea of the person judging and not in any
efficient cause whatever. Hence the above named principle may be
called a *maxim* for judging the intrinsic purposiveness of organisms.

It is common knowledge that scientists who dissect plants and
animals, seeking to investigate their structure and to see into the
reasons why and the end for which they are provided with such and
such parts, why the parts have such and such a position and interconnexion, and why the internal form is precisely what it is, adopt the
above maxim as absolutely necessary. So they say that nothing in
such forms of life is in *vain*, and they put the maxim on the same
footing of validity as the fundamental principle of all natural science,
that *nothing* happens *by chance*. They are, in fact, quite as unable to

free themselves from this teleological principle as from that of general physical science. For just as the abandonment of the latter would leave them without any experience at all, so the abandonment of the former would leave them with no clue to assist their observation of a type of natural things that we have already come to think under the concept of natural ends.

Indeed this concept leads reason into an order of things entirely different from that of a mere mechanism of nature, which *mere mechanism* no longer proves adequate in this domain. An idea must, it is thought, underlie the possibility of the natural product. But this idea is an absolute unity of the representation, whereas the material is a plurality of things that of itself can afford no definite unity of composition. Hence, if that unity of the idea is actually to serve as the *a priori* determining ground of a natural law of the causality of such a form of the composite, the end of nature must be made to extend to *everything* contained in its product. For if once we lift such an effect out of the sphere of the blind mechanism of nature and relate it *as a whole* to a supersensible ground of determination, we must then estimate it out and out on this principle. We have no reason for assuming the form of such a thing to be still partly dependent on blind mechanism, for with such confusion of heterogeneous principles every reliable rule for judging things would disappear. 377

It is no doubt the case that in an animal body, for example, many parts might be explained as accretions on simple mechanical laws (as skin, bone, hair). Yet the cause that accumulates the appropriate material, modifies and fashions it, and deposits it in its proper place, must always be judged teleologically. Hence, everything in the body must be regarded as organized, and everything, also, in a certain relation to the thing is itself in turn an organ.

§ 67
The principle on which nature in general is judged teleologically as a system of ends

WE have said above that the *extrinsic* purposiveness of natural things affords no adequate justification for taking them as ends of nature to explain the reason of their existence, or for treating their contingently purposive effects as ideally the grounds of their existence on the principle of final causes. Thus we are not entitled to consider

rivers as natural ends then and there, because they facilitate communication amongst peoples in inland countries, or *mountains*, because
they contain the sources of the rivers and hold stores of snow for the
378   maintenance of their flow in dry seasons, or, similarly, the *slope* of
the land, that carries down these waters and leaves the country dry.
For, although this configuration of the earth's surface is very necessary for the origination and sustenance of the vegetable and animal
kingdoms, yet intrinsically it contains nothing the possibility of
which should make us feel obliged to invoke causality according
to ends. The same applies to plants utilized or enjoyed by man; or
to animals, as the camel, the ox, the horse, dog, etc., which are so vari-
ously employed, sometimes as servants of man, sometimes as food
for him to live on, and mostly found quite indispensable. The external relationship of things that we have no reason to regard as ends in
their own right can only be hypothetically judged as purposive.

There is an essential distinction between judging a thing as a
natural end in virtue of its intrinsic form and regarding the real
existence of this thing as an end of nature. To maintain the latter
view we require, not merely the concept of a possible end, but a
knowledge of the final end (*scopus*) of nature. This involves our referring nature to something supersensible, a reference that far transcends any teleological knowledge we have of nature; for, to find the
end of the real existence of nature itself, we must look beyond nature.
That the origin of a simple blade of grass is only possible on the rule
of ends is, to our human faculty of judging, sufficiently proved by its
internal form. But let us lay aside this consideration and look only to
the use to which the thing is put by other natural beings—which
means that we abandon the study of the internal organization and
look only to external purposive relations to ends. We see, then, that
the grass is required as a means of existence by cattle, and cattle,
similarly, by man. But we do not see why after all it should be necessary that human beings should in fact exist (a question that might
not be so easy to answer if we were to consider the New Hollanders
or Fuegians*). We do not then arrive in this way at any categorical
end. On the contrary all such purposive relation is made to rest on a
condition that must be displaced to an ever-retreating horizon. This
condition is the unconditional condition—the existence of a thing as
a final end—which, as such, lies entirely outside the study of the
world on physico-teleological lines. But, then, such a thing is not a

natural end either, since it (or its entire genus) is not to be regarded as a product of nature.

Hence it is only in so far as matter is organized that it necessarily involves the concept of it as a natural end, because here it possesses a form that is at once specific and a product of nature. But, brought so far, this concept necessarily leads us to the idea of aggregate nature as a system following the rule of ends, to which idea, again, the whole mechanism of nature has to be subordinated on principles of reason— at least for the purpose of testing phenomenal nature by this idea. The principle of reason is one which it is competent for reason to use as a merely subjective principle, that is as a maxim: everything in the world is good for something or other; nothing in it is in vain; we are entitled, indeed encouraged, by the example that nature affords us in its organic products, to expect nothing from it and its laws but what is purposive when things are viewed as a whole.

It is evident that this is a principle to be applied not by the deter- mining, but only by the reflective, power of judgement, that it is regulative and not constitutive, and that all that we obtain from it is a clue to guide us in the study of natural things. These things it leads us to consider in relation to a ground of determination already given, and in the light of a new uniformity, and it helps us to extend physical science according to another principle, that, namely, of final causes, yet without interfering with the principle of the mechanism of physical causality. Furthermore, this principle is altogether silent on the point of whether anything judged according to it is, or is not, an end of nature *by design*: whether, that is, the grass exists for the sake of the ox or the sheep, and whether these and the other things of nature exist for the sake of man. We do well to consider even things that are unpleas- ant to us, and that in particular connexions are counter-purposive, from this point of view also. Thus, for example, one might say that the vermin which plague human beings in their clothes, hair, or beds, may, by a wise provision of nature, be an incitement towards clean- liness, which is of itself an important means for preserving health. Or the mosquitoes and other stinging insects that make the wilds of America so trying for the savages, may be so many goads to urge these primitive people to drain the marshes and bring light into the dense forests that shut out the air, and, by so doing, as well as by the tillage of the soil, to render their abodes more sanitary. Even what appears to man to be contrary to nature in his own internal organization

379

affords, when treated on these lines, an interesting, and sometimes even instructive, outlook into a teleological order of things, to which mere unaided study from a physical point of view apart from such a principle would not lead us. Some people say that people or animals that have a tapeworm receive it as a sort of compensation to make good some deficiency in their vital organs. Now, just in the same way, I would ask if dreams (from which our sleep is never free, although we rarely remember what we have dreamed), may not be a regulation of nature adapted to ends. For when all the muscular forces of the body are relaxed dreams serve the purpose of internally stimulating the vital organs by means of the imagination and the great activity which it exerts (an activity that in this state generally give rise to an affect). This seems to be why imagination is usually more actively at work in the sleep of those who have gone to bed at night with an overfilled stomach, just when this stimulation is most needed. Hence, I would suggest that without this internal stimulating force and fatiguing unrest that makes us complain of our dreams, which in fact, however, are probably curative, sleep, even in a sound state of health, would amount to a complete extinction of life.

Once the teleological judging of nature, supported by the natural ends actually presented to us in organic beings, has entitled us to form the idea of a great system of the ends of nature, we may regard even natural beauty from this point of view, such beauty being an accordance of nature with the free play of our cognitive faculties as engaged in grasping and judging its appearance. For then we may look upon it as an objective purposiveness of nature in its entirety as a system of which man is a member. We may regard it as a favour[3] that nature has extended to us, that besides giving us what is useful it has dispensed beauty and charms in such abundance, and for this we may love it, just as we view it with respect because of its immensity, and feel ourselves ennobled by such contemplation—just as if nature had erected and decorated its splendid stage with this precise purpose in its mind.

[3] In the Part on aesthetic judgement the statement was made: *we could regard nature with favour* because we take a delight in its form that is altogether free (disinterested). For in this judgement of mere taste no account is taken of any end for which these natural beauties exist: whether to excite pleasure in us, or irrespective of us as ends. But in a teleological judgement we pay attention to this relation; and so we can *regard it as a favour of nature*, that it has been disposed to promote our culture by exhibiting so many beautiful forms.

The general drift of the present section is simply this: once we have discovered a capacity in nature for bringing forth products that can only be thought by us according to the concept of final causes, we advance a step farther. Even products which do not (either as to 381 themselves or the relation, however purposive, in which they stand) make it necessarily incumbent upon us to go beyond the mechanism of blind efficient causes and seek out some other principle on which they are possible, may nevertheless be justly judged as forming part of a system of ends. For the idea from which we started is one which, when we consider its foundation, already leads beyond the world of the senses, and then the unity of the supersensible principle must be treated, not as valid merely for certain species of natural beings, but as similarly valid for the whole of nature as a system.

§ 68

The principle of teleology considered as an inherent principle of natural science

THE principles of a science may be inherent in that science itself, and are then termed indigenous (*principia domestica*). Or they may rest on concepts that can only be encountered outside that science, and are *foreign* principles (*peregrina*). Sciences containing the latter principles rest their doctrines on auxiliary propositions (*lemmata*), that is, they obtain some concept or other, and with this concept some basis for a regular procedure, that is borrowed from another science.

Every science is a system in its own right; and it is not sufficient that in it we construct according to principles, and so proceed technically, but we must also set to work architectonically with it as a separate and independent building. We must treat it as a self-subsisting whole, and not as a wing or section of another building—although we may subsequently make a passage to or fro from one part to another.

Hence if we supplement natural science by introducing the concept of God into its context for the purpose of rendering the purposiveness of nature explicable, and if, having done so, we turn round and use this purposiveness in order to prove that there is a God, then both natural science and theology are deprived of all intrinsic substance. This deceptive crossing and re-crossing from one side to the other involves both in uncertainty, because their boundaries are thus allowed to overlap.

The expression, an end of nature, is of itself sufficient to obviate this confusion and prevent our confounding natural science or the occasion it affords for a *teleological* judging of its objects with the contemplation of God, and hence with a *theological* demonstration. It is not to be regarded as a matter of no consequence that the above expression should be confused with that of a divine end in the ordering of nature, or that the latter should even be passed off as the more appropriate and the one more becoming to a pious soul, on the ground that, say what we will, it must eventually come back to our deriving these purposive forms in nature from a wise Author of the universe. On the contrary we must scrupulously and modestly restrict ourselves to the term that expresses just as much as we know, and no more—namely, an end of nature. For before we arrive at the question of the cause of nature itself, we find in nature and in the course of its generative processes examples of such products produced in nature according to known empirical laws. It is according to these laws that natural science must judge its objects, and, consequently, it must seek within itself for this causality according to the rule of ends. Therefore this science must not overleap its bounds for the purpose of claiming for itself, as an indigenous principle, one to whose concept no experience can be adequate, and upon which we are not authorized to venture until after natural science has been brought to completion.

Natural qualities that are demonstrable *a priori*, and so reveal their possibility on universal principles without any aid from experience, may involve a technical purposiveness. Yet, being absolutely necessary, they cannot be credited to natural teleology at all. Natural teleology forms part of physics, and is a method applicable to the solution of the problems of physics. Arithmetical and geometrical analogies, also universal mechanical laws, however strange and worthy of our admiration the union in a single principle of a variety of rules apparently quite disconnected may seem, have no claim on that account to rank as teleological grounds of explanation in physics. They may deserve to be brought under review in the universal theory of the purposiveness of the things of nature in general, but, if so, this is a theory that would have to be assigned to another science, namely metaphysics. It would not form an inherent principle of natural science: whereas in the case of the empirical laws of the natural ends which organisms present it is not only permissible, but even unavoidable, to use the teleological *mode of judging* as a principle of natural science in respect of a peculiar class of its objects.

For the purpose of keeping strictly within its own bounds physics entirely ignores the question whether natural ends are ends *designedly* or *undesignedly*. To deal with that question would be to meddle in the 383 affairs of others—namely, in what is the business of metaphysics. Suffice it that there are objects whose one and only *explanation* is on natural laws that we are unable to conceive otherwise than by adopting the idea of ends as principle, objects which, in their intrinsic form, and with nothing more in view than their internal relations, are *cognizable* in this way alone. It is true that in teleology we speak of nature as if its purposiveness were a thing of design. But to avoid all suspicion of presuming in the slightest to mix up with our sources of knowledge something that has no place in physics at all, namely a supernatural cause, we refer to design in such a way that, in the same breath, we attribute this design to nature, that is to matter. Here no room is left for misinterpretation, since, obviously, no one would ascribe design, in the proper sense of the term, to a lifeless material. Hence our real intention is to indicate that the word design, as here used, only signifies a principle of reflective, and not of determining, judgement, and consequently is not meant to introduce any special ground of causality, but only to assist the employment of reason by supplementing investigation on mechanical laws by the addition of another method of investigation, so as to make up for the inadequacy of the former even as a method of empirical research that has for its object all particular laws of nature. Therefore, when teleology is applied to physics, we speak with perfect justice of the wisdom, the economy, the forethought, the beneficence of nature. But in so doing we do not convert nature into an intelligent being, for that would be absurd; but neither do we dare to think of placing another being, one that is intelligent, above nature as its architect, for that would be presumptuous.[4] On the contrary our only intention is to designate in this way a kind of natural causality on an analogy with our own

[4] The German word *vermessen* (presumptuous) is a good word* and full of meaning. A judgement in which we forget to take stock of the extent of our powers of understanding may sometimes sound very modest, while yet it presumes a great deal, and is really very presumptuous. Of this type are the majority of those by which we purport to exalt divine wisdom by furnishing the works of creation and preservation with designs that are really intended to do honour to the individual wisdom of our own subtle intellects.

causality in the technical employment of reason, for the purpose of keeping in view the rule upon which certain natural products are to be investigated.

384 But why, then, is it that teleology does not usually form a special part of theoretical natural science, but is relegated to theology by way of a propaedeutic or transition? This is done in order to keep the study of the mechanical aspect of nature in close connexion to what we are able so to subject to our observation or experiment that we could ourselves produce it like nature, or at least produce it according to similar laws. For we have complete insight only into what we can make and accomplish according to our concepts. But to effect by means of art a presentation similar to organization, as an intrinsic end of nature, infinitely surpasses all our powers. And as for such extrinsic arrangements of nature as are considered purposive (e.g. winds, rains, etc.), physics certainly studies their mechanism, but it is quite unable to exhibit their relation to ends so far as this relation purports to be a condition necessarily attaching to a cause. For this necessity in the nexus does not touch the constitution of things, but turns wholly on the combination of our concepts.

SECOND DIVISION
Dialectic of Teleological Judgement

---

§ 69
What is an antinomy of judgement?

DETERMINING judgement does not possess any principles of its own
upon which *concepts of objects* are grounded. It is not autonomous; for
it merely *subsumes* under given laws, or concepts, as principles. Just
for this reason it is not exposed to any danger from inherent antinomy and does not run the risk of a conflict of its principles. Thus the
transcendental power of judgement, which was shown to contain the
conditions of subsumption under categories, was not independently
nomothetic. It only specified the conditions of sensuous intuition upon
which reality, that is, application, can be ascribed to a given concept
as a law of the understanding. In the discharge of this office it could
never fall into a state of internal disunion, at least in the matter of
principles.

But the *reflective* power of judgement has to subsume under a law
that is not yet given. It has, therefore, in fact only a principle of
reflection upon objects for which we are objectively at a complete loss
for a law, or concept of the object, sufficient to serve as a principle
covering the particular cases as they come before us. Now as there is
no permissible employment of the cognitive faculties apart from
principles, reflective judgement must in such cases be a principle to
itself. As this principle is not objective and is unable to introduce any
basis of cognition of the object sufficient for the required purpose
of subsumption, it must serve as a mere subjective principle for the
employment of our cognitive faculties in a purposive manner, namely,
for reflecting upon objects of a particular kind. Reflective judgement
has, therefore, its maxims applicable to such cases—maxims that are
in fact necessary for obtaining a knowledge of the natural laws to be
found in experience, and which are directed to assist us in arriving at
concepts, be these even concepts of reason, wherever such concepts
are absolutely required for the mere purpose of coming to know nature
in its empirical laws.—Between these necessary maxims of reflective

judgement a conflict may arise, and consequently an antinomy. This affords the basis of a dialectic; and if each of the mutually conflicting maxims has its foundation in the nature of our cognitive faculties, this dialectic may be called a natural dialectic, and it constitutes an unavoidable illusion which it is the duty of critical philosophy to expose and to resolve lest it should deceive us.

§ 70

Exposition of this Antinomy

IN dealing with nature as the sum of objects of outer sense, reason is able to rely upon laws some of which are prescribed by understanding itself *a priori* to nature, while others are capable of indefinite extension by means of the empirical determinations occurring in experience. For the application of the laws prescribed *a priori* by understanding, that is, of the *universal* laws of material nature in general, judgement does not need any special principle of reflection; for there it is determining, an objective principle being furnished to it by understanding. But in respect of the particular laws with which we can become acquainted through experience alone, there is such a wide scope for diversity and heterogeneity that judgement must be a principle to itself, even for the mere purpose of searching for a law and seeking one out in the phenomena of nature. For it needs such a principle as a guiding thread, if it is even to hope for a consistent body of empirical knowledge based on a thorough-going lawfulness of nature—that is a unity of nature in its empirical laws. Now from the fact of this contingent unity of particular laws it may come to pass that judgement acts upon two maxims in its reflection, one of which it receives *a priori* from mere understanding, but the other of which is prompted by particular experiences that bring reason into play to conduct a judging

387 of corporeal nature and its laws according to a particular principle. What happens then is that these two different maxims seem to all appearance incompatible with one another, and a dialectic arises that throws judgement into confusion as to the principle of its reflection.

The first maxim of such reflection is the *thesis*: All production of material things and their forms must be judged as possible on mere mechanical laws.

The second maxim is the *antithesis*: Some products of material nature cannot be judged as possible on mere mechanical laws (that is, for judging them quite a different law of causality is required, namely, that of final causes).

If now these regulative principles of investigation were converted into constitutive principles of the possibility of the objects themselves, they would read thus:

Thesis: All production of material things is possible on mere mechanical laws.

Antithesis: Some production of such things is not possible on mere mechanical laws.

In this latter form, as objective principles for determining judgement, they would contradict one another, so that one of the pair would necessarily be false. But that would then be an antinomy certainly, though not one of judgement, but rather a conflict in the legislation of reason. But reason is unable to prove either one or the other of these principles: seeing that we can have no *a priori* determining principle of the possibility of things on mere empirical laws of nature.

On the other hand, looking to the maxims of reflective judgement as first set out, we see that they do not in fact contain any contradiction at all. For if I say: I must *judge* the possibility of all events in material nature, and, consequently, also all forms considered as its products, on mere mechanical laws, I do not thereby assert that they *are solely possible in this way*, that is, to the exclusion of every other kind of causality. On the contrary this assertion is only intended to indicate that I *ought* at all times to *reflect* upon these things *according to the principle* of the simple mechanism of nature, and, consequently, push my investigation with it as far as I can, because unless I make it the basis of research there can be no knowledge of nature in the true sense of the term at all. Now this does not stand in the way of the second maxim when a proper occasion for its employment presents itself—that is to say, in the case of some natural forms (and, at their instance, in the case of nature as a whole), we may, in our reflection 388 upon them, follow the trail of a principle which is radically different from explanation by the mechanism of nature, namely the principle of final causes. For reflection according to the first maxim is not in this way superseded. On the contrary we are directed to pursue it as far as we can. Further it is not asserted that those forms were not possible on the mechanism of nature. It is only maintained that *human reason*, adhering to this maxim and proceeding on these lines, could never discover any basis for what constitutes the specific character of a natural end, whatever additions it might make in this way to its knowledge of natural laws. This leaves it an open question, whether in the unknown inner ground of nature itself the physico-mechanical and the purposive connections present in the same things may not cohere in a single principle; it being only our reason that is not in a position to unite them in such a principle, so that our judgement, consequently, remains *reflective*, not determining, that is, acts on a subjective ground, and not according to an objective principle of the possibility of things in their inherent nature, and, accordingly, is compelled to conceive a different principle from that of the mechanism of nature as a ground of the possibility of certain forms in nature.

§ 71

Introduction to the solution of the above antinomy

WE are wholly unable to prove the impossibility of the production of organized natural products in accordance with the simple mechanism of nature. For we cannot see into the first and inner ground of the infinite multiplicity of the particular laws of nature, which, being only known empirically, are for us contingent, and so we are absolutely incapable of reaching the intrinsic and all-sufficient principle of the possibility of a nature—a principle which lies in the supersensible. But may not the productive capacity of nature be just as adequate for what we judge to be formed or connected according to the idea of ends as it is for what we believe merely calls for consideration of nature as a mechanism? Or may it be that in fact things are genuine natural ends (as we must necessarily judge them to be), and as such founded upon an original causality of a completely different kind, which cannot be contained 389 in material nature or its intelligible substrate, namely, the causality of an architectonic understanding? What has been said shows that these are questions upon which our reason, very narrowly restricted in respect of the concept of causality if this concept has to be specified *a priori*, can give absolutely no information.—But that, relatively to our cognitive faculties, the mere mechanism of nature is also unable to furnish any explanation of the production of organisms, is a matter just as indubitably certain. *For reflective judgement*, therefore, this is a perfectly sound principle: that for the clearly manifest nexus of things according to final causes, we must think a causality distinct from mechanism, namely a world-cause acting according to ends, that is, an intelligent cause—however rash and undemonstrable a principle this might be *for determining judgement*. In the first case the principle is a simple maxim of judgement. The concept of causality which it involves is a mere idea to which we in no way undertake to concede reality, but only make use of it to guide a reflection that still leaves the door open for any available mechanical explanation, and that never strays from the sensible world. In the second case the principle would be an objective principle. Reason would prescribe it and judgement would have to be subject to it and determine itself accordingly. But in that case reflection wanders from the world of the senses into transcendent regions, and possibly gets led astray.

All semblance of an antinomy between the maxims of the strictly physical, or mechanical, mode of explanation and the teleological, or technical, rests, therefore, on our confusing a principle of reflective with one of determining judgement. The *autonomy* of the former, which is valid merely subjectively for the use of our reason in respect of particular empirical laws, is mistaken for the *heteronomy* of the second, which has to conform to the laws, either universal or particular, given by the understanding.

§ 72

The various kinds of systems dealing with the purposiveness of nature

No one has ever yet questioned the correctness of the principle that when judging certain things in nature, namely organisms and their possibility, we must look to the concept of final causes. Such a principle is admittedly necessary even where we require no more than a *guiding-thread* for the purpose of becoming acquainted with the character of these things by means of observation, without presuming to investigate their first origin. Hence the question can only be, whether this principle is merely subjectively valid, that is, a mere maxim of judgement, or is an objective principle of nature. On the latter alternative there would belong to nature another type of causality beyond its mechanism and its simple dynamical laws, namely, the causality of final causes, under which natural causes (dynamical forces) would stand only as intermediate causes.

Now this speculative question or problem might well be left without any answer or solution. For, if we content ourselves with speculation

390

within the bounds of the mere knowledge of nature, the above maxims are ample for its study as far as human powers extend, and for probing its deepest secrets. So it must be that reason harbours some presentiment, or that nature, so to speak, gives us a hint. With the help of this concept of final causes, might we not be able to take a step, we are prompted to think, beyond and above nature, and connect it to the supreme point in the series of causes? Why not relinquish the investigation of nature (although we have not advanced so very far with it) or, at least, lay it temporarily aside, and try first to discover whither that stranger in natural science, the concept of natural ends, would lead us?

Now at this point, certainly, the undisputed maxim above mentioned would inevitably introduce a problem that opens up a wide field for controversy. For it may be alleged that the nexus of natural ends *proves* the existence of a special kind of causality for nature. Or it may be contended that this nexus, considered in its true nature and on objective principles, is, on the contrary, identical with the mechanism of nature, or rests on one and the same ground, though in the case of many natural products this ground often lies too deeply buried for our investigation. Hence, as is contended, we have recourse to a subjective principle, namely art, or causality according to ideas, in order to introduce it, on an analogy, as the basis of nature—an expedient that in fact proves successful in many cases, in some certainly seems to fail, but in no case entitles us to introduce into natural science a kind of agency different from causality on mere mechanical laws of nature.—Now, in giving to the procedure, or causal operation of nature, the name of technic, on account of the suggestion of an end which we find in its products, we propose to divide this technic into such as is *designed* (*technica intentionalis*) and such as is *undesigned* (*technica naturalis*). The former is intended to convey that nature's capacity for production by final causes must be considered a special kind of causality; the latter that this capacity is at bottom identical with natural mechanism, and that the contingent coincidence with our concepts of art and their rules is a mere subjective condition of our judging this capacity, and is thus erroneously interpreted as a special kind of natural generation.

To speak now of the systems that offer an explanation of nature on the point of final causes, one cannot fail to perceive that they all, without exception, controvert one another dogmatically. In other words they conflict concerning objective principles of the possibility of things, whether this possibility be one due to causes acting designedly or merely undesignedly. They do not contest the subjective maxim of mere judgement upon the cause of the purposive products in question. In the latter case *disparate* principles might very well be reconciled, whereas, in *the former, contradictorily opposed* principles annul one another and are mutually inconsistent.

The systems in respect of the technic of nature, that is, of nature's power of production on the rule of ends, are of two kinds: that of the *idealism* and that of the *realism* of natural ends. The former maintains that all purposiveness on the part of nature is *undesigned*; the latter, that some purposiveness, namely that of organized beings, is *designed*. From the latter the hypothetical consequence may be inferred, that the technic of nature is also designed in what concerns all its other products relatively to nature in its entirety, that is, is an end.

1. The *idealism* of purposiveness (I am here all along referring to objective purposiveness) is either that of the *accidentality* or *fatality* of the determination of nature in the purposive form of its products. The former principle fixes on the relation of matter to the physical basis of its form, namely dynamical laws; the latter on its relation to the hyperphysical basis of matter and nature as a whole. The system of *accidentality*, which is attributed to Epicurus or Democritus,* is, in its literal interpretation, so manifestly absurd that it need not detain us. On the other hand, the system of *fatality*, of which Spinoza is the accredited author,* although it is to all appearances much older, rests upon something supersensible, into which our insight, accordingly, is unable to penetrate. It is not so easy to refute: the reason being that its conception of the original being is quite unintelligible. But this much is clear, that on this system the purposive connexion in the world must be regarded as undesigned. For, while it is derived from an original being, it is not derived from its intelligence, and consequently not from any design on its part, but from the necessity of the nature of this being and the unity of the world flowing from that nature. Hence it is clear, too, that the fatalism of purposiveness is also an idealism of purposiveness.

2. The *realism* of the purposiveness of nature is also either physical or hyperphysical. The *former* bases natural ends on the analogue of a faculty acting designedly, that is, on the *life of matter*—this life being either inherent in it or else bestowed upon it by an inner animating

principle or world-soul. This is called *hylozoism.** The *latter* derives such ends from the original source of the universe. This source it regards as an intelligent Being producing with design—or essentially and fundamentally living. It is *theism.*[5]

§ 73
None of the above systems does what it professes to do

WHAT is the aim and object of all the above systems? It is to explain our teleological judgements about nature. To do so they adopt one or other of two courses. One side denies their truth, and consequently describes them as an idealism of nature (represented as art). The other side recognizes their truth, and promises to demonstrate the possibility of a nature according to the idea of final causes.

1. The systems that contend for the idealism of the final causes in nature fall into two classes. One class does certainly concede to the principle of these causes a causality according to dynamical laws (to which causality the natural things owe their purposive existence). But it denies to it *intentionality*—that is, it denies that this causality is determined designedly to this its purposive production, or, in other words, that an end is the cause. This is the explanation adopted by Epicurus. It completely denies and abolishes the distinction between a technic of nature and its mere mechanism. Blind chance is accepted as the explanation, not only of the agreement of the generated products with our concepts, and, consequently, of the technic of nature, but even of the determination of the causes of this development on dynamical laws, and, consequently, of its mechanism. Hence nothing is explained, not even the illusion in our teleological judgements, so that the alleged idealism in them is left altogether unsubstantiated.

Spinoza, as the representative of the other class, seeks to release us from any inquiry into the ground of the possibility of ends of nature, and to deprive this idea of all reality, by refusing to allow that such

---

[5] We see from this how, as in most speculative matters of pure reason, the schools of philosophy have, in the way of dogmatic assertions, usually attempted every possible solution of the problem before them. Thus in the case of the purposiveness of nature, at one time a *lifeless matter*, or again a *lifeless God*, at another, a *living matter*, or else a *living God*, have been tried. Nothing is left to us except, if needs be, to break away from all these *objective assertions*, and weigh our judgement *critically* in its mere relation to our cognitive faculties. By so doing we may procure for their principle a validity which, if not dogmatic, is yet that of a maxim, and ample for the reliable employment of our reason.

ends are to be regarded as products at all. They are, rather, accidents inhering in an original being. This being, he says, is the substrate of the natural things, and, as such, he does not ascribe to it causality in respect of them, but simply subsistence. Thanks, then, to the unconditional necessity both of this being and of all the things of nature, as its inherent accidents, he assures to the natural forms, it is true, that unity of ground necessary for all purposiveness, but he does so at the expense of their contingency, apart from which no *unity of end* is thinkable. In eliminating this unity he eliminates all *trace of design*, and leaves the original ground of the things of nature divested of all intelligence.

But Spinozism does not effect what it intends. It intends to furnish an explanation of the purposive connection of natural things, which it does not deny, and it refers us simply to the unity of the subject in which they all inhere. But suppose we grant it this kind of existence for the beings of the world, such ontological unity is not then and there a *unity of end* and does not make it in any way intelligible. The latter is, in fact, quite a special kind of unity. It does not follow from the interconnexion of things in one subject, or of the beings of the world in an original being. On the contrary, it implies emphatically some relation to a *cause* possessed of intelligence. Even if all the things were to be united in one *simple* subject, yet such unity would never exhibit a purposive relation unless these things were understood to be, first, inner *effects* of the substance as a *cause*, and, secondly, effects of it as cause by *virtue of its intelligence*. Apart from these formal conditions all unity is mere necessity of nature, and, when it is ascribed nevertheless to things that we represent as outside one another, blind 394 necessity. But if what the scholastics call the transcendental perfection of things, in relation to their own proper essence—a perfection according to which all things have inherent in them all the requisites for being the thing they are and not any other thing—is to be termed a natural purposiveness, we then get a childish playing with words in the place of concepts. For if all things must be thought as ends, then to be a thing and to be an end are identical, so that, all said and done, there is nothing that specially deserves to be represented as an end.

This makes it evident that by resolving our concept of natural purposiveness into the consciousness of our own inherence in an all-embracing, though at the same time simple, being, and by seeking the form of purposiveness in the unity of that being, Spinoza must have intended to maintain the idealism of the purposiveness and not its realism. But even this he was unable to accomplish, for the mere representation of the unity of the substrate can never produce the idea of purposiveness, even if it is undesigned.

2. Those who not merely maintain the *realism* of natural ends, but purport even to explain it, think they can detect a special type of causality, namely that of causes operating intentionally. Or, at least, they think they are able to perceive the possibility of such causality— for unless they did they could not set about trying to explain it. For even the most daring hypothesis must rely at least on the *possibility* of its assumed foundation being *certain*, and the concept of this foundation must be capable of being assured its objective reality.

But the possibility of a living matter is quite inconceivable. The very conception of it involves self-contradiction, since lifelessness, *inertia*, constitutes the essential characteristic of matter. Then if the possibility of a matter endowed with life and of the whole of nature conceived as an animal is invoked in support of the hypothesis of a purposiveness of nature in the macrocosm, it can only be used with the utmost reserve in so far as it is manifested empirically in the organization of nature in the microcosm. Its possibility can in no way be perceived *a priori*. Hence there must be a vicious circle in the explanation, if the purposiveness of nature in organized beings is sought to be derived from the life of matter and if this life in turn is only to be known in organized beings, so that no concept of its possibility can be formed apart from such experience. Hence hylozoism does not perform what it promises.

Finally *theism* is equally incapable of substantiating dogmatically the possibility of natural ends as a key to teleology. Yet the source of its explanation of them has this advantage over all others, that by attributing an intelligence to the original Being it adopts the best mode of rescuing the purposiveness of nature from idealism, and introduces an intentional causality for its production.

For theism would first have to succeed in proving to the satisfaction of determining judgement that the unity of end in matter is an impossible result of the mere mechanism of nature. Otherwise it is not entitled definitely to locate its ground beyond and above nature. But the farthest we can get is this. The first and inner ground of this very mechanism being beyond our ken, the constitution and limits of our cognitive faculties are such as to preclude us from in any way looking to matter with a view to finding in it a principle of determinate purposive relations. We are left, on the contrary, with no alternative way of judging nature's products as natural ends other than that which resorts to a supreme Intelligence as the cause of the world. But this is not a ground for determining judgement, but only for reflective judgement, and it is absolutely incapable of authorizing us to make any objective assertion.

§ 74

The impossibility of treating the concept of a technic of nature dogmatically springs from the inexplicability of a natural end

EVEN though a concept is to be placed under an empirical condition we deal dogmatically with it, if we regard it as contained under another concept of the object—this concept forming a principle of reason—and determine it in accordance with the latter. But we deal merely critically with the concept if we only regard it in relation to our cognitive faculties and, consequently, to the subjective conditions of thinking it, without undertaking to decide anything as to its object. Hence the dogmatic treatment of a concept is treatment which is authoritative for determining judgement: the critical treatment is such as is authoritative merely for reflective judgement.

Now the concept of a thing as a natural end is one that subsumes nature under a causality that is only thinkable by the aid of reason, and so subsumes it for the purpose of letting us judge on this principle of what is given of the object in experience. But in order to make use of this concept dogmatically for determining judgement we should have first to be assured of its objective reality, as otherwise we could not subsume any natural thing under it. The concept of a thing as a natural end is, however, certainly one that is empirically conditioned, that is, is one only possible under certain conditions given in experience. Yet it is not one to be abstracted from these conditions, but, on the contrary, it is only possible on a rational principle in the judging of the object. Being such a principle, we have no insight into its objective reality, that is to say, we cannot perceive that an object answering to it is possible. We cannot establish it dogmatically; and we do not know whether it is a merely conjectured and objectively empty concept (*conceptus ratiocinans*), or whether it is a rational concept, supplying a basis of knowledge and confirmed by reason (*conceptus ratiocinatus*). Hence it cannot be treated dogmatically on behalf of determining judgement. In other words, it is not only impossible to decide whether or not things of nature, considered as natural ends, require for their production a causality of a quite peculiar kind, namely an intentional causality, but the very question is quite out of order. For the concept of a natural end is altogether unprovable by reason in respect of its objective reality, which means that it is not constitutive for determining judgement, but merely regulative for reflective judgement.

That this concept is not provable is clear from the following considerations. Being a concept of a *natural product*, it involves natural necessity. Yet it also involves in one and the same thing, considered as an end, an accompanying contingency in the form of the object in respect of mere laws of nature. Hence, if it is to escape self-contradiction, besides containing a basis of the possibility of the thing in nature it must further contain a basis of the possibility of this nature itself and of its reference to something that is not an empirically cognizable nature, namely to something supersensible, and, therefore, to what is not cognizable by us at all. Otherwise in judging of its possibility, we should not have to judge it in the light of a kind of causality different from that of natural mechanism. Accordingly the concept of a thing as a natural end is transcendent *for determining judgement* if its object is viewed by reason—although for reflective
397 judgement it may be immanent in respect of objects of experience. Objective reality, therefore, cannot be procured for it on behalf of determining judgement. Hence we can understand how it is that all systems that are ever devised with a view to the dogmatic treatment of the concept of natural ends or of nature as a whole that owes its consistency and coherence to final causes, fail to decide anything whatever either by their objective affirmations or by their objective denials. For, if things are subsumed under a concept that is merely problematic, the synthetic predicates attached to this concept—as, for example, in the present case, whether the natural end which we suppose for the production of the thing is designed or undesigned—must yield judgements about the object of a similar problematic character, whether they be affirmative or negative, since one does not know whether one is judging about what is something or nothing. The concept of a causality through ends, that is, ends of art, has certainly objective reality, just as that of a causality according to the mechanism

of nature has. But the conception of a causality of nature following the rule of ends, and still more of such a Being as is utterly incapable of being given to us in experience—a Being regarded as the original source of nature—while it may no doubt be thought without self-contradiction, is nevertheless useless for the purpose of dogmatic definitive assertions. For, since it is incapable of being extracted from experience, and besides is unnecessary for its possibility, there is nothing that can give any guarantee of its objective reality. But even if this could be assured, how can I reckon among products of nature things that are definitely posited as products of divine art, when it was the very incapacity of nature to produce such things according to its own laws that necessitated the appeal to a cause distinct from nature?

§ 75

The concept of an objective purposiveness of nature is a critical principle of reason for the use of reflective judgement

BUT then it is one thing to say: The production of certain things of nature, or even of nature as a whole, is only possible through the agency of a cause that pursues designs in determining itself to action. It is an entirely different thing to say: *By the peculiar constitution of my cognitive faculties* the only way I can judge of the possibility of those things 398 and of their production is by conceiving for that purpose a cause working designedly, and, consequently, a being whose productivity is analogous to the causality of an understanding. In the former case I desire to ascertain something about the object, and I am bound to prove the objective reality of a concept I have assumed. In the latter case it is only the employment of my cognitive faculties that is determined by reason in accordance with their peculiar character and the essential conditions imposed both by their range and their limitations. The first principle is, therefore, an *objective* principle intended for determining judgement. The second is a subjective principle for the use merely of reflective judgement, of which it is, consequently, a maxim that reason prescribes.

In fact, if we desire to pursue the investigation of nature with diligent observation, if only in its organized products, we cannot avoid the necessity of ascribing the concept of design to nature. We have in this concept, therefore, a maxim absolutely necessary for the empirical employment of our reason. But once such a guide for the study of nature has been adopted, and its application verified, it is obvious that we must at least try this maxim of judgement also on nature as a whole, because many of its laws might be discoverable in the light of this maxim which otherwise, with the limitations of our insight into its mechanism, would remain hidden from us. But in respect of the latter employment, useful as this maxim of judgement is, it is not indispensable. For nature as a whole is not given to us as organized—in the very strict sense above assigned to the word. On the other hand, in respect of those natural products that can only be judged as designedly formed in the way they are, and not otherwise, the above maxim of reflective judgement is essentially necessary, if for no other purpose, to obtain an empirical knowledge of their intrinsic character. For the very notion that they are organized things is itself impossible unless we associate with it the notion of a production by design.

Now where the possibility of the real existence or form of a thing is represented to the mind as subject to the condition of an end, there is bound up indissolubly with the concept of the thing the concept of its contingency in accordance with natural laws. For this reason those natural things which we consider to be only possible as ends 399 constitute the foremost proof of the contingency of the universe. Alike for the popular understanding and for the philosopher they are, too, the only valid argument for its dependence upon and its origin from an extramundane Being, and from one, moreover, that the above purposive form shows to be intelligent. Thus they indicate that teleology must look to a theology for a complete answer to its inquiries.

But suppose teleology brought to the highest pitch of perfection, what would it all prove in the end? Does it prove, for example, that such an intelligent Being really exists? No; it proves no more than this, that by the constitution of our cognitive faculties, and, therefore, in bringing experience into touch with the highest principles of reason, we are absolutely incapable of forming any concept of the possibility of such a world unless we think a highest cause *operating designedly*. We are unable, therefore, objectively to substantiate the proposition: There is an intelligent original Being. On the contrary, we can only do so subjectively for the employment of our power of judgement in its reflection on the ends in nature, which are incapable of being thought on any other principle than that of the intentional causality of a highest cause.

Should we desire to establish the major premiss dogmatically from teleological grounds, we should become entangled in inextricable difficulties. For then these reasonings would have to be supported by the thesis: The organized beings in the world are not possible otherwise than by virtue of a cause operating designedly. But are we to say that because we can only push forward our investigation into the causal nexus of these things and recognize the conformity to law which it displays by following the idea of ends, we are also entitled to presume that for every thinking and knowing being the same holds true as a necessary condition, and as one, therefore, attaching to the object instead of merely to the subject, that is, to our own selves? For this is the inevitable position that we should have to be prepared to take up. But we could not succeed in carrying such a point. For, strictly speaking, we do not *observe* the ends in nature as designed. We only *read* this concept *into* the facts as a guide to judgement in its reflection upon the products of nature. Hence these ends are not given to us by the object. It is even impossible for us *a priori* to warrant the eligibility of such a concept if it is taken to possess objective reality. We can get absolutely nothing, therefore, out of the thesis beyond a proposition resting only on subjective conditions, that is to say the conditions of reflective judgement adapted to our cognitive faculties. If this proposition were to be expressed in objective terms and as valid dogmatically, it would read: There is a God. But all that is permissible for us human beings is the narrow formula: We cannot conceive or render intelligible to ourselves the purposiveness that must be introduced as the basis even of our knowledge of the intrinsic possibility of many natural things, except by representing it, and, in general, the world, as the product of an intelligent cause—in short, of a God. 400

Now supposing that this proposition, founded as it is upon an indispensably necessary maxim of our power of judgement, is perfectly satisfactory from every *human* point of view and for any use to which we can put our reason, whether speculative or practical, I should like to know what loss we suffer from our inability to prove its validity for higher beings also—that is to say, to substantiate it on pure objective grounds, which unfortunately are beyond our reach. It is, I mean, quite certain that we can never get a sufficient knowledge of organized beings and their inner possibility, much less get an explanation of them, by looking merely to mechanical principles of nature.

Indeed, so certain is it, that we may confidently assert that it is absurd for human beings even to entertain any thought of so doing or to hope that maybe another Newton may some day arise, to make intelligible to us even the genesis of but a blade of grass from natural laws that no design has ordered. Such insight we must absolutely deny to mankind. But, then, are we to think that a source of the possibility of organized beings amply sufficient to explain their origin without having recourse to a design, *could* never be found buried among the secrets even of nature, were we able to penetrate to the principle upon which it specifies its familiar universal laws? This, in its turn, would be a presumptuous judgement on our part. For how do we expect to get any knowledge on the point? Probabilities drop entirely out of count in a case like this, where the question turns on judgements of pure reason. On the question, therefore, whether or not any being acting designedly stands behind what we properly term natural ends, as a world cause, and consequently, as Author of the world, we can pass no objective judgement whatever, whether it be affirmative or negative. This much alone is certain, that if we ought, for all that, to form our judgement on what our own proper nature permits us to see, that is, subject to the conditions and restrictions of our reason, we are utterly unable to ascribe the possibility of such natural ends to any other source than an intelligent Being. This alone squares with the maxim of our reflective judgement, and, therefore, with a subjective ground that is nevertheless ineradicably bound to the human race.

401

§ 76
Remark

THE following consideration is one that justly merits detailed elaboration in transcendental philosophy, but it can only be introduced here as an explanatory digression, and not as a step in the main argument.

Reason is a faculty of principles, and the unconditioned is the ultimate goal at which it aims. The understanding, on the other hand, is at its disposal, but always only under a certain condition that must be given. But, without concepts of the understanding, to which objective reality must be given, reason can pass no objective (synthetic) judgements whatever. As theoretical reason it is absolutely devoid of any constitutive principles of its own. Its principles, on the contrary, are merely regulative. It will readily be perceived that once reason advances beyond the reach of the understanding it becomes extravagant. It displays itself in ideas—that have certainly a foundation as regulative principles—but not in objectively valid concepts. The understanding, however, unable to keep pace with it and yet requisite in order to give validity in respect of objects, restricts the validity of these ideas to the judging subject, though to the subject in a comprehensive sense, as inclusive of all who belong to the human race. In other words it limits their validity to the terms of this condition: From the nature of our human faculty of knowledge, or, to speak in the broadest terms, even according to any concept that we are able *to form for ourselves* of the capacity of a finite intelligent being in general, it must be conceived to be so and cannot be conceived otherwise—terms which involve no assertion that the foundation of such a judgement lies in the object. We shall submit some examples which, while they certainly possess too great importance and are also too full of difficulty to be here forced at once on the reader as propositions that have been proved, may yet offer some food for reflection, and may elucidate the matters upon which our attention is here specially engaged.

Human understanding cannot avoid the necessity of drawing a distinction between the possibility and the actuality of things. The reason for this lies in our own selves and the nature of our cognitive faculties. For were it not that two entirely heterogeneous factors, the understanding for concepts and sensuous intuition for the corresponding objects, are required for the exercise of these faculties, there 402 would be no such distinction between the possible and the actual. This means that if our understanding were intuitive it would have no objects but such as are actual. Concepts, which are merely directed to the possibility of an object, and sensuous intuitions, which give us something and yet do not thereby let us cognize it as an object, would both cease to exist. Now the whole distinction which we draw between the merely possible and the actual rests upon the fact that possibility signifies the position of the representation of a thing relatively to our concept, and, in general, to our capacity of thinking, whereas actuality signifies the positing of the thing in its intrinsic existence apart from this concept. Accordingly the distinction of possible from actual things is one that is merely valid subjectively for human understanding. It arises from the fact that even if something does not exist, we may yet always give it a place in our thoughts, or if there is something of which we have no concept we may nevertheless imagine it given. To say, therefore, that things may be possible without being actual, that from mere possibility, therefore, no conclusion whatever as to actuality can be drawn, is to state propositions that hold true for human reason, without such validity proving that this distinction lies in the things themselves. That this inference is not to be drawn from the propositions stated, and that, consequently, while these are certainly valid even of objects, so far as our cognitive faculties in their subjection to sensuous conditions are also occupied with objects of the senses, they are not valid of things generally, is apparent when we look to the demands of reason. For reason never withdraws its challenge to us to adopt something or other existing with unconditioned necessity—a primal ground—in which there is no longer to be any difference between possibility and actuality, and our understanding has absolutely no concept to answer to this idea—that is, it can discover no way of representing to itself any such thing or of forming any notion of its mode of existence. For if understanding *thinks* it—let it think it how it will—then the thing is represented merely as possible. If it is conscious of it as given in intuition, then it is actual, and no thought of any possibility enters into the case. Hence the concept of an absolutely necessary being, while doubtless an indispensable idea of reason, is for human understanding an unattainable problematic concept. Nevertheless it is valid for the employment of our cognitive faculties according to their peculiar structure; consequently not so for the object nor, as that would mean, for every knowing being. For I cannot take for granted that thought and intuition are two distinct conditions subject to which every being exercises its cognitive faculties, and, therefore, that things 403 have a possibility and actuality. An understanding into whose mode of cognition* this distinction did not enter would express itself by saying: All objects that I know *are*, that is, exist; and the possibility of some that did not exist, in other words, their contingency supposing them to exist, and, therefore, the necessity that would be placed in contradistinction to this contingency, would never enter into the imagination of such a being. But what makes it so hard for our understanding with its concepts to rival reason is simply this, that the very thing that reason regards as constitutive of the object and adopts as its principle is for understanding, in its human form, extravagant, that is, impossible under the subjective conditions of its knowledge.—In this state of affairs, then, this maxim always holds true, that once the knowledge of objects exceeds the capacity of the understanding we must always conceive them according to the subjective conditions necessarily attaching to our human nature in the exercise of its faculties. And if—as must needs be the case with extravagant concepts—judgements passed in this manner cannot be constitutive principles determining the character of the object, we shall yet be left with regulative principles whose function is immanent and reliable, and which are adapted to the human point of view.

We have seen that in the theoretical study of nature reason must assume the idea of an unconditioned necessity of the original ground of nature. Similarly in the practical sphere it must presuppose its own causality as unconditioned (in respect of nature), in other words, its freedom, since it is conscious of its own moral command. Now here the objective necessity of action as duty is, however, regarded as opposed to that which it would have as an event if its source lay in nature instead of in freedom or rational causality. So the action, with its absolute necessity of the moral order, is looked on as physically wholly contingent—that is, we recognize that what *ought* necessarily to happen, frequently does not happen. Hence it is clear that it only springs from the subjective character of our practical faculty that the moral laws must be represented as commands, and the actions conformable to them as duties, and that reason expresses this necessity not as an '*is*' (an event) but as an 'ought to be' (as obligation). This would not occur if reason and its causality were considered as independent of sensibility, that is, as free from the subjective condition of its application to objects in nature, and as being, consequently, a cause in an intelligible world perfectly harmonizing with the moral law. For in such a world there would be no difference between 404 obligation and act, or between a practical law as to what is possible through our agency and a theoretical law as to what we make actual. However, although an intelligible world in which everything is actual by reason of the simple fact that, being something good, it is possible, is for us an extravagant concept—as is also freedom itself, the formal condition of that world—yet it has its proper function. For while, in this respect, it is useless for the purpose of any constitutive principle determining an object and its objective reality, it yet serves as a universal *regulative principle*. This is due to the constitution of our partly sensuous nature and capacity, which makes it valid for us and, so far as we can imagine from the constitution of our reason, for all intelligent beings that are in any way bound to this sensible world. But this principle does not objectively determine the nature of freedom as a form of causality: it converts, and converts with no less validity than if it did so determine the nature of that freedom, the rule of actions according to that idea into a command for everyone.

Similarly, as to the case before us, we may admit that we should find no distinction between the mechanism and the technic of nature, that is, its purposive connections, were it not for the character of our understanding. Our understanding must move from the universal to the particular. In respect of the particular, therefore, judgement can recognize no purposiveness, or, consequently, pass any determinate judgements, unless it is possessed of a universal law under which it can subsume that particular. But the particular by its very nature contains something contingent in respect of the universal. Yet reason demands that there shall also be unity in the synthesis of the particular laws of nature, and, consequently, conformity to law—and a derivation *a priori* of the particular from the universal laws in point of their contingent content is not possible by any defining of the concept of the object. Now the above conformity to law on the part of the contingent is termed purposiveness. Hence it follows that the concept of a purposiveness of nature in its products, while it does not touch the determination of objects, is a necessary concept for the human power of judgement, in respect of nature. It is, therefore, a subjective principle of reason for the use of judgement, and one which, taken as regulative and not as constitutive, is as necessarily valid for our *human judgement* as if it were an objective principle.

§ 77

The peculiarity of human understanding that makes the concept of a natural end possible for us

IN the foregoing Remark we have noted peculiarities belonging to our faculty of cognition—even to our higher faculty of cognition—which we are easily misled into treating as objective predicates to be transferred to the things themselves. But these peculiarities relate to ideas to which no commensurate object can be given in experience, and which thus could only serve as regulative principles in the pursuit of experience. The concept of a natural end stands, no doubt, on the same footing as regards the source of the possibility of a predicate like this—a source which can only be ideal. But the result attributable to this source, namely the product itself, is nevertheless given in nature, and the concept of a causality of nature, regarded as a being acting according to ends, seems to convert the idea of a natural end into a constitutive teleological principle. Herein lies a point of difference between this and all other ideas.

But this difference lies in the fact that the idea in question is a principle of reason for the use, not of understanding, but of judgement, and is, consequently, a principle solely for the application of an understanding in the abstract to possible objects of experience. Moreover, this application only affects a field where the judgement passed cannot be determining but simply reflective. Consequently, while the object may certainly be given in experience, it cannot even be *judged determinately*—to say nothing of being judged with complete adequacy—in accordance with the idea, but can only be made an object of reflection.

The difference turns, therefore, on a peculiarity of *our* (human) understanding relative to our power of judgement in reflecting on things in nature. But, if that is the case, then we must have here an underlying idea of a possible understanding different from the human. (And there was a similar implication in the *Critique of Pure Reason*.* We were bound to have present to our minds the thought of another possible form of intuition, if ours was to be deemed one of a special kind, one, namely, for which objects were only to rank as phenomena.) Were this not so it could not be said that certain natural products *must*, from the particular constitution of our understanding, be *considered by us*—if we are to conceive the possibility of their production—as having been produced designedly and as ends, yet without this statement involving any demand that there should, as a matter of fact, be a particular cause present in which the representation of an end acts as determining ground, or, therefore, without involving any assertion as to the powers of an understanding different from the human. This is to say, the statement does not deny that a superhuman understanding may be able to discover the source of the possibility of such natural products even in the mechanism of nature, that is, in the mechanism of a causal nexus for which an understanding is not positively assumed as cause. 406

Hence what we are here concerned with is the relation which *our* understanding bears to the power of judgement. We have, in fact, to examine this relation with a view to finding a certain element of contingency in the constitution of our understanding, so as to note it as a peculiarity of our own in contradistinction to other possible kinds of understanding.

This contingency turns up quite naturally in the *particular* which judgement has to bring under the *universal* supplied by the concepts of the understanding. For the particular is not determined by the universal of *our* (human) understanding. Though different things may agree in a common characteristic, the variety of forms in which they may be presented to our perception is contingent. Our understanding is a faculty of concepts. This means that it is a discursive understanding for which the character and variety to be found in the particular given to it in nature and capable of being brought under its concepts must certainly be contingent. But now intuition is also a factor in knowledge, and a faculty of *complete spontaneity of intuition* would be a cognitive faculty distinct from sensibility and wholly independent of it. Hence it would be an understanding in the widest sense of the term. Thus we are also able to imagine an *intuitive* understanding—negatively, or simply as not discursive—which does not move, as ours does with its concepts, from the universal to the particular and so to the individual. Such an understanding would not experience the above contingency in the way nature and understanding accord in natural products subject to *particular* laws. But it is just this contingency that makes it so difficult for our understanding to reduce the multiplicity of nature to the unity of knowledge. Our understanding can only accomplish this task through the harmonizing of the features of nature with our faculty of concepts—a most contingent accord. But an intuitive understanding has no such work to perform.

Accordingly our understanding is peculiarly circumstanced in respect of the power of judgement. For in cognition by means of the understanding the particular is not determined by the universal. 407 Therefore the particular cannot be derived from the universal alone. Yet in the multiplicity of nature, and through the medium of concepts and laws, this particular has to accord with the universal in order to be capable of being subsumed under it. But under the circumstances mentioned this accord must be very contingent and must exist without any determinate principle to guide our judgement.

Nevertheless we are able at least to conceive the possibility of such an accord of the things in nature with the power of judgement—an accord which we represent as contingent, and, consequently, as only possible by means of an end directed to its production. But, to do so, we must at the same time imagine an understanding different from our own, relative to which—and, what is more, without starting to attribute an end to it—we may represent the above accord of natural laws with our power of judgement, which for our understanding is only thinkable when ends are introduced as a middle term effecting the connexion, as *necessary*.

It is, in fact, a distinctive characteristic of our understanding, that in its cognition—as, for instance, of the cause of a product—it moves from the *analytic universal* to the particular, or, in other words, from concepts to given empirical intuitions. In this process, therefore, it determines nothing in respect of the multiplicity of the particular. On the contrary, understanding must wait for the subsumption of the empirical intuition—supposing that the object is a natural product—under the concept, to furnish this determination for the faculty of judgement. But now we are also able to form a notion of an understanding which, not being discursive like ours, but intuitive, moves from the *synthetic universal*, or intuition of a whole as a whole, to the particular—that is to say, from the whole to the parts. To render possible a definite form of the whole a *contingency* in the synthesis of the parts is not implied by such an understanding or its representation of the whole. But that is what our understanding requires. It must advance from the parts as the universally conceived principles to different possible forms to be subsumed under the latter as consequences. Its structure is such that we can only regard a real whole in nature as the effect of the concurrent dynamical forces of the parts. How then may we avoid having to represent the possibility of the whole as dependent upon the parts in a manner conformable to our discursive understanding? May we follow what the standard of the intuitive or archetypal understanding prescribes, and represent the possibility of the parts as both in their form and synthesis dependent upon the whole? But the very peculiarity of our understanding in question prevents this being done in such a way that the whole contains the source of the possibility of the nexus of the parts. This would be self-contradictory in knowledge of the 408 discursive type. But the *representation* of a whole may contain the source of the possibility of the form of that whole and of the nexus of the parts which that form involves. But, now, the whole would in that case be an effect or *product* the *representation* of which is looked on as the *cause* of its possibility. But the *product* of a cause whose determining ground is merely the representation of its effect is termed an end. Hence it follows that it is simply a consequence flowing from the particular character of our understanding that we should represent products of nature as possible according to a different type of causality from that of the physical laws of matter, that is, as only possible according to ends and final causes. In the same way we explain the fact that this principle does not touch the question of how such things themselves, even considered as phenomena, are possible on this mode of production, but only concerns the judging of them that is possible to our understanding. On this view we see at the same time why it is that in natural science we are far from being satisfied with an explanation of natural products by means of a causality according to ends. For in such an explanation all we ask for is a judging of natural generation as adapted to our critical faculty, or reflective judgement, instead of one adapted to the things themselves on behalf of determining judgement. Here it is also quite unnecessary to prove that an *intellectus archetypus* like this is possible. It is sufficient to show that we are led to this idea of an *intellectus archetypus* by contrasting with it our discursive understanding that has need of images (*intellectus ectypus*) and noting the contingent character of a faculty of this form, and that this idea involves nothing self-contradictory.

Now where we consider a material whole and regard it as in point of form a product resulting from the parts and their powers and capacities of self-integration (including as parts any foreign material introduced by the co-operative action of the original parts), what we represent to ourselves in this way is a mechanical generation of the whole. But from this view of the generation of a whole we can elicit no concept of a whole as end—a whole whose intrinsic possibility emphatically presupposes the idea of a whole as that upon which the very nature and action of the parts depend. Yet this is the representation which we must form of an organized body. But, as has just been shown, we are not to conclude from this that the mechanical generation of an organized body is impossible. For that would amount to saying that it is impossible, or, in other words, self-contradictory, *for any understanding* to form a representation of such a unity in the conjunction of the manifold without also making the idea of this unity its producing cause, that is, without representing the production as designed. At the same time this is the conclusion that we should in fact have to draw were we entitled to look on material beings as things in themselves. For in that case the unity constituting the basis of the possibility of natural formations would only be the unity of space. But space is not a real ground of the generation of things. It is only their formal condition—although from the fact that no part in it can be determined except in relation to the whole (the representation of which, therefore, underlies the possibility of the parts) it has some resemblance to the real ground of which we are in search. But then it is at least possible to regard the material world as a mere phenomenon, and to think something which is not a phenomenon, namely a thing in itself, as its substrate. And this we may rest upon a corresponding intellectual intuition, albeit it is not the intuition that we possess. In this way a supersensible real ground, although for us unknowable, would be procured for nature, and for the nature of which we ourselves form part. Everything, therefore, which is necessary in this nature as an object of the senses we should judge according to mechanical laws. But the accord and unity of the particular laws and of their resulting subordinate forms, which we must deem contingent in respect of mechanical laws—these things which exist in nature as an object of reason, and, indeed, nature in its entirety as a system, we should also consider in the light of teleological laws. Thus we should estimate nature on two kinds of principles. The mechanical mode of explanation would not be excluded by the teleological as if the two principles contradicted one another.

Further, this gives us an insight into what we might doubtless have easily conjectured independently, but which we should have found it difficult to assert or prove with certainty. It shows us that while the principle of a mechanical derivation of natural products displaying purposiveness is consistent with the teleological principle, it in no way enables us to dispense with it. We may apply to a thing which we have to judge as a natural end, that is, to an organized being, all the laws of mechanical generation known or yet to be discovered, we may even hope to make good progress in such researches, but we can never get rid of the appeal to a completely different source of generation for the possibility of a product of this kind, namely that of a causality by ends. It is utterly impossible for human reason, or for any finite reason qualitatively resembling ours, however much it may surpass it in degree, to hope to understand the generation even of a blade of grass from mere mechanical causes. For if judgement finds the teleological nexus of causes and effects quite indispensable for the possibility of an object like this, be it only for the purpose of studying it under the guidance of experience, and if a ground involving relation to ends and adequate for external objects as phenomena altogether eludes us, so that we are compelled, although this ground lies in nature, to look for it in the supersensible substrate of nature, all possible insight into which is, however, cut off from us: it is absolutely impossible for us to obtain any explanation at the hand of nature itself to account for any synthesis displaying purposiveness. So by the constitution of our human faculty of knowledge it becomes necessary to look for the supreme source of this purposiveness in an original understanding as the cause of the world.

§ 78

The union of the principle of the universal mechanism of matter
with the teleological principle in the technic of nature

It is of infinite importance to reason to keep in view the mechanism which nature employs in its productions, and to take due account of it in explaining them, since no insight into the nature of things can be attained apart from that principle. Even the concession that a supreme Architect has directly created the forms of nature in the way they have existed from all time, or has predetermined those which in their course of development regularly conform to the same type, does not further our knowledge of nature one whit. The reason is that we are wholly ignorant of the ideas or mode of agency of such a supreme Being, in which the principles of the possibility of the natural beings are supposed to be contained, and so cannot explain nature in this way moving from above downwards, that is *a priori*. On the other hand our explanation would be simply tautological if, relying on the purposiveness found, as we believe, in the forms of objects of experience, we should set out from these forms and move from below upwards, that is *a posteriori*, and with a view to explaining such purposiveness should appeal to a cause acting in accordance with ends. We should be cheating reason with mere words—not to mention the fact that where, by resorting to explanation of this kind, we get lost in the extravagant speculation beyond the reach of natural science, reason is betrayed into poetic enthusiasm, the very thing which it is its pre-eminent calling to prevent.

On the other hand, it is an equally necessary maxim of reason not 411 to overlook the principle of ends in the products of nature. For although this principle does not make the way in which such products originate any more comprehensible to us, yet it is a heuristic principle for the investigation of the particular laws of nature. And this remains true even though it be understood that, as we confine ourselves rigorously to the term natural ends, even where such products manifestly exhibit a designed purposive unity, we do not intend to make any use of the principle in order to explain nature itself— that is to say, in speaking of natural ends, pass beyond the bounds of nature in quest of the source of the possibility of those products. However, inasmuch as the question of this possibility must be addressed sooner or later, it is just as necessary to conceive a special type of causality for it—one not to be found in nature—as to allow that the mechanical activity of natural causes has its special type. For the receptivity for different forms over and above those which matter is capable of producing by virtue of such mechanism must be supplemented by a spontaneity of some cause—which cannot, therefore, be matter—as in its absence no reason can be assigned for those forms. Of course before reason takes this step it must exercise due caution and not seek to explain as teleological every technic of nature— meaning by this a formative capacity of nature which displays (as in the case of regularly constructed bodies) purposiveness of structure for our mere apprehension. On the contrary it must continue to regard such technic as possible on purely mechanical principles. But to go so far as to exclude the teleological principle, and to want to keep always to mere mechanism, even where reason, in its investigation into the manner in which natural forms are rendered possible by their causes, finds a purposiveness of a character whose relation to a different type of causality is apparent beyond all denial, is equally unscientific. It inevitably sends reason on a fantastical and roving expedition among powers of nature that are only cobwebs of the brain and quite unthinkable, in just the same way as a merely teleological mode of explanation that pays no heed to the mechanism of nature would turn reason visionary.

These two principles are not capable of being applied in conjunction to one and the same thing in nature as co-ordinate truths available for the explanation or deduction of one thing by or from another. In other words they are not to be united in that way as dogmatic and constitutive principles affording insight into nature on behalf of determining judgement. If I suppose, for instance, that a maggot is to be regarded as a product of the mere mechanism of matter, that is of a new formative process which a substance brings about by its own unaided resources when its elements are liberated as the result of decomposition, I cannot then turn round and derive 412 the same product from the same substance as a causality that acts from ends. Conversely, if I suppose that this product is a natural end, I am precluded from relying on its mechanical generation, or adopting such generation as a constitutive principle for judging the product in respect of its possibility, and thus uniting the two principles. For each mode of explanation excludes the other—even supposing that objectively both grounds of the possibility of such a product rest on a single foundation, provided this foundation was not what we were thinking of. The principle which is to make possible the compatibility of the above pair of principles, as principles to be followed in judging nature, must be placed in what lies beyond both (and consequently beyond the possible empirical representation of nature), but in what nevertheless contains the ground of the representation of nature. It must, in other words, be placed in the supersensible, and to this each of the two modes of explanation must be referred. Now the only concept we can have of the supersensible is the indeterminate conception of a ground that makes possible the judging of nature according to empirical laws. Beyond this we cannot go: by no predicate can we determine this concept any further. Hence it follows that the union of the two principles cannot rest on one basis of *explanation* setting out in so many terms how a product is possible on given laws so as to satisfy *determining* judgement, but can only rest on a single basis of *exposition* elucidating this possibility for *reflective* judgement. For explanation means derivation from a principle, which must, therefore, be capable of being clearly cognized and specified. Now the principle of the mechanism of nature and that of its causality according to ends, when applied to one and the same product of nature, must cohere in a single higher principle and flow from it as their common source, for if this were not so they could not both enter consistently into the same survey of nature. But if this principle, which is objectively common to both, and which, therefore, justifies the association of its dependent maxims of natural research, is of such a kind that, while it can be indicated, it can never be definitely cognized or clearly specified for employment in particular cases as they arise, then no explanation can be extracted from such a principle. There can be no clear and definite derivation, in other words, of the possibility of a natural product, as one possible on those two heterogeneous principles. Now the principle common to the mechanical derivation, on the one hand, and the teleological, on the other, is the *supersensible*, which we must introduce as the basis of nature as phenomenon. But of this we are unable from a theoretical point of view to form the slightest positive determinate concept. How, therefore, in the light of the supersensible as a principle, nature 413 in its particular laws constitutes a system for us, and one capable of being cognized as possible both on the principle of production from physical causes and on that of final causes, is a matter which does not admit of any explanation. All we can say is that if it happens that objects of nature present themselves, whose possibility is incapable of being conceived by us on the principle of mechanism—which always has a claim upon a natural being—unless we rely on teleological principles, it is then to be presumed that we may confidently study natural laws on lines following both principles—according as the possibility of the natural product is cognizable to our understanding from one or other principle—without being disturbed by the apparent conflict that arises between the principles upon which our judging of the product is formed. For we are at least assured of the possibility of both being reconciled, even objectively, in a single principle, inasmuch as they deal with phenomena, and these presuppose a supersensible ground.

We have seen that the principles both of nature's mechanical operation and of its teleological or designed technique, as bearing upon one and the same product and its possibility, may alike be subordinated to a common higher principle of nature in its particular laws. Nevertheless, this principle being *transcendent*, the narrow capacity of our understanding is such that the above subordination does not enable us to unite the two principles *in the explanation* of the same natural generation, even where, as is the case with organized substances, the intrinsic possibility of the product is only *intelligible* by means of a causality according to ends. Hence we must keep to the statement of the principle of teleology above given. So we say that by the constitution of our human understanding no causes but those acting by design can be adopted as grounds of the possibility of organized beings in nature, and the mere mechanism of nature is quite insufficient to explain these its products; and we add that this implies no desire to decide anything by that principle in respect of the possibility of such things themselves.

This principle, we mean to say, is only a maxim of reflective, not of determining judgement. Hence, it is only valid subjectively for us, not objectively to explain the possibility of things of this kind themselves—in which things themselves both modes of generation might easily spring consistently from one and the same ground. Furthermore, unless the teleologically-conceived mode of generation were supplemented by a concept of a concomitantly presented mech-
414 anism of nature, such genesis could not be judged as a product of nature at all. Hence, we see that the above maxim immediately involves the necessity of a union of both principles in the judging of things as natural ends. But this union is not to be directed to substituting one principle, either wholly or in part, in the place of the other. For in the room of what is regarded, by us at least, as only possible by design, mechanism cannot be assumed, and in the room of what is cognized as necessary in accordance with mechanism, such contingency as would require an end as its determining ground cannot be assumed. On the contrary we can only subordinate one to the other, namely mechanism to designed technique. And on the transcendental principle of the purposiveness of nature this may readily be done.

For where ends are thought as the sources of the possibility of certain things, means have also to be supposed. Now the law of the efficient causality of a means, considered *in its own right*, requires nothing that presupposes an end, and, consequently, may be both mechanical and yet a subordinate cause of designed effects. Hence, looking only to organic products of nature, but still more if, impressed by the endless multitude of such products, we go on and adopt, at least on an allowable hypothesis, the principle of design, in the connexion of natural causes following particular laws, as a *universal principle* of reflective judgement in respect of the whole of nature, namely the world, we may imagine a great and even universal interconnexion of mechanical and teleological laws in the generative processes of nature. Here we neither confuse nor transpose the principles upon which such processes are judged. For in a teleological judgement, even if the form which the matter assumes is judged as only possible by design, yet the matter itself, considered as to its nature, may also be subordinated, conformably to mechanical laws, as means to the represented end. At the same time, inasmuch as the basis of this compatibility lies in what is neither the one nor the other, neither mechanism nor purposive nexus, but is the supersensible substrate of nature which is hidden from our view, for our human reason the two modes of representing the possibility of such objects are not to be fused into one. On the contrary, we are unable to judge their possibility otherwise than as one grounded in accordance with the nexus of final causes upon a supreme understanding. Thus the teleological mode of explanation is in no way prejudiced.

But now it is an open question, and for our reason must always remain an open question, how much the mechanism of nature contributes as means to each final design in nature. Further, having regard to the above-mentioned intelligible principle of the possibility of a nature in general, we may even assume that nature is possible in all respects on both kinds of law, the physical laws and those of final causes, as universally consonant laws, although we are quite unable to see how this is so. Hence, we are ignorant how far the mechanical mode of explanation possible for us may penetrate. This much only is certain, that no matter what progress we may succeed in making with it, it must still always remain inadequate for things that we have once recognized to be natural ends. Therefore, by the constitution of our understanding we must subordinate such mechanical grounds, one and all, to a teleological principle.

Now this is the source of a privilege and, owing to the importance of the study of nature on the lines of the principle of mechanism for the theoretical employment of our reason, the source also of a duty. We may and should explain all products and events of nature, even the most purposive, so far as lies in our power, on mechanical lines— and it is impossible for us to assign the limits of our powers when confined to the pursuit of inquiries of this kind. But in so doing we

415

must never lose sight of the fact that among such products there are those which we cannot even subject to investigation except under the conception of an end of reason. These, if we respect the essential nature of our reason, we are obliged, despite those mechanical causes, to subordinate in the last resort to a causality according to ends.

Theory of the Method of Teleological Judgement

§ 79
Whether teleology must be treated as a branch of natural science

EVERY science must have its definite position in the complete encyclo-pedia of the sciences. If it is a philosophical science its position must be assigned to it either in the theoretical or the practical division. Further, if its place is in the theoretical division, then the position assigned to it must either be in natural science—which is its proper position when it considers things capable of being objects of experience—consequently in physics proper, psychology, or cosmology, or else in theology—as the science of the original source of the world as the sum of all objects of experience.

Now the question arises: What position does teleology deserve? Is it a branch of natural science, properly so called, or of theology? A branch of one or the other it must be; for no science can belong to the transi-tion from one to the other, because this only signifies the articulation or the organization of the system and not a position in it.

That it does not form a constituent part of theology, although the use that may there be made of it is most important, is evident from the nature of the case. For its objects are the productions of nature and their cause; and, although it points to this cause as a ground residing beyond and above nature, namely a Divine Author, yet it does not do so for determining judgement. It only points to this cause in the inter-ests of reflective judgement engaged in surveying nature, its purpose being to guide our judging of the things in the world by means of the idea of such a ground, as a regulative principle, in a manner adapted to our human understanding.

But just as little does it appear to form a part of natural science. For this science requires determining, and not merely reflective, prin-ciples for the purpose of assigning objective grounds of natural effects. As a matter of fact, also, the theory of nature, or the mechanical expla-nation of its phenomena by efficient causes, is in no way helped by considering them in the light of the correlation of ends. The exposition of the ends pursued by nature in its products, so far as such ends form a system according to teleological concepts, belongs strictly speaking only to a description of nature that follows a particular guiding thread. Here reason does fine work, and work that is full of practical purposiveness from various points of view. But it gives no information whatever as to the origin and intrinsic possibility of these forms. Yet this is what specially concerns the theoretical science of nature.

Teleology, therefore, in the form of a science, is not a branch of doctrine at all, but only of critique, and of the critique of a particular cognitive faculty, namely that of judgement. But it does contain *a priori* principles, and to that extent it may, and in fact must, specify the method by which nature has to be judged according to the principle of final causes. In this way the science of its methodical application exerts at least a negative influence upon the procedure to be adopted in the theoretical science of nature. It also in the same way affects the metaphysical bearing which this science may have on theology, when the former is treated as a propaedeutic to the latter.

§ 80

The necessary subordination of the principle of mechanism to the teleological principle in the explanation of a thing regarded as a natural end

OUR *right to aim at* an explanation of all natural products on simply mechanical lines is in itself quite unrestricted. But the constitution of our understanding, as engaged upon things in the shape of natural ends, is such that our *power* of *meeting all demands* from the unaided resources of mechanical explanation is not only very limited, but is also circumscribed within clearly marked bounds. For by a principle of judgement that adopts the above procedure alone nothing whatever can be accomplished in the way of explaining natural ends. For this reason our judging of such products must also at all times be subordinated to a teleological principle.

418   Hence there is reason, and indeed merit, in pursuing the mechanism of nature for the purpose of explaining natural products so far as this can be done with probable success, and in fact never abandoning this attempt on the ground that it is *intrinsically* impossible to encounter the purposiveness of nature along this road, but only on the ground that it is impossible *for us* as human beings. For in order to succeed along

this line of investigation we should require an intuition different from our sensuous intuition and a determinate knowledge of the intelligible substrate of nature—a substrate from which we could show the reason of the very mechanism of phenomena in their particular laws. But this wholly surpasses our capacity.

So where it is established beyond question that the concept of a natural end applies to things, as in the case of organized beings, if the investigator of nature is not simply to waste his labour, he must always in judging them accept some original organization or other as fundamental. He must consider that this organization avails itself of the very mechanism above mentioned for the purpose of producing other organic forms, or for evolving new structures from those given—such new structures, however, always issuing from and in accordance with the end in question.

It is praiseworthy to employ a comparative anatomy and go through the vast creation of organized natural beings in order to see if there is not discoverable in it something resembling a system, especially with respect to the principle of their productions. For otherwise we should be obliged to content ourselves with the mere principle of judging—which tells us nothing that gives any insight into the production of such beings—and to abandon in despair all claim to *insight into nature* in this field. When we consider the agreement of so many genera of animals in a certain common schema, which apparently underlies not only the structure of their bones, but also the arrangement of their remaining parts, and when we find here the wonderful simplicity of the original plan, which has been able to produce such an immense variety of species by the shortening of one part and the lengthening of another, by the involution of this part and the evolution of that, there gleams upon the mind a ray of hope, however faint, that the principle of the mechanism of nature, apart from which there can be no natural science at all, may yet enable us to arrive at some explanation in the case of organic life. This analogy of forms, which in all their differences seem to be produced in accordance with a common type, strengthens the suspicion that they have an actual kinship due to descent from a common parent. This we might trace in the gradual approxima- 419 tion of one animal species to another, from that in which the principle of ends seems best authenticated, namely from man, back to the polyp, and from this back even to mosses and lichens, and finally to the lowest perceivable stage of nature. Here we come to crude matter;

and from this, and the forces which it exerts in accordance with mechanical laws (laws resembling those by which it acts in the formation of crystals) seems to be developed the whole technic of nature which, in the case of organized beings, is so incomprehensible to us that we feel obliged to imagine a different principle for its explanation.

Here the *archaeologist* of nature is at liberty to go back to the traces that remain of nature's earliest revolutions, and, appealing to all he knows of or can conjecture about its mechanism, to trace the genesis of that great family of living things (for it must be pictured as a family if there is to be any foundation for the consistently coherent affinity mentioned). He can suppose that the womb of mother earth as it first emerged, like a huge animal, from its chaotic state, gave birth to creatures whose form displayed less purposiveness, and that these again bore others which adapted themselves more perfectly to their native surroundings and their relations to each other, until this womb, becoming rigid and ossified, restricted its birth to definite species incapable of further modification, and the multiplicity of forms was fixed as it stood when the operation of that fruitful formative power had ceased. — Yet, for all that, he is obliged eventually to attribute to this universal mother an organization suitably constituted with a view to all these forms of life, for unless he does so, the possibility of the purposive form of the products of the animal and plant kingdoms is quite unthinkable.[1] But when he does attribute all this to nature he has only pushed the explanation a stage farther back. He cannot pretend to have made the genesis of those two kingdoms intelligible independently of the condition of final causes.

420

---

[1] An hypothesis of this kind may be called a daring venture on the part of reason; and there are probably few even among the most acute scientists to whose minds it has not sometimes occurred. For it cannot be said to be absurd, like the *generatio aequivoca*, which means the generation of an organized being from crude inorganic matter. It never ceases to be *generatio univoca* in the widest acceptation of the word, as it only implies the generation of something organic from something else that is also organic, although, within the class of organic beings, differing specifically from it. It would be as if we supposed that certain water animals transformed themselves by degrees into marsh animals, and from these after some generations into land animals. In the judgement of plain reason there is nothing *a priori* self-contradictory in this. But experience offers no example of it. On the contrary, as far as experience goes, all generation known to us is *generatio homonyma*. It is not merely *univoca* in contradistinction to generation from an unorganized substance, but it brings forth a product which in its very organization is of like kind with that which produced it, and a *generatio heteronyma* is not met with anywhere within the range of our experience.

Even as regards the alteration which certain individuals of the organized genera contingently undergo, where we find that the character thus altered is transmitted and taken up into the generative power, we can form no other plausible judgement of it than that it is an occasional development of a purposive capacity originally present in the species with a view to the preservation of the kind. For in the complete inner purposiveness of an organized being, the generation of its like is intimately associated with the condition that nothing shall be taken up into the generative force which does not also belong, in such a system of ends, to one of its undeveloped original capacities. Once we depart from this principle we cannot know with certainty whether many constituents of the form at present found in a species may not be of equally contingent and purposeless origin, and the principle of teleology, that nothing in an organized being which is preserved in the propagation of the species should be judged as devoid of purposiveness, would be made very unreliable and could only hold good for the parent stock, to which our knowledge does not reach.

In reply to those who feel obliged to adopt a teleological principle of critical judgement, that is an architectonic understanding in the case of all such natural ends, *Hume* raises the objection* that one might ask with equal justice how such an understanding is itself possible. By this he means that one may also ask how it is possible that there should be such a teleological coincidence in one being of the manifold faculties and properties presupposed in the very concept of an understanding which also possesses a productive power. But there is nothing in this point. For the whole difficulty that besets the question as to the genesis of a thing that involves ends and that is solely comprehensible by their means rests upon the demand for unity in the source of the synthesis of the multiplicity of *externally existing* elements in this product. For, if this source is laid in the understanding of a productive cause regarded as a simple substance, the above question, as a teleological problem, is abundantly answered, whereas if the cause is merely sought in matter, as an aggregate of many externally existing substances, the unity of principle requisite for the intrinsically purposive form of its complex structures is wholly absent. The *autocracy* of matter in productions that for our understanding are only conceivable as ends, is a word with no meaning.

This is the reason why those who look for a supreme ground of the possibility of the objectively purposive forms of matter, and yet do not concede an understanding to this ground, choose nevertheless to make the world-whole either an all-embracing substance (pantheism), or else—what is only the preceding in more defined form—a complex of many determinations inhering in a single *simple substance* (Spinozism). Their object is to derive from this substance that *unity* of source which all purposiveness presupposes. And in fact, thanks to their purely onto-logical concept of a simple substance, they really do something to sat-isfy *one* condition of the problem—namely, that of the unity implied in the reference to an end. But they have nothing to say on the sub-ject of the *other* condition, namely the relation of the substance to its consequence regarded as an *end*, this relation being what gives to their ontological ground the more precise determination which the problem demands. The result is that they in no way answer the *entire* problem. Also for our understanding it remains absolutely unanswer-able except on the following terms. First, the original source of things must be pictured by us as a simple substance. Then its attribute, as simple substance, in its relation to the specific character of the natural forms whose source it is—the character, namely, of purposive unity—must be pictured as the attribute of an intelligent substance. Lastly, the relation of this intelligent substance to the natural forms must, owing to the contingency which we find in everything which we im-agine to be possible only as an end, be pictured as one of *causality*.

§ 81

The association of mechanism with the teleological principle which we apply to the explanation of a natural end considered as a product of nature

WE have seen from the preceding section that the mechanism of nature is not sufficient to enable us to conceive the possibility of an organized being, but that it must ultimately be subordinated to a cause acting by design—or, at least, that the type of our cognitive faculty is such that we must conceive it to be so subordinated. But just as little can the mere teleological source of a being of this kind enable us to consider and to judge it as at once an end and a product of nature. With that teleological source we must further associate the mechanism of nature as a sort of instrument of a cause acting by design and to whose ends nature is subordinated even in its mechanical laws. The possibility of such a union of two completely different types of causality, namely that of nature in its universal conformity to law and that of an idea which restricts nature to a particular form of which nature, as nature, is in no way the source, is something which our reason does not comprehend. For it resides in the supersensible substrate of nature, of which we are unable to make any definite affirmation, further than that it is the self-subsistent being of which we know merely the phenomenon. Yet, for all that, this principle remains in full and undiminished force, that everything which we assume to form part of phenomenal nature and to be its product must be thought as connected with nature according to mechanical laws. For, apart from this type of causality, organized beings, although they are ends of nature, would not be natural products.

Now supposing we adopt the teleological principle of the production of organized beings, as indeed we cannot avoid doing, we may base their internally purposive form either on the *occasionalism* or on the *pre-establishment* of the cause. According to occasionalism the Supreme Cause of the world would directly supply the organic formation, stamped with the impress of its own idea, on the occasion of each impregnation, to the commingling substances united in the generative process. On the system of pre-establishment the Supreme Cause would only endow the original products of its wisdom with the inherent capacity by means of which an organized being produces another after its own kind, and the species preserves its continuous existence, whilst the loss of individuals is ever being repaired through the agency of a nature that simultaneously labours towards their destruction. If the occasionalism of the production of organized beings is assumed, all co-operation of nature in the process is entirely lost, and no room is left for the exercise of reason in judging of the possibility of products of this kind. So we may take it for granted that no one will embrace this system who cares anything for philosophy.

Again the system of pre-establishment may take either of two forms. 423 Thus it treats every organized being produced from one of its own kind either as its *educt* or as its *product*. The system which regards the generations as educts is termed that of *individual preformation*, or, sometimes, the *theory of evolution*; that which regards them as products is called the system of *epigenesis*. The latter may also be called the system of *generic preformation*, inasmuch as it regards the productive capacity of the parents, in respect of the inner purposive tendency that would be part of their original stock, and, therefore, the specific form, as still having been *virtualiter* preformed. On this statement the opposite theory of individual preformation might also more appropriately be called the *theory of involution* (or *encasement*).

The advocates of the *theory of evolution* exclude all individuals from the formative force of nature, for the purpose of deriving them directly from the hand of the creator. Yet they would not venture to describe the occurrence on the lines of the hypothesis of occasionalism, so as to make the impregnation an idle formality, which takes place whenever a supreme intelligent cause of the world has made up his mind to form a foetus directly with his own hand and relegate to the mother the mere task of developing and nourishing it. They would avow adherence to the theory of preformation; as if it were not a matter of indifference whether a supernatural origin of such forms is allowed to take place at the start or in the course of the world-process. They fail to see that in fact a whole host of supernatural contrivances would be spared by acts of creation as occasion arose, which would be required if an embryo formed at the beginning of the world had to be preserved from the destructive forces of nature, and had to keep safe and sound all through the long ages till the day arrived for its development, and also that an incalculably greater number of such preformed entities would be created than would be destined ever to develop, and that all those would be so many creations thus rendered superfluous and in vain. Yet they would like to leave nature some role in these operations, so as not to lapse into an unmitigated hyperphysics that can dispense with all explanation on naturalistic lines. Of course they would still remain unshaken in their hyperphysics; so much so that they would discover even in miscarriages—which yet cannot possibly be deemed ends of nature—a marvellous purposiveness, even if it be directed to no better end than that of being a purposiveless purposiveness intended to set some chance anatomist at his wit's end, and make him fall on his knees with admiration. However, they would be absolutely unable to

424 make the generation of hybrids fit in with the system of preformation, but would be compelled to allow to the seed of the male creature, to which in other cases they had denied all but the mechanical property of serving as the first means of nourishment for the embryo, a further and additional formative force directed to ends. And yet they would not concede this force to either of the two parents when dealing with the complete product of two creatures of the same genus.

As against this, even supposing we failed to see the enormous advantage on the side of the advocate of *epigenesis* in the matter of empirical evidence in support of this theory, still reason would antecedently be strongly prepossessed in favour of this line of explanation. For as regards things the possibility of whose origin can only be represented to the mind according to a causality of ends, epigenesis nonetheless regards nature as at least itself productive in respect of the continuation of the process, and not as merely unfolding something. Thus with the least possible expenditure of the supernatural it entrusts to nature the explanation of all steps subsequent to the original beginning. But it refrains from determining anything as to this original beginning, which is what baffles all the attempts of physics, no matter what chain of causes it adopts.

No one has rendered more valuable services in connexion with this theory of epigenesis than Herr Hofr. *Blumenbach.** This is as true of what he has done towards establishing the correct principles of its application—partly by setting due bounds to an overly free employment of it—as it is of his contributions to its proof. He makes organic substance the starting-point for physical explanation of these formations. For to suppose that crude matter, obeying mechanical laws, was originally its own architect, that life could have sprung up from the nature of what is void of life, and matter have spontaneously adopted the form of a self-maintaining purposiveness, he justly declares to be contrary to reason. But at the same time he leaves to the mechanism of nature, in its subordination to this inscrutable *principle* of a primordial *organization*, an indeterminable yet also unmistakable function. The capacity of matter here required he terms—in contradistinction to the simply mechanical *formative force* universally residing in it—in the case of an organized body a *formative impulse*, standing, so to speak, under the higher guidance and direction of the above principle.

§ 82

The teleological system in the extrinsic relations of organisms

BY extrinsic purposiveness I mean the purposiveness that exists where one thing in nature subserves another as means to an end. Now even things which do not possess any intrinsic purposiveness, and whose possibility does not imply any, such as earth, air, water, and the like, may nevertheless extrinsically, that is in relation to other beings, be very well adapted to ends. But then those other beings must in all cases be organized, that is be natural ends, for unless they are ends the former could not be considered means. Thus water, air, and earth cannot be regarded as means to the emergence of mountains. For intrinsically there is nothing in mountains that calls for a source of their possibility according to ends. Hence their cause can never be referred to such a source and represented under the predicate of a means subservient thereto.

Extrinsic purposiveness is an entirely different concept from that of intrinsic purposiveness, the latter being connected with the possibility of an object irrespective of whether its actuality is itself an end or not. In the case of an organism we may further inquire: For what end does it exist? But we can hardly do so in the case of things in which we recognize the simple effect of the mechanism of nature. The reason is that in the case of organisms we have already represented to ourselves a causality according to ends—a creative understanding—to account for their intrinsic purposiveness, and have referred this active faculty to its determining ground, the design. One extrinsic purposiveness is the single exception—and it is one intimately bound up with the intrinsic purposiveness of an organization. It does not leave open the question as to the ulterior end for which the nature so organized must have existed, and yet it lies in the extrinsic relation of a means to an end. This is the organization of the two sexes in their mutual relation with a view to the propagation of their species. For here we may always ask, just as in the case of an individual: Why was it necessary for such a pair to exist? The answer is: In this pair we have what first forms an *organizing* whole, though not an organized whole in a single body.

Now when it is asked to what end a thing exists, the answer may take one or other of two forms. It may be said that its existence and generation have no relation whatever to a cause acting designedly. Its origin is 426 then always understood to be derived from the mechanism of nature. Or it may be said that its existence, being that of a contingent natural entity, has some ground or other involving design. And this is a thought which it is difficult for us to separate from the concept of a thing that is organized. For inasmuch as we are compelled to rest its intrinsic possibility on the causality of final causes and an idea underlying this causality, we cannot but think that the real existence of this product is also an end. For where the representation of an effect is at the same time the ground determining an intelligent efficient cause to its production, the effect so represented is termed an *end*. Here, therefore, we may either say that the end of the real existence of a natural being of this kind is inherent in itself, that is, that it is not merely an end, but also a *final end*; or we may say that the final end lies outside it in other natural beings, that is, that its real existence, which is adapted to ends, is not itself a final end, but is necessitated by its being at the same time a means.

But if we go through the whole of nature we do not find in it, as nature, any being capable of laying claim to the distinction of being the final end of creation. In fact it may even be proved *a priori*, that what might do perhaps as an *ultimate end* for nature, endowing it with any conceivable qualities or properties we choose, could nevertheless in its character of a natural thing never be a final end.

Looking to the vegetable kingdom we might at first be induced by the boundless fertility with which it spreads itself abroad upon almost every soil to think that it should be regarded as a mere product of the mechanism which nature displays in its formations in the mineral kingdom. But a more intimate knowledge of its indescribably wise organization precludes us from entertaining this view, and drives us to ask: For what purpose do these forms of life exist? Suppose we reply: For the animal kingdom, which is thus provided with the means of sustenance, so that it has been enabled to spread over the face of the earth in such a manifold variety of genera. The question again arises: For what purpose then do these herbivores exist? The answer would be something like this: For the carnivores, which are only able to live on what itself has animal life. At last we come down to the question: What is the end and purpose of these and all the preceding natural kingdoms? For man, we say, and the multifarious uses to which his intelligence teaches him to put all these forms of life. He is the ultimate end of creation here upon earth, because he is the one and only being upon it that is able to form a concept of ends, and from an aggregate of things purposively fashioned to construct by the aid of his reason a system of ends. 427

We might also follow the chevalier Linné* and take the seemingly opposite course. Thus we might say: The herbivorous animals exist for the purpose of checking the profuse growth of the vegetable kingdom by which many species of that kingdom would be choked; the carnivores for the purpose of setting bounds to the voracity of the herbivores; and finally man exists so that by pursuing the latter and reducing their numbers a certain equilibrium between the productive and destructive forces of nature may be established. So, on this view, however much man might in a certain relation be judged as end, in a different relation he would in turn only rank as a means.

If we adopt the principle of an objective purposiveness in the manifold variety of the specific forms of terrestrial life and in their extrinsic relations to one another as beings with a structure adapted to ends, it is only rational to go on and imagine that in this extrinsic relation there is also a certain organization and a system of the whole kingdom of nature following final causes. But experience seems here to give the lie to the maxim of reason, more especially as regards an ultimate end of nature—an end which nevertheless is necessary to the possibility of such a system, and which we can only place in man. For, so far from making man, regarded as one of the many animal species, an ultimate end, nature has no more exempted him from its destructive than from its productive forces, nor has it made the smallest exception to its subjection of everything to a mechanism of forces devoid of an end.

The first thing that would have to be expressly appointed in a system ordered with a view to a purposive whole of natural beings upon the earth would be their habitat—the soil or the element upon or in which they are intended to thrive. But a more intimate knowledge of the nature of this basic condition of all organic production shows no trace of any causes but those acting altogether without design, and in fact tending towards destruction rather than calculated to promote genesis of forms, order, and ends. Land and sea not only contain memorials of mighty primeval disasters that have overtaken both them and all their living forms, but their entire structure—the strata of the land and the coastlines of the sea—has all the appearance of being the outcome of the wild and all-subduing forces of a nature working in a state of chaos. However wisely the configuration, elevation and slope of the land may now seem to be adapted for the reception of water from the air, for the subterranean channels of the springs that well up between the diverse layers of earth (suitable for various products) and for the course of the rivers, yet a closer investigation of them shows that they have resulted simply as the effect partly of volcanic eruptions, partly of floods, or even of invasions of the ocean. And this is not only true as regards the genesis of this configuration, but more particularly of its subsequent transformation, attended with the disappearance of its primitive organic productions.[2] If now the abode for all these forms of life—the lap of the land and the bosom of the deep—points to none but a wholly undesigned mechanical generation, how can we, or what right have we to ask for or to maintain a different origin for these latter products? And even if man, as the most minute examination of the remains of those devastations of nature seems, in Camper's judgement,* to prove, was not caught up in such revolutions, yet his dependence upon the remaining forms of terrestrial life is such that, if a mechanism of nature whose power overrides these others is admitted, he must be regarded as included within its scope, although his intelligence, to a large extent at least, has been able to save him from its work of destruction.

But this argument seems to go beyond what it was intended to prove. For it would seem to show not merely that man could not be an ultimate end of nature or, for the same reason, the aggregate of the organized things of terrestrial nature be a system of ends, but that even the products of nature previously deemed to be natural ends could have no other origin than the mechanism of nature.

But, then, we must bear in mind the results of the solution above 429 given of the antinomy of the principles of the mechanical and teleological generation of organic natural beings. These principles, as we there saw, are merely principles of reflective judgement in respect of formative nature and its particular laws, the key to whose systematic correlation is not in our possession. They tell us nothing definite as to the origin of the things in their own intrinsic nature. They only assert that by the constitution of our understanding and our reason we are unable to conceive the origin in the case of beings of this kind otherwise than in the light of final causes. The utmost persistence possible, even a boldness, is allowed us in our endeavours to explain them on mechanical lines. More than that, we are even summoned by

---

[2] If the name of *natural history*, now that it has once been adopted, is to continue to be used for the description of nature, we may give the name of *archaeology* of *nature*, as contrasted with art, to that which the former literally indicates, namely an account of the bygone or *ancient* state of the earth—a matter on which, though we dare not hope for any certainty, we have good ground for conjecture. Fossil remains would be objects for the archaeology of nature, just as rudely cut stones, and things of that kind, would be for the archaeology of art. For, as work is actually being done in this department, under the name of a theory of the earth, steadily though, as we might expect, slowly, this name would not be given to a purely imaginary study of nature, but to one to which nature itself invites and summons us.

reason to do so, albeit we know we can never succeed with such an explanation—not because there is an inherent inconsistency between the mechanical generation and an origin according to ends, but for subjective reasons involved in the particular type and limitations of our understanding. Lastly, we saw that the reconciliation of the two modes of representing the possibility of nature might easily lie in the supersensible principle of nature, both external and internal. For the mode of representation based on final causes is only a subjective condition of the exercise of our reason in cases where it is not seeking to know the proper judgement to form of objects arranged merely as phenomena, but is bent rather on referring these phenomena, principles and all, to their supersensible substrate, for the purpose of recognizing the possibility of certain laws of their unity, which are incapable of being represented by the mind otherwise than by means of ends (of which reason also possesses examples of the supersensuous type).

§ 83

The ultimate end of nature as a teleological system

WE have shown in the preceding section that, looking to principles of reason, there is ample ground—for reflective, though not of course for determining, judgement—for letting us judge man as not merely a natural end, such as all organized beings are, but as the being upon this earth who is the *ultimate end* of nature, and the one in relation to whom all other natural things constitute a system of ends. What now is the end in man, and the end which, as such, is intended to be promoted by means of his connexion with nature? If this end is something which must be found in man himself, it must either be of such a kind that man himself may be satisfied by means of nature and its beneficence, or else it is the aptitude and skill for all manner of ends for which he may employ nature both external and internal. The former end of nature would be the *happiness* of man, the latter his *culture*.

The conception of happiness is not one which man abstracts more or less from his instincts and so derives from the animality within him. It is, on the contrary, a mere *idea* of a state, and one to which he seeks to make his actual state of being adequate under purely empirical conditions—an impossible task. He projects this idea himself, and, thanks to his understanding and its complex relations with imagination and the senses, projects it in such different ways, and even alters his concept so often, that even if nature were a complete slave to his free power of choice, it would nevertheless be utterly unable to adopt any definite, universal and fixed law by which to accommodate itself to this fluctuating concept and so bring itself into accord with the end that each individual arbitrarily sets before himself. But even if we sought to reduce this concept to the level of the true wants of nature in which our species is in complete and fundamental accord, or, trying the other alternative, sought to increase to the highest level man's skill in accomplishing his imagined ends, nevertheless what man means by happiness, and what in fact constitutes his peculiar ultimate natural end, as opposed to the end of freedom, would never be attained by him. For his own nature is not so constituted as to rest or be satisfied in any possession or enjoyment whatever. Then external nature is far from having made a particular favourite of man or from having preferred him to all other animals as the object of its beneficence. For we see that in its destructive operations—plague, famine, flood, cold, attacks from animals great and small, and all such things—it has as little spared him as any other animal. But, besides all this, the discord of inner *natural tendencies* betrays him into further misfortunes of his own invention, and reduces other members of his species, through the oppression of lordly power, the barbarism of wars, and the like, to such misery, while he himself does all he can to work destruction on his race, that, even with the utmost goodwill on the part of external nature, its end, supposing it were directed to the happiness of our species, would never be attained in a system of terrestrial nature, because our own nature is not capable of it. Man, therefore, is always but a link in the chain of natural ends. True, he is a principle in respect of many ends to which nature seems to have predetermined 431 him, seeing that he makes himself so; but, nevertheless, he is also a means towards the preservation of the purposiveness in the mechanism of the remaining members. As the single being upon earth that possesses understanding, and, consequently, a capacity for setting before himself ends of his deliberate choice, he is certainly titular lord of nature, and, supposing we regard nature as a teleological system, he is born to be its ultimate end. But this is always on the terms that he has the intelligence and the will to give to it and to himself such a reference to ends as can be self-sufficing independently of nature, and, consequently, a final end. Such an end, however, must not be sought in nature.

But, where in man, at any rate, are we to place this *ultimate end* of nature? To discover this we must seek out what nature can supply for the purpose of preparing him for what he himself must do in order to be a final end, and we must segregate it from all ends whose possibility rests upon conditions that man can only await at the hand of nature. Earthly happiness is an end of the latter kind. It is understood to mean the sum of all possible human ends attainable through nature whether in man or external to him. In other words it is the material substance of all his earthly ends and what, if he converts it into his entire end, renders him incapable of positing a final end for his own existence and of harmonizing therewith. Therefore of all his ends in nature, we are left only with a formal, subjective condition, that, namely, of the aptitude for setting ends before himself at all, and, independent of nature in his power of determining ends, of employing nature as a means in accordance with the maxims of his free ends generally. This alone remains as what nature can effect relative to the final end that lies outside it, and as what may therefore be regarded as its ultimate end. The production in a rational being of an aptitude for any ends whatever of his own choosing, consequently of the aptitude of a being in his freedom, is *culture*. Hence it is only culture that can be the ultimate end which we have cause to attribute to nature in respect of the human race. His individual happiness on earth, and, we may say, the mere fact that he is the chief instrument for instituting order and harmony in non-rational external nature, are ruled out.

But not every form of culture can fill the office of this ultimate end of nature. *Skill* is a culture that is certainly the principal subjective condition of the aptitude for the furthering of ends of all kinds, yet it is incompetent for giving assistance to the *will* in its determination and choice of its ends. But this is an essential factor, if an aptitude for ends 432 is to have its full meaning. This latter condition of aptitude, involving what might be called culture by way of training (discipline), is negative. It consists in the liberation of the will from the despotism of desires whereby, in our attachment to certain natural things, we are rendered incapable of exercising a choice of our own. This happens when we allow ourselves to be enchained by impulses with which nature only provided us that they might serve as guidance to prevent our neglecting, or even impairing, the animal element in our nature, while yet we are left free enough to tighten or slacken them, to lengthen or shorten them, as the ends of our reason demand.

Skill can hardly be developed in the human race otherwise than by means of inequality among human beings. For the majority, in a mechanical kind of way that calls for no special art, provide the necessities of life for the ease and convenience of others who apply themselves to the less necessary branches of culture in science and art. These keep the masses in a state of oppression, with hard work and little enjoyment, though in the course of time much of the culture of the higher classes spreads to them also. But with the advance of this culture—the culminating point of which, where devotion to what is superfluous begins to be prejudicial to what is indispensable, is called luxury— misfortunes increase equally on both sides. With the lower classes they arise by force of domination from without, with the upper from seeds of discontent within. Yet this splendid misery is connected with the development of natural tendencies in the human race, and the end pursued by nature itself, even if it is not our end, is thereby attained. The formal condition under which nature can alone attain this its real end is the existence of a constitution so regulating the mutual relations of men that the abuse of freedom by individuals striving one against another is opposed by a lawful authority centred in a whole, called a *civil community*. For it is only in such a constitution that the greatest development of natural tendencies can take place. In addition to this we should also need a *cosmopolitan* whole—had men but the ingenuity to discover such a constitution and the wisdom voluntarily to submit themselves to its constraint. It would be a system of all states that are in danger of acting injuriously to one another. In its absence, and with the obstacles that ambition, love of power, and avarice, especially 433 on the part of those who hold the reins of authority, put in the way even of the possibility of such a scheme, *war* is inevitable. Sometimes this results in states splitting up and resolving themselves into lesser states, sometimes one state absorbs other smaller states and endeavours to build up a larger unit. But if on the part of men war is a thoughtless undertaking, being stirred up by unbridled passions, it is nevertheless a deep-seated, maybe far-seeing, attempt on the part of supreme wisdom, if not to found, yet to prepare the way for a rule of law governing the freedom of states, and thus bring about their unity in a system established on a moral basis. And, in spite of the terrible calamities which it inflicts on the human race, and the hardships, perhaps even greater, imposed by the constant preparation for it in time of peace, yet—as the prospect of the dawn of an abiding reign

of national happiness keeps ever retreating farther into the distance—
it is one further spur for developing to the highest pitch all talents that
minister to culture.*

We turn now to the discipline of inclinations. In respect of these our
natural capacities are very purposively adapted to the performance of
our essential functions as an animal species, but the inclinations are
a great impediment to the development of our humanity. Yet here
again, in respect of this second requisite for culture, we see nature
striving on purposive lines to give us that education that renders us
receptive to higher ends than it can itself afford. The preponderance
of evil which a taste refined to the extreme of idealization, and which
even luxury in the sciences, considered as food for vanity, diffuses
among us as the result of the crowd of insatiable inclinations which
they beget, is indisputable. But, while that is so, we cannot fail to
recognize the end of nature—ever more and more to prevail over the
rudeness and violence of inclinations that belong more to the animal
part of our nature and are most inimical to education that would fit
us for our higher vocation (inclinations towards enjoyment), and to
make way for the development of our humanity. Fine art and the sciences, if they do not make man morally better, yet, by conveying a
pleasure that admits of universal communication and by introducing
polish and refinement into society, make him civilized. Thus they do
much to overcome the tyrannical propensities of the senses, and so
prepare man for a sovereignty in which reason alone shall have sway.
Meanwhile the evils visited upon us, now by nature, now by the trucu-
lent egoism of man, evoke the energies of the soul, and give it strength
and courage to submit to no such force, and at the same time allow
us to sense that in the depths of our nature there is an aptitude for
higher ends.[3]

---

[3] The value of life for us, measured simply by *what we enjoy* (by the natural end of the
sum of all our inclinations, that is by happiness), is easy to decide. It is less than nothing.
For who would enter life afresh under the same conditions? Who would even do so according to a new, self-devised plan (which should, however, follow the course of nature), if it
also were merely directed to enjoyment? We have shown above what value life receives
from what it involves when lived according to the end with which nature is occupied in
us, and which consists in *what we do*, not merely what we enjoy, we being, however, in that
case always but a means to an undetermined final end. There remains then nothing but the
worth which we ourselves assign to our life by what we not only do, but do with a view
to an end so independent of nature that the very existence of nature itself can only be an
end subject to the condition so imposed.

§ 84

The final end of the existence of a world, that is, of creation itself

A *final end* is an end that does not require any other end as condition of its possibility.

If the simple mechanism of nature is accepted as the explanation of its purposiveness, it is not open to us to ask: For what end do the things in the world exist? For on such an idealistic system we have only to reckon with the physical possibility of things,—and things that it would be mere sophistry to imagine as ends. Whether we refer this form of things to chance, or whether we refer it to blind necessity, such a question would in either case be meaningless. But if we suppose the purposive nexus in the world to be real, and assume a special type of causality for it, namely the activity of a cause *acting designedly*, we cannot then stop short at the question: What is the end for which things in the world, namely organized beings, possess this or that form, or are placed by nature in this or that relation to other things? On the contrary, once we have conceived an understanding that must be regarded as the cause of the possibility of such forms as they are actually found in things, we must go on and seek in this understanding for an objective 435 ground capable of determining such productive understanding to the production of an effect of this kind. That ground is then the final end for which such things exist.

I have said above that the final end is not an end which nature would be competent to realize or produce in terms of its idea, because it is one that is unconditioned. For in nature, as a thing of the senses, there is nothing whose determining ground, discoverable in nature itself, is not always in turn conditioned. This is not merely true of external or material nature, but also of our internal or thinking nature—it being of course understood that I am only considering what in us is strictly nature. But a thing which by virtue of its objective characterization is to exist necessarily as the final end of an intelligent cause, must be of such a kind that in the order of ends it is dependent upon no further or other condition than simply its idea.

Now we find in the world beings of only one kind whose causality is teleological, or directed to ends, and which at the same time are beings of such a character that the law according to which they have to determine ends for themselves is represented by them themselves as unconditioned and not dependent on anything in nature, but as necessary in itself. The being of this kind is man, but man regarded as noumenon. He is the only natural creature whose peculiar objective characterization is nevertheless such as to enable us to recognize in him a supersensible faculty—his *freedom*—and to perceive both the law of the causality and the object of freedom which that faculty is able to set before itself as the highest end—the highest good in the world.

Now it is not open to us in the case of man, considered as a moral agent, or similarly in the case of any rational being in the world, to ask the further question: For what end (*quem in finem*) does he exist? His existence inherently involves the highest end—the end to which, as far as in him lies, he may subject the whole of nature, or against which at least he must not deem himself subjected to any influence on its part.— Now assuming that things in the world are beings that are dependent in point of their real existence, and, as such, stand in need of a supreme cause acting according to ends, then man is the final end of creation. For without man the chain of mutually subordinated ends would have no ultimate point of reference. Only in man, and only in him as the individual being to whom the moral law applies, do we find unconditional legislation in respect of ends. This legislation, therefore, is what alone 436 qualifies him to be a final end to which entire nature is teleologically subordinated.[4]

---

[4] It would be possible for the happiness of the rational beings in the world to be an end of nature, and, were it so, it would also be the *ultimate* end of nature. At least it is not obvious *a priori* why nature should not be so ordered, for, so far as we can see, happiness is an effect which it would be quite possible for nature to produce by means of its mechanism. But morality, or a causality according to ends that is subordinate to morality, is an absolutely impossible result of natural causes. For the principle that determines such causality to action is supersensible. In the order of ends, therefore, it is the sole principle possible which is absolutely unconditioned in respect of nature, and it is what alone qualifies the subject of such causality to be the *final end* of creation, and the one to which the whole of nature is subordinated. *Happiness*, on the other hand, as an appeal to the testimony of experience revealed in the preceding section, so far from being a *final end of creation*, is not even an *end of nature* as regards man in preference to other creatures. It may always be that individual human beings will make it their ultimate subjective end. But if seeking for the final end of creation, I ask: For what end was it necessary that human beings should exist? my question then refers to an objective supreme end, such as the highest reason would demand for their creation. If, then, to this question we reply: So that beings may exist upon whom that supreme Cause may exercise this beneficence, we then belie the condition to which the reason of man subjects even his own inmost wish for happiness, namely, harmony with his own inner moral legislation. This proves that happiness can only be a conditional end, and, therefore, that it is only as a moral being that man can

§ 85

Physico-Theology

Physico-Theology is the attempt* on the part of reason to infer the supreme cause of nature and its attributes from the *ends* of nature—ends which can only be known empirically. A *moral theology*, or ethico-theology, would be the attempt to infer that cause and its attributes from the moral end of rational beings in nature—an end which can be known *a priori*.

The former naturally precedes the latter. For if we seek to infer a world-cause from the things in the world by *teleological* arguments, we must first of all be given ends of nature. Then for these ends so given we must afterwards look for a final end, and this final end obliges us to seek the principle of the causality of the supreme cause in question. 437

Much natural research can, and indeed must, be conducted in the light of the teleological principle without our having occasion to inquire into the source of the possibility of the purposive activity which we meet with in various products of nature. But should we now desire to form also a concept of this source, we are then in the position of having absolutely no available insight that can penetrate beyond our mere maxim of reflective judgement. According to this maxim, given but a single organized product of nature, then the structure of our cognitive faculty is such that the only source which we can conceive it to have is one that is a cause of nature itself—whether of nature as a whole or even only of this particular portion of it—and that derives from an understanding the requisite causality for such a product. This is a critical principle which doubtless brings us no whit farther in the explanation of natural things or their origin. Yet it discloses to our view a prospect that extends beyond the horizon of nature and points to our being able perhaps to determine more closely the concept of an original being that otherwise appears so unfruitful.

Now I say that no matter how far physico-teleology may be pushed, it can never disclose to us anything about a *final end* of creation; for

be the final end of creation; while, as regards his state of being, happiness is only incident thereto as a consequence proportionate to the measure of his harmony with that end, as the end of his existence.

it never even begins to look for a final end. Thus it can justify, no doubt, the concept of an intelligent world-cause as a concept which subjectively—that is in relation to the nature of our cognitive faculty alone—is effective to explain the possibility of things that we can render intelligible to ourselves in the light of ends. But neither from a theoretical nor a practical point of view can it determine this concept any further. Its attempt falls short of its proposed aim of affording a basis of theology. To the last it remains nothing but a physical teleology: for the purposive connection which it recognizes is only, and must only, be regarded as subject to natural conditions. Consequently it can never institute an inquiry into the end for which nature itself exists—this being an end whose source must be sought outside nature. Yet it is upon the definite idea of this end that the definite conception of such a supreme intelligent world-cause, and, consequently, the possibility of a theology, depend.

Of what use are the things in the world to one another? What good is the manifold in a thing to this thing? How are we entitled to assume that nothing in the world is in vain, but that, provided we grant that certain things, regarded as ends, ought to exist, everything serves some purpose or other *in nature*? All these questions imply that in respect of our judgement reason has at its command no other principle 438 of the possibility of the object which it is obliged to judge teleologically than that of subordinating the mechanism of nature to the architectonic of an intelligent author of the world; and directed to all these issues the teleological survey of the world plays its part nobly and fills us with intense admiration. But inasmuch as the data, and, consequently, the principles, for determining such a concept of an intelligent world-cause, regarded as the supreme artist, are merely empirical, they do not allow us to infer any other attributes belonging to it than those which experience reveals to us as manifested in its effects. But as experience is unable to embrace the whole of nature as a system, it must frequently find support for arguments which, to all appearances, conflict with that concept and with one another. Yet it can never lift us above nature to the end of its real existence or thus raise us to a definite concept of such a higher intelligence—even if it were in our power empirically to survey the entire system considered as mere nature.

If the problem which physico-theology has to solve is set to a lower key, then its solution seems an easy matter.* Thus we may think of an intelligent being possessing a number of superlative attributes, without the full complement of those necessary for establishing a nature harmonizing with the greatest possible end, and to all beings of this description—of whom there may be one or more—we might be extravagant enough to apply the concept of a *Deity*. Or, if we let it pass as of no importance to supplement by arbitrary additions the proofs of a theory where the grounds of proof are deficient; and if, therefore, where we have only reason to assume *much* perfection (and what, then, is much for us?) we deem ourselves entitled to take *all possible* perfection for granted:—then physical teleology has important claims to the distinction of affording the basis of a theology. But what is there to lead, and, more than that, authorize us to supplement the facts of the case in this way? If we are called on to point out what it is, we shall seek in vain for any ground of justification in the principles of the theoretical employment of reason. For such employment emphatically demands that for the purpose of explaining an object of experience we are not to ascribe to it more attributes than we find in the empirical data for the possibility of the object. On closer investigation we should see that underlying our procedure is an idea of a Supreme Being, which rests on an entirely different employment of reason, namely its practical employment, and that it is this idea, which exists in us *a priori*, that impels us to supplement the defective representation of an original ground of the ends in nature afforded by physical teleology, and enlarge it to the concept of a Deity. When we saw this, we should not erroneously imagine that we had evolved this idea, and, with it, a theology by means of the theoretical employment of reason in the physical cognition of the world— much less that we had proved its reality. 439

One cannot blame the ancients so very much for imagining that, while there was great diversity among their gods, both in respect of their power and of their purposes and dispositions, they were all, not excepting the sovereign head of the gods himself, invariably limited in human fashion. For on surveying the order and course of the things in nature they certainly found ample reason for assuming something more than mere mechanism as its cause and for conjecturing the existence of purposes on the part of certain higher causes, which they could only conceive to be superhuman, behind the machinery of this world. But, since they encountered both the good and evil, the purposive and the counter purposive, very much interspersed, at least to human eyes, and could not take the liberty of assuming, for the sake of the arbitrary idea of an all-perfect author, that there were nevertheless mysteriously wise and beneficent ends, of which they did not see the evidence, underlying all this apparent antagonism, their judgement on the supreme world-cause could hardly be other than it was, so long, that is, as they followed maxims of the mere theoretical employment of reason with strict consistency. Others who were physicists* and in that character desired to be theologians also, thought that they would give full satisfaction to reason by providing for the absolute unity of the principle of natural things, which reason demands, by means of the idea of a being in which, as sole substance, the whole assemblage of those natural things would be contained only as inhering modes. While this substance would not be the cause of the world by virtue of its intelligence, it would nevertheless be a subject in which all the intelligence on the part of the beings in the world would reside. Hence, although it would not be a being that produced anything according to ends, it would be one in which all things—owing to the unity of the subject of which they are mere determinations—must necessarily be interconnected in a purposive manner, though independently of any end or design. Thus they introduced the idealism of final causes, by converting the unity, so difficult to deduce, of a number of substances standing in a purposive connexion, from a causal dependence *on one* substance into the unity of inherence *in one*. Looked at from the side of the beings that inhere, this system became *pantheism*, and from the side of the sole subsisting subject, as original being, it 440 became, by a later development, *Spinozism*. Thus in the end, instead of solving the problem of the primary source of the purposiveness of nature, it regarded the whole question as idle, for the conception of such purposiveness, being shorn of all reality, was reduced to a simple misinterpretation of the universal ontological conception of a thing in the abstract.

So we see that the conception of a Deity, such as would meet the demands of our teleological judging of nature, can never be developed according to mere theoretical principles of the employment of reason— and these are the only principles upon which physico-theology relies. For, suppose we assert that all teleology is a delusion on the part of the power of judgement in its judging of the causal nexus of things and take refuge in the sole principle of a mere mechanism of nature.

Then nature only appears to us to involve a universal relation to ends, owing to the unity of the substance that contains it as no more than the multiplicity of its modes. Or, suppose that instead of adopting this idealism of final causes, we wish to adhere to the principle of the realism of this particular type of causality. Then—no matter whether we base natural ends on a number of intelligent original beings or on a single one—the moment we find ourselves with nothing upon which to ground the conception of realism but empirical principles drawn from the actual nexus of ends in the world, on the one hand we cannot help accepting the fact of the discordance with purposive unity of which nature presents many examples, and on the other hand, we can never obtain a sufficiently determinate concept of a single intelligent cause—so long as we keep to what mere experience entitles us to extract—to satisfy any sort of theology whatever which will be of use theoretically or practically.

It is true that physical teleology urges us to go in quest of a theology. But it cannot produce one—however far we carry our investigations of nature, or help out the nexus of ends discovered in it with ideas of reason (which for physical problems must be theoretical). We may pose the reasonable question: What is the use of our basing all these arrangements on a great, and for us unfathomable, intelligence, and supposing it to order this world according to its intentions, if nature does not and cannot ever tell us anything as to the final aim in view? For apart from a final purpose we are unable to relate all these natural ends to a common point of reference, or form an adequate teleological principle, be it for combining all the ends in a known system, or be it for framing such a conception of the supreme Intelligence, as cause of a nature like this, as could act as a standard for our judge- ment in its teleological reflection upon nature. I should have, it is true, in that case an *artistic intelligence* for miscellaneous ends, but no *wisdom* for a final end, which nevertheless is what must, properly speaking, contain the ground by which such intelligence is determined. I require a final end, and it is only pure reason that can supply this *a priori* for all ends in the world are empirically conditioned and can contain nothing that is absolutely good, but only what is good for this or that purpose regarded as contingent. Such a final end alone would instruct me how I am to conceive the supreme cause of nature—what attributes I am to assign to it, and in what degree, and how I am to

441

conceive its relation to nature—if I am to judge nature as a teleological system. In the absence, then, of a final end, what liberty or what authority have I to extend at will such a very limited concept of that original intelligence as I can base on my own poor knowledge of the world, or my concept of the power of this original being to realize its ideas, or of its will to do so, and so forth, and expand it to the idea of an all-wise and infinite being? Were I able to do this theoretically it would presuppose omniscience in myself to enable me to see into the ends of nature in their entire context, and in addition to conceive all other possible schemes, as compared with which the present would have to be judged on reasonable grounds to be the best. For without this perfected knowledge of the effect, my reasoning can arrive at no definite concept of the supreme cause—which is only to be found in that of an intelligence in every respect infinite, that is, in the concept of a Deity—or establish a basis for theology.

Hence, allowing for all possible extension of physical teleology, we may keep to the principle set out above and say that the constitution and principles of our cognitive faculty are such that we can only conceive nature, in respect of those of its arrangements that are familiar to us and display purposiveness, as the product of an intelligence to which it is subjected. But whether this intelligence may also have had a final purpose in view in the production of nature and in its constitution as a whole, which final purpose in that case would not reside in nature as the sensible world, is a matter that the theoretical study of nature can never disclose. On the contrary, however great our knowledge of nature, it remains an open question whether that supreme cause is the original source of nature as a cause acting throughout according to a final end, or whether it is not rather such a source by virtue of an intelligence that is determined by the simple necessity of its nature to the production of certain forms (by analogy to what we call the artistic

442 instinct in animals). The latter version does not involve our ascribing even wisdom to such intelligence, much less wisdom that is supreme and conjoined with all other properties requisite for ensuring the perfection of its product.

Hence physico-theology is a misconceived physical teleology. It is of no use to theology except as a preparation or propaedentic, and is only sufficient for this purpose when supplemented by a further principle on which it can rely. But it is not, as its name would suggest, sufficient, even as a propaedentic, if taken by itself.

§ 86
Ethico-Theology

THERE is a judgement which even the commonest understanding finds irresistible when it reflects upon the existence of the things in the world and the existence of the world itself. It is the verdict that all the manifold forms of life, co-ordinated though they may be with the greatest art and concatenated with the utmost variety of purposive adaptations, and even the entire complex that embraces their numerous systems, incorrectly called worlds, would all exist for nothing, if man, or rational beings of some sort, were not to be found in their midst. Without man, in other words, the whole of creation would be a mere wilderness, a thing in vain, and have no final end. Yet it is not man's cognitive faculty, that is, theoretical reason, that forms the point of reference which alone gives its worth to the existence of all else in the world—as if the meaning of his presence in the world was that there might be someone in it that could make it an object of *contemplation*. For if this contemplation of the world brought to light nothing but things without a final end, the existence of the world could not acquire a worth from the fact of its being known. A final end of the world must be presupposed as that in relation to which the contemplation of the world may itself possess a worth. Neither is it in relation to the feeling of pleasure or the sum of such feelings that we can think that there is a given final end of creation, that is to say, it is not by well-being, not by enjoyment, whether bodily or mental, not, in a word, by happiness, that we value that absolute worth. For the fact that man, when he does exist, makes happiness his own final purpose, affords us no conception of any reason why he should exist at all, or of any worth he himself possesses, for which his existence should be made agreeable to him. Hence man must already be presupposed to be the final end of creation, in order that we may have a rational ground to explain why nature, when regarded as an absolute whole according to principles of ends, must be in accord with the conditions of his happiness.—Accordingly it is only the faculty of desire that can give the required point of reference—yet not that faculty which makes man dependent upon nature (through sensuous impulses), that is, not that in respect of which the worth of his existence is dependent upon what

443

he receives and enjoys. On the contrary it is the worth which he alone can give to himself, and which consists in what he does—in the manner in which and the principles upon which he acts in the *freedom* of his faculty of desire, and not as a link in the chain of nature. In other words a good will is that whereby man's existence can alone possess an absolute worth, and in relation to which the existence of the world can have a *final end*.

Even the popular verdict of sound human reason, once its reflection is directed to this question and pressed to consider it, is in complete accord with the judgement that it is only as a moral being that man can be a final end of creation. What, it will be said, does it all avail, that this man has so much talent, that he is even so active in its employment and thus exerts a useful influence upon social and public life, and that he possesses, therefore, considerable worth alike in relation to his own state of happiness and in relation to what is good for others, if he has not a good will? Looked at from the point of view of his inner self, he is a contemptible object; and, if creation is not to be altogether devoid of a final end, such a man, though as man he is part of creation, must nevertheless, as a bad man dwelling in a world subject to moral laws, forfeit, in accordance with those laws, his own subjective end, that is happiness, as the sole condition under which his existence can cohere with the final end.

Now if we find instances in the world of an order adapted to ends, and if, as reason inevitably requires, we subordinate the ends which are only conditionally ends, to one that is unconditioned and supreme, that is to a final end, we readily see, to begin with, that we are then not dealing with an end of nature, included within nature taken as existent, but with the end of the existence of nature itself, with all its orderly adaptations included. Consequently we see the question is one of the ultimate *end of creation*, and, more precisely, of the supreme condition under which alone there can be a final end, or, in other words, of the ground that determines a highest intelligence to the production of the beings in the world.

444   It is, then, only as a moral being that we acknowledge man to be the end of creation. Hence we have, first of all, a reason, or at least the primary condition, for regarding the world as a consistent whole of interconnected ends, and as a *system* of final causes. Now the structure of our reason is such that we necessarily refer natural ends to an intelligent world-cause. Above all, then, we have *one principle* applicable

to this relation, enabling us to think the nature and attributes of this first cause considered as supreme ground in the kingdom of ends, and to form a definite concept of it. This is what could not be done by physical teleology, which was only able to suggest vague concepts of such a ground—concepts which this vagueness made as useless for practical as for theoretical employment.

With such a definite principle as this, of the causality of the original being, we shall not have to regard it merely as an intelligence and as legislating for nature, but as the sovereign head legislating in a moral kingdom of ends. In relation to the *highest good*, which is alone possible under his sovereignty, namely the existence of rational beings under moral laws, we shall conceive this original being to be *omniscient*, so that even our inmost dispositions—wherein lies the distinctive moral worth in the actions of rational beings in the world—may not be hid from him. We shall conceive him as *omnipotent*, so that he may be able to adapt entire nature to this highest end; as both *all-good* and *just*, since these two attributes, which unite to form *wisdom*, constitute the conditions under which a supreme cause of the world can be the source of the greatest good under moral laws. Similarly the other remaining transcendental attributes, such as *eternity*, *omnipresence*, and so forth (for goodness and justice are moral attributes), all attributes that are presupposed in relation to such a final end, will have to be regarded as belonging to this original being.—In this way *moral* teleology supplements the deficiency of *physical* teleology, and for the first time establishes a *theology*. For physical teleology, if it is not to borrow secretly from moral teleology, but is to proceed with strict logical rigour, can from its own unaided resources establish nothing but a demonology, which does not admit of any definite concept.

But the principle which, because of the moral and teleological significance of certain beings in the world, refers the world to a supreme cause as Deity, does not establish this relation by being simply a completion of the physico-teleological argument, and therefore by adopting this necessarily as its foundation. On the contrary it can rely on *its own* resources, and urges attention to the ends of nature and 445 inquiry after the incomprehensibly great art that lies hidden behind its forms, so as to give to the ideas produced by pure practical reason an incidental confirmation in natural ends. For the conception of beings of the world subject to moral laws is an *a priori* principle upon which man must necessarily judge himself. Furthermore, if there is

a world-cause acting designedly and directed to an end, the moral
relation above mentioned must just as necessarily be the condition of
the possibility of a creation as is the relation determined by physical
laws—that is, supposing that such an intelligent cause has also a final
end. This is a principle which reason regards even *a priori* as one that
is necessary for its teleological judging of the existence of things. The
whole question, then, is reduced to this: Have we any ground capable
of satisfying reason, speculative or practical, to justify our attributing
a *final end* to the supreme cause that acts according to ends? For that,
judging by the subjective character of our reason, or even by anything
we can at all imagine of the reason of other beings, such final end could
be nothing but *man as subject to moral laws*, may be taken *a priori* as a
matter of certainty; whereas we are wholly unable to cognize *a priori*
what are the ends of nature in the physical order, and above all it is
impossible to see that a nature could not exist apart from such ends.

Remark

Imagine a person at the moment when his mind is disposed to moral
feeling! If, amid beautiful natural surroundings, he is in calm and
serene enjoyment of his existence, he feels within him a need—a need
of being grateful for it to someone. Or, at another time, in the same
frame of mind, he may find himself in the stress of duties which he can
only perform and will perform by submitting to a voluntary sacrifice;
then he feels within him a need—a need of having, in so doing, carried
out something commanded of him and obeyed a Supreme Lord. Or he
may in some thoughtless manner have diverged from the path of duty,
though not so as to have made himself answerable to others; yet
words of stern self-reproach will then fall upon an inward ear, and he
will seem to hear the voice of a judge to whom he has to render account.
In a word, he needs a moral Intelligence; because he exists for an end,
and this end demands a Being as the cause both of himself and the world
with that end in view. It is waste of labour to go burrowing behind
these feelings for motives; for they are immediately connected with
the purest moral disposition: *gratitude*, *obedience*, and *humiliation*—
that is, submission before a deserved chastisement—being special
modes of the mind's attunement to duty. It is merely that the mind
inclined to give expansion to its moral disposition here voluntarily
imagines an object that is not in the world, in order, if possible, to
prove its dutifulness before such an object also. Hence it is at least

possible—and, besides, there is in our moral habits of thought a foundation for so doing—to form a representation of a pure moral need for the existence of a being, whereby our morality gains in strength or even obtains—at least on the side of our representation—an extension of area, that is to say, is given a new object for its exercise. In other words, it is possible to admit a moral legislator existing apart from the world, and to do so without regard to theoretical proof, and still less to self-interest, but on a purely moral ground, which, while of course only subjective, is free from all foreign influence, on the mere recommendation of a pure practical reason that legislates for itself alone. It may be that such a disposition of the mind is but a rare occurrence, or, again, does not last long, but rather is fleeting and of no permanent effect, or, it may be, passes away without the mind bestowing a single thought upon such a shadowy image, and without troubling to reduce it to clear concepts. Yet the source of this disposition is unmistakable. It is the original moral predisposition of our nature, as a subjective principle, that will not let us be satisfied, in our consideration of the world, with the purposiveness which it derives through natural causes, but leads us to introduce into it an underlying supreme cause governing nature according to moral laws.— In addition to the above there is the fact that we feel ourselves urged by the moral law to strive after a universal highest end, while yet we feel ourselves, and all nature too, incapable of its attainment. Further, it is only so far as we strive after this end that we can judge ourselves to be in harmony with the final end of an intelligent world-cause—if such there be. Thus we have a pure moral ground derived from practical reason for admitting this cause (since we may do so without self-contradiction), if for no better reason, in order that we may not run the risk of regarding such striving as quite idle in its effects, and of allowing it to flag in consequence.

Let us restate what we intended to convey here by all these obser-   447
vations. While *fear* doubtless in the first instance may have been able to produce *gods*, that is demons, it is only *reason* by its moral principles that has been able to produce the concept of *God*—and it has been able to do so despite the great ignorance that has usually prevailed in what concerns the teleology of nature, or the considerable doubt that arises from the difficulty of reconciling by a sufficiently established principle the mutually conflicting phenomena that nature presents. Further, the inner *moral* destination of man's existence

supplements the shortcomings of natural knowledge, by directing us to join to the thought of the final end of the existence of all things—an end the principle of which only satisfies reason from an *ethical* point of view—the thought of the supreme cause as endowed with attributes whereby it is empowered to subject the whole of nature to that single purpose, and make it merely instrumental thereto. In other words it directs us to think the supreme cause as a *Deity*.

§ 87

The moral proof of the existence of God

WE have a *physical teleology* that affords evidence sufficient for our theoretical reflective judgement to enable us to admit the existence of an intelligent world-cause. But in ourselves, and still more in the general concept of a rational being endowed with freedom of its causality, we find a *moral teleology*. But as our own relation to an end, together with the law governing it, may be determined *a priori*, and consequently cognized as necessary, moral teleology does not stand in need of any intelligent cause outside ourselves to explain this intrinsic conformity to law any more than what we consider purposive in the geometrical properties of figures (their adaptation for all possible kinds of employment by art) lets us look beyond to a supreme understanding that imparts this purposiveness to them. But this moral teleology deals with us for all that as beings of the world and, therefore, as beings associated with other things in the world; and the same moral laws enjoin us to turn our consideration to these other things in the world, regarded either as ends, or as objects in respect of which we ourselves are the final end. This moral teleology, then, which deals with the relation of our own causality to ends, or even to a final end that must be proposed by us in the world, as well as with the reciprocal relation subsisting between the world and that moral end and 448 the possibility of realizing it under external conditions—a matter upon which no physical teleology can give us any guidance—raises a necessary question. For we must ask: Does this moral teleology oblige our rational judgement to go beyond the world and seek for an intelligent supreme principle in respect of the relation of nature to the moral side of our being, so that we may form a representation of nature as displaying purposiveness in relation also to our inner moral legislation and its possible realization? Hence there is certainly a moral teleology. It is as necessarily implicated with the *nomothetic* of freedom on the one hand, and that of nature on the other, as with civil legislation is implicated the question of where the executive authority is to be sought. In fact there is here the same implication as is to be found in everything in which reason has to assign a principle of the actuality of a certain uniform order of things that is only possible according to ideas.—We shall begin by exhibiting how from the above moral teleology and its relation to physical teleology reason advances to *theology*. Having done so, we shall make some observations on the possibility and conclusiveness of this mode of reasoning.

If we assume the existence of certain things, or even only of certain forms of things, to be contingent, and consequently to be only possible by means of something else as their cause, we may then look for the supreme source of this causality, and, therefore, for the unconditioned ground of the conditioned, either in the physical or the teleological order—that is, we may look either to the *nexus effectivus* or to the *nexus finalis*. In other words, we may ask which is the supreme productive cause, or we may ask what is the supreme or absolutely unconditioned end of such a cause, that is, what in general is the final end for which it produces these or all its products. In the latter question it is obviously taken for granted that this cause can form a representation of the end, and is consequently an intelligent being, or at least that it must be conceived by us as acting according to the laws of such a being.

Now, supposing we follow the teleological order, there is a *fundamental principle* to which even the most ordinary human intelligence is obliged to give immediate assent. It is the principle that if there is to be a *final end* at all, which reason must assign *a priori*, then it can only be *man*—or any rational being in the world—*standing under moral laws*.[5] For—and this is the verdict of everyone—if the world only consisted of lifeless beings, or even consisted partly of living, but yet non-rational 449

[5] I say deliberately: *under* moral laws. It is not man *in accordance* with moral laws, that is to say, human beings living in conformity with such laws, that is the final end of creation. For to use the latter expression would be to assert more than we know, namely, that it is in the power of an author of the world to ensure that man should always conform to the moral laws. But this presupposes a concept of freedom and of nature—of which latter alone we can think an external author—that implies an insight into the supersensible substrate of nature and its identity with what is rendered possible in the world by causality through freedom. Such insight far exceeds that of our reason. It is only of *man under moral laws* that we are able to affirm, without transcending the limits of our insight, that

beings, the existence of such a world would have no worth whatever, because there would exist in it no being with the least conception of what worth is. On the other hand, if there were even rational beings, and if nevertheless their reason were only able to set the worth of the existence of things in the bearing which nature has upon them, that is, in their well-being, instead of being able to procure such a worth for themselves from original sources, that is, in their freedom, then there would be, it is true, relative ends in the world, but no absolute end, since the existence of rational beings of this kind would still always remain devoid of an end. It is, however, a distinctive feature of the moral laws that they prescribe something for reason in the form of an end apart from any condition, and consequently in the very form that the concept of a final end requires. Therefore the existence of a reason like this, that in the order of ends can be the supreme law to itself, in other words the real existence of rational beings subject
450   to moral laws, can alone be regarded as the final end of the existence of a world. But if this is not so, then either no end whatever in the cause underlies the existence of the world or else only ends without a final end.

The moral law is the formal rational condition of the employment of our freedom, and, as such, of itself alone lays its obligation upon us, independently of any end as its material condition. But it also defines for us a final end, and does so *a priori*, and makes it obligatory upon us to strive towards its attainment. This end is the *highest good in the world* possible through freedom.

The subjective condition under which man, and, as far as we can at all conceive, every rational finite being also, is able under the above

his existence forms the final end of the world. This statement also accords perfectly with the verdict of human reason in its reflection upon the course of the world from a moral standpoint. We believe that even in the case of the wicked we perceive the traces of a wise design in things if we see that the wanton criminal does not die before he has suffered the just punishment of his misdeeds. According to our conceptions of free causality, good or bad conduct depends upon ourselves. But where we think that the supreme wisdom in the government of the world lies, is in the fact that the occasion for the former, and the result following from both, is ordained according to moral laws. In the latter consists, properly speaking, the honour of God, which is therefore not inappropriately termed by theologians the ultimate end of creation.—We should add that when we make use of the word creation, we only take it to mean what is spoken of here, namely, the cause of the *existence* of a *world*, or of the things in it, that is, substances. This is also what the strict meaning of the word conveys—*actuatio substantiae est creatio*. Consequently it implies no assumption of a cause that acts freely and that is therefore intelligent. The existence of such an intelligent cause is what we are set upon proving.

law to set before himself a final end, is happiness. Consequently the highest possible physical good in the world, and the one to be furthered so far as in us lies as the final end, is *happiness*—subject to the objective condition that the individual harmonizes with the law of *morality*, regarded as worthiness to be happy.

But by no faculty of our reason can we represent to ourselves these two requisites for the final end proposed to us by the moral law to be *connected* by means of mere natural causes and also conformed to the idea of the final end in contemplation. Accordingly, if we do not bring the causality of any other means besides nature into alliance with our freedom, the concept of the *practical necessity* of such an end through the application of our powers does not accord with the theoretical concept of the *physical possibility* of its realization.

Consequently we must assume a moral world-cause, that is, an author of the world, if we are to set before ourselves a final end in conformity with the requirements of the moral law. And as far as it is necessary to set such an end before us, so far, that is in the same degree and upon the same ground, it is necessary to assume an author of the world, or, in other words, that there is a God.[6]

This proof, to which we may easily give the form of logical precision, does not imply that it is as necessary to assume the existence of 451 God as it is to recognize the validity of the moral law, and that, consequently, one who is unable to convince himself of the former may deem himself absolved from the obligations imposed by the latter. No! all that must be abandoned in that case is the *aim* of realizing the final end in the world by the pursuit of the moral law (the happiness of rational beings harmoniously associated with such pursuit, as the highest good in the world). Every rational being would still have to continue to recognize himself as firmly bound by the precept of morality, for its laws are formal and command unconditionally, paying no regard to

[6] This moral argument is not intended to supply an *objectively* valid proof of the existence of God. It is not meant to demonstrate to the sceptic that there is a God, but that he *must adopt* the assumption of this proposition as a maxim of his practical reason, if he wishes to think in a manner consistent with morality.—Further, the argument is not intended to affirm that it is necessary *for the purpose of morality* to assume that the happiness of all rational beings in the world is proportioned to their morality. On the contrary it is *by virtue of morality* that the assumption is necessitated. Consequently it is an argument that is sufficient *subjectively* and for moral beings.*

ends (as the material content of the will). But the one requirement of the final end, as prescribed by practical reason to the beings of the world, is an irresistible end planted in them by their nature as finite beings. Reason refuses to countenance this end except as subject to the moral law *as* inviolable *condition*, and would only have it made universal in accordance with this condition. Thus it makes the furtherance of happiness in agreement with morality the final end. To promote this end—so far, in respect of happiness, as lies in our power—is commanded us by the moral law, whatever the outcome of this endeavour may be. The fulfilment of duty consists in the form of the earnest will, not in the intervening causes that contribute to success.

Suppose, then, that an individual, influenced partly by the weakness of all the speculative arguments that are thought so much of, and partly by the number of irregularities he finds in nature and the moral world, becomes persuaded of the proposition: There is no God; nevertheless in his own eyes he would be a worthless creature if he chose on that account to regard the laws of duty as simply fanciful, invalid, and non-obligatory, and resolved boldly to transgress them. Again, let us suppose that such a man were able subsequently to convince himself of the truth of what he had at first doubted; he would still remain worthless if he held to the above way of thinking. This is so, were he even to fulfil his duty as punctiliously as could be desired, so far as actual actions are 452 concerned, but were to do so from fear or with a view to reward, and without an inward reverence for duty. Conversely, if, as a believer in God, he observes his duty according to his conscience, uprightly and disinterestedly, yet if whenever, to try himself, he puts before himself the case of his haply being able to convince himself that there is no God, he straight away believes himself free from all moral obligation, the state of his inner moral disposition could then only be bad.

Let us then, as we may, take the case of a righteous man, such, say, as Spinoza, who considers himself firmly persuaded that there is no God and—since in respect of the object of morality a similar result ensues—no future life either. How will he judge his individual intrinsic purposiveness that is derived from the moral law which he reveres in practice? He does not require that its pursuit should bring him any personal benefit either in this or any other world. On the contrary his will is disinterestedly to establish only that good to which the holy law directs all his energies. But he is circumscribed in his endeavour. He may, it is true, expect to find a chance concurrence now and again, but he can never expect to find in nature a uniform agreement—a consistent agreement according to fixed rules, answering to what his maxims are and must be subjectively, with that end which yet he feels himself obliged and urged to realize. Deceit, violence, and envy will always be rife around him, although he himself is honest, peaceable, and benevolent; and the other righteous individuals that he meets in the world, no matter how deserving they may be of happiness, will be subjected by nature, which takes no heed of such deserts, to all the evils of want, disease, and untimely death, just as are the other animals on the earth. And so it will continue to be until one yawning grave devours them all—just and unjust, there is no distinction in the grave—and hurls them back into the abyss of the aimless chaos of matter from which they were first drawn—they that were able to believe themselves the final end of creation.—Thus the end which this right-minded man would have, and ought to have, in view in his pursuit of the moral law, would certainly have to be abandoned by him as impossible. But perhaps he resolves to remain faithful to the call of his inner moral vocation and would not willingly permit the respect with which he is immediately inspired to obedience by the moral law be weakened owing to the nullity of the one ideal final end that answers to its high demand—which could not happen without doing injury to his moral disposition. If so he must assume the existence of 453 a *moral* author of the world, that is, of a God. As this assumption at least involves nothing intrinsically self-contradictory he may quite readily make it from a practical point of view, that is to say, at least for the purpose of framing a conception of the possibility of the final end morally prescribed to him.

§ 88
Limitation of the validity of the moral proof

PURE reason, regarded as a practical faculty, a capacity, that is to say, for determining the pure employment of our causality by means of ideas, or pure rational concepts, not only possesses in its moral law a principle which is regulative of our actions, but by virtue of that law it furnishes at the same time an additional principle which, from a subjective point of view, is constitutive. This principle is contained in the concept of an object which reason alone is able to think, and which is meant to be realized in the world through our actions in conformity to that law. The idea of a final end in the employment of freedom in obedience to moral laws has, therefore, a reality that is subjectively *practical*. We are determined *a priori* by reason to further what is best for the world as far as this lies within our power. This consists in the union of the greatest welfare of the rational beings in the world with the supreme condition of their good, or, in other words, by the union of universal happiness with the strictest morality. Now the possibility of one of the factors of this final end, namely that of happiness, is empirically conditioned. It depends upon how nature is constituted—on whether nature harmonizes or not with this end. It is, therefore, from a theoretical point of view problematic; whereas the other factor, namely morality, in respect of which we are independent of the co-operation of nature, is *a priori* assured of its possibility and is dogmatically certain. Accordingly, the fact that we have a final end set before us *a priori* does not meet all the requirements of the objective and theoretical reality of the concept of the final end of rational beings in the world. It is further requisite that creation, that is, the world itself, should, in respect of its existence, have a final end. If we were able to prove *a priori* that it has such an end, this would supplement the subjective reality of the final end by a reality that is objective. For if creation has a final end at all we cannot conceive it otherwise than as harmonizing necessarily with our moral faculty, which is what alone makes the concept of an end possible. But, 454 now, we do find in the world what are certainly ends. In fact physical teleology exhibits ends in such abundance that if we let reason guide our judgement we have after all justification for assuming, as a principle upon which to investigate nature, that there is nothing whatever in nature that has not got its end. Yet in nature itself we search in vain for its own final end. Hence, just as the idea of this final end resides only in reason, so it is only in rational beings that such an end itself can and must be sought as an objective possibility. But the practical reason of these beings does not merely assign this final end: it also determines this concept in respect of the conditions under which a final end of creation can alone be thought by us.

Now the question arises: Is it not possible to substantiate the objective reality of the concept of a final end in a manner that will meet the theoretical requirements of pure reason? This cannot indeed be done apodictically for determining judgement. Yet may it not be done sufficiently for the maxims of theoretical judgement in so far as it is reflective? This is the least that could be demanded of speculative philosophy, which undertakes to connect the ethical end with natural ends by means of the idea of a single end. Yet even this little is still far more than it can ever accomplish.

Let us look at the matter from the standpoint of the principle of theoretical reflective judgement. To account for the purposive products of nature are we not justified in assuming a supreme cause of nature, whose causality in respect of the actuality of nature, or whose act of creation, must be regarded as specifically different from that which is required for the mechanism of nature, or, in other words, as the causality of an understanding? If we are, then, on the above principle, we should say that we were also sufficiently justified in attributing to this original being, not merely ends prevalent throughout nature, but also a final end. This does not serve the purpose of proving the existence of such a being, yet, at least, as was the case in the physical teleology, it is a justification sufficient to convince us that to make the possibility of such a world intelligible to ourselves we must not merely look to ends, but must also ascribe its existence to an underlying final end.

But a final end is simply a concept of our practical reason and cannot be inferred from any data of experience for the purpose of forming a theoretical judgement of nature, nor can it be applied to the cognition of nature. The only possible use of this concept is for practical reason according to moral laws; and the final end of creation 455 is such a constitution of the world as harmonizes with what we can only definitely specify according to laws, namely with the final end of our pure practical reason and of this, moreover, in so far as it is intended to be practical.—Now, by virtue of the moral law which enjoins this final end upon us, we have reason for assuming from a practical point of view, that is for the direction of our energies towards the realization of that end, that it is possible, or, in other words, practicable. Consequently we are also justified in assuming a nature of things harmonizing with such a possibility—for this possibility is subject to a condition which does not lie in our power, and without the assistance of nature the realization of the final end would be impossible. Hence, we have a moral justification for supposing that where we have a world we have also a final end of creation.

This does not yet bring us to the inference from moral teleology to a theology, that is, to the existence of a moral author of the world, but only to a final end of creation, which is defined in the above manner. Now must we, to account for this creation, that is, for the existence of things conformable to a *final end*, in the first place admit an intelligent being, and, in the second place, not merely an intelligent being—as had to be admitted to account for the possibility of such things in nature as we are compelled to judge as *ends*—but one that is also *moral*, as author of the world, and consequently a *God*? This admission involves a further inference, and one of such a nature that we see that it is intended for the power of judging by concepts of practical reason, and, being so, is drawn for reflective, not for determining judgement. It is true that with us morally practical reason is essentially different in its principles from technically practical reason. But, while this is so, we cannot pretend to see that the same distinction must also hold in the case of the supreme world-cause, if it is assumed to be an intelligence, and that a peculiar type of causality is required on its part for the final end, different from that which is requisite simply for natural ends, or, that we have, consequently, in our final end, not merely a *moral ground* for admitting a final end of creation, as an effect, but also a *moral being*, as the original source of creation. But it is quite competent for us to assert that *the nature of our faculty of reason is such* that without an author and governor of the world, who is also a moral lawgiver, we are wholly unable to render intelligible to ourselves the possibility of a purposiveness, related *to the moral law* and its object, such as exists in this final end.

456   The actuality of a supreme morally legislative author is, therefore, sufficiently proved simply *for the practical employment* of our reason, without determining anything theoretically in respect of its existence. For reason has an end which is prescribed independently by its own peculiar legislation. To make this end possible it requires an idea which removes, sufficiently for reflective judgement, the obstacle which arises from our inability to carry such legislation into effect when we have a mere physical conception of the world. In that way this idea acquires practical reality, although for speculative knowledge it fails of every means that would procure it reality from a theoretical point of view for explaining nature or determining its supreme cause. For theoretical reflective judgement an intelligent world-cause was sufficiently proved by physical teleology from the ends of nature. For practical reflective judgement moral teleology effects the same by means of the

concept of a final end, which it is obliged to ascribe to creation from a practical point of view. The objective reality of the idea of God, regarded as a moral author of the world, cannot, it is true, be substantiated by means of physical ends *alone*. Nevertheless, when the knowledge of those ends is associated with that of the moral end, the maxim of pure reason which directs us to pursue unity of principles so far as we are able to do so lends considerable importance to these ends for the purpose of reinforcing the practical reality of that idea by the reality which it already possesses from a theoretical point of view for judgement.

In this connexion there are two points which it is most necessary to note for the purpose of preventing a misunderstanding which might easily arise. In the first place these attributes of the supreme being can only be *thought* by us on an analogy. For how are we to investigate its nature when experience can show us nothing comparable? In the second place, such attributes also only enable us to think a supreme being, not to *cognize* it or to predicate them of it in a more or less theoretical manner. For this could only be done on behalf of determining judgement, as a faculty of our reason in its speculative aspect, and for the purpose of discerning the *intrinsic nature* of the supreme world-cause. But the only question that concerns us here is as to what concept we have, by the structure of our cognitive faculties, to form of this being, and whether we have to admit its existence on account of an end, which pure practical reason, apart from any such assumption, enjoins upon us to realize as far as in us lies, and for which we seek likewise to procure simply practical reality, that is to say, merely to be able to regard an envisaged effect as possible. It may well be that this concept is extravagant for speculative reason. The attributes also which by means of it we ascribe to the being in question may, objectively used, involve a covert anthropomorphism. Yet the object which we have in view in employing them is not that we wish to determine the nature of that being by reference to them—a nature which is inaccessible to us—but rather that we seek to use them for determining our own selves and our will. We may name a cause after the concept which we have of its effect—though only in respect of the relation in which it stands to this effect. And we may do this without on that account seeking to define intrinsically the inherent nature of that cause by the only properties known to us of causes of that kind, which properties

457

must be given to us by experience. We may, for instance, ascribe to the soul, among other properties, a *vis locomotiva**, because physical movements are actually initiated, the cause of which lies in the mind's activity of representing them. But this we do without on that account meaning to attribute to the soul the only kind of dynamical forces of which we have any knowledge—that is, those involving attraction, pressure, impact, and, consequently, motion, forces which always presuppose a being extended in space. Now in just the same way we have to assume *something* that contains the ground of the possibility and practical reality, or practicability, of a necessary moral final end. But, looking to the character of the effect expected therefrom, we may conceive this 'something' as a wise being ruling the world according to moral laws. And, in conformity with the character of our cognitive faculties, we are obliged to conceive it as a cause of things that is distinct from nature, for the sole purpose of expressing the *relation* in which this being that transcends all our cognitive faculties stands to the object of *our* practical reason. Yet in so doing we do not mean on that account to ascribe to this being theoretically the only causality of this kind familiar to us, namely an understanding and a will. Nor indeed, even as to the causality which we think exists in this being in respect of what is *for us* a final end, we do not mean to differentiate it objectively, as it exists in this being itself, from the causality in respect of nature and all its purposive determinations. On the contrary we only presume to be able to admit this distinction as one subjectively necessary for our cognitive faculty, constituted as it is, and as valid for reflective, and not for objectively determining judgement. But, once the question touches practical issues, a *regulative* principle of this kind—one for prudence or wisdom to follow—which directs us to act in conformity with something, as an end, the possibility of which, by the character of our cognitive faculties, can only be conceived by us in a certain manner, then becomes also *constitutive*. In other words it is practically determining, whereas the very same principle regarded as one upon which to judge the objective possibility of things is in no way theoretically determining, or, in other words, does not imply that the only type of possibility which our thinking faculty recognizes may also be predicated of the object of our thought. On the contrary it is a mere *regulative* principle for the use of reflective judgement.

Remark

This moral proof is not in any sense a newly discovered argument, but at the most only an old one in a new form. For its germ was lying in the human mind when our reason first quickened into life, and it only grew and developed with the progressive culture of that faculty. The moment human beings began to reflect upon right and wrong— at a time when they as yet cast but a heedless regard at the purposiveness of nature, and when they took advantage of it without imagining the presence of anything but nature's accustomed course—one inevitable judgement must have forced itself upon them. It could never be a matter of indifference, whether a person has acted fairly or falsely, with equity or with violence, albeit to his life's end, as far at least as human eye can see, his virtues have brought him no reward, and his transgressions no punishment. It seems as though they perceived a voice within them say that it must make a difference. So there must also have been a lurking notion, however obscure, of something after which they felt themselves bound to strive, and with which such a result would be wholly discordant, or with which, once they regarded the course of the world as the sole order of things, they would then be unable to reconcile that inner vocation of their minds. Now crude as are the various notions they might form of the way in which such an irregularity could be put straight—and it is one that must be far more revolting to the human mind than the blind chance which some have sought to make the underlying principle of their judgement of nature—there is only one principle upon which they could even conceive it possible for nature to harmonize with the moral law within them. It is that of a supreme cause ruling the world according to moral laws. For a final end within, that is set before them as a duty, and a nature without, that has no final end, though in it the former end is to be actualized, are in open contradiction. I admit they might hatch many absurdities concerning the inner nature of that world-cause. But that relation to the moral order in the government of the world always remained the same as is universally comprehensible to the most untutored reason, so far as it treats itself as practical, though speculative reason is far from being able to keep 459 pace with it.—Further, in all probability, it was this moral interest that first aroused attentiveness to beauty and the ends of nature. This would be admirably calculated to strengthen the above idea, though it could not supply its foundation. Still less could it dispense with the moral interest; for it is only in relation to the final end that the very study of the ends of nature acquires that immediate interest displayed to so great an extent in the admiration bestowed upon nature without regard to any ensuing advantage.

§ 89

The use of the moral argument

THE fact that, in respect of all our ideas of the supersensible, reason is restricted to the conditions of its practical employment, is of obvious use in connexion with the idea of God. It prevents *theology* from losing itself in the clouds of THEOSOPHY, i.e. in transcendent conceptions that confuse reason, or from sinking into the depths of DEMONOLOGY, i.e. an anthropomorphic mode of representing the supreme being. Also it keeps *religion* from falling into *theurgy*, which is a fanatical delusion that a feeling can be communicated to us from other supersensible beings and that we in turn can exert an influence on them, or into *idolatry*, which is a superstitious delusion that one can make oneself acceptable to the supreme being by any other means than that of a moral disposition.[7]

For if the vanity or presumption of those who would argue about what lies beyond the sensible world is allowed to determine even the smallest point theoretically, and so as to extend our knowledge; if any boast is permitted of shedding light upon the existence and constitution of the divine nature, its intelligence and will, and the laws of both these and the attributes which issue therefrom and influence the world: then I should like to know at what precise point the line is going to be 460 drawn for these pretensions of reason. From whatever source such light is derived still more may be expected—if, as the idea is, we only rack our brains. Yet it is only on some principle that bounds can be set to such claims—it is not enough simply to appeal to our experience of the fact that all attempts of the sort have so far miscarried; for

---

[7] A religion is never free from the imputation of idolatry, in a practical sense, so long as the attributes with which it endows the supreme being are such that anything that man may do can be taken as in accordance with God's will on any other all-sufficing condition than that of morality. For however pure and free from sensuous images the form of that concept may be from a theoretical point of view, yet, with such attributes, it is from a practical point of view depicted as an idol—the character of God's will, that is to say, is represented anthropomorphically.

that is no disproof of the possibility of a better result. But the only principle possible in this case is either that of admitting that in respect of the supersensible absolutely nothing can be determined theoretically (unless solely by way of bare negation), or that of supposing the existence in our reason of an as yet untapped mine of who knows how vast and enlightening information reserved for us and our posterity.—But the result, so far as concerns religion—that is, morality in relation to God as lawgiver—would be that morality, supposing that the theoretical knowledge of God has to take the lead, must then conform to theology. Thus not only will an extrinsic and arbitrary legislation on the part of a supreme being have to be introduced in place of an immanent and necessary legislation of reason, but, even in such legislation, all the defects of our insight into the divine nature must spread to the ethical code, and religion in this way be divorced from morality and perverted.

What now of the hope of a future life? It is open to us to look to the final end which, in obedience to the injunction of the moral law, we have ourselves to fulfil, and to adopt it as a guiding thread for the verdict of reason concerning our vocation—a verdict which is therefore only regarded as necessary or worthy of acceptance from a practical point of view. But if, instead of so doing, we consult our faculty of theoretical knowledge, then the same lot befalls psychology in this connexion as befell theology in the case above. It supplies no more than a negative conception of our thinking being. It tells us that not one of the operations of the mind or manifestations of inner sense can be explained on materialistic lines; that, accordingly, no illuminating or determining judgement as to the separate nature of what thinks, or of the continuance or discontinuance of its personality after death, can possibly be made on speculative grounds by any exercise of our faculty of theoretical knowledge, Thus everything is here left to the teleological judging of our existence from a point of view that is necessary in the practical sphere, and to the assumption of the continuance of our existence, as a condition required by the final end that is absolutely imposed upon us by reason. Hence in our negative result we see at once a gain—a gain that at first sight no doubt appears a loss. For just as theology can never become theosophy, so rational *psychology* can never become *pneumatology*, as a science that 461 extends our knowledge, nor yet, on the other hand, be in danger of lapsing into any sort of *materialism*. On the contrary we see that it is really a mere anthropology of the inner sense, a knowledge, that is to say, of our thinking self *as alive*, and that, in the form of a theoretical cognition, it also remains merely empirical. But, as concerned with the problem of our eternal existence, rational psychology is not a theoretical science at all. It rests upon a single inference of moral teleology, just as the entire necessity of its employment arises out of moral teleology and our practical vocation.

§ 90

The type of assurance in a teleological proof of the existence of God

WHETHER a proof is derived from immediate empirical presentation of what is to be proved, as in the case of proof by observation of the object or by experiment, or whether it is derived *a priori* by reason from principles, what is primarily required of it is that it should not *persuade*, but *convince*, or at least tend to convince. The argument or inference, in other words, should not be simply a subjective, or aesthetic, ground of assent—a mere semblance—but should be objectively valid and a logical source of knowledge. If it is not this, intelligence is taken in, not won over. An illusory proof of the type in question is brought forward in natural theology—maybe with the best of intentions, but nevertheless with a deliberate concealment of its weakness. The whole host of arguments for an origin of the things of nature according to the principle of ends is marshalled before us, and capital is made out of the purely subjective ground of human reason. The latter is inclined, by its very character, wherever it can do so without contradiction, to think one single principle in place of several. Also, where this principle only provides one, or, it may be, a large proportion, of the terms necessary for defining a concept, it supplements this or these by adding the others, so as to complete the concept of the thing by an arbitrary extension. For naturally, when we find such a number of products of nature pointing us to an intelligent cause, should we not suppose one single such cause in preference to supposing a plurality of them? And why, then, stop at great intelligence, might, and so forth, in this cause, and not rather endow it with omniscience and omnipotence, and, in a word, regard it as one that contains an ample source of such attributes for all possible things? And why not go on and ascribe to this single all-powerful primordial being, not merely the intelligence necessary for the laws and products of nature, but also the supreme ethical and practical reason that belongs to a moral world-cause? For by this completion of the concept we are supplied with a principle that meets the joint requirements alike of insight into nature and moral wisdom—and no objection of the least substance can be brought against the possibility of such an idea. If now, in the course of this argument, the moral springs that stir the mind are touched, and a lively interest imparted to them with all the force of rhetoric—of which they are quite worthy—a persuasion arises of the objective sufficiency of the proof, and, in most cases where it is used, an even beneficent illusion that disdains any examination of its logical accuracy, and in fact abhors and sets its face against logical criticism, as if it sprang from some impious misgiving.—Now there is really nothing to say against all this, so long as we only take popular expediency into consideration. But we cannot and should not be deterred from the analysis of the proof into the two heterogeneous elements which this argument involves, namely into so much as pertains to physical, and so much as pertains to moral teleology. For the fusing of both elements prevents our recognizing where the real nerve of the proof lies, or in what part or in what way it must be reshaped, so that its validity may be able to be upheld under the most searching examination—even though on some points we should be compelled to confess that reason sees but a short way. Hence, the philosopher finds it his duty—supposing that he were even to pay no regard to what he owes to sincerity—to expose the illusion, however wholesome, which such a confusion can produce. He must segregate what is mere matter of persuasion from what leads to conviction—two modes of assent that differ not merely in degree but in kind—so as to be able to present openly in all its clearness the attitude which the mind adopts in this proof, and to subject it frankly to the most rigorous test.

Now a proof which is directed towards conviction may be of one or other of two kinds. It may be intended to decide what the object is *in itself*, or else what it is *for us*, that is, for man in the abstract, according to the rational principles on which it is necessarily judged 463 by us. It may, in other words, be a proof κατ' ἀλήθειαν or one κατ' ἄνθρωπον *—taking the latter word in the broad sense of man in the abstract. In the first case it is grounded on principles adequate for determining judgement, in the second on such as are adequate merely for reflective judgement. Where, in the latter case, a proof rests simply on theoretical principles, it can never tend towards conviction. But if

292 Critique of Teleological Judgement

it is grounded on a practical principle of reason, one which, consequently, is universal and necessary, it may well lay claim to a conviction that is sufficient from a practical point of view, that is to a moral
conviction. But a proof *tends towards conviction*, though without producing conviction, if it merely puts us on the road to conviction.
This it does where it only involves objective sources of conviction
which, while as yet insufficient to produce certitude, are nevertheless
of such a kind that they are not subjective grounds of judgement,
which, as such, serve merely for persuasion.

Now all arguments that establish a theoretical proof are sufficient
either: (1) for proof by logically rigorous *syllogistic inferences*; or,
where this is not the case, (2) for inference by *analogy*; or, should
even such inference be absent, still (3) for *probable opinion*; or, finally,
for what is least of all, (4) the assumption of a merely possible source
of explanation as an *hypothesis*.—Now I assert that all arguments without exception that tend towards theoretical conviction, are powerless
to produce any assurance of the above type, from its highest degree to
its lowest, *where* the proposition that is to be proved is the existence of
an original being, regarded as a God in the sense appropriate to the
complete content of this concept, that is to say, regarded as a *moral*
author of the world, and, consequently, in such a way that the final end
of creation is at once derived from him.

1. The critique has abundantly shown* how the matter stands as
regards proof in *strict logical form*—advancing, that is, from universal to particular. No intuition corresponding to the concept of a being
which has to be sought beyond nature is possible for us. So far, therefore, as that concept has to be determined theoretically by synthetic
predicates, it always remains for us a problematical concept. Hence, there
exists absolutely no cognition of such a being that would in the smallest
degree enlarge the reach of our theoretical knowledge. The particular
conception of a supersensible being cannot possibly be subsumed in
any way under the universal principles of the nature of things, so as
to allow of its being determined by inference from those principles,
464 for they are solely valid for nature as an object of the senses.

2. In the case of two dissimilar things we may admittedly form some
concept of one of them by an *analogy*[8] which it bears to the other, and

---

[8] *Analogy*, in a qualitative sense, is the identity of the relation subsisting between
grounds and consequences—causes and effects—so far as such identity subsists despite
the specific difference of the things, or of those properties, considered in themselves

do so even on the point on which they are dissimilar; but from that in which they are dissimilar we cannot draw any *inference* from one to the other on the strength of the analogy—that is, we cannot transfer the mark of the specific difference to the second. Thus on the analogy of the law of the equality of action and reaction in the mutual attraction and repulsion of bodies I am able to picture to my mind the   465 social relations of the members of a commonwealth regulated by civil laws; but I cannot transfer to these relations the former specific determinations, that is, physical attraction and repulsion, and ascribe them to the citizens, so as to constitute a system called a state.—In the same way the causality of the original being may, in its relation to the things of the world, regarded as natural ends, quite properly be conceived on the analogy of an intelligence, regarded as the source of the forms of certain products that we call works of art. For this is only done in the interests of the theoretical or practical use which our cognitive faculty has to make of this concept when dealing with the things in the world. But from the fact that with the beings of the

(i.e. apart from this relation), which are the source of similar consequences. Thus when we compare the formative activities of the lower animals with those of man, we regard the unknown source of such effects in the former case, as compared with the known source of similar effects produced by man, that is by reason, as the analogon of reason. By this we mean to imply that while the source of the formative capacity of the lower animals, to which we give the name of instinct, is in fact specifically different from reason, yet, comparing, say, the constructive work of beavers and human beings, it stands in a like relation to its effect.—But this does not justify me in inferring that, because man employs *reason* for what he constructs, beavers must possess reason also, and in calling this an *inference* from analogy. But from the similar mode of activity on the part of the lower animals, the source of which we are unable directly to perceive, compared with that of man, of which we are immediately conscious, we may quite correctly infer, *on the strength of the analogy*, that the lower animals, like man, act according to *representations*, and are not machines, as Descartes contends, and that, despite their specific difference, they are living beings and as such generally kindred to man. The principle that authorizes us to draw this inference lies in the fact that we have exactly the same reason for putting the lower animals in this respect in the same genus with human beings as in man for putting human beings, so far as we look at them from the outside and compare their acts, in the same genus with one another. There is *par ratio** here. In the same way the causality of the supreme world-cause may be conceived on the analogy of an understanding, if we compare its final products in the world with the formative works of man, but we cannot, on the strength of the analogy, infer such human attributes in the world-cause. For the principle that would make such a mode of reasoning possible is absent in this case, namely the *paritas rationis* for including the supreme being and man, in relation to their respective causalities, in one and the same genus. The causality of the beings in the world which, like causality by means of understanding, is always sensuously conditioned, cannot be transferred to a being which has no generic concept in common with man beyond that of a thing in the abstract.

world intelligence must be ascribed to the cause of an effect that is considered artificial, we are wholly unable to infer by analogy that, in relation to nature, the very same causality that we perceive in man belongs also to the being which is entirely distinct from nature. The reason is that this touches the precise point of dissimilarity between a cause that is sensuously conditioned in respect of its effects and a supersensible original being. This dissimilarity is implied in the very concept of such a supersensible being, and the distinguishing feature cannot therefore be transferred to it.—In this very fact, that I am required to conceive the causality of the Deity only on the analogy of an understanding—a faculty which is not known to us in any other being besides man, subjected, as he is, to the conditions of sensibility—lies the prohibition that forbids me to ascribe to God an understanding in the proper sense of the word.[9]

3. There is no room for *opinion* in *a priori* judgements. Such judgements, on the contrary, enable us to cognize something as quite certain, or else give us no cognition at all. But even where the given premisses from which we start are empirical, as are the natural ends in the present case, yet they cannot help us to form any opinion that extends beyond the sensible world, and to such rash judgements we cannot accord the least claim to probability. For probability is a fraction of a possible certainty distributed over a particular series of grounds—the grounds of the possibility within the series being compared with the sufficient ground of certainty, as a part is compared with a whole. Here the insufficient ground must be capable of being increased to the point of sufficiency. But these grounds, being the determining grounds of the certainty of one and the same judgement, must be of the same order. For unless they are, they would not, when taken together, form a quantum—such as certainty is. Thus one component part cannot lie within the bounds of possible experience, and another lie beyond all possible experience. Consequently, since premisses that are simply empirical do not lead to anything supersensible, nothing can supplement the imperfection of such an empirical series. Not the smallest approximation, therefore, occurs in the attempt to reach the supersensible, or a knowledge of it, from such premisses; and consequently no

466

---

[9] This does not involve the smallest loss to our representation of the relation in which this being stands to the world, so far as concerns the consequences, theoretical or practical, of this concept. To seek to inquire into the intrinsic nature of this being is a curiosity as senseless as it is idle.

probability enters into a judgement about the supersensible, when it rests on arguments drawn from experience.

4. If anything is intended to serve as an *hypothesis* for explaining the possibility of a given phenomenon, then at least the possibility of that thing must be perfectly certain. We give away enough when, in the case of an hypothesis, we waive the knowledge of actual existence— which is affirmed in an opinion put forward as probable—and more than this we cannot surrender. At least the possibility of what we make the basis of an explanation must be open to no doubt, otherwise there would be no end to empty fictions of the brain. But it would be taking things for granted without anything whatever to go upon, if we were to assume the possibility of a supersensible being defined according to positive concepts, for no one of the conditions requisite for cognition, so far as concerns the element dependent on intuition, is given. Hence, all that is left as the criterion of this possibility is the principle of contradiction—which can only prove the possibility of the thought and not of the object which is thereby thought.

The net result is that for the existence of the original being, regarded as a Deity, or of the soul, regarded as an immortal spirit, it is absolutely impossible for human reason to obtain any proof from a theoretical point of view, so as to produce the smallest degree of assurance. And there is a perfectly intelligible reason for this, since we have no available material for defining the idea of the supersensible, seeing that we should have to draw that material from things in the world of the senses, and then its character would make it utterly inappropriate to the supersensible. In the absence, therefore, of all determination, we are left merely with the conception of a non-sensible something containing the ultimate ground of the sensible world. This constitutes no cognition of its intrinsic nature, such as would extend our concept of this ground.

§ 91

The type of assurance produced by a practical faith

IF we look merely to the manner in which something can be an object of knowledge (*res cognoscibilis*) *for us*, that is, having regard to the subjective nature of our powers of representation, we do not in that case compare our concepts with the objects, but merely with our faculties of cognition and the use that they are able to make of the given representation from a theoretical or practical point of view. So the question whether something is a cognizable entity or not, is a question which touches, not the possibility of the things themselves, but the possibility of our knowledge of them.

Things which can be *known* are of three kinds:* *matters of opinion* (*opinabile*), *matters of fact* (*scibile*), *and matters of faith* (*mere credibile*).

1. The objects of mere ideas of reason, being wholly incapable of presentation, on behalf of theoretical knowledge, in any possible experience whatever, are to that extent also things altogether *unknowable*, and, consequently, we cannot even *form an opinion* about them. For to form an opinion *a priori* is absurd on the face of it and the straight road to pure figments of the brain. Either our *a priori* proposition is certain, therefore, or it involves no element of assurance at all. Hence, *matters of opinion* are always objects of an empirical knowledge that is at least intrinsically possible. They are, in other words, objects belonging to the sensible world, but objects of which an empirical knowledge is impossible *for us* because the degree of empirical knowledge we possess is as it is. Thus the ether of our modern physicists—an elastic fluid interpenetrating all other substances and completely permeating them—is a mere matter of opinion, yet it is in all respects of such a kind that it could be perceived if our external senses were sharpened to the highest degree, but its presentation can never be the subject of any observation or experiment. To assume rational inhabitants of other planets is a matter of opinion; for if we could get nearer the planets, which is intrinsically possible, experience would decide whether such inhabitants are there or not; but as we never shall get so near to them, the matter remains one of opinion. But to entertain an opinion that there exist in the material universe pure unembodied thinking spirits is mere romancing—supposing, I mean, that we dismiss from our notice, as well we may, certain phenomena that have been passed off for such.*

468   Such a notion is not a matter of opinion at all, but an idea pure and simple. It is what remains when we abstract from a thinking being all that is material and yet leave it in possession of its thought. But whether, when we have taken away everything else, the thought—which we only know in man, that is in connexion with a body—would still remain, is a matter we are unable to decide. A thing like this is a *sophistical entity* (*ens rationis ratiocinantis*), not an *entity of reason*

(*ens rationis ratiocinatae*). With the latter it is anyway possible to substantiate the objective reality of its concept, at least in a manner sufficient for the practical employment of reason, for this employment, which has its peculiar and apodictically certain *a priori* principles, in fact demands and postulates that concept.

2. The objects that answer to concepts whose objective reality can be proved are *matters of fact*[10] (*res facti*). Such proof may be afforded by pure reason or by experience, and in the former case may derive from theoretical or practical data of reason, but in all cases it must be effected by means of an intuition corresponding to the relevant concepts. Examples of matters of fact are the mathematical properties of geometrical magnitudes, for they admit of *a priori presentation* for the theoretical employment of reason. Further, things or qualities of things that are capable of being verified by experience, whether it be one's own personal experience or that of others (supported by evidence), are in the same way matters of fact.—But there is this notable point, that one idea of reason, strange to say, is to be found among the matters of fact—an idea which does not of itself admit of any presentation in intuition, or, consequently, of any theoretical proof of its possibility. The idea in question is that of *freedom*. Its reality is the reality of a particular kind of causality (the concept of which would be transcendent if considered theoretically), and as a causality of that kind it admits of verification by means of practical laws of pure reason and in the actual actions that take place in obedience to them, and, consequently, in experience.—It is the only one of all the ideas of pure reason whose object is a matter of fact and must be included among the *scibilia*.

3. Objects that must be thought *a priori*, either as consequences or 469 as grounds, if pure practical reason is to be used as duty commands, but which are transcendent for the theoretical use of reason, are mere *matters of faith*. Such is the *highest good* which has to be realized in the world through freedom—a concept whose objective reality cannot be proved in any experience possible for us, or, consequently, so as to satisfy the requirements of the theoretical employment of

---

[10] I here extend the concept of a matter of fact beyond the usual meaning of the term, and, I think, rightly. For it is not necessary, and indeed not practicable, to restrict this expression to actual experience where we are speaking of the relation of things to our cognitive faculties, as we do not need more than a merely possible experience to enable us to speak of things as objects of a definite kind of knowledge.

reason, while at the same time we are enjoined to use it for the purpose of realizing that end through pure practical reason in the best way possible, and, accordingly, its possibility must be assumed. This effect which is commanded, *together with the only conditions on which its possibility is conceivable by us*, namely the existence of God and the immortality of the soul, are *matters of faith* (*res fidei*) and, moreover, are of all objects the only ones that can be so called.[11] For although we have to believe what we can only learn by *testimony* from the experience of others, yet that does not make what is so believed in itself a matter of faith, for with *one* of those witnesses it was personal experience and matter of fact, or is assumed to have been so. In addition it must be possible to arrive at knowledge by this path—the path of historical belief; and the objects of history and geography, as, in general, everything that the nature of our cognitive faculties makes at least a possible subject of knowledge, are to be classed among matters of fact, not matters of faith. It is only objects of pure reason that can be matters of faith at all, and even they must then not be regarded as objects simply of pure speculative reason; for this does not enable them to be reckoned with any certainty whatever among matters, or objects, of that knowledge which is possible for us. They are ideas, that is concepts, whose objective reality cannot be guaranteed theoretically. On the other hand, the supreme final end to be realized by us, which is all that can make us worthy of being ourselves the final end of a creation, is an idea that has objective reality for us in practical matters, and is a matter in this sense. But since we cannot procure objective reality for this concept from a theoretical point of view, it is a mere matter of faith on the part of pure reason, as are also God and immortality, the latter being the sole conditions under which, owing to the character of our human reason, we are able to conceive the possibility of that effect of the use of our freedom according to law. But assurance in matters of faith is an assurance from a purely practical point of view. It is a moral faith that proves nothing for pure rational knowledge as theoretical, but only for it as practical and directed to the fulfilment of its obligations. It in no way extends either

470

---

[11] Being a matter of faith does not make a thing an *article of faith*, if by articles of faith we mean such matters of faith as one can be bound to *acknowledge*, inwardly or outwardly— a kind therefore that does not enter into natural theology. For, being matters of faith, they cannot, like matters of fact, depend on theoretical proofs, and, therefore, the assurance is a free assurance, and it is only as such that it is compatible with the morality of the subject.

speculation or the practical rules of prudence based upon the principle of self-love. If the supreme principle of all moral laws is a postulate, this involves the possibility of its supreme object, and, consequently, the condition under which we are able to conceive such possibility, being also postulated. This does not make the cognition of the latter any knowledge or any opinion of the existence or nature of these conditions, as a mode of theoretical knowledge, but a mere assumption, confined to practical matters and commanded in practical interests, on behalf of the moral use of our reason.

If we were able with any plausibility to make the ends of nature which physical teleology sets before us in such abundance the basis of a *determinate* concept of an intelligent world-cause, the existence of this being would not even then be a matter of faith. For as it would not be assumed on behalf of the performance of our duty, but only for the purpose of explaining nature, it would simply be the opinion and hypothesis best suited to our reason. Now the teleology in question does not lead in any way to a determinate concept of God. On the contrary such a concept can only be found in that of a moral author of the world, because this alone furnishes the final end to which we can assign ourselves only so far as we live in accordance with what the moral law prescribes to us as the final end, and, consequently, imposes upon us as a duty. Hence, it is only by relation to the object of our duty, as the condition which makes its final end possible, that the concept of God acquires the privilege of figuring in our assurance as a matter of faith. On the other hand, this very same concept cannot make its object valid as a matter of fact, for although the necessity of duty is quite plain for practical reason, yet the attainment of its final end, so far as it does not lie entirely in our own hands, is merely assumed in the interests of the practical employment of reason, and, therefore, is 471 not practically necessary in the way duty itself is.[12]

[12] The final end which we are enjoined by the moral law to pursue is not the ground of duty. For duty lies in the moral law which, being a formal practical principle, directs categorically, irrespective of the objects of the faculty of desire—the material content of willing—and, consequently, of any end whatever. This formal character of our actions—their subordination to the principle of universal validity—which alone constitutes their intrinsic moral worth, lies entirely in our own power; and we can quite easily make abstraction from the possibility or the impracticability of the ends that we are obliged to promote in accordance with that law—for they only form the extrinsic worth of our actions. Thus we put them out of consideration, as what does not lie altogether in our own power, in order to concentrate our attention on what rests in our own hands. But the object in

Faith as *habitus*, not as *actus*,* is the moral attitude of reason in its
assurance of the truth of what is beyond the reach of theoretical
knowledge. It is the steadfast principle of the mind, therefore, according to which the truth of what must necessarily be presupposed as the
condition of the supreme final end being possible is assumed as true in
consideration of the fact that we are under an obligation to pursue that
end[13]—and assumed notwithstanding that we have no insight into
472 its possibility, though likewise none into its impossibility. Faith, in
the plain acceptation of the term, is a confidence of attaining a purpose the furthering of which is a duty, but whose achievement is a
thing of which we are unable to *perceive* the possibility—or, consequently, the possibility of what we can alone conceive to be its conditions. Thus the faith that has reference to particular objects is
entirely a matter of morality, provided such objects are not objects of
possible knowledge or opinion, in which latter case, and above all in
matters of history, it must be called credulity and not faith. It is a free

view—the furthering of the final end of all rational beings, namely, happiness so far as it
is consistent with duty—is nevertheless imposed upon us by the law of duty. But speculative reason does not in any way perceive the practicability of that object—whether we look
at it from the standpoint of our own physical power or from that of the co-operation of
nature. On the contrary, so far as we are able to form a rational judgement on the point,
speculative reason must, apart from the assumption of the existence of God and immortality, regard it as a baseless and idle, though well-intentioned, expectation, to hope that
mere nature, internal or external, will from such causes bring about such a result of
our good conduct, and could it have perfect certainty as to the truth of this judgement,
it would have to look on the moral law itself as a mere delusion of our reason in respect
of practical matters. But speculative reason is fully convinced that the latter can never
happen, whereas those ideas whose object lies beyond nature may be thought without
contradiction. Hence for the sake of its own practical law and the task which it imposes,
and, therefore, in respect of moral concerns, it must recognize those ideas to be real, in
order not to fall into self-contradiction.

[13] It is a confidence in the promise of the moral law. But this promise is not regarded
as one involved in the moral law itself, but rather as one which we import into it, and so
import on morally adequate grounds. For a final end cannot be commanded by any law of
reason, unless reason, though it be with uncertain voice, also promises its attainability, and
at the same time authorizes assurance as to the sole conditions under which our reason can
imagine such attainability. The very word *fides* expresses this; and it must seem suspicious how this expression and this particular idea find a place in moral philosophy, since
it was first introduced with Christianity, and its acceptance might perhaps seem only a
flattering imitation of the language of the latter. But this is not the only case in which this
wonderful religion has in the great simplicity of its statement enriched philosophy with far
more definite and purer concepts of morality than morality itself could have previously
supplied. But once these concepts are found, they are *freely* approved by reason, which
adopts them as concepts at which it could quite well have arrived itself and which it
might and ought to have introduced.

assurance, not of any matter for which dogmatic proofs can be found for theoretical determining judgement, nor of what we consider a matter of obligation, but of that which we assume in the interests of a purpose which we set before ourselves in accordance with laws of freedom. But this does not mean that it is adopted like an opinion formed on inadequate grounds. On the contrary it is something that is grounded in reason (though only in relation to its practical employment), and *adequately so in this regard*. For without it, when the moral attitude comes into collision with theoretical reason and fails to satisfy its demand for a proof of the possibility of the object of morality, it forfeits all its stability, and wavers between practical commands and theoretical doubts. To be *incredulous* is to adhere to the maxim of placing no reliance on testimony; but a person is *unbelieving* who denies all validity to the above ideas of reason because their reality has no theoretical foundation. Hence, such a person judges dogmatically. But a dogmatic *unbelief* cannot stand side by side with a moral maxim governing the attitude of the mind—for reason cannot command one to pursue an end that is recognized to be nothing but a fiction of the brain. But the case is different with a *doubtful faith*. For with such a faith the want of conviction from grounds of speculative reason is only an obstacle—one which a critical insight into the limits of this faculty can deprive of any influence upon conduct and for which it can make amends by   473
a paramount practical assurance.

If we desire to replace certain mistaken efforts in philosophy, and to introduce a different principle, and gain influence for it, it gives great satisfaction to see just how and why such attempts were bound to miscarry.

God, *freedom*, and the *immortality of the soul* are the problems to whose solution, as their ultimate and unique goal, all the laborious preparations of metaphysics are directed. Now it was believed that the doctrine of freedom was only necessary as a negative condition for practical philosophy, whereas that of God and the nature of the soul, being part of theoretical philosophy, had to be proved independently and separately. Then each of those two concepts was subsequently to be united with what is commanded by the moral law (which is only possible on terms of freedom) and a religion was to be arrived at in this way. But we perceive at once that such attempts were bound to miscarry.

For from simple ontological concepts of things in the abstract, or of the existence of a necessary being, we can form absolutely no concept of an original being determined by predicates which admit of being given in experience and which are therefore available for cognition. But should the concept be founded on experience of the physical purposiveness of nature, it could then in turn supply no proof adequate for morality or, consequently, the cognition of a God. Just as little could knowledge of the soul drawn from experience—which we can only obtain in this life—furnish a concept of its spiritual and immortal nature, or, consequently, one that would satisfy morality. *Theology* and *pneumatology*, regarded as problems framed in the interests of sciences pursued by a speculative reason, lie in their very implication beyond all our faculties of knowledge, and cannot, therefore, be established by means of any empirical data or predicates.—These two concepts, both that of God and that of the soul (in respect of its immortality), can only be defined by means of predicates which, although they themselves derive their possibility entirely from a supersensible source, must, for all that, prove their reality in experience, for this is the only way in which they can make possible a cognition of a wholly supersensible being.—Now the only concept of this kind to be found in human reason is that of the free-
474 dom of man subject to moral laws and, in conjunction therewith, to the final end which freedom prescribes by means of these laws. These laws and this final end enable us to ascribe, the former to the author of nature, the latter to man, the properties which contain the necessary conditions of the possibility of both. Thus it is from this idea that an inference can be drawn to the existence and the nature of both God and the soul—beings that otherwise would be entirely hidden from us.

  Hence, the source of the failure of the attempt to attain to a proof of God and immortality by the merely theoretical route lies in the fact that no knowledge of the supersensible is possible if the path of natural concepts is followed. The reason why the proof succeeds, on the other hand, when the path of morals, that is, of the concept of freedom, is followed, is because from the supersensible, which in morals is fundamental (i.e. as freedom), there arises a definite law of causality. By means of this law the supersensible here not only provides material for the knowledge of the other supersensible, that is of the moral final end and the conditions of its practicability, but it also reveals its own reality, as a matter of fact, in actions. For that very reason, however, it is unable to afford any valid argument other than from a practical point of view—which is also the only one needful for religion.

There is something very remarkable in the way this whole matter stands. Of the three ideas of pure reason, God, freedom, and immortality, that of freedom is the one and only concept of the supersensible which (owing to the causality implied in it) proves its objective reality in nature by its possible effect there. By this means it makes possible the connexion of the two other ideas with nature, and the connexion of all three to form a religion. We are thus ourselves possessed of a principle which is capable of determining the idea of the supersensible within us, and, in that way, also of the supersensible without us, so as to constitute knowledge—a knowledge, however, which is only possible from a practical point of view. This is something of which mere speculative philosophy—which can only give a simply negative concept even of freedom—must despair. Consequently the concept of freedom, as the fundamental concept behind all unconditionally-practical laws, can extend reason beyond the bounds to which every (theoretical) concept of nature must remain hopelessly restricted.

IF we ask how the moral argument, which only proves the existence of God as a matter of faith for practical pure reason, ranks with the other arguments in philosophy, the value of the entire stock of the latter may be readily judged. It turns out that we are left with no choice here, but that philosophy in its theoretical capacity must of its own accord resign all its claims in the face of an impartial critique.

Philosophy must lay the first foundations of all assurance on what is matter of fact, unless such assurance is to be entirely baseless. Hence, the only difference that can arise in the proof is on the point of whether an assurance in the consequence inferred from this matter of fact may be based upon it in the form of *knowledge* for theoretical cognition or in the form of *faith* for practical cognition. All matters of fact come under the head either of the *concept of nature*, which proves its reality in objects of the senses that are given, or might be given, antecedently to all concepts of nature; or else of the *concept of freedom*, which sufficiently reveals its reality by the causality of reason in respect of certain effects in the sensible world that are possible by means of that causality—a causality which reason indisputably postulates in the moral law. Now the concept of nature—which pertains merely to theoretical cognition—is either metaphysical and wholly *a priori*; or physical, that is *a posteriori* and of necessity only conceivable by means of determinate experience. Hence, the metaphysical concept of nature—which does not presuppose any determinate experience—is ontological.

Now *the ontological proof* of the existence of God drawn from the concept of an original being may take one or other of two paths. It may start from the ontological predicates which alone enable that being to be completely defined in thought, and thence infer its absolutely necessary existence. Or it may start from the absolute necessity of the existence of something or other, whatever it may be, and thence infer the predicates of the original being. For an original being implies in accordance with its very concept—if such a being is not derived from anything else—the unconditional necessity of its own existence and (if this necessity may be formulated to the mind) its determination in and through the concept itself. Now these two requirements were both supposed to be found in the concept of the ontological idea of an *ens realissimum* or *superlatively real being*. Thus there arose two metaphysical arguments.

The proof which is based on the purely metaphysical concept of nature—the strictly ontological proof, as it is called— started from the concept of the superlatively real being and thence inferred its absolutely necessary existence, the argument being that unless it existed it would lack one reality, namely, existence.—The other, which is also called the metaphysico-*cosmological* proof, started from the necessity of the existence of something or other—and as much as that I must certainly concede, since an existence is given to me in my own self-consciousness—and thence inferred its complete determination as the superlatively real being. For, as was argued, while all that has existence is determined in all respects, what is absolutely necessary—that is, what we have to cognize as such, and, consequently, cognize *a priori*—must be completely determined *through its concept*; but such thorough determination can only be found in the concept of a superlatively real thing. The sophistries in both these inferences need not be exposed here, as that has already been done in another place. All I need now say is that, let such proofs be defended with all the forms of dialectical subtlety you please, yet they will never reach out beyond the schools and enter into every-day life or be able to exert the slightest influence on ordinary healthy intelligence.

The proof which is founded on a concept of nature, which, while it can only be empirical, is yet intended to lead beyond the bounds of nature as the sum of sensible objects, can only be the proof derived from the *ends* of nature. Though the concept of these ends, no doubt, cannot be given *a priori*, but only through experience, this proof promises such a concept of the original ground of nature as alone, of all those that we can conceive, is appropriate to the supersensible—the concept, namely, of a supreme intelligence as cause of the world. And in point of fact, so far as principles of reflective judgement go, that is to say, in respect of our human faculty of cognition, it is as good as its word.—But, now, is this proof in a position to give us that concept of a *supreme* or independent, intelligent being, when further understood as that of a God, that is an author of a world subject to moral laws, and so as, therefore, to be sufficiently definite for the idea of a final end of the existence of the world? That is the question on which

476

everything turns, whether we are looking for a theoretically adequate concept of the original being on behalf of our knowledge of nature as a whole, or for a practical concept for religion.

This argument, drawn from physical teleology, is deserving of all respect. It appeals to the intelligence of the ordinary person with the same convincing force as it does to the most subtle thinker; and a Reimarus won undying honour for himself* by elaborating this line of thought, which he did with his characteristic profundity and clear-477 ness in that work of his which has not yet been excelled.—But what is the source of the powerful influence which this proof exerts upon the mind, and exerts especially on a calm and perfectly voluntary assent arising from the cool judgement of reason (for emotion and exaltation of the mind produced by the wonders of nature may be put down to persuasion)? Is it physical ends, which all point to an inscrutable intelligence in the world-cause? No, they would be an inadequate source, as they do not satisfy the needs of reason or an inquiring mind. For reason asks: For what end do all those things of nature exist which exhibit a kind of art? And for what end does man himself exist—man with whose consideration we are inevitably brought to a halt, he being the ultimate end of nature, so far as we can conceive? Why does this universal nature exist, and what is the final end of all its wealth and variety of art? To suggest that it was made for enjoyment, or to be gazed at, contemplated and admired—which if the matter ends there, amounts to no more than enjoyment of a particular kind—as though enjoyment was the ultimate and final end of the presence here of the world and of man himself, cannot satisfy reason. For a personal worth, which man can only give to himself, is presupposed by reason, as the sole condition upon which he and his existence can be a final end. In the absence of this personal worth—which alone yields a definite concept—the ends of nature do not dispose of the question. In particular they cannot offer any *definite concept* of the supreme being as an all-sufficient (and for that reason one and, in the strict sense of the term, *supreme*) being, or of the laws according to which its intelligence is cause of the world.

That the physico-teleological proof produces conviction just as if it were also a theological proof is, therefore, not due to the use of ideas of the ends of nature as furnishing so much empirical evidence of a *supreme* intelligence. On the contrary it is the moral evidence, which dwells in every human being and touches him so deeply, that insinuates itself into our reasoning. One does not stop at the being that manifests itself with such incomprehensible art in the ends of nature, but one goes on to ascribe to it a final end, and, consequently, wisdom—although the perception of such natural ends does not entitle one to do this. Thus the above argument is arbitrarily supplemented in respect of its inherent defect. It is, therefore, really the moral proof that alone produces the conviction, and even this only does so from the point of view of moral considerations to which everyone so inwardly assents. The sole merit of the physico-teleological proof is that it leads the mind in its contemplation of the world to take the path of ends, and guides it in this way to an *intelligent* author of the world. At this point, then, the moral relation to ends and the idea of a like lawgiver and author of the world, in the form of a theological concept, though in truth purely an extraneous addition, seems to grow quite naturally out of the physico-teleological evidence. 478

Here we may let the matter rest at the popular *statement of the case*. For where ordinary sound understanding confuses two distinct principles, and draws its correct conclusion in point of fact only from one of them, it generally finds it difficult, if their separation calls for much reflection, to dissociate one from the other as heterogeneous principles. But, besides, the moral argument for the existence of God does not, strictly speaking, merely as it were *supplement* the physico-teleological so as to make it a complete proof. Rather is it a distinct proof which *compensates* for the failure of the latter to produce conviction. For the physico-teleological argument cannot in fact do anything more than direct reason in its judging of the source of nature and its contingent but admirable order, which is only known to us through experience, and draw our attention to a cause that acts according to ends and is as such the source of nature—a cause which through the character of our cognitive faculty we must conceive as intelligent—and in this way make us more susceptible to the influence of the moral proof. For what the latter concept needs is so essentially different from anything that is to be found in or taught by concepts of nature that it requires a special premiss and proof entirely independent of the foregoing if the concept of the original being is to be specified sufficiently for theology and its existence is to be inferred.—The moral proof (which of course only proves the existence of God when we take the practical, though also indispensable, side of reason into account) would, therefore, continue to retain its full force were we to meet with no material at all in the world, or only ambiguous material, for physical teleology. We can imagine rational beings finding themselves in the midst of a nature such as to show no clear trace of organization, but only the effects of a mere mechanism of crude matter, so that, looking to them and to the variability of some merely contingently purposive forms and relations, there would appear to be no reason for inferring an intelligent author. In this nature there would then be nothing to suggest a physical teleology. And yet reason, while receiving no instruction here from concepts of nature, would find in the concept of freedom, and the ethical ideas grounded upon it, a ground, sufficient for practice, for postulating the concept of the original being appropriate to those ideas, that is, as a Deity, and nature, including even our own existence, as a final end answering to freedom and its laws, and for doing so in consideration of the indispensable command of practical reason.—However the fact that in the actual world abundant material for physical teleology exists to satisfy the rational beings in it—a fact not antecedently necessary—serves as a desirable confirmation of the moral argument, so far as nature can adduce anything analogous to the ideas of reason (moral ideas in this case). For the concept of a supreme cause that possesses intelligence—a concept that is far from sufficient for a theology—acquires by that means such reality as is sufficient for reflective judgement. But this concept is not required as a foundation of the moral proof; nor can the latter proof be used for completing the former, which of itself does not point to morality at all, and making it *one* entire proof by continuing the train of reasoning on the same fundamental lines. Two such heterogeneous principles as nature and freedom cannot but yield two different lines of proof—while the attempt to derive the proof in question from nature will be found inadequate for what is meant to be proved.

If the premises of the physico-teleological argument could really sustain the proof sought, the result would be very gratifying to speculative reason. For they would afford hope of producing a theosophy—that being the name one would have to give to a theoretical knowledge of the divine nature and its existence sufficient for explaining both the constitution of the world and the distinctive scope of moral laws. Similarly if psychology were sufficient to enable us to attain to a knowledge of the immortality of the soul, it would open the door to a pneumatology which would be equally acceptable to reason. But, however much it might flatter the vanity of an idle curiosity, neither of the two fulfils the desire of reason in respect of theory, which would have to be based on a knowledge of the nature of things. But whether they do not better fulfil their ultimate objective purpose, the first in the form of theology, the second in the form of anthropology, when both are grounded on the moral principle, namely that of freedom, and adapted, therefore, to the practical employment of reason, is a different question, and one which we have here no need to pursue further.

480

But the reason why the physico-teleological argument does not furnish what theology requires is that it does not, and cannot, yield any concept of the original being that is sufficiently determinate for that purpose. Such a concept has to be derived entirely from a different quarter, or (at least) you must look elsewhere to supplement the defects of the concept by what is an arbitrary addition. You infer an intelligent world-cause from the great purposiveness of natural forms and their relations. But what is the degree of this intelligence? Beyond doubt you cannot assume that it is the highest possible intelligence; for to do so you would have to see that a greater intelligence than that of which you perceive any evidence in the world is inconceivable, which means attributing omniscience to yourself.* In the same way you infer from the greatness of the world a very great might on the part of its author. But you will acknowledge that this has only comparative significance for your power of comprehension and that, since you do not know all that is possible, so as to compare it with the magnitude of the world, so far as known to you, you cannot infer the omnipotence of its author from so small a standard, and so forth. Now this does not bring you to any determinate concept of an original being suitable for a theology. For that concept can only be found in the thought of the totality of the perfections associated with an intelligence, and for this merely *empirical* data can give you no assistance whatever. But apart from a determinate concept of this kind you can draw no inference to a *single* intelligent original being; whatever your purpose, you can only suppose one.—Now, certainly, one may quite readily give you the liberty of making an arbitrary addition—since reason raises no valid objection—and saying that where one meets with so much perfection one may well suppose all perfection to be united in a unique world-cause; because reason can turn such a definite principle to better account both theoretically and practically. But then you cannot cry up this concept of the original being as one which you have proved, since you have only assumed it in the interests of a better employment of reason. Hence all lament or impotent rage on account of the supposed enormity of casting a doubt on the conclusiveness of your chain of reasoning is idle bluster. For it would very much like us to believe that the doubt that is freely expressed as to the validity of your argument is a questioning of sacred truth, so that under this cover its weakness may pass unnoticed.

On the other hand, moral teleology, whose foundations are no less firm than those of physical teleology, and which in fact should be regarded as in a better position, seeing that it rests *a priori* on principles that are inseparable from our reason, leads to what the possibility of a theology requires, namely to a definite *concept* of the supreme cause as one that is the cause of the world in its accordance with moral laws, and, consequently, of such a cause as satisfies our moral final end. Now that is a cause that requires nothing less than omniscience, omnipotence, omnipresence, and so forth, as the natural attributes characterizing its operation. These attributes must be thought as connected to the moral final end which is infinite, and accordingly as adequate to that end. Thus moral teleology alone can furnish the concept of a *unique* author of the world suitable for a theology.

In this way theology also leads directly to *religion*, that is *the recognition of our duties as divine commands.** For it is only the recognition of our duty and of its content—the final end enjoined upon us by reason—that was able to produce a determinate concept of God. This concept is, therefore, from its origin indissolubly connected with a sense of obligation to that being. On the other hand, even supposing that by pursuing the theoretical path one could arrive at a determinate concept of the original being, namely, as simple cause of nature, one would afterwards encounter considerable difficulty in finding valid proofs for ascribing to this being a causality in accordance with moral laws, and might, perhaps, not be able to do so at all without resorting to arbitrary interpolation. Yet, if the concept of such causality is left out, that would-be theological concept can form no basis for the support of religion. Even if a religion could be established on these theoretical lines, yet in what touches our own disposition, which is the essential element in religion, it would really be a different religion from one in which the concept of God and the (practical) conviction of his existence springs from our fundamental ideas of morality. For if omnipotence, omniscience, and so forth on the part of an author of the world were concepts given to us from another quarter, and if, regarded in that light, we had to take them for granted for the purpose only of applying our concepts of duties to our relation to such author, then these latter concepts would inevitably betray strong traces of compulsion and forced submission. But what of the alternative? What if the final end of our true vocation is presented to our minds quite freely, and through the prescription of our own reason, by a reverence for the moral law? Why, then, we accept into our moral perspective a cause harmonizing with that end and with its accomplishment, and accept 482 it with deepest veneration—wholly different from any pathological fear—and we willingly bow down before it.[1]

But why should it be of any consequence to us to have a theology at all? Well, as to this, it is quite obvious that it is not necessary for the extension or rectification of our knowledge of nature or, in fact, for any theory whatever. We need theology solely on behalf of religion, that is to say, of the practical or, in other words, moral employment of our reason, and need it as a subjective requirement. Now if it turns out that the one and only argument which leads to a determinate concept of the object of theology is itself a moral argument, the result will not seem strange. But, more than that, we shall not feel that the assurance produced by this line of proof falls in any way short of the ultimate intention it has in view, provided we are clear on the point that an argument of this kind only proves the existence of God in a way that satisfies our moral vocation, that is, from a practical point of view. Speculation does not here display its force in any way, nor does it enlarge the borders of its realm. Also the surprise at the fact that we here assert the possibility of a theology, and the alleged contradiction in that assertion with what the critique of speculative reason argued with respect to the categories, will disappear on close inspection. What that critique claimed was that the categories can only produce knowledge when applied to sensible objects, and that they can in no way do so when applied to the supersensible. But let it be observed that while the categories are here used on behalf of the knowledge of God, they are so

---

[1] Both the admiration for beauty and the emotion excited by the profuse variety of ends of nature, which a reflective mind is able to feel prior to any clear representation of an intelligent author of the world, have something about them akin to a *religious* feeling. Hence they seem primarily to act upon the moral feeling (of gratitude and veneration towards the unknown cause) by means of a kind of judging analogous to the moral kind, and therefore to affect the mind by exciting moral ideas. It is then that they inspire that admiration which is fraught with far more interest than mere theoretical observation can produce.

used solely for practical, not for theoretical purposes, that is they are not directed to the intrinsic, and for us inscrutable, nature of God. —Let me take this opportunity of putting an end to the misinterpretation of the above doctrine in the critique—a doctrine which is very necessary, but which, to the chagrin of blind dogmatists, relegates reason to its proper bounds. In this regard I here append the following elucidation.

If I ascribe *motive* force to a body, and conceive it, therefore, by 483 means of the category of *causality*, then at the same time and by the same means I *cognize* it; that is to say, I determine the concept which I have of it as an object in general by means of what applies to it in the concrete as an object of sense (this being the condition of the possibility of the relation in question). Thus, suppose the dynamical force that I ascribe to it is that of repulsion, then—even though I do not as yet place beside it another body against which it exerts this force—I may predicate of it a place in space, further an extension or space possessed by the body itself, and, besides, a filling of this space by the repelling forces of its parts, and, finally, the law regulating this filling of space—I mean the law that the force of repulsion in the parts must decrease in the same ratio as the extension of the body increases, and as the space which it fills with the same parts and by means of this force is enlarged.—On the other hand, if I form a notion of a supersensible being as *prime mover*, and thus employ the category of causality in consideration of the same mode of action in the world, namely, the movement of matter, I must not then conceive it to be at any place in space, or to be extended, indeed I am not even to conceive it as existing in time at all or as coexistent with other beings. Accordingly, I have no forms of thought whatever that could interpret to me the condition under which movement derived from this being as its source is possible. Consequently from the predicate of cause, as prime mover, I do not get the least concrete cognition of it: I have only the representation of a something containing the source of the movements in the world. And as the relation in which this something, as cause stands to these movements, does not give me anything further that belongs to the constitution of the thing which is cause, it leaves the concept of this cause quite empty. The reason is, that with predicates that only get their object in the sensible world I may no doubt advance to the existence of something that must contain the source of these predicates, but I cannot advance to the determination of the concept of this something as a supersensible being, a concept that excludes all those predicates. If, therefore, I make the category of causality determinate by means of the concept of a *prime mover*, it does not help me in the slightest to cognize what God is. But maybe I shall fare better if I take a line from the order of the world and proceed, not merely to *think* the causality of the supersensible being as that of a supreme *intelligence*, but also to *cognize* it by means of this determination of the concept in question; for then the troublesome terms of space and extension drop out.—Beyond all doubt the great purposiveness present in the world compels us to *think* that there is a supreme 484 cause of this purposiveness and one whose causality has an intelligence behind it. But this in no way entitles us to *ascribe* such intelligence to that cause. (Thus, for instance, we are obliged to think the eternity of God as an existence throughout all time, because we can form no other concept of mere existence than that of a magnitude, or in other words, than as duration. Similarly we have to think the divine omnipotence as an existence in all places, in order to interpret to ourselves God's immediate presence in respect of things external to one another. All this we do without, however, being at liberty to ascribe any of these thought-forms to God as something we could cognize in him.) If I determine the causality of man in respect of certain products that are only explicable by reference to intentional purposiveness by conceiving it as an intelligence on his part, I need not stop there, but I can ascribe this predicate to him as a familiar attribute of man and thereby cognize him. For I know that intuitions are given to the senses of man, and by means of understanding are brought under a concept and thus under a rule; that this concept contains only the common characteristic, letting the particular drop out, and is therefore discursive; that the rules for bringing representations under the general form of a consciousness are given by understanding in advance of those intuitions, and so on. Accordingly, I ascribe this attribute to man as one whereby I *cognize* him. But supposing, now that I seek to *think* a supersensible being (God) as intelligence, while this is not merely permissible but unavoidable if I am to exercise certain functions of my reason, I have no right whatever to flatter myself that I am in a position to ascribe intelligence to that being and thereby to *cognize* it by one of its attributes. For in that case I must omit all the above conditions under which I know an intelligence. Consequently, the predicate that is only available for the determination of man is quite inapplicable to a supersensible object. Hence we are quite unable to cognize what God is by means of any such definite causality. And it is so with all categories. They can have no significance whatever for knowledge theoretically considered, unless they are applied to objects of possible experience.—But I am able to think even a supersensible being on the analogy of an understanding—indeed must do so when I look to certain other considerations—without, however, thereby desiring to cognize it theoretically. I refer to the case of this mode of its causality having to do with an effect in the world that involves an aim which is morally necessary but for sensuous beings is unrealizable. For in that case a knowledge of God and his existence, that is to say a theology, is possible by means of attributes and determinations of this causality merely conceived in him according to analogy, and this knowledge has all requisite reality in a practical relation, but also *in respect only of this relation*, that is, in relation to morality.—An ethical theology is therefore quite possible. For while morality without theology may certainly carry on with its own rule, it cannot do so with the final purpose which this very rule enjoins, unless it throws reason to the winds as regards this purpose. But a theological ethics—on the part of pure reason—is impossible, seeing that laws which are not originally given by reason itself, and the observance of which it does not bring about as a practical capacity, cannot be moral. In the same way a theological physics would be a monstrosity, because it would not bring forward any laws of nature but rather ordinances of a supreme will, whereas a physical, or, properly speaking, physico-teleological, theology can at least serve as a propaedeutic to theology proper, since by means of the study of natural ends, of which it presents a rich supply, it awakens us to the idea of a final end which nature cannot exhibit. Consequently it can make us alive to the need of a theology which should define the concept of God sufficiently for the highest practical employment of reason, though it cannot produce a theology or furnish demonstrations adequate for its support.

APPENDIX

The 'First Introduction' to the *Critique of Judgement*

I. *Philosophy as a System*

IF philosophy is a *system* of rational knowledge through concepts, this already suffices to distinguish it from a critique of pure reason, for although the latter includes a philosophical investigation into the possibility of this kind of knowledge, it does not form part of such a system, but rather projects and examines the very idea of this system in the first place.

We must begin by dividing the system into its formal and material parts, the first of which (logic) merely treats the form of thought in a system of rules, while the second (the real part) systematically considers the objects that are thought in so far as rational cognition of them is possible through concepts.

Now this real system of philosophy itself can only be divided into *theoretical* and *practical* philosophy, in accordance with the original difference in their respective objects and with the essential distinction, deriving from this, in the principles of a science that includes them. One part, therefore, must be the philosophy of nature, the other part the philosophy of morals; while the former may also contain empirical principles, the latter can never contain anything but pure *a priori* principles (since freedom cannot possibly be an object of experience).

But there is a major and prevailing misconception, one very damaging to the way in which we approach the science itself,* with regard to the meaning of the *practical* character that permits something to be assigned to *practical philosophy*. It has been deemed proper to include diplomacy and political economy, the rules of household management, and those of general behaviour, prescriptions concerning diet and the health of body and soul alike (and indeed why not all the arts and professions?) within practical philosophy since all of these contain a body of practical propositions. But while practical propositions are distinguished from theoretical propositions, which contain the possibility and the determinations of things, not by their content but by a difference in the way we represent them, merely those which consider *freedom* under laws are so distinguished. All the rest are simply applications of the theory of the nature of things to the way in which we can produce them according to a principle, that is to say, their possibility represented as resulting from a voluntary act (which equally belongs to the realm of natural causes). Thus the solution of the problem in mechanics—to discover the respective lengths of the arms of a lever if a given force is to be in equilibrium with a given weight—is certainly expressed as a practical formula, but one which contains no more than the theoretical proposition: in a state of equilibrium the lengths of the arms of the lever are inversely proportional to the former. It is simply that this relationship, since it is an effect of a cause governed (through our own choice) by the *representation* of that relation, is thought as possible. And the same holds for all practical propositions that are concerned only with the production of objects. If someone offers prescriptions for promoting happiness and discusses, for example, what one must do to be happy, then it is only the inner conditions of the possibility of being happy—temperance, moderation of the inclinations in order not to yield to passion, etc.—which are represented as relevant to the nature of the subject, together with the way we can produce this balance through our own efforts. Consequently, all this is derived directly from the relation between the theory of the object and that of our own nature (ourselves as cause). Since the practical prescription is here distinguished

197   from a theoretical one by its formula rather than by its content, no special type of philosophy is required to investigate such a connection of ground and consequent. In short, all practical propositions which derive what can occur in nature from the power of our own choice as a cause belong to theoretical philosophy as knowledge of nature. Only those propositions which give freedom its law are specifically differentiated by their content from the former propositions. One can say of the first kind that they constitute the practical part of a *philosophy of nature*, while the latter alone lay the foundation of a special *practical philosophy*.

Remark

It is very important to divide philosophy precisely according to its parts, and to that end not to include amongst the members of this systematic division something that is only a consequence or an application of it to given cases and that thus requires no special principles.

Practical propositions are distinguished from theoretical ones either with regard to their principles or their consequences. In the latter case, they do not comprise a particular part of science, but belong to the theoretical part of science as consequences of a particular kind that derive from it. Now the possibility of things under the laws of nature differs essentially and in principle from their possibility under laws of freedom. But this difference does not lie in the fact that in the latter case we locate the cause in a will, while in the former case we locate it in the things themselves external to the will. For if the will obeys no other principles than those in accordance with which, as merely natural laws, the understanding grasps the possibility of the object, and the proposition implying the possibility of something as an effect of the causality of voluntary action can be described as a 'practical'

proposition, we still cannot claim that this proposition is remotely distinguished, in principle, from the theoretical propositions which concern the nature of things; and it must therefore borrow its principle from the latter   198
in order to present the representation of an object in reality.

Thus practical propositions, the content of which concerns merely the possibility of a represented object (through voluntary action), are simply an application of a thorough theoretical knowledge and cannot comprise a special part of a science. A 'practical' geometry, considered as a separate science, is a nonsense, however many practical propositions this pure science may contain, most of which, as problems, require special instruction for their solution. The problem of constructing a square with a given side and a given right angle is a practical proposition, but it is purely a consequence of the relevant theory. Nor can the art of surveying (*agrimensoria*) ever presume the title of a practical geometry or ever be described as a special part of geometry itself, but belongs amongst the scholia of the latter, namely the employment of this science for purposes of commerce.[1]

Even in a science of nature, in so far as it rests upon empirical principles, namely physics in the proper sense, the practical procedures for discovering the hidden laws of nature, under the name of 'experimental physics', can never justify the (equally nonsensical) name of 'practical physics' as a part of natural philosophy. For the principles according to which we perform our   199
experiments must themselves always be derived from our knowledge of nature, and thus from theory. And exactly the same is true of the practical precepts concerning the voluntary production of a certain state of mind within ourselves (e.g. the arousing or taming of the imagination, or the pacifying or subduing of the inclinations). There is no practical *psychology* as a special part of the philosophy of human nature since the principles for a possible, artfully produced, state of mind must be borrowed from those concerning the possible determinations of the character of our nature, and although these consist of practical propositions they still do not comprise a practical part of psychology, but belong simply to its scholia precisely because they possess no special principles.

In general, practical propositions (whether they be pure *a priori* or empirical), if they immediately imply the possibility of an object through

---

[1] This pure and therefore sublime science seems to forfeit something of its dignity in conceding that, as elementary geometry, it requires *implements* for the construction of its concepts, albeit only two, namely the compass and the ruler; these constructions alone are called 'geometrical', while those of higher geometry are called 'mechanical' because more complex mechanical devices are required to construct the concepts of the latter. But what we understand in the former case is not the actual implements (*circinus et regola*),* which can never render the relevant figures with mathematical precision, but rather the simplest ways in which the imagination can exhibit the latter *a priori*, something which cannot be matched by any instrument

our own power of choice, always belong to our knowledge of nature and thus to the theoretical part of philosophy. Only those propositions which directly present the determination of an act as necessary, simply by representing its form (in accordance with laws in general), regardless of the material content of the envisaged object, can and must possess their own special principles (in the idea of freedom), and although the concept of an object of the will (the highest good) is grounded on precisely these principles, this object still only belongs indirectly, as a consequence, to the practical precept (henceforth described as a 'moral' one). Moreover, the possibility of the highest good cannot properly be grasped through any knowledge of nature (or theory). Thus it is only such propositions which belong to a special part of a system of rational cognition under the name of practical philosophy.

In order to avoid ambiguity, all of the remaining practical propositions, regardless of the science with which they may be connected, can be called 200 *technical* rather than practical ones. For they belong to the *art* of realizing what is envisaged, something which, in the case of a complete theory, is always merely an extension of the latter and never an independent part of any kind of precept. In this sense all precepts of skill are technical[2] and therefore belong to our theoretical knowledge of nature and derive from the latter.

But in what follows we shall also employ the term 'technic'* where the objects of nature are merely *judged as if* their possibility depended upon 201 art. In such cases the judgements are neither theoretical nor practical (in the sense just described) since they determine nothing with regard to the character of the object or to the way in which we produce the latter; rather nature itself is thereby judged, though merely in analogy with art, and indeed in a subjective relation to our faculty of cognition rather than in an

---

[2] This is the place to correct an error which I committed* in the *Groundwork for the Metaphysics of Morals*. For after asserting that the imperatives of skill command only conditionally, under the condition of ends that are merely possible, i.e. *problematic*, I described such practical precepts as 'problematical imperatives', an expression which obviously harbours a contradiction. I should have called them *technical* imperatives, i.e. imperatives of art. The *pragmatic* imperatives, or rules of prudence, which command under the condition of an *actual* and thus even subjectively necessary end, are now also included under the technical imperatives (for what is prudence other than the skill of being able to use free human beings, and even one's own natural dispositions and inclinations, for one's own intentions?). It is only because the end which we ascribe to ourselves and to other human beings, namely that of one's own happiness, cannot be counted amongst the merely arbitrary ends, that we are justified in designating these technical imperatives in a special way. For the task requires not merely that we specify the means of executing an end, as in technical imperatives, but that we also determine what constitutes the end itself (happiness), whereas in the case of general technical imperatives this is presupposed as already known.

objective relation to the objects. Here we shall not indeed describe the judgements themselves as technical, but rather the power of judgement upon whose laws these judgements are grounded, and in conformity with this nature itself will also be called 'technical'. Since this technic includes no propositions of an objectively determining character, it does not constitute a part of doctrinal philosophy, but only part of the critique of our cognitive faculties.

II. *The System of the Higher Cognitive Faculties which lies at the Basis of Philosophy*

IF we are speaking of the division not of *philosophy*, but of our *faculty for a priori cognition through concepts* (the higher faculty), i.e. of a critique of pure reason with respect solely to its capacity for thinking (leaving the pure form of intuition out of consideration), then the systematic representation of the capacity for thought falls into three parts: first, the capacity for knowledge of the *universal* (of rules)—*the understanding*; secondly, the capacity for *subsuming the particular under the universal*—the *power of judgement*; and thirdly, the capacity for *determining* the particular through the universal (the derivation from principles)—*reason*.

The critique of pure *theoretical* reason, dedicated to uncovering the sources of all knowledge a priori (and thus also of the intuitive aspect which belongs to reason), furnished the laws of *nature*, the critique of practical reason furnished the laws of *freedom*, and thus the a priori principles of all philosophy appear to have been entirely dealt with already.

But if the understanding furnishes a priori laws of nature, while reason furnishes those of freedom, then we may expect by analogy that the power of judgement, which mediates the relationship of the other two faculties, will likewise afford its own special a priori principles which will perhaps form the basis for a particular division of philosophy, and that the latter, as a system, can only be composed of two parts.

Yet the power of judgement is such a peculiar, and by no means independent, faculty of cognition that it provides neither concepts, as does the understanding, nor ideas, as does reason, for any object whatsoever, because it is merely a power of subsuming under concepts that are given from elsewhere. If, therefore, there were any rule or concept that sprang originally from the power of judgement, it would have to be a concept of things *in nature in so far as nature conforms to our power of judgement*; it would thus concern that character of nature of which we can form no other concept than that its organization conforms to our capacity for subsuming the particular given laws under more general ones which are not given. In other words, this would have to be the concept of a purposiveness of nature that

furthers our capacity to know nature in so far as we must be able to judge
203 the particular to be contained under the universal and to subsume it under
the concept of nature as one.

A concept of this kind is that of *experience as a system in accordance with empirical laws*. For although experience forms a system under *transcendental* laws, which comprise the condition of the possibility of experience in general, one might yet be presented with such an *infinite multiplicity* of empirical laws and so great a *heterogeneity of natural forms* in particular experience that the concept of a system in accordance with these (empirical) laws would necessarily appear alien to the understanding, and neither the possibility nor still less the necessity of such a unified whole would be conceivable. Yet particular experience, which is thoroughly coherent under constant principles, also demands this systematic connection of empirical laws through which it becomes possible for the power of judgement to subsume the particular under the universal, while always remaining within the empirical sphere and advancing to the highest empirical laws and the forms of nature that correspond to them. Hence the *aggregate* of particular experiences must be regarded as a *system* since without this presupposition no thoroughly lawlike interconnection, i.e. no empirical unity of these experiences,[3] could be established.

204   This lawfulness, which is in itself contingent (as far as all the concepts of the understanding are concerned) and which the power of judgement (merely for its own advantage) presumes and presupposes in nature, is a formal purposiveness of nature which we in fact *assume* in the latter, but which forms the basis neither for a theoretical knowledge of nature nor for a practical principle of freedom; nonetheless, it provides a principle for judging and investigating nature with regard to the general laws through which we arrange the particular cases of experience in order to bring out

---

[3] The possibility of an experience in general is the possibility of empirical cognitions as synthetic judgements. Thus it cannot be derived *analytically* from the mere comparison of perceptions (as is commonly believed) since the combination of two different perceptions in the concept of an object (for its cognition) is a *synthesis*, one which makes empirical *cognition*, i.e. experience, possible only in accordance with principles of the synthetic unity of appearances, i.e. in accordance with principles which permit the latter to be brought under the categories. Now these empirical cognitions, in accordance with what they necessarily have in common (namely those transcendental laws of nature), constitute an analytic unity of all experience, but not that synthetic unity of experience as a system which binds together under a principle the empirical laws even in regard to their differences (and where their multiplicity may be endless). What the category is with respect to every particular experience, that is what the purposiveness or fitness of nature is to our power of judgement (even with regard to its particular laws), and that is why nature is represented as not merely mechanical, but also as technical, a concept that certainly does not determine synthetic unity objectively, but still subjectively furnishes principles which serve to guide our enquiries into nature.

the systematic connection required for coherent experience and which we have an *a priori* ground for assuming.

The concept which springs originally from the power of judgement and belongs peculiarly to it is therefore that of nature as *art* or, in other words, the concept of the *technic of nature* with respect to its *particular* laws. This concept does not supply the foundation for any theory and no more implies any knowledge of objects and their characteristics than does logic, but merely furnishes a principle for advancing in accordance with empirical laws through which the investigation of nature becomes possible. This does not   205 enrich our knowledge of nature with any specific objective law, but merely provides the basis for a maxim of the power of judgement, namely to observe in accordance with it and thereby to unify the forms of nature.

Philosophy, as a doctrinal system of the knowledge of both nature and freedom, is not endowed with any new division here since this representation of nature as art is a mere idea which serves as the principle for our investigations into nature and thus merely enables the subject to introduce systematic interconnection into the aggregate of empirical laws as such wherever possible in so far as we attribute to nature a relationship to this need of ours. On the other hand, our concept of the technic of nature, as a heuristic principle for judging it, will belong to the critique of our cognitive faculty; this critique indicates what cause we have for representing the technic of nature in this way, what the origin of this idea may be, whether it is to be found in an *a priori* source, and likewise what the range and limits of its employment may be. In short, such an enquiry will belong to the system of the critique of pure reason, but not to doctrinal philosophy.

III. *The System of All the Faculties of the Human Mind*

WE can trace all the powers of the human mind, without exception, back to three: the *faculty of cognition*, the *feeling of pleasure and displeasure*, and the *faculty of desire*. Now it is true that philosophers, who otherwise deserve   206 unstinting praise for the thoroughness of their thinking, have sought to explain this distinction away as a purely apparent one and to bring all the faculties under that of cognition alone. But it is very easily demonstrated, and it has already been obvious for some time, that this attempt to bring unity to the plurality of the faculties—one that was otherwise undertaken in a genuinely philosophical spirit—is futile. For there always remains a great difference between representations which belong to knowledge, as related merely to the object and to the unity of our consciousness of these representations, and likewise between the objective relation in which they belong to the faculty of desire when regarded as the cause of the reality of the object, and representations which merely stand in relation to the subject, when they afford their own grounds for merely maintaining their existence in the subject, and to that extent are regarded in relation to the feeling of pleasure. This latter is not a case of knowledge at all, nor does it furnish any knowledge, although it may presuppose something of the kind as a determining ground.

The connection between knowledge of an object and the feeling of pleasure or displeasure occasioned by its existence, or the way in which the faculty of desire resolves to bring the object into existence, can certainly be known empirically, but since this connection is not based on any *a priori* principle, the powers of the mind to that extent constitute only an *aggregate* rather than a system. Now one can certainly elicit an *a priori* connection between the feeling of pleasure and the other two faculties, and if we connect an *a priori* cognition, namely the rational concept of freedom, to the faculty of desire as its determining ground, we can at the same time discover subjectively within this objective determination a feeling of pleasure contained in the determination of the will. But the cognitive faculty is not linked to the faculty of desire in this way *by means of* pleasure or displeasure since here the pleasure does not precede the latter faculty, but either only follows after its determination or is perhaps nothing but the sensation of this capacity of the will to be determined by reason itself; pleasure therefore is not a particular feeling or a unique form of receptivity which would demand a particular domain for itself amongst the properties of the mind. But since the analysis of the powers of the mind incontestably reveals a feeling of pleasure which is independent of any determination by the faculty of desire and can instead furnish a basis for determinations of the latter, the connection between this faculty and the other two within a single system implies that this feeling of pleasure, like the other two faculties, rests on *a priori* principles rather than on merely empirical grounds. Thus, for the idea of philosophy as a system, we still require a *critique* (though not a doctrine) *of the feeling of pleasure and displeasure* to the extent that is not empirically grounded.

Now since the *faculty of cognition through concepts* finds its *a priori* principle in the pure understanding (in its concept of nature), and the *faculty of desire* finds its *a priori* principle in pure reason (in its concept of freedom), there remains amongst the general properties of the mind an intermediate faculty or receptivity, namely the *feeling of pleasure and displeasure*, just as there remains amongst the higher cognitive faculties a certain intermediate power, namely that of judgement. What is more natural than to suspect that the latter will also contain *a priori* principles for the former?

Without descrying anything further about the possibility of this connection, we can certainly already recognize here a kind of fitness between the power of judgement and the feeling of pleasure, which can serve as the determining ground for the latter or find such a ground within it. For while the understanding and reason, in the *division of the faculty of cognition through concepts*, relate their representations to objects in order to acquire concepts of the latter, the power of judgement relates solely to the subject and for its own part produces no concepts of objects. Similarly, while in the *general division of the powers of the mind in general* both the cognitive faculties and the faculty of desire contain an *objective* relation to representations, the feeling of pleasure and displeasure, by contrast, is merely a receptivity with respect to a state of the subject; thus if the power of judgement is to determine anything on its own part, this could only be the feeling of pleasure, and conversely, if the latter is to possess an *a priori* principle at all, this will only be found in the power of judgement.

IV. *Experience as a System for the Power of Judgement*

WE observed in the *Critique of Pure Reason* that nature in its entirety, as the sum of all objects of experience, comprises a system according to transcendental laws, ones which the understanding itself furnishes *a priori* (namely for appearances in so far as, connected in one consciousness, they are to constitute experience). In precisely the same way, experience must also ideally form a system of possible empirical knowledge in accordance with universal as well as particular laws, in so far as this is objectively possible at least in principle. The unity of nature under a principle of the thoroughgoing connection of everything contained in this sum of all appearances requires this. To this extent we are to regard experience in general as a system under transcendental laws of the understanding, rather than as a mere aggregate.

But it does not follow from this that nature is a system that is *comprehensible* for the human faculty of cognition with respect to *empirical* laws as well, and that the thoroughgoing systematic interconnection of its appearances in one experience, and thus experience itself as a system, is possible for human beings. For the variety and diversity of empirical laws might be so great that while it would still be possible in part to connect our perceptions in one experience in accordance with particular laws that we happen to have discovered already, it would never be possible to bring these empirical laws themselves together under a common principle, if it were the case, as is perfectly possible (as far as the understanding can tell us *a priori*), that the variety and diversity of these laws, and of the corresponding forms of nature, were infinitely great and we were thus confronted by a crude and chaotic aggregate revealing no trace of system whatsoever, even if we still had to presuppose a system in accordance with transcendental laws.

For the *unity of nature in space and time* and the unity of our possible experience are one and the same because the former is a sum of mere appearances (kinds of representation) which only possesses objective reality in experience, and the latter must be possible as a system under empirical laws if we are to think the former as a system (as indeed we must). It is therefore a subjectively necessary, transcendental *presupposition* that this dismaying and limitless diversity of empirical laws and this heterogeneity of natural forms does not belong in nature, but that, instead, nature is fitted for experience as an empirical system through the affinity of particular laws under more general ones.

Now this presupposition is the transcendental principle of the power of judgement. For the latter is not merely the faculty of subsuming the particular under the universal whose concept is given, but also, conversely, that of discovering the universal for the particular. But the understanding, in its transcendental *legislation* for nature, ignores the whole manifold of possible empirical laws. It considers only the conditions of the possibility of experience in general with respect to its formal character. In the understanding, therefore, we cannot discover the aforementioned principle of the affinity of particular laws of nature. The power of judgement alone, to which it falls to bring particular laws under higher, though still empirical, principles, while also taking account of the diversity of these laws under the same universal laws of nature, must take such a principle as the basis of its procedure. For in groping about amongst the forms of nature, whose reciprocal agreement with common empirical but higher laws would otherwise be regarded by the power of judgement as entirely contingent, it would be even more contingent if *individual perceptions* lent themselves so luckily to formulation in terms of an empirical law; but it would be all the more contingent if manifold empirical laws simply happened to be fitted for the systematic unity of our knowledge of nature in a *wholly interconnected* possible experience, unless, by means of an *a priori* principle, we presupposed nature to possess such a form.

All of the current formulae: nature takes the shortest path—*she does nothing in vain*—*she makes no leaps in the manifold of forms* (*continuum formarum*)—*she is rich in species but poor in genera*, and so forth, are nothing but this same transcendental expression of the power of judgement that lays down for itself a principle for experience as a system and thus for its own needs. Neither the understanding nor reason can establish such a law of nature *a priori*. For although we can perhaps see that nature conforms, in its purely formal laws, to our understanding (and thus becomes an object of experience in general), with respect to the plurality and heterogeneity of the particular laws of nature it is free of all restrictions legislated by our faculty of cognition. It is a sheer assumption on the part of the power of judgement, for the sake of its own employment in advancing continuously from particular empirical laws to more general, though still empirical, ones in order to consolidate empirical laws, which establishes that principle. Under no circumstances can such a principle be set to the account of experience since only under this assumption is it possible to order experience in a systematic fashion.

v. *The Reflective Power of Judgement*

THE power of judgement can be regarded either as a mere faculty for *reflecting* on a given representation, in accordance with a certain principle, for producing a concept that is thereby made possible, or as a faculty for *determining* an underlying concept by means of an *empirical* representation. In the first case, we are dealing with the *reflective*, in the second case, with the *determining* power of judgement. But to *reflect* (to deliberate) is to compare and combine given representations either with other representations or with our faculty of cognition in relation to a concept that is thereby made possible. The reflective power of judgement is also what is called the faculty of judging (*facultas diiudicandi*).

Now *reflecting* (which even occurs in animals, albeit only instinctively: not in relation to a resulting concept, but to an inclination yet to be determined) requires a principle just as much as the act *of determining* in which the underlying concept of the object prescribes the rule to the power of judgement and thus assumes the place of the principle.

The principle of reflection upon given objects of nature is that empirically determinate *concepts* can indeed be found for all things in nature;[4] or,

---

[4] At first glance this principle does not look like a synthetic and transcendental proposition, but rather appears to be tautological and to belong to mere logic. For the latter teaches us how we can compare a given representation with others and form a concept by abstracting what it shares with others as a characteristic mark for general use. But logic tells us nothing about whether for each object nature must also show many others that can be compared with it in similarity of form; on the contrary, this condition for the possibility of applying logic to nature is a principle of representing nature, as system for our power of judgement, in which the manifold, divided into genera and species, makes it possible for us, through comparison, to bring all the forms of nature that we may encounter to concepts (of greater or lesser generality). Now the understanding certainly teaches us (though also through synthetic principles) how to think of all things in nature as contained in a transcendental system in accordance with *a priori* concepts (the categories); but the power of judgement, which (as reflective) also seeks out concepts for empirical representations as such, must assume therefore in addition that nature in its boundless multiplicity has hit upon a division into genera and species which makes it possible for our power of judgement to find concordance amongst the natural forms which it compares with one another, and to arrive at empirical concepts, and their interconnection, by ascending to more general, though still empirical, concepts; i.e. the power of judgement presupposes a system of nature in accordance with empirical laws as well, and does so *a priori*, and therefore by means of a transcendental principle.

212 in other words, that in the products of nature one can always presuppose a form which is possible under universal laws that are accessible to our knowledge. For if we were not entitled to assume this, and were unable to base our treatment of empirical representations upon this principle, all reflection would be undertaken in a merely blind and random fashion with no legitimate expectation that it could harmonize with nature.

With respect to the universal concepts of nature, under which a concept of experience (without particular empirical determination) is possible in the first place, reflection already possesses a guide in the concept of nature in general, i.e. in the understanding. And the power of judgement requires no special principle of reflection, but *schematizes* nature *a priori* and applies these schemata to every empirical synthesis, something without which no judgements of experience would be possible. In this case, the power of judgement, in its reflection, is also determining and its transcendental schematism simultaneously serves it as a rule under which the given empirical intuitions can be subsumed.

213 But for those concepts which have to be found for given empirical intuitions in the first place, and which presuppose a special law of nature through which alone *particular* experience is possible, the power of judgement requires a peculiar, equally transcendental principle for its reflection. And one cannot in turn refer this power to empirical laws which are already known, something which would transform reflection into a mere comparison with empirical forms for which one already possesses the relevant concepts. For the question is how, by comparing perceptions, one could ever hope to arrive at empirical concepts that capture what is common to a variety of natural forms, if (as is entirely conceivable) nature had bestowed so great a heterogeneity upon the immense variety of its empirical laws, that all, or almost all, comparison would be useless for discovering any coherence or hierarchical order in the plurality of species and genera. All comparison of empirical representations, in order to discover in natural things empirical laws and the corresponding *specific* forms and, through comparison of these with others, to discover *generically corresponding* forms, presupposes that nature has observed in its empirical laws a certain economy, fitted for our power of judgement, and a similarity amongst its forms which we can comprehend. And this presupposition, as an *a priori* principle of the power of judgement, must precede all such comparison.

The reflective power of judgement thus works with given appearances to bring them under empirical concepts of determinate natural things not
214 schematically, but *technically*; not merely mechanically, like a tool controlled by the understanding and the senses, but *artistically*, according to the universal but nonetheless indeterminate principle of a purposive and systematic ordering of nature. Our power of judgement is favoured, as it were, by the conformity of the particular laws of nature (about which the understanding is

silent) to the possibility of experience as a system, which is a presupposition without which we have no hope of finding our way in the labyrinth of the multiplicity of possible particular laws. Thus the power of judgement itself makes the *technic of nature* into the principle of its reflection *a priori*, without being able to explain or determine it more precisely or to possess an objective determining ground for the universal concepts of nature (through a cognition of things in themselves), but only in order to facilitate its reflection in accordance with its own subjective laws and needs while remaining in harmony with the laws of nature in general.

But the principle of the reflective power of judgement, through which nature is thought as a system under empirical laws, is to be considered merely as a principle *for the logical employment of the power of judgement*, and while it is indeed a transcendental principle with regard to its origin, it serves merely to regard nature *a priori* as qualified for a *logical system* in its multiplicity under empirical laws.

The logical form of a system consists simply in the division of given general concepts (like the concept of nature in general here) through which we think, according to a certain principle, the particular (here the empirical) in its diversity as contained in the universal. If one proceeds empirically and ascends from the particular to the universal, a *classification* of the manifold is required, i.e. a comparison of several classes each of which is determined by a distinct concept. When the classification is complete with respect to the common characteristic, its subsumption under higher classes (genera) proceeds until one reaches the concept which contains the principle of the entire classification (and constitutes the highest genus). If, on the other hand, one begins with the universal concept, in order to descend to the particular by means of exhaustive division, the procedure is described as the *specification* 215 of the manifold* under a given concept, since one is moving here from the highest genus towards the lower one (subgenera or species) and from species to subordinate species. Instead of employing the everyday expression that one must specify the particular which stands under the universal, it is more exact to say that one is *specifying the general concept* since the manifold is here ordered under the latter. This is because the genus, logically considered, is, as it were, the matter or raw substrate which nature works into particular species and subspecies through multiple determinations. Thus one can say that *nature specifies itself* according to a certain principle (or the idea of a system), on analogy with the way in which jurists use the word when speaking of the specification of certain raw material of their own.[5]

Now it is clear that the reflective power of judgement, given its character, cannot undertake to *classify* the whole of nature in accordance with its

---

[5] The Aristotelian school also called the *genus* matter, but the *specific difference* the form.

empirical varieties unless it assumes that nature itself *specifies* its transcendental laws in accordance with some principle or other. This principle can be none other than that of suitability for the faculty of the power of judgement itself in finding sufficient kinship amongst the infinite multiplicity of things under possible empirical laws as to bring them under empirical concepts (classes) and these in turn under more universal laws (higher genera), and thus to arrive at an empirical system of nature. Since this kind of classification is not a matter of ordinary empirical knowledge, but rather an artistic knowledge, nature, in so far as it is thought as specifying itself in accordance with such a principle, is here also regarded as *art*. The power of judgement thus necessarily carries with it *a priori* a principle of the *technic* of nature, which is distinct from the *nomothetic* of nature through transcendental laws of the understanding since the latter can validate its principle as law, while the former can do so only as a necessary presupposition.[6]

216   The special principle of the power of judgement is therefore this: *nature specifies its universal laws as empirical ones, in accordance with the form of a logical system, on behalf of the power of judgement.*

It is here that the concept of a *purposiveness* of nature arises, and indeed as a characteristic concept of the reflective power of judgement, rather than of reason, since the end is posited not in the object but solely in the subject, and indeed in the subject's mere capacity for reflection. We describe something as 'purposive' if its existence seems to presuppose an antecedent representation of the thing in question. But natural laws that are so constituted and interrelated as if the power of judgement had designed them to satisfy its own requirements resemble the case in which the possibility of things presupposes the representation of them as a ground. Thus the power of judgement, by means of its principle, thinks a purposiveness in nature in the specification of its forms through empirical laws.

It is not these forms themselves, however, that are thereby thought as purposive, but only their relation to one another and their fitness, even in their great multiplicity, for a logical system of empirical concepts. Even if nature revealed to us no more than this logical purposiveness, we should still have cause for admiring nature in this regard since we are unable to find any ground for this in the universal laws of the understanding themselves. Yet hardly anyone but a transcendental philosopher would be capable of such admiration, and even he could identify no determinate case where

---

[6] Could Linnaeus* possibly have hoped to outline a system of nature if he had had to worry whether, on finding a stone that he called granite, this might differ in its internal constitution from every other apparently identical one, so that all he could ever hope to encounter were individual things merely isolated, as it were, for the understanding, but never a class of things which could be brought under the concepts of genus and species?

this purposiveness is manifested *in concreto*, but would have to think it solely in general terms.

VI. *The Purposiveness of Natural Forms as so many Particular Systems* 217

THAT nature, in its empirical laws, should so specify itself as is requisite for the possibility of experience as a single system of empirical knowledge, implies that this form of nature contains a logical purposiveness, i.e. that of its conformity with the subjective conditions of the power of judgement concerning the possible coherence of empirical concepts in the totality of one experience. But this does not entitle us to infer any adaptation of nature to a real purposiveness in its products, i.e. to the generation of individual things as systems. For these could always be mere aggregates, as far as intuition can tell, and still be subject to empirical laws which cohere with others in a logically divisible system without having to assume for their individual possibility a specially identified concept and thus a teleology of nature as their basis. It is in this way that we regard earths, stones, minerals etc. as mere aggregates and devoid of any purposive form, but as nevertheless so related in their inner character and the grounds of their possibility as objects of knowledge that they lend themselves to classification as a system of nature under empirical laws, even though *in themselves* they display no systematic form.

By an *absolute purposiveness* of natural forms I therefore understand that external configuration or internal structure of such forms which are so constituted that their possibility is necessarily grounded in an idea of the same within our power of judgement. For purposiveness is conformity to law on the part of something which is contingent. Nature works *mechanically*, as *mere nature*, in producing aggregates, but it works *technically*, i.e. *artistically*, in producing systems, for example, crystals, all sorts of flower forms, or the 218 internal structure of plants and animals. The difference between these two ways of judging natural beings lies simply in the *reflective* power of judgement which certainly can and perhaps must proceed to do what the *determining* power of judgement (governed by principles of reason) does not concede to the latter with respect to the possibility of objects, and it might be the case that the determining power of judgement is capable of tracing everything back to a mechanical explanation. For it is quite possible that the *explanation* of a given appearance, governed by objective principles of reason, may be *mechanical*, while the rule for judging the same object, according to subjective principles of reflection, may be *technical*.

In fact the principle of the power of judgement, namely the purposiveness of nature in the specification of its universal laws, may not extend so far that we can infer the production of *natural forms that are purposive in themselves* (because even without them the system of nature under empirical laws, which is all that the power of judgement is justified in postulating, is possible), and this is something that must always be given through experience; but since we have reason to suppose a principle of the purposiveness of nature in its particular laws, it is still always *possible* and permissible, if experience shows us purposive forms amongst its products, to ascribe this to the same ground on which the first type of purposiveness may rest.

Even though this ground itself might lie in the supersensible and wholly transcend the domain of our possible insights into nature, we have nevertheless accomplished something in so far as the power of judgement offers us a transcendental principle of the purposiveness of nature in relation to the purposiveness of natural forms which we encounter in experience. If this is not sufficient to account for the possibility of such forms, at least it still permits us to apply such a special concept as that of purposiveness to nature and its conformity to law, even though this principle cannot be an objective concept of nature but is simply derived from the subjective relation of nature to one of the faculties of the mind.

219   VII. *The Technic of the Power of Judgement as the Ground of the Idea of a Technic of Nature*

As we have shown above, it is the power of judgement which first makes it possible, and indeed necessary, to think, in addition to the mechanical necessity of nature, a purposiveness in nature. Without this assumption systematic unity in the complete classification of particular forms under empirical laws would be impossible. We have shown, in the first place, that the principle of purposiveness, being only a subjective principle of the division and specification of nature, determines nothing with regard to the forms of nature's products. In this respect, the purposiveness in question would remain merely conceptual and would supply a maxim suggesting the unity of empirical laws of nature for the logical employment of the power of judgement in experience, furthering the application of reason to its objects. But there would be no natural products, as such, whose form corresponds with this particular kind of systematic unity, namely that according to a representation of an end. The *causality* of nature with respect to the form of its products as ends I would describe as the *technic* of nature. It is opposed to the mechanism of nature, which consists in the connection of the manifold without any concept underlying the specific character of this connection, just as certain lifting devices, such as a lever or an inclined plane, which can also exercise their intended effect as a means to an end without presupposing any idea, are called machines rather than products of art because while they can indeed be used purposively, their possibility is not dependent upon this use.

The first question at this point is this: how can the technic of nature be *perceived* in its products? Precisely because it is not a category, the concept of purposiveness is in no way a concept that is constitutive of experience, and nor is it any determination of an appearance appropriate to an empir- 220 ical *concept* of the object. We perceive purposiveness in our power of judgement in so far as it merely reflects upon a given object, perhaps on the empirical intuition of the same, to bring it under some (as yet undetermined) concept, or upon the concept of experience itself, to bring the laws it contains under common principles. Thus it is essentially the *power of judgement* that is technical. Nature is therefore represented as technical only to the extent that it harmonizes with this procedure and makes it necessary. We shall shortly indicate how the concept of reflective judgement, which makes possible the inner perception of a purposiveness of representations, can also be applied to the representation of the object as contained under it.[7]

Now to each empirical concept there belong three acts of the spontaneous faculty of cognition: 1. the apprehension (*apprehensio*) of the manifold of intuition; 2. the synthesis, i.e. the synthetic unity of the consciousness of this manifold in the concept of an object (*apperceptio comprehensiva*); 3. the presentation (*exhibitio*) in intuition of the object corresponding to this concept. The first act requires imagination, the second requires reason and the third requires the power of judgement which, where an empirical concept is involved, is the determining power of judgement.

But since in simple reflection on perception it is not a question of reflecting on a determinate concept, but in general only of reflecting on the rule concerning perception as an aid to the understanding, as a faculty of concepts, it is evident in the case of a merely reflective judgement that the imagination and the understanding are regarded in their necessary relationship to one another with respect to power of judgement in general, in contrast to their actual relationship in a given perception.

If, then, the form of a given object in empirical intuition is such that the *apprehension* of its manifold in the imagination agrees with the presentation of a concept of the understanding (regardless of which concept), then 221 in simple reflection the understanding and the imagination harmonize with one another for the furtherance of their work and the object is perceived as purposive with respect to the power of judgement alone. The purposiveness itself is therefore considered as merely subjective since a determinate concept of the object is thereby neither required nor produced, and the judgement involved is not a cognitive one. Such a judgement is called an *aesthetic judgement of reflection.*

---

[7] We put, it is said, final causes into things, we do not draw them, as it were, out of our perception of things.

If, on the other hand, empirical concepts and laws conforming to the mechanism of nature are already given, and the power of judgement compares such a concept of the understanding with reason and its principle of the possibility of a system, then if this form is encountered in the object the purposiveness is judged to be *objective* and the thing is called a *natural end*, since in the previous case things were only judged to be indeterminately purposive *natural forms*. A judgement on the objective purposiveness is called *teleological*. This is a *cognitive judgement*, but it belongs only to the reflective and not to the determining power of judgement. For in general the technic of nature, whether it be merely *formal* or *real*, is only a relation of things to our power of judgement, in which alone we can find the idea of the purposiveness of nature that we attribute to nature itself merely in relation to that power.

VIII. *The Aesthetic of the Faculty of Judging*

THE expression 'an aesthetic kind of representation' is completely unambiguous if we understand it to signify the relation of the representation to the object as appearance with a view to the cognition of the object. For in this case the expression 'aesthetic' means that the form of sensibility (i.e. how the subject is affected) is necessarily attached to the representation and is thus unavoidably transferred to the object (though only as phenomenon). Consequently there can be a transcendental aesthetic* as a science that

222 belongs to the faculty of cognition. It has long been customary, however, to describe a mode of representation as 'aesthetic', i.e. as sensuous, also to signify our intention of relating a representation not to the faculty of cognition, but rather to our feeling of pleasure and displeasure. Although we are also accustomed (in accordance with this nomenclature) to calling this feeling a 'sense' (a modification of our state), since we lack an alternative expression, it is nonetheless not an objective sense the determination of which is employed for *cognition* of an object (for to intuit or otherwise perceive something with pleasure is not a simple relation of the representation to the object but rather involves a receptivity on the part of the subject); on the contrary, it contributes nothing whatsoever to our knowledge of objects. There can therefore be no aesthetic science of feeling, as there is indeed an aesthetic of the faculty of cognition, because all the determinations of feeling are of purely subjective significance. A certain ambiguity, therefore, inevitably clings to the expression 'aesthetic kind of representation' if it is understood now to mean that which arouses pleasure or displeasure and now to concern merely the cognitive faculty, in so far as it involves sensuous intuition, with regard to the knowledge of objects as appearances.

This ambiguity can, however, be removed if we apply the expression 'aesthetic' neither to intuition nor to the representations of the understanding, but solely to the acts of the *power of judgement*. An *aesthetic judgement*, if we intended to employ it for objective knowledge, would be so blatantly contradictory that this expression is a sufficient insurance against misinterpretation. For intuitions can indeed be sensuous, but judgements certainly belong only to the understanding (taken in the broader sense), and to *judge* aesthetically or sensuously, in so far as this purports to be *knowledge* of an object, is therefore a contradiction where sensibility meddles in the affairs of the understanding and (through a *vitium subreptionis*)* gives a false direction to the latter. An *objective* judgement, by contrast, is always brought about through the understanding alone and cannot therefore be called an aesthetic 223 one. Consequently our transcendental aesthetic of the faculty of judgement was certainly able to speak of sensory intuitions, but could never speak of aesthetic judgements because, since it is concerned solely with cognitive judgements that determine an object, all of its judgements must be logical ones. The expression 'an aesthetic judgement of an object' therefore signifies that a given representation is indeed related to an object, but such a judgement conveys the determination of the subject and its feeling rather than that of the object. As far as the power of judgement is concerned, the understanding and the imagination are regarded in relationship with one another, and this relationship can be considered (as happened in the transcendental schematism of the power of judgement) as objective and cognitive. But this same relationship of two cognitive faculties can also be regarded purely subjectively, in so far as one of them helps or hinders the other in the selfsame representation and thereby affects the *state of the mind*, and is thus a relationship that can be *sensed* (something encountered in the independent employment of no other faculty of cognition). Now although this sensation is not a sensuous representation of an object, it can nonetheless be ascribed to sensibility since it is subjectively connected with the sensuous rendering of the concepts of the understanding through the power of judgement, as a sensuous representation of how the state of the subject is affected by an act of that faculty. A judgement can be termed 'aesthetic', i.e. sensuous (according to its subjective effect rather than to its determining ground), even though an act of (objective) judging is an act of the understanding (as a higher faculty of cognition in general) rather than one of sensibility.

Every *determining* judgement is *logical* because its predicate is a given objective concept. A merely *reflective* judgement about a particular object, however, *can be aesthetic* if the judgement, even before it contemplates comparing the object with others, and with no concept antecedent to the given intuition, unites the imagination (which merely apprehends the object) with the understanding (which produces a general concept) and perceives a relationship between the two cognitive faculties which forms the subjective and merely sensitive condition of the objective employment of the power 224 of judgement (namely the mutual harmony of these two faculties). But an aesthetic sensuous judgement is also possible, where the predicate of the judgement *cannot be* a concept of an object because it does not belong to the cognitive faculty at all, as in the example: 'The wine is pleasant'—for here the predicate expresses the relation of a representation directly to the feeling of pleasure, and not to the faculty of cognition.

An aesthetic judgement can thus in general be defined as that kind of judgement whose predicate can never be cognitive, i.e. involve a concept of an object, although it may contain the general subjective conditions for cognition in general. Sensation is the determining ground in this kind of judgement. But there is only one unique, so-called, sensation which can never become the concept of an object, and this is the feeling of pleasure and displeasure. This is purely subjective since, by contrast, all other sensations can be employed with a view to cognition. An aesthetic judgement, therefore, is one whose determining ground lies in a sensation that is immediately connected with the feeling of pleasure and displeasure. In an aesthetic judgement of the senses it is that sensation that is immediately produced by the empirical intuition of the object, whereas in aesthetic judgements of reflection it is that sensation produced in the subject by the harmonious play between the two cognitive faculties of the power of judgement, the imagination and the understanding, when the former's capacity for apprehension and the latter's capacity for presentation reciprocally further one another in a given representation. In such a case, this relation, merely through its form, causes a sensation which is the determining ground of a judgement. This judgement is consequently described as 'aesthetic' and is connected with the feeling of pleasure as subjective purposiveness (without a concept).

Whereas aesthetic judgements of the senses express material purposiveness, aesthetic judgements of reflection express formal purposiveness. But since aesthetic judgements of the senses do not relate to the faculty of cognition at all, but only relate immediately through the senses to the feeling of pleasure, it is only aesthetic judgements of reflection that we can regard as grounded on principles peculiar to the power of judgement. For if reflection upon a given representation precedes the feeling of pleasure (as the deter-
225 mining ground of the judgement), then the subjective purposiveness is *thought* before it is *felt* in its effect; and in that respect an aesthetic judgement belongs, by virtue of its principles, to the higher faculty of cognition, and indeed to the power of judgement under whose subjective but universal conditions the representation of the object is subsumed. But since a merely subjective condition of a judgement permits no determinate concept of its determining ground, this ground can only be furnished through the feeling of pleasure, though in such a way that the aesthetic judgement is

always a judgement of reflection. This is the case because, by contrast, a judgement that assumes no comparison of the representation with the cognitive faculties and their cooperative effect in the power of judgement is an aesthetic judgement of the senses. The latter also relates a given representation to the feeling of pleasure (though not by means of the power of judgement and its principle). It is only in the treatise itself that the characteristic feature which allows us to specify this difference can be identified, namely the claim of the judgement to universal validity and necessity. For if an aesthetic judgement inevitably implies the latter, it thereby also claims that its determining ground must *lie not merely in the feeling* of pleasure and displeasure alone, but *equally in a rule* belonging to the higher cognitive faculties, and here specifically in a rule belonging to the power of judgement, which thereby legislates *a priori* with respect to the conditions of reflection and demonstrates *autonomy*. This autonomy, however, is not objective (like that of the understanding with respect to the theoretical laws of nature, or that of reason concerning the laws of freedom), i.e. by means of concepts of things or of possible actions, but is merely subjective and valid for a judgement derived from feeling, a judgement which, if it can lay claim to universal validity, indicates its origin as based upon *a priori* principles. We should properly have to describe this legislation as *heautonomy* since the power of judgement furnishes the law neither for nature nor for freedom but solely for itself, and is not a faculty of producing concepts of objects, but only of comparing specific cases with concepts supplied to it from elsewhere and of stating the subjective conditions of the possibility of this connection *a priori*.

It is precisely this which also explains why judgement, when it is merely reflective and is not based upon a concept of the object, is expressed in an act which is immediately related only to sensation (something which transpires 226 with no other higher faculty) and which, like all sensation, is always accompanied by pleasure or displeasure, instead of consciously relating the given representation to its own rule. And this is because the rule itself is only subjective, and agreement with it can only be recognized in something which also merely expresses a relation to the subject, namely sensation, as the characteristic feature and determining ground of the judgement. This is why it is also called an 'aesthetic' judgement, so that all our judgements can be divided, according to the order of the higher cognitive faculties, into *theoretical*, *aesthetic*, and *practical* ones, where under aesthetic judgements only those of reflection are to be understood since they alone are related to a principle of the power of judgement, whereas by contrast aesthetic judgements of the senses are immediately concerned solely with the relation of representations to inner sense considered as a feeling.

Remark

It is especially important at this point to elucidate the explanation of pleasure as a sensuous representation of the *perfection* of an object. According to
this explanation an aesthetic judgement of the senses or one of reflection
would invariably be a cognitive judgement of the object since perfection is
a determination that presupposes a concept of the object. Hence a judgement attributing perfection to an object could not be distinguished from
other logical judgements, except perhaps, as some allege, through the
'confused' character attaching to the concept (which is how some presume
to describe sensibility). But this can never constitute any specific distinction
amongst judgements. For otherwise a countless host of judgements, not
only those belonging to the understanding but also especially to reason,
would also have to be described as aesthetic because an object is thereby determined through a confused concept, as in judgements concerning right and
wrong since few people (even including philosophers) possess a clear concept
227 of what right is.[8] A sensuous representation of perfection is a contradiction
in terms, and if the harmonious unification of the manifold is to be
described as perfection this must be represented through a concept if it is
properly to bear the name of perfection. If one were to regard pleasure and
displeasure as nothing but a cognition of things through the understanding
(though one unconscious of its own concepts), and claim that they only
seem to be mere sensations, then we should have to describe this way of
judging things as entirely intellectual rather than as aesthetic (sensuous);
the senses would then basically be nothing but a judging understanding
(albeit one without sufficient consciousness of its own acts) and the aesthetic kind of representation would no longer be specifically distinguished
from logical kind of representation. And since the boundary between the

---

[8] In general one can say that things can never be regarded as *specifically different* from
one another by virtue of a quality which passes over into another one merely through an
increase or decrease in degree. As far as the difference in the distinctness or confused-
ness of concepts is concerned, this depends solely on the degree to which we are conscious of their distinguishing features and that corresponds to the amount of attention
directed to them. Hence, in this respect, one kind of representation is not specifically
different from any other. But intuition and concept are specifically distinct from one
another for neither can pass over into the other, however much our consciousness of
each, and of their characteristic features, may wax or wane. The greatest indistinctness
in a kind of conceptual representation (that of 'right' for example) still retains the
specific difference deriving from its origin in the understanding, while the greatest distinctness in intuition cannot bring it one whit closer to the former, for this latter kind of
representation has its seat in sensibility. Logical distinctness is also utterly different from
aesthetic distinctness, and the latter may obtain even though we do represent the object
to ourselves through concepts at all, that is to say, even though the representation, as an
intuition, is sensuous.

two could never be drawn with precision, this difference of nomenclature would be quite useless. (No mention will be made here of this mystical way of representing the things of the world, one which recognizes no sensuous intuition distinct from concepts and thus leaves it with nothing but an intuitive understanding.)

But one might still ask: does not our concept of the purposiveness of nature mean exactly the same as what is affirmed by the concept of *perfection*,* and is the empirical consciousness of subjective purposiveness, or the feeling of pleasure we take in certain objects, not simply the sensuous intuition of a perfection, as some like to explain pleasure in general?

My answer is this: *perfection*, as the mere completeness of a plurality in   228 so far as it together constitutes a unity, is an ontological concept which is the same as that of totality (allness) of a composite (through coordination of the manifold in an aggregate, or its simultaneous subordination as a series of grounds and consequences) and has nothing whatsoever to do with the feeling of pleasure or displeasure. *The* perfection of a thing with respect to the relation between its manifold and the concept of the thing is only formal. But if I speak of *a* perfection (and there can be many such in a thing grasped under the same concept), it is always grounded in the concept of something as an end to which the ontological concept of the unification of the manifold is applied. This end need not, however, be a practical end, one which presupposes or includes a pleasure in the existence of the object, but can also belong to technic; it thus concerns merely the possibility of things and is *the conformity to law of an intrinsically contingent combination of the manifold* in the object. As an example we may consider the purposiveness which is necessarily thought in the possibility of a regular hexagon for it is entirely contingent that six equal lines on a plane should intersect at precisely equal angles and this lawlike combination presupposes a concept which, as a principle, makes it possible. This kind of objective purposiveness observed in things of nature (and especially in organized beings) is now thought as objective and material and necessarily carries with it the concept of an end of nature (actual or imputed) in relation to which we also attribute perfection to things; judgement in this regard is called 'teleological' and carries with it no feeling of pleasure whatsoever, just as the latter is not to be looked for in any judgement that concerns mere causal connection.

The concept of perfection as objective purposiveness thus has nothing whatsoever to do with the feeling of pleasure and the latter has nothing whatsoever to do with the former. For judging the former a *concept* of an object is necessarily required, whereas for judging the latter no concept is needed and purely empirical intuition can suffice. The representation of subjective purposiveness in an object, on the other hand, is even the same as the feeling of pleasure (without involving an abstracted concept of any

purposive relation) and there is a great gulf between these two kinds of
229 purposiveness. If what is subjectively purposive is to be objective as well,
a much more far-reaching investigation is required, not only of practical
philosophy but also of the technic, whether it be that of nature or of art. That
is to say: to find perfection in a thing requires reason, to find a thing agreeable
only requires the senses, to encounter beauty in a thing requires nothing
but reflection (devoid of any concept) upon a given representation.

The aesthetic faculty of reflection thus judges only about the subjective
purposiveness (not the perfection) of the object, and the question now arises
whether it judges only *by means of* the pleasure or displeasure which is felt
here, or whether it even judges *about* the latter, so that the judgement simultaneously determines that pleasure or displeasure *must* be combined with the
representation of the object.

This question, as we have already indicated, cannot yet be decided adequately at this point. It is only through the exposition of such judgements,
furnished in the treatise itself, that we shall be able to conclude whether or
not they possess a universal validity and necessity which permits them to be
derived from a determining ground *a priori*. In that case, a judgement would
indeed determine something *a priori* by means of the sensation of pleasure
or displeasure, but it would also simultaneously determine something
a priori through the faculty of cognition (namely the power of judgement)
by means of the universality of a rule for combining the feeling with a
given representation. On the other hand, if a judgement contained nothing but the relation between the representation and the feeling (without
the mediation of any cognitive principle), as is the case with an aesthetic
judgement of the senses (which is neither a cognitive judgement nor a judgement of reflection), then all aesthetic judgements would belong in the merely
empirical domain.

For the moment we can note that no transition from cognition to the
feeling of pleasure takes place through concepts of objects (in so far as the
latter are to relate to that feeling), and that we cannot therefore expect to
determine *a priori* the influence which a given representation exercises on
the mind; and further, as we already noted in the *Critique of Practical Reason*,
that the representation of a universal lawfulness of willing must simultaneously determine the will and thereby also awaken the feeling of respect, as a
law contained, and indeed *a priori* contained, in our moral judgements, even
though this feeling still cannot be derived from concepts. In the same way
230 we shall see that aesthetic judgements of reflection contain the concept of
a formal but subjective purposiveness of objects, resting on an *a priori*
principle which is fundamentally the same as the feeling of pleasure, but
which cannot be derived from any concepts to whose possibility in general

the power of representation stands in relation when it affects the mind in reflecting on an object.

An explanation of this feeling, considered in general and without distinguishing whether it accompanies sense perception, reflection, or a determination of the will, must be transcendental.[9] It can be expressed as follows: *pleasure* is a *state* of the mind in which a representation is in harmony with itself, as a ground for simply preserving this state itself (for the state in which the powers of the mind mutually further one another in a representation does preserve itself) or else for producing its object. In the first case, the judgement concerning the given representation is an aesthetic

231

[9] It is worth attempting a transcendental definition of concepts which are employed as empirical principles if one has cause to suspect that they share kinship with the pure faculty of cognition *a priori*. Thus one proceeds like the mathematician who greatly facilitates the solution of his problem by leaving the empirical data indeterminate and bringing the mere synthesis of the latter under the expressions of pure arithmetic. But an objection has been raised against a similar definition of mine concerning the faculty of desire (*Critique of Practical Reason*, Preface): namely that it cannot be defined as *the capacity for causing, through its representations, the existence of the objects of these representations* since mere *wishes* are also desires, although we can readily see that they are incapable of producing their objects. But this simply proves that there are also determinations of the faculty of desire where it stands in contradiction with itself. This is certainly a noteworthy phenomenon for empirical psychology (as is the observed influence of prejudices on the understanding for logic), but it should not disturb the definition of the faculty desire objectively considered, namely as it is in itself, before it diverted from its own determination in some way or other. For in fact a human being can desire, in the liveliest and most persistent fashion, something that he is nonetheless convinced he cannot achieve, or that is even utterly impossible, like wishing undone something that has already transpired, or longing for a burdensome time to us to pass more quickly, and so forth. It is also important for morality to warn emphatically against such hollow and fantastic desires which are often nourished by novels, and sometimes by not dissimilar mystical notions of a more-than-human perfection and fanatical blessedness. But the very effect which such hollow longings and desires, that cause the heart to swell and languish, exert upon the mind, weakening it through exhaustion of its forces, are enough to prove that while these forces are repeatedly incited through such representations to realize their object, the mind just as often sinks back into an awareness of its own impotence. It is a task of no little significance for anthropology to investigate why nature has planted within us a disposition to the fruitless expenditure of our powers in such hollow wishes and longings (which certainly play a great role in human life). Here, as everywhere else, it seems to me that nature has proceeded wisely. For if the representation of an object had never led us to exercise our powers before ascertaining the adequacy of our capacity to produce the object, those powers would surely remain largely unused. For we ordinarily come to know our powers only through the attempt to use them. Nature has thus connected the exercise of power to the representation of an object even before we become aware of our capacity, and the latter is often first brought forth through the very effort which initially appeared to the mind itself as an idle wish. Now it falls to wisdom to put limits on this instinct, but it will never succeed in eradicating it or ever desire to do so.

judgement of reflection. In the second case, however, it is an aesthetic-pathological or aesthetic-practical judgement. It can readily be seen here that pleasure and displeasure, since they are not kinds of cognition, cannot be explained in their own right, and ask to be felt rather than understood; and that one can only explain them, and then only inadequately, through the influence which a representation exercises by means of this feeling upon the activity of the powers of the mind.

IX. *Teleological Judging*

BY the term '*formal* technic of nature' I intended to express the purposiveness of nature in intuition, whereas by the term '*real* technic of nature' I understand the purposiveness of nature in accordance with concepts. The former yields purposive structures for the power of judgement, i.e. a form in the representation of which the imagination and the understanding are spontaneously and reciprocally harmonious with respect to the possibility of a concept. The latter indicates the concept of things as natural ends, i.e. as things whose inner possibility presupposes a purpose, and therefore a concept, which is the underlying condition of the causality of their production.

The power of judgement itself can provide and construct purposive forms for intuition *a priori* when it devises such forms for apprehension as are suitable for the presentation of a concept. But ends, i.e. representations which are themselves regarded as conditions for the causal production of their objects (as effects), must in general be given from elsewhere before the power of judgement concerns itself with harmonizing with the conditions of the manifold; and if there are to be any natural ends, we must be able to regard certain things in nature as if they were products of a cause whose activity could only be determined through a *representation* of the object. But we cannot determine *a priori* precisely how, and in what variety of ways, things are possible with respect to their causes since for this we require knowledge of empirical laws.

A judgement concerning purposiveness in things of nature as a ground of their possibility (as natural ends) is called a *teleological judgement*. Although *a priori* aesthetic judgements are not possible, we nonetheless encounter *a priori* principles in the necessary idea of the systematic unity of experience, and they include the concept of the formal purposiveness of nature for our power of judgement; and this reveals *a priori* the possibility of aesthetic judgements of reflection that are based upon *a priori* principles. Nature is necessarily harmonious, not merely with respect to the agreement of its transcendental laws with our *understanding*, but also with respect to the agreement of its empirical laws with the *power of judgement* and the capacity of the latter to present an empirical apprehension of the forms of nature by means of the imagination. This agreement simply serves for the further-ance of experience, and the formal purposiveness of experience with respect to the ultimate harmony of nature (with the power of judgement) is thereby revealed as necessary. But if nature, as the object of teleological judgement, is also to be thought in agreement with the causality of *reason*, under the concept of an end which reason fashions for itself, then that is more than can be attributed to the power of judgement alone; the power of judgement can, of course, contain its own *a priori* principles for the form of intuition, but not for concepts of the production of things. The concept of a real *end of nature* thus falls completely beyond the scope of the power of judgement, taken simply on its own. For the latter, as a separate cognitive power, consid-ers only how two faculties (the imagination and the understanding) are related in a representation prior to the formation of a concept and thereby perceives the subjective purposiveness of the object for its apprehension (through the imagination) by the cognitive faculties. Thus in the teleological purposiveness of things as natural ends, which can only be represented through concepts, the power of judgement will have to relate the under-standing to reason (something unnecessary for experience in general) in order to be able to represent things as ends of nature.

The aesthetic judging of natural forms might, without supplying a con-cept underlying the object, discover simply through intuitive and empirical apprehension certain objects occurring in nature to be purposive, i.e. merely in relation to the subjective conditions of the power of judgement. Aesthetic judging would therefore neither require a concept of an object nor produce one; that is why it would not interpret these objects in an objective judge-ment as natural ends, but merely as purposive under a subjective relation to the power of representation. This purposiveness of forms can be called 234 *figurative*, and the technic of nature with respect to these forms can also be designated accordingly (*technica speciosa*).*

On the other hand, teleological judgement presupposes a concept of the object and judges the possibility of the latter according to a law that connects cause and effect. This technic of nature might therefore be called *plastic*, if this word were not already now commonly used with reference both to nat-ural beauty and to the purposes of nature. Thus one could, if one wishes, also call it an *organic technic* of nature, an expression which then designates the concept of purposiveness not merely for the mode in which we represent them but also for the possibility of the objects themselves.

The most essential and most important thing for this section, however, is the demonstration that the concept *of final causes* in nature, which sep-arates the teleological judging of nature from judging it in accordance with universal mechanical laws, is a concept which belongs merely to the power of judgement and not to the faculties of understanding or reason. Thus if the concept of natural ends were also to be employed in an objective sense, as an *intention of nature*, this employment would already be sophistical and could never be grounded within experience. For although experience exhibits ends, nothing can demonstrate that these are also intentions, and thus anything pertaining to teleology that is encountered in experience contains nothing but the relation of its objects to the power of judgement, and in fact to a fundamental principle of the latter, through which it legislates for itself (and not for nature)—namely as the reflective power of judgement.

The concept of ends and of purposiveness is indeed a concept of reason, in so far as one attributes to reason the ground of the possible existence of an object. But the purposiveness of nature, or even the concept of things as natural ends, places reason into relation with these things as their cause, although through experience we have no knowledge of the ground of the possibility of things. For it is only in *products of art* that we can become aware of the causality of reason with respect to objects, which are therefore called ends or described as purposive, and to call reason 'technical' in this regard conforms to our experience of the causality of our own powers. But to rep-

235   resent nature as technical on analogy with reason (and thus to ascribe pur-posiveness, and thus even ends, *to nature*) involves a specific concept which can never be encountered within experience, and which is only introduced by the power of judgement in its reflection upon objects in order to organize experience, as indicated by this concept, under specific laws, namely those of the possibility of a system.

For all purposiveness in nature can be regarded either as *natural* (*forma finalis naturae spontanea*) or as *intentional* (*intentionalis*). Experience on its own justifies only the first way of representing purposiveness, while the second is a hypothetical way of explaining it which goes beyond any concept of things as natural ends. The former concept of things as ends of nature originally belongs to the *reflective* power of judgement (as logically rather than aesthetically reflective), while the latter belongs to the *determining* power of judgement. In the first case reason is certainly also required, albeit only for the sake of experience that is to be organized in accordance with principles (thus in its *immanent* employment), whereas the second case requires reason to lose itself in extravagant demands (in its transcendent employment).

We can and should endeavour, to the best of our ability, to investigate nature as causally connected in experience according to purely mechanical laws, since it is these which furnish the true grounds of physical explana-tion and their interconnection constitutes rational scientific knowledge of nature. But amongst nature's products we find specific and very widely dis-tributed genera which contain within themselves a connection of efficient causes that we can only ground in the concept of an end if we wish to have

ordered experience at all, i.e. observation according to a principle that is
adequate to their inner possibility. If we were to judge their form and its
possibility merely according to mechanical laws, where the idea of the effect
must be regarded not as the ground of the possibility of the cause but rather
the reverse, it would be impossible, simply from the specific form of these
natural things, to derive an empirical concept which would allow us to pass
from this inner structure, as cause, to the effect, since the parts of these
machines are the cause of the effect which they manifest not in so far as each
part has a separate ground of its own, but only in so far as they all share one   236
common ground of their possibility. It is entirely contrary to the nature of
physico-mechanical causes that the whole should be the cause of the possibility of the causality of the parts, for the parts must already be given if we
are to grasp the possibility of a whole on the basis of the latter; and further,
the particular representation of a whole, a representation that precedes the
possibility of the parts, is a mere idea and is called an 'end' if it is regarded
as the ground of a causality. Thus it is clear that if there are such products
of nature, it is impossible to investigate their character or their cause even
within experience (let alone to explain them through reason) without representing their form and their causality as determined according to a principle of ends.

Now it is clear in such cases that the concept of an objective purposiveness of nature serves merely to assist *reflection* on an object, and not
its *determination* through the concept of an end, and that a teleological
judgement concerning the inner possibility of a product of nature is a merely
reflective, not a determining judgement. Thus when we say, for example,
that the crystalline lens in the eye has the *purpose* of focusing, through a secondary refraction, the light rays emanating from a certain point into a point
on the retina, we are merely saying that we think the representation of a
purpose in the causal action of nature in producing the eye because such
an idea serves as a principle for conducting our investigation concerning
this part of the eye, and thus also assists us to devise possible means of
enhancing the relevant effect. But this does not yet involve attributing
to nature a causality in accordance with a representation of ends, i.e. an
intentional action, which latter would involve a determining teleological
judgement, and as such a transcendent one, that introduces a causality
lying beyond the bounds of nature.

The concept of natural ends is therefore merely a concept of the reflective
power of judgement for the sake of exploring the causal connection in
objects of experience. Employing a teleological principle for the explanation
of the inner possibility of certain natural forms leaves it undecided whether
their purposiveness is *intentional* or *unintentional*. A judgement asserting
either one or the other conclusion would be a determining rather than a

237 reflective one, and the concept of an end of nature would then no longer be a mere *concept of the power of judgement*, for immanent (empirical) employment, but would be bound up with a *concept of reason*, of an intentionally acting cause set over nature, irrespective of whether we wished to pass an affirmative or a negative judgement in this case.

x. *The Search for a Principle of the Technical Power of Judgement*

IF we are seeking for a general ground of explanation for events, this may be found either in an empirical principle, or an *a priori* principle, or in a combination of both. This can be seen from the physico-mechanical explanations of the events occurring in the material world, which take their principles partly from universal (rational) natural science and partly from that science which contains the empirical laws of motion. It is the same when we seek psychological grounds of explanation for the behaviour of the mind, but with the difference that, as far as I am aware, these principles are wholly empirical with one exception, namely that of the continuity of all changes which underlies these perceptions *a priori* (since time, which has only one dimension, is the formal condition of inner intuition). But this contributes virtually nothing to the process of explanation because the general theory of time does not furnish sufficient material for an entire science, unlike the pure theory of space (geometry).

If it were important to explain how what we call 'taste' first arose amongst human beings, why it has been affected by certain things more than others, or how it has brought forth judgements of beauty under varying regional and social circumstances, which have allowed it to grow into a luxury, and so forth, we should have to seek the relevant principles of explanation mainly in psychology (which in a case like this invariably means nothing but empirical psychology). Thus moral teachers expect 238 psychologists to explain the curious phenomenon of miserliness which places an absolute value upon the mere possession of the means for a more than comfortable condition of life (or for any other goal) while resolving never to use them, or to explain that craving for honour on the part of those who take reputation itself as their only goal and direct their precepts less to moral laws themselves than to the removal of obstacles which impede the influence of such laws. In this connection we must confess that psychological explanations are in a very sorry state as compared with physical ones, that hypotheses are infinitely available here, that given three explanations, we can also always easily imagine a fourth equally convincing one. Hence there is a host of alleged psychologists of this kind who are adept at identifying the causes for every movement or affection of the mind that is aroused by plays, poetic images, or objects of nature, and who even bestow the name of philosophy upon their ingenuity in finding a scientific explanation for the most ordinary natural events of the material world, although they thereby reveal not merely an absence of real knowledge, but also perhaps of any capacity for attaining it. To furnish psychological observations (as Burke did in his treatise on the beautiful and the sublime),* and thus to gather material for the systematic connection of empirical rules in the future without here making any attempt to understand them, is probably the sole true duty of an empirical psychology which will probably never legitimately aspire to the rank of a philosophical science.

But if a judgement presents itself as universally valid, and thereby positively lays claim to *necessity*, this professed necessity may rest either upon concepts of the object *a priori* or upon the subjective conditions of underlying concepts *a priori*; thus if we grant the claim of such a judgement, it would be quite absurd to justify it by explaining the origin of the judgement psychologically. This would be self-defeating since if the desired explanation were fully accomplished, it would prove that the judgement can claim no necessity whatsoever precisely because its empirical origin has now been identified.

Now aesthetic judgements of reflection (which we shall later analyse under the name of judgements of taste) are of the type we have just described. They claim to be necessary, and they assert not that everyone does indeed so judge—for then they would be open to explanation by empirical psychology—but rather that everyone *should* so judge, and this implies that they possess their own *a priori* principle. If the relation to such a principle, one which claims necessity for itself, were not intrinsic to these judgements, we should have to assume that a judgement should be regarded as universally valid because it is actually so regarded, as confirmed by observation, and, conversely, that the fact that everyone does judge in a certain manner implies that they *should* so judge, and this is a patent absurdity. 239

Aesthetic judgements of reflection do indeed reveal the difficulty that they are not based upon concepts at all and thus cannot be derived from any determinate principle, for in that case they would be logical judgements. The subjective representation of purposiveness is not supposed to be a concept of an end. But a relation to an *a priori* principle can and must invariably hold wherever a judgement claims necessity; and here we are concerned solely with this claim and its possibility in so far as a critique of reason is precisely thereby encouraged to seek out the underlying, though indeterminate, principle at work here. And reason can successfully discover this principle and recognize it as one which subjectively and *a priori* underlies the judgement in question, although it can never be a determinate concept of an object.

Thus one is compelled to admit that a teleological judgement is grounded in an *a priori* principle and would be impossible without such a principle, although we only discover the purpose of nature in judgements of this sort through experience and could never become aware without experience that things of this kind are even possible. For a teleological judgement, although it connects a determinate concept of an end, upon which it grounds the possibility of certain products of nature, with the representation of the object (something that does not happen in an aesthetic judgement), it still merely remains a reflective judgement, as in the former case. A teleological judgement does not presume to assert, with respect to this objective purposiveness, that nature (or any other being working through nature) in fact acts *intentionally*, i.e. that in nature or its cause the thought of an end determines causality, but merely that we must employ the mechanical laws of nature in accordance with this analogy (the relation of cause and effect) in order to recognize the possibility of such objects and acquire a concept of them capable of furnishing a single systematic and coherent structure in experience.

A teleological judgement compares the concept of a natural product as it is with what it *ought to be*. Here the judgement of the possibility of the natural product is based upon a previous *a priori* concept (of an end). There is no difficulty in representing the possibility of something in this way where the products of art are concerned. But to conceive that a product of nature *ought* to be something or other, and thus to judge whether it actually is so or not, itself presupposes a principle which could not have been derived from experience (which only tells us what things are).

We are immediately aware through experience that we see by means of the eye, and we likewise learn through experience of the internal and external structure of the eye, which define the conditions of its possible use, and therefore of its causality under mechanical laws. But I can also make use of a stone either to crush something or to build something, etc., and these effects can also be related to their causes as specific ends. Yet this does not permit me to say that the stone ought to be used for building. But with regard to the eye I judge that it *ought* to be adapted to seeing, and although its form, the character of all its parts, and their composition, when judged in accordance with merely mechanical laws, are entirely contingent as far as my own power of judgement is concerned, I nevertheless think that its form and structure manifest a certain necessity, namely one that accords with a concept which precedes the formative causes of the organ in question and without which I am incapable of conceiving of the possibility of this natural product under any mechanical laws of nature (something that is not the case with the stone). This 'ought' therefore implies a necessity which is clearly differentiated from that physico-mechanical necessity through which a thing is

possible under the laws of efficient causes alone (with any preceding idea), 241
and it can no more be determined through mere empirical and physical
laws than the necessity belonging to aesthetic judgements can be determined through psychological ones.

Thus all judgements concerning the purposiveness of nature, whether
they be aesthetic or teleological, are subject to *a priori* principles, and indeed
to those belonging specifically and exclusively to the power of judgement,
because they are merely reflective rather than determining judgements. And
that is precisely why they also belong to a critique of pure reason (understood
in the most general sense). Teleological judgements require this critique
more than aesthetic judgements do since the former, left to themselves, only
encourage reason to draw potentially extravagant conclusions, whereas the
latter demand careful investigation only to guard against their own principle leading to an exclusive preoccupation with the empirical and thereby
forfeiting their claims to a universally valid necessity.

XI. *The Encyclopedic Introduction of the Critique of Judgement into the System of the Critique of Pure Reason*

EVERY introduction to an exposition serves either to introduce a proposed
doctrine or to introduce the doctrine itself into a system in which it belongs
as a part. The first kind of introduction precedes the doctrine, while the
second should properly only constitute its conclusion and indicate its
place, according to fundamental principles, in the body of doctrines with
which it is connected through common principles. The former approach
is a *propaedeutic* introduction, while the second can be called an *encyclopedic* one.

Propaedeutic introductions are the customary ones, which prepare the
way for the proposed doctrine by drawing the preliminary knowledge that is
requisite from other already existing doctrines or sciences in order to facilitate the transition in question. If they are so designed as to distinguish
carefully between the special principles of the novel doctrine (*domestica*) and 242
those belonging to some other doctrine (*peregrinis*),* they serve to demarcate
the boundaries of the sciences—a precaution which cannot be recommended too highly since without it no thoroughness, especially with regard
to philosophical knowledge, can be hoped for.

An encyclopedic introduction, however, presupposes not the existence
of a related doctrine that is preparatory to the newly promulgated doctrine, but rather the idea of a system which will only be completed through
the latter. This cannot be accomplished by raking over or collecting up the
many things that have been discovered on the path of research, but only
when we are able to specify completely the subjective or objective sources

of a certain kind of cognition through the formal concept of a whole which equally contains the principle of a complete *a priori* division. Thus one can easily see why encyclopedic introductions, useful though they might be, are nonetheless so rare.

The faculty whose distinctive principle will be sought out and discussed here (the power of judgement) is of a very special kind in that it produces, on its own account, no knowledge whatsoever, whether theoretical or practical, and, despite its *a priori* principle, contributes nothing to transcendental philosophy as an objective doctrine, but simply constitutes the connection between two other higher cognitive faculties (understanding and reason). Hence in determining the principles of this faculty, which lends itself only to a critique and is incapable of becoming a doctrine, I may be permitted to relinquish the order of argument that is otherwise always necessary and offer a brief encyclopedic introduction. This is not an introduction to the system of the *sciences* of pure reason, but merely to the *critique* of all the faculties of the mind which can be determined *a priori* and in so far as they constitute a system within the mind, an approach which thus serves to unite a propaedeutic introduction with an encyclopedic one.

The introduction of the power of judgement into the system of the pure faculties of cognition through concepts rests entirely upon its distinctive transcendental principle: that nature in specifying the transcendental laws 243 of the understanding (the principles of its possibility as nature in general), i.e. the manifold of its empirical laws, operates in accordance with the idea of its own systematic division and thus facilitates the possibility of experience as an empirical system. This suggests first, and indeed *a priori*, the concept of a conformity to law, i.e. a purposiveness of nature, which is objectively contingent but subjectively necessary (for our cognitive faculties). Even if this principle determines nothing with respect to the particular forms of nature, since the purposiveness of the latter can only be given empirically, a judgement concerning such forms nonetheless acquires a claim to necessity and universal validity, as a merely reflective judgement, through the relation between the subjective purposiveness of the given representation for the power of judgement and the *a priori* principle of the power of judgement of nature's purposiveness in its empirical conformity to law in general. Thus an aesthetic reflective judgement can be regarded as resting upon an *a priori* principle (although it is not determining) and the power of judgement will thereby find itself entitled to a place within the critique of the higher faculties of pure cognition.

The concept of a purposiveness of nature (as a technical purposiveness which is essentially different from a practical one), if it is not simply to be the fraudulent substitution of *what we make of nature* for what *nature is*, is a concept distinct from all dogmatic philosophy (theoretical and practical) and is grounded merely on that principle of the power of judgement which precedes empirical laws and first renders possible their coherence within the unity of a system of such laws. It is therefore clear, with respect to the two ways of employing the reflective power of judgement (the aesthetic and the teleological), that only the judgement which precedes any concept of the object, namely the reflective aesthetic judgement, possesses its determining ground in the power of judgement, unmixed with any other faculty of cognition; on the other hand, a teleological judgement on the concept of a natural end, even if it merely employs the principle of the reflective rather than the determining power of judgement, can only be made by combining reason with empirical concepts. It is thus easy to show the possibility of a teleological judgement on nature without having to base it upon any special principle of the power of judgement since this possibility merely 244 follows from the principle of reason. By contrast, the possibility of a mere judgement of reflection, which is aesthetic yet nonetheless grounded on an *a priori* principle, i.e. a judgement of taste, if it can actually be shown to have a justifiable claim to universal validity, certainly does require a critique of the power of judgement as a faculty with distinctive transcendental principles (like reason and the understanding), and only in this way does it qualify for inclusion within the system of the pure faculties of cognition. This is because an aesthetic judgement, while it presupposes no concept of its object, nonetheless ascribes purposiveness and indeed universal validity to it. Thus the principle for this can only lie in the power of judgement itself since a teleological judgement, by contrast, presupposes a concept of the object, which reason brings under the principle of teleological connection, although only in so far as the power of judgement employs this concept of an end of nature in a merely reflective rather than in a determining judgement.

The power of judgement thus reveals itself in taste alone, and indeed in that concerning objects of nature, as a faculty possessing its own distinctive principle, and it thereby claims a place in the general critique of the higher faculties of cognition which one might not otherwise have believed it deserves. But once we concede that the faculty of the power of judgement can set *a priori* principles for itself, it also becomes necessary to determine its proper range. And for this completion of the task of critique we must recognize that both the aesthetic and the teleological capacities are contained within a single faculty and rest upon the same principle, for the teleological judgement concerning things of nature also belongs, along with the aesthetic judgement, to the reflective rather than to the determining power of judgement.

The critique of taste, however, which is otherwise employed merely for the improvement or strengthening of taste itself, fills a lacuna within the system of our cognitive faculties if one considers it from a transcendental perspective, and thus opens up the striking and, it seems to me, highly encouraging prospect of a complete system of all the powers of the mind in their relationship not merely to the sensuous but also to the supersensible domain, without thereby effacing the boundaries which have been set to their use in this respect by the most rigorous critique. It may perhaps prove helpful for the reader, and facilitate a clearer view of the structure of the investigations which follow, if I here furnish an outline of their systematic connection with one another, although, like the whole of the section, it should properly assume its place at the end of the treatise itself.

All of the faculties of the mind can be traced back to these three:

> *the faculty of cognition*
> *the feeling of pleasure and displeasure*
> *the faculty of desire*

The cognitive faculty, although it does not always function as cognition (since a representation belonging to this faculty can also be a pure or empirical intuition without reference to concepts), nonetheless invariably underlies the exercise of all the faculties. If we thus consider the general capacity for knowledge in accordance with principles, we can correlate the powers of the mind with the following higher faculties:

> *the faculty of cognition*   *the understanding*
> *the feeling of pleasure and displeasure*   *the power of judgement*
> *the faculty of desire*   *reason*

We find that the understanding possesses specific *a priori* principles for the faculty of cognition, the power of judgement possesses such principles only for the feeling of pleasure and displeasure, while reason possesses such principles merely for the faculty of desire. These formal principles serve to ground a necessity which is partly objective and partly subjective, but which also possesses objective validity in part because it is subjective, in so far as these principles determine, through the higher faculties here correlated with them, the corresponding powers of the mind:

the faculty of cognition	*the understanding*	*lawfulness*
the feeling of pleasure and displeasure	*the power of judgement*	*purposiveness*
the faculty of desire	*reason*	*purposiveness which is also law* (*obligation*)

Finally, associated with these *a priori* grounds of the possibility of forms, we also find the following products corresponding to them:

Faculties of the mind	Higher faculties of cognition	A priori principles	Products
faculty of cognition	the understanding	lawfulness	nature
feeling of pleasure and displeasure	the power of judgement	purposiveness	art
faculty of desire	reason	purposiveness which is also law (*obligation*)	morality

NATURE thus grounds its lawfulness on *a priori* principles of the understanding as the *faculty of cognition*; *ART* is guided *a priori* in its *purposiveness* in accordance with the *power of judgement* in relation to the *feeling of pleasure and displeasure*; lastly, *MORALITY* (as the product of freedom) stands under the idea of a form *of purposiveness* which is qualified for universal law as the determining ground of *reason* with respect to the *faculty of desire*. The judgements which arise in this way from *a priori* principles that are peculiar to each of the fundamental faculties of the mind are *theoretical*, *aesthetic*, and *practical* judgements respectively.

Thus we uncover a system of the powers of the mind in their relation to nature and to freedom, both of which possess their own distinctive *determining a priori* principles and which therefore constitute the two parts of philosophy as a doctrinal system (theoretical and practical philosophy), as well as a transition from the *sensible* substrate of the former to the *intelligible* substrate of the latter by means of the power of judgement which connects both parts through a distinctive principle of its own; this transition is accomplished through the critique of a faculty (the power of judgement) whose function is simply connective and which cannot therefore furnish any knowledge on its own account or make any contribution to doctrine, but whose judgements—called *aesthetic* (possessing merely subjective principles) as distinct from those called *logical* (whether theoretical or practical) which necessarily possess objective principles—are of a special kind in that they 247 relate sensuous intuitions to an idea of nature whose conformity to law cannot be understood except in relation to a supersensible substrate. The proof of this will be produced in the course of the treatise itself.

We shall not call the critique of this faculty with respect to the former type of judgement an *aesthetic* (understood as a doctrine of the senses) but a *critique of aesthetic judgement*. This is because the meaning of the former expression is too broad, since it can also signify the sensuous character of the *intuition* which belongs to theoretical cognition and which furnishes the material for logical (objective) judgements. That is why we have earlier defined the expression 'aesthetic' exclusively as a predicate belonging to intuition in the context of cognitive judgements. But there is no danger of misunderstanding if we call the power of judgement 'aesthetic' precisely because it does not relate the representation of an object to concepts, and thus does not relate a judgement to cognition at all (being merely reflective rather than determining). For although intuitions are sensuous (aesthetic) for the logical power of judgement, they must nevertheless first be raised to the level of concepts in order to contribute to the knowledge of objects, something which is not the case for the aesthetic power of judgement.

XII. *The Division of the Critique of Judgement*

DIVIDING the domain of a certain kind of cognition in order to present it as a system has an importance that is rarely recognized, but also involves a commonly misunderstood difficulty. If we regard the parts of such a possible whole as already complete in themselves, the division is made *mechanically*, simply for the sake of comparing the parts, and the resulting whole becomes an *aggregate* (rather as cities do when land is divided amongst prospective settlers according to the individual designs of each without any regulation). But if we can and should presuppose an idea of whole, according to a certain principle, and prior to the determination of the parts, the division must be made *scientifically*, and it is only in this way that the whole becomes a system. And this is always required where the domain of *a priori* knowl-
248 edge is concerned (which together with its principles rests upon a special legislative faculty on the part of the subject), for in such cases the range within which these laws can be employed, and therefore also the number and the relationship of the parts to knowledge as a whole, are determined *a priori* through the distinctive character of this faculty. But no properly grounded division can be produced without simultaneously *producing* the whole itself and already presenting it completely in all its parts, though only of course under the rule of *critique*. Nothing further is then required to bring it into the systematic form of a *doctrine* (in so far as this cognitive faculty can by its nature furnish such a thing) except the *thoroughness* of its application and the elegant *precision* of its connection to particular content.

Now in order to divide a critique of the power of judgement (a faculty which, although grounded on *a priori* principles, can never furnish the material for a doctrine), we must fundamentally recognize that it is only the reflective, not the determining, power of judgement which possesses its own *a priori* principles. The former proceeds merely *schematically*, under the laws of another faculty (the understanding), while the latter proceeds merely *technically*, under its own laws. The procedure of the latter is based upon the principle of a technic of nature, and consequently upon a concept of purposiveness in nature which must be presupposed *a priori*. Although the reflective power of judgement, in accordance with its own principle, must assume this purposiveness to be only subjective, i.e. relatively to this faculty itself, it still carries with it the concept of a *possible* objective purposiveness, i.e. the conformity to law on the part of the things of nature as natural ends.

A purposiveness that is judged merely subjectively, which is not therefore based on any concept, and in so far as it is merely subjectively judged never can be based on one, is a relation to the feeling of pleasure and displeasure, and the judgement concerning this relation is *aesthetic* (and this is indeed the only possible way of judging aesthetically). When this feeling merely accompanies the sensuous representation of the object, i.e. the sensation of the object, the aesthetic judgement is empirical, and while it certainly requires a specific receptivity, it calls for no specific power of judgement; and if, furthermore, the latter were assumed to be determining, it would also have to be grounded in a concept of an end, and the purposiveness, as objective, would therefore have to be judged logically rather than aesthetically. For these reasons are compelled to recognize that the aesthetic power of judgement, as a special faculty, is nothing but the *reflective power of judgement*, and that the feeling of pleasure (which cannot be distinguished from the representation *of subjective purposiveness*) must not be 249 regarded as derived from or related by an *a priori* principle either to the sensation in an empirical representation of the object or to the concept of the object. This feeling can only therefore be regarded as connected with reflection and the form (the distinctive activity of the power of judgement) through which it advances from empirical intuitions to general concepts. The *aesthetic* of the reflective power of judgement will therefore constitute one part of the critique of this faculty, just as the *logic* of the same faculty, under the name of *teleology*, will constitute the other part. In both cases, however, nature itself is considered as technical, i.e. as purposive with respect to its products, on the one hand subjectively, merely with regard to the mode of representation of the subject, and on the other hand as objectively purposive in relation to the possibility of the object itself. We shall see hereafter that the purposiveness of form in the realm of appearance is *beauty* and that the faculty for judging it is *taste*. It would seem to follow from this that the division of the critique of the power of judgement, into its aesthetic and its teleological part, must comprise solely the *theory of taste* and that of *physical ends* (the judging of things in the world as natural ends).

But all *purposiveness*, whether subjective or objective, can be divided into *inner* and *relative* purposiveness; the former is based upon the representation of the object as such, while the latter is based simply upon the contingent *use* of the object. Thus the form of the object can be perceived, in the first place, in mere intuition without regard to any concepts, as purposive for the reflective power of judgement, and in this case subjective purposiveness is ascribed to the thing and to nature itself. In the second place, the perception of the object may reveal for reflection absolutely no purposiveness of its form as such, although the representation of the object can certainly arouse the feeling of a purposiveness lying *a priori* in the subject (perhaps the supersensible determination of the powers of the subject) and thereby ground an aesthetic judgement which is also related to an *a priori* principle (though only a subjective one), but not, as in the first case, relative to the *purposiveness of nature* with regard to the subject, but only to a possible teleological *use* of certain sensuous intuitions, by virtue of their form, through the merely reflective power of judgement. The first kind of judgement therefore ascribes *beauty* to the objects of nature, while the second ascribes *sublimity* to them, and in both cases merely by means of aesthetic (reflective) judgements devoid of any concept of an object, merely with regard to subjective purposiveness. But no special technic of nature would be presupposed for the second kind since it depends merely on a contingent use of a representation that is contributory not to cognition of an object but to a different feeling, namely that of the inner purposiveness in the constitution of the powers of the mind. Yet judgement concerning the sublimity of nature would not be excluded from the aesthetic division of the reflective power of judgement because it too expresses a subjective purposiveness that does not rest upon the concept of an object.

It is just the same with regard to the objective purposiveness of nature, i.e. the possibility of things as natural ends where we judge only in accordance with concepts of the latter, i.e. judge not aesthetically (in relation to the feeling of pleasure and displeasure) but logically, in what we call a teleological judgement. Objective purposiveness is grounded either on the inner possibility of the object or on the relative possibility of its external consequences. In the first case, a teleological judgement considers the *perfection* of a thing in accordance with an end which lies within it (since the manifold is here interrelated reciprocally as both end and means). In the second case, a teleological judgement extends only to the *usefulness* of a natural object, namely its correspondence to a purpose which lies in other things.

Thus the critique of the aesthetic power of judgement comprises, firstly, the critique of *taste* (the faculty of judging the beautiful) and, secondly, the critique of the *feeling of spirit*, for that is how I would initially describe the faculty of representing sublimity in certain objects. Since the faculty of the teleological power of judgement relates its representation of purposiveness to the object not by means of feeling but through concepts, no special terms are required in order to distinguish the faculties it implies, whether we are speaking of inner or relative (though in both cases objective) purposiveness; for the teleological power of judgement here relates its reflection entirely to reason (rather than to feeling).

But we should note that it is the technic of nature—and not that of the human powers of representation that we call *art* (in the proper sense of the word)—with respect to which we are here investigating purposiveness as a regulative concept of the power of judgement. We are not seeking for the principle of artistic beauty or of artistic perfection, although one could call the process of nature 'technical', i.e. quasi artistic, if we regard it as technical (or plastic) as represented on analogy with the comparable causality of art. For we are concerned here with the principle of the merely reflective power of judgement, rather than with the determining power of judgement (which underlies all human works of art), and in this case purposiveness must therefore be regarded as *unintentional* and can thus only be ascribed to nature. The judgement of artistic beauty will subsequently have to be regarded as a mere derivative of those principles which underlie the judgement concerning natural beauty.

The critique of the reflective power of judgement with respect to nature will thus consist of two parts: the critique of the *aesthetic faculty* and the critique of the *teleological faculty* of judging the things of nature.

The first part will contain two books, of which the first will be the critique of *taste* or of the judging of the *beautiful*, and the second the critique of *the feeling of the spirit* (in the mere reflection upon an object) or of the judging of the *sublime*.

The second part likewise contains two books, the first of which will bring under principles the judging of things as natural ends with respect to their *inner possibility*, while the other will do the same for the judgement concerning their *relative purposiveness*.

Each of these books will contain two sections, an *analytic* and a *dialectic* of the faculty of judging.

The analytic will attempt to furnish in the same number of chapters first the *exposition* and then the *deduction* of the concept of a purposiveness of nature.

EXPLANATORY NOTES

References to Kant's *Critique of Pure Reason* are given in standard form, indicating the original pagination of the first (A) and/or second (B) edition of the text (which is also reproduced in the Academy and subsequent editions and translations of the work).

PART I

3 *Preface to the First Edition*: the second edition of 1793 reprinted the text of the 1790 edition of the third *Critique* with generally minor changes of an orthographic and stylistic kind. Significant differences between the two editions will be indicated at the relevant points.

6 *the metaphysics of nature and of morals*: Kant is referring to his project of a new kind of metaphysics (an immanent 'metaphysics of experience' rather than a transcendent 'dogmatic' metaphysics), namely a rigorous transcendental analysis of the first principles underlying natural science and morality. He had already published his *Groundwork for the Metaphysics of Morals* in 1785, and made a contribution to a transcendental metaphysics of nature in his *Metaphysical Principles of Natural Science* in 1786. The *Metaphysics of Morals* followed in 1797.

13 *O mihi praeteritos, etc.*: A citation from Virgil's *Aeneid* (viii. 560): 'O mihi praeteritos referat si Iuppiter annos' ('If only Jupiter could give me back those vanished years').

15 *the judgement which subsumes the particular . . . is determining*: Meredith's older term 'determinant' for Kant's use *of reflektierend* has been replaced throughout with the term 'determining'. Both these forms will be found in the Anglophone secondary literature on Kant's work.

then the judgement is simply reflective: Meredith's term for Kant's use of *reflektierend* has been retained throughout. The term has also been rendered in English as 'reflecting' and again both forms can be found in the secondary discussions of the third *Critique*.

16 *the purposiveness of its form*: as indicated in the *Note on the Text, Translation, and Revision* Meredith's older term 'finality' and the corresponding adjectival form 'final' have been replaced throughout by the now more standard rendering of 'purposiveness' and 'purposive' for Kant's *Zweckmäßigkeit* and *zweckmäßig* respectively.

32 *quodlibet ens est aut A aut non A*: traditional Latin formulation of the logical law of non-contradiction: 'any being whatsoever is either A or non-A'.

35 *In my search for the moments*: Kant is using the term 'moment' (*das Moment*) in a technical sense. It has nothing to do with temporal succession and signifies a fundamental aspect or dimension that can be analysed in relation

to a complex phenomenon. The term is related to the Latin *momentum* and originally derives from physics and mechanics. It is frequently used in a philosophical context by Hegel and thinkers in the dialectical tradition, such as Adorno.

36 *with an accompanying sensation of delight*: Meredith's rendering of Kant's term *das Wohlgefallen* as 'delight' and of the corresponding verbal form *gefallen* as 'to please' have been retained throughout. Other translators have employed 'satisfaction' and 'to please' or variations on 'like' or 'liking'.

that Iroquois sachem: Kant alludes to an anecdote related by a French Jesuit traveller François-Xavier Charlevoix in his *History and General Description of New France* of 1744.

inveigh with the vigour of a Rousseau: Kant is thinking of the general attitudes of Jean-Jacques Rousseau (1712–78), and his criticism of artificial civilization and luxury in his *Discourse on the Origin and Foundations of Inequality amongst Men* of 1755.

55 *Assuming with Euler*: Leonard Euler (1707–83), a renowned Swiss mathematician and physicist, who defended a wave theory of light and presented his scientific views in popular epistolary form.

60 *designs à la grecque*: 'in the Greek manner'.

65 *the famous Doryphorus of Polycletus ... and Myron's Cow*: celebrated Greek sculptures from the fifth century BC. The Doryphoros, the spear-bearer by Polycletus of Argos, and the bronze cow of Myron of Eleutherae were regarded as perfect classical models of proportion and were widely reproduced and discussed by artists and writers, including Goethe.

71 *General Remark on the First Section of the Analytic*: the remark strictly speaking refers to the first 'book' (the Analytic of the Beautiful).

73 *Marsden in his description of Sumatra*: William Marsden (1754–1836), English philologist and orientalist whose *History of Sumatra* (1783) was translated into German in 1785.

82 *Savary's observations in his account of Egypt*: Nicolas Savary (1750–88), French orientalist and Egyptologist, published his *Lettres sur l'Égypte* in 1787.

95 *as Herr von Sassure relates*: Horace Bénédict de Saussure (1740–99) was a Swiss geographer, botanist, and traveller, who described his experiences in his voluminous *Voyages dans les Alpes* of 1779–86.

107 *Burke, who deserves to be called the foremost author*: Edmund Burke (1729–97) published his *Philosophical Enquiry into the Origin of our Ideas of the Sublime and Beautiful* in 1757. For the original passage quoted from the German translation, see part IV, section vii.

109 *The deduction of aesthetic judgements*: here as elsewhere Kant uses the term 'deduction', derived from legal terminology, in his specifically critical sense of exhibiting the right to make a certain type of universal claim. See *Critique of Pure Reason* A 84–92.

114 *then let him adduce Batteux or Lessing*: Charles Batteux (1713–80), prominent French theorist of the arts, and Gotthold Ephraim Lessing (1729–81), influential German writer, critic, and controversialist whose most important contribution to aesthetics was his treatise *Laokoon* of 1766 comparing the limits and possibilities of different arts and their respective media.

115 *Thus although critics, as Hume says*: Kant is referring to Hume's essay 'The Sceptic' in his *Essays, Moral and Political* of 1741–2: 'There is something approaching to principles in mental taste, and critics can reason and dispute more plausibly than cooks or perfumers.'

126 *a posse ad esse non valet consequentia*: 'there is no valid inference from the possible to the actual.'

132 *it is only production through freedom . . . that should be termed art*: Kant is using 'art' (*Kunst*) here in the broad sense as a specifically human skill for shaping or fabricating a 'work' (corresponding to the Latin 'ars' and the Greek 'technē').

133 *Camper describes very exactly*: Kant is alluding to Peter Camper (1722–89), a Dutch anatomist and naturalist who also wrote a treatise on *The Best Form for Shoes*.

134 *only beautiful art*: the German expression for the 'fine arts', as they had come to be distinguished from handicraft and the artisanal domain in general, like the equivalent contemporary terms in the romance languages, is the 'beautiful arts'. The repudiation of the idea of a comparable beautiful form of 'science' is directed primarily against the aesthetician Alexander Gottlieb Baumgarten (1714–62).

138 *So all that Newton has set forth in his immortal work*: Kant is alluding to Newton's great treatise on *The Mathematical Principles of Natural Philosophy* of 1687.

Wieland: Christoph Martin Wieland (1733–1813), influential and prolific German poet, translator, and critic whose *History of Agathon* is regarded as the earliest example of the *Bildungsroman* (novel relating the personal and cultural development of its protagonist).

141 *things that in nature would be ugly or displeasing*: a thought that is already clearly expressed by Aristotle in a famous passage of his *Poetics* (chapter IV: 1448*b*).

144 *When the great king expresses himself in one of his poems*: Kant is referring to King Frederick II of Prussia (1712–86), 'Frederick the Great', whose poem he cites in a slightly free and vaguely poetical prose German translation (possibly his own). The French original runs as follows:

> Oui, finissons sans trouble, et mourons sans regrets,
> En laissant l'Univers comblé de nos bienfaits.
> Ainsi l'Astre du jour, au bout de sa carrière,
> Répand sur l'horizon une douce lumière,
> Et les derniers rayons qu'il darde dans les airs
> Sont les derniers soupirs qu'il donne à l'Univers

145 *So, for example, a certain poet says*: Kant quotes from P. L. Withof (1725–89) and his *Academic Poems*, which appeared in 1782. The original has 'goodness' where Kant writes 'virtue'.

Segner made use of this idea: Kant is referring to Johann Andreas von Segner (1704–77), German mathematician and natural philosopher, and the frontispiece to his *Introduction to the Theory of Nature* of 1754.

148 *Hume, in his history, informs the English*: Kant is referring to David Hume's *History of England* (1754–62).

150 *formative arts*: the common German expression 'die bildende Kunst' has no precise equivalent in English and reflects a traditional interest in defining the fine arts in terms of their relevant medium, and therefore the kind of specific content and expression open to them. 'Formative' art fundamentally involves the deliberate artistic shaping or treatment of a medium in the context of spatial perception and thus includes architecture, sculpture, landscape gardening, and painting, as Kant's following remarks make clear.

156 *the vir bonus dicendi peritus*: 'an excellent man and skilled speaker'.

159 *And so, perhaps, Epicurus was not wide of the mark*: Epicurus was famous for identifying 'happiness' with 'pleasure' and arguing that all human beings inevitably pursue the latter under one form or another as their ultimate goal.

162 *Voltaire said that heaven has given us two things*: Kant alludes to a line in the long poem *Henriade* by Voltaire (1694–1778).

164 *A person . . . is said to have humours*: Meredith attempts to capture Kant's play on the different senses of the words *launisch* ('moody') and the (now antiquated) *launicht* ('humorous').

176 *the halo in the grotto of Antiparos*: Antiparos is a small Greek island famous for an impressive stalactite cavern.

179 *subiectio sub adspectum*: submission to view.

183 *education in what are called the humaniora*: the humanities.

the befitting social character of mankind: Meredith, like most modern translators, follows the reading of the second edition of the text. The first edition has 'happiness' (*Glückseligkeit*) rather than 'social character' (*Geselligkeit*).

PART II

191 *Plato, himself a master of this science*: Kant alludes to the 'enthusiasm' with which Plato was inspired by the apparently innate and immutable character of mathematical truths to develop his metaphysical 'theory of ideas' and the pre-existence of the soul.

he could derive all that Anaxagoras inferred: Athenian philosopher (*c.*500–428 BC) who espoused a teleological view of the world as under the governance of mind or intelligence (*nous*).

198 *vestigium hominis video*: the Latin means 'I see the trace of a human being'. It appears to be a reference to a story related by Vitruvius in his treatise *On Architecture* (Preface to book VI): 'Aristippus, the Socratic philosopher, suffered shipwreck and was cast up on the shore at Rhodes where he glimpsed geometrical figures traced in the sand and is said to have cried out to his companions: There is hope for I see the traces of men.'

203 *a complete transformation, recently undertaken, of a great people*: it is unclear whether Kant is alluding here to the American Revolution of 1776–83 or revolutionary developments that had begun in France in 1789.

206 *the New Hollanders or Fuegians*: the indigenous inhabitants of Australia and Tierra del Fuego respectively.

211 *The German word vermessen (presumptuous) is a good word*: the German word suggests a hybristic loss or transgression of due 'measure'.

219 *The system . . . attributed to Epicurus or Democritus*: the Greek thinkers Democritus of Abdera (*c*.460–*c*.370 BC) and Epicurus (341–271 BC) denied immortality and presented a broadly materialist explanation of all things in terms of matter, motion, and the void. Epicurus appears in Dante's *Inferno* as he 'who set down the world to chance'.

   the system of fatality, of which Spinoza is the accredited author: like Fichte after him, Kant regards the metaphysical monism presented by Spinoza (1632–77) in his *Ethics* as ultimately indistinguishable from a 'fatalistic' determinism that submerges the finitely free rational subject in the anonymous mechanism of nature and replaces the practical autonomy of the will with a contemplative relation to the absolute.

220 *This is called hylozoism*: the theory of an original living matter or primal stuff that has been ascribed to the first Greek philosophers of nature and to modern pantheistic thinkers like Giordano Bruno.

230 *An understanding into whose mode of cognition*: see *Critique of Pure Reason* B 139 and the following note.

233 *And there was a similar implication in the Critique of Pure Reason*: for Kant's discussion of the possible idea of an 'archetypal intellect' which, unlike 'our' human cognition, is not intrinsically finite and dependent upon sensuous intuition and could generate its objects simply through thinking them, see *Critique of Pure Reason* B 307–9.

249 *Hume raises the objection*: Kant may be alluding here to Hume's discussion of religious questions in *An Enquiry concerning Human Understanding* (section 11) or possibly to the latter's *Dialogues concerning Natural Religion* (part V).

253 *Herr. Hofr. Blumenbach*: important German naturalist and zoologist Johann Friedrich Blumenbach (1752–1848) who published an influential treatise *On the Formative Impulse and the Process of Reproduction* in 1781. 'Epigenesis' is the modern theory that an individual living being develops by means of the gradual differentiation and elaboration of a fertilized egg cell, as contrasted with the older biological theory of 'preformation' which sees

the development of the individual as the unfolding and extension of an originally complete organic form.

255 *We might also follow the chevalier Linné*: Kant is referring to the celebrated Carl von Linné (1707–78), better known by the Latinized form of Linnaeus, the Swedish naturalist chiefly remembered for his contributions to botanical classification and his metaphor of the 'three kingdoms' of mineral, vegetable, and animal nature. His most influential works were his *System of Nature* (1st ed. 1735) and *The Genera of Plants* (1737).

257 *And even if man . . . seems, in Camper's judgement*: see note to p. 133.

262 *developing to the highest pitch all talents that minister to culture*: Kant also presents the ideas presented in the preceding paragraph in his late essays, particularly in his *Idea for a Universal History from a Cosmopolitan Point of View* (1784) and his *On Perpetual Peace* of 1795.

265 *Physico-Theology is the attempt*: for Kant's first discussion of physico-theology in a fully 'critical' context see the *Critique of Pure Reason* A 620–30.

266 *its solution seems an easy matter*: Kant's objections to the traditional argument from design in natural theology in this paragraph closely parallel those of Hume in *An Enquiry concerning Human Understanding* (section 11) and in his *Dialogues concerning Natural Religion* (though it is unknown whether Kant was familiar with the latter work, which had appeared in German translation in 1781).

268 *Others who were physicists*: by physicists here Kant probably means 'natural philosophers' of a monistic kind from the ancient Milesian cosmologists, like Thales and Anaximenes, who tried to explain the world from a single primal stuff or principle, to metaphysical thinkers like Spinoza, who identified God and Nature and interpreted everything as an expression of the one and only ultimate 'substance'.

279 This note was added by Kant in the 2nd edn.

286 *vis locomotiva*: Latin term denoting a vital or 'moving force'.

291 κατ' ἀλήθειαν . . . κατ' ἄνθρωπον: the Greek expressions signify 'according to the truth' (intrinsically) and 'according to the human perspective'.

292 *The critique has abundantly shown*: Kant is here referring back to his analysis in the *Critique of Pure Reason* A 631–42.

293 *par ratio*: Latin expression meaning 'the same grounds'.

296 *Things which can be known are of three kinds*: Kant discusses these distinctions in the *Critique of Pure Reason* A 820–31. There is an intrinsic ambiguity about the German word *Glauben* which may mean 'belief' (whether it is true or not) in an everyday empirical sense or 'faith' in the moral or religious sense of believing 'in' someone or something.

certain phenomena that have been passed off for such: Kant may well be alluding here to the theosophical speculations of Emanuel Swedenborg (1688–1772), whose pretensions to theoretical knowledge he had treated highly ironically in his early work *Dreams of a Spirit-Seer Elucidated through the Dreams of Metaphysics* of 1766.

300 *Faith as habitus, not as actus*: faith as an 'attitude' rather than as an 'act', i.e. in terms of a general disposition seeking to promote the realization of the good, not in terms of ritual acts or a confessional creed.

306 *a Reimarus won undying honour for himself*: Hermann Samuel Reimarus (1694–1768), Professor of Oriental Languages in Hamburg and a well-known deist thinker in his time. He defended the teleological argument for God as the intelligent author of the world in his *Treatises concerning the Pre-eminent Truths of Natural Religion* of 1754 and also discussed biological questions from a philosophical point of view in his *General Reflections concerning the Instincts of Animals* of 1760. Soon after his death Lessing created something of a scandal (the 'controversy of the fragments') by publishing extracts from his unpublished manuscripts that contained devastating criticism of 'revealed' religion and the authority of scripture. Kant knew the texts in question but was unaware of Reimarus's authorship which was only clearly established in the early nineteenth century.

309 *this means attributing omniscience to yourself*: Kant may be implicitly alluding here to Hume's arguments in *An Enquiry concerning Human Understanding* (section VII: 'Of the Idea of necessary Connexion').

310 *the recognition of our duties as divine commands*: Kant briefly presented this exclusively moral-practical conception of God's 'commandments' in the first *Critique* (A 818–19) and the second *Critique* (Ak. 6: 153), but only developed it at length in *Religion within the Bounds of Reason Alone* in 1793.

'FIRST INTRODUCTION'

315 *the science itself*: Kant is referring to philosophy itself as the 'science' or systematic articulation of the fundamental principles governing experience and knowledge in general.

317 *circinus et regola*: compass and ruler.

318 *the term 'technic'*: a term derived from the Greek word *techne* indicating a craft, art, or productive capacity.

   an error which I committed: Kant is referring to his earlier discussion of different kinds of imperatives in the *Groundwork* (Ak. 4: 414ff.)

327 *the specification of the manifold*: see *Critique of Pure Reason* A 652.

328 *Linnaeus*: see note to p. 255.

332 *there can be a transcendental aesthetic*: Kant is alluding to his earlier use of the term 'aesthetic' in his 'transcendental aesthetic' in the *Critique of Pure Reason* A 19–49. In that context aesthetic signifies 'pertaining to the conditions of sensuous intuition', i.e. to space and time as the forms of pure intuition that define human receptivity or sensibility.

333 *through a vitium subreptionis*: through a 'fallacy of subreption', i.e. the substitution of a concept of something sensuous for a concept of something intellectual in character. See *Critique of Pure Reason* A260–92.

337 *the concept of perfection*: Kant is alluding to the ideas of A. G. Baumgarten.

341 *technica speciosa*: technic in respect of appearance.

345 *as Burke did in his treatise on the beautiful and the sublime*: see note to p. 107 above.

347 *domestica . . . pergrinis*: 'native' and 'foreign' principles respectively.

BILINGUAL GLOSSARY

German–English

German	English
die Abgötterei	idolatry
der Abgrund	abyss
die Absicht	intention, aim
absichtlich	intentional
die Achtung	respect
adhärierend	adherent
der Affekt	affect
affizieren	to affect
die Allegorie	allegory
allgemein	universal
allgemeingültig	universally valid
die Allgemeinheit	universality
angemessen	suitable, fitting
die Angemessen- heit	suitability
angenehm	agreeable
das Angenehme	the agreeable
anhängend	dependent
die Anlage	potential, disposition
der Anreiz	stimulus
anschauen	to intuit
die Anschauung	intuition
der Anschein	semblance
ansinnen	to impute
der Anspruch	claim
die Arbeit	labour
die Art	kind, species
die Ästhetik	the aesthetic
ästhetisch	aesthetic
das Attribut	attribute
der Ausdruck	expression
die Baukunst	architecture
bedingen	to condition
die Bedingung	condition
das Begehrungs- vermögen	faculty of desire
die Begierde	desire
der Begriff	concept
der Beifall	approval, assent
das Beispiel	example
die Beistimmung	assent, agreement
beleben	to enliven
die Belebung	animation, enlivening
bestimmen	to determine
bestimmend	determining
die Bestimmung	determination, vocation
der Bestimmungs- grund	determining ground
die Betrachtung	contemplation
beurteilen	to judge
die Beurteilung	judging
die Bewunderung	admiration
die Bezeichnung	designation
das Bild	image
bilden	to form
die bildende Kunst	formative art
die Bildhauerei	sculpture
die Bildung	formation, form
die Bildungstrieb	formative impulse
das Bildwerk	piece of sculpture
billigen	to approve
die Billigung	approbation
der Boden	territory
der Charakter- ismus	mark
darstellen	to present
die Darstellung	presentation
das Dasein	existence
die Dichtkunst	poetry, literature
disputieren	to dispute
die Doktrin	doctrine
die Ehrfurcht	reverence
die Eigenschaft	property
die Eigentüm- lichkeit	peculiarity, distinctiveness
die Einbildungs- kraft	imagination
die Eingebung	inspiration
die Einhelligkeit	agreement, accord

einstimmig	concordant
die Einstimmig-keit	agreement, concordance
der Ekel	disgust
empfänglich	receptive, susceptible
die Empfäng-lichkeit	receptivity, susceptibility
die Empfindelei	sentimentality
empfinden	to sense, to feel
die Empfindung	sensation
die Endursache	final cause
der Endzweck	final end
der Enthusiasmus	enthusiasm
die Entschlossen-heit	resoluteness
entspringen	to arise, spring
das Erhabene	the sublime
die Erhebung	elevation
erkennen	to cognize, to know
die Erkenntnis	cognition, knowledge
das Erkenntnis-urteil	cognitive judgement
das Erkenntnis-vermögen	faculty of cognition
erregen	to arouse
erscheinen	to appear
die Erscheinung	appearance
die Erschüt-terung	shaking
exemplarisch	exemplary
die Existenz	existence
das Feld	field
figürlich	figural
fühlen	to feel
der Furcht	fear
furchtbar	fearful
die Gattung	genus
der Gaumen-geschmack	taste of the palate
das Gebiet	realm
gebieten	to command
das Gebot	command
gefallen	to please
das Gefühl	feeling
der Gegenstand	object
der Geist	spirit
geistreich	inspired
der Gemeinsinn	common sense
das Gemüt	mind
die Gemüts-stimmung	disposition/temper of the mind
das Genie	genius
genießen	to enjoy
der Genuß	enjoyment
die Geschick-lichkeit	skill
der Geschmack	taste
das Geschmacks-urteil	judgement of taste
das Geschöpf	creature
das Gesetz	law
die Gesetzgebung	legislation, jurisdiction
gesetzmäßig	conformable to law
die Gesetz-mäßigkeit	conformity to law
die Gestalt	shape, figure
die Gesundheit	health
die Gewalt	violence, dominion
der Glaube	faith, belief
gleichgültig	indifferent
das Glied	member
die Glückseligkeit	happiness
gräßlich	horrible
die Grenze	limit, bound
die Grenzlosigkeit	boundlessness
die Größe	magnitude
der Grundsatz	fundamental principle
gültig	valid
die Gültigkeit	validity
die Gunst	favour
das Gute	the good
das höchste Gut	the highest good
das Handwerk	handicraft
der Hang	tendency, propensity
hemmen	to check, inhibit
die Hemmung	inhibition
die Humanität	humanity
die Idee	idea
der Inbegriff	sum
indemonstrabel	indemonstrable

inexponibel	inexponible
das Interesse	interest
die Kluft	gulf
die Klugheit	prudence
die Kontemplation	contemplation
der Körper	body
die Kultur	culture, cultivation
die Kunst	art
künstlich	artistic, artificial
das Kunstwerk	work of art
die Laune	humour
launicht	humorous
launisch	moody, full of humours
das Leben	life
das Lebensgefühl	feeling of life
leiden	to suffer
die Leidenschaft	passion
der Leitfaden	clue, guide
letzter Zweck	ultimate end
die Liberalität	liberality
die Lohnkunst	remunerative art
die Lust	pleasure
die Macht	might
die Malerkunst	(art) painting
die Maschine	machine, device
der Maßstab	standard
die Maxime	maxim
der Mensch	man, human being
die Menschheit	mankind
die Mißbilligung	disapprobation
das Mißfallen	aversion
mitteilbar	communicable
die Mitteilbarkeit	communicability
mitteilen	to communicate
das Mittel	means
das Mittelglied	middle term
das Moment	moment
moralisch-praktisch	morally-practical
die Moralität	morality
das Muster	model
musterhaft	exemplary
die Nachäffung	aping
nachahmen	to imitate
der Nachahmer	imitator
die Nachahmung	imitation
die Nachmachung	copying
die Nachfolge	following
die Naturgabe	natural endowment
die Neigung	inclination
die Nützlichkeit	usefulness
das Nützliche	the useful
das Objekt	object
die Ohnmacht	helplessness, impotence
das Organ	organ
die Organisation	organisation
der Organismus	organism
die Originalität	originality
die Pflicht	duty
die Phantasie	fantasy
die Plastic	plastic art
das Prinzip	principle
die Quelle	source
das Reale	the real
reflektierend	reflective
die Reflexion	reflection
die Regel	rule
das Reich	kingdom
der Reiz	charm
reizen	to charm
der Richter	judge
der Richtmaß	standard, criterion
rühren	to move, to touch
die Rührung	emotion
der Satz	proposition
schätzen	to estimate
die Schätzung	estimation
der Schauer	awe, dread
der Schein	illusion, semblance
der Scheu	dread
der Schmerz	pain
der Schmuck	finery
schön	beautiful
das Schöne	the beautiful
die Schönheit	beauty
die Schöpfung	creation
die Schranke	restriction
der Schreck	terror

die Schwärmerei	fanaticism, enthusiasm	überschwenglich	extravagant
		übersinnlich	supersensible
die Selbst- erhaltung	self-preservation	das Übersinnliche	the supersensible
		überreden	to persuade
die Selbst- schätzung	self-esteem	die Überredung	persuasion
		übertreffen	to surpass
sinnlich	sensuous	überzeugen	to convince
der Sinn	sense	die Überzeugung	conviction
die Sinne	the senses	das Unbedingte	the unconditioned
der Sinnenschein	sensuous semblance	die Unbegrenzt- heit	limitlessness
die Sinnlichkeit	sensibility		
die Sitten	morals	die Unermeß- lichkeit	unmeasurability
die Sittlichkeit	morals		
die Seele	soul	das Ungeheure	the monstrous
das Spiel	play	uninteressiert	disinterested
spielen	to play	die Unlust	displeasure
die Spontaneität	spontaneity	die Unparteilich- keit	impartiality
der Sprung	leap		
der Spur	trace	die Unwider- stehlichkeit	irresistibility
der Staatskörper	body politic		
die Stimmung	disposition, temper, mood	unzweckmäßig	non-purposive
		die Unzweck- mäßigkeit	non-purposive character
stimmen	to agree, to dispose		
streiten	to contend	das Urbild	archetype
das Subjekt	subject	die Ursache	cause
das Substrat	substrate	das Urteil	judgement
das Symbol	symbol	urteilen	to judge
symbolisch	symbolic	die Urteilskraft	judgement
das Talent	talent	vergnügen	to gratify
die Technik	technic	das Vergnügen	gratification
technisch- praktisch	technically-practical	die Verknüpfung	connection
		das Vermögen	faculty
die Teilnehmung	participation	die Vernunft	reason
das Teilnehmungs- gefühl	feeling of sympathy	die Vernünftelei	subtlety
		vernünftelnd	sophistical, rationalizing
die Teleologie	teleology		
teleologisch	teleological	die Vernünftidee	idea of reason
die Totalität	totality	die Versinn- lichung	sensuous rendering
der Trieb	impulse, drive		
der Triebfeder	incentive, spring		
übereinstimmen	to agree, to harmonize	der Verstand	understanding
die Überein- stimmung	agreement, harmony	die Verwandt- schaft	kinship, similarity
		die Verwun- derung	astonishment
der Übergang	transition		
die Überlegen- heit	pre-eminence, superiority	vollkommen	perfect

die Vollkommen-heit	perfection	der Wohnplatz	abode
voraussetzen	to presuppose	das Zeichen	sign
die Voraussetzung	presupposition	die Zeichnung	design
die Vorschrift	precept	die Zerstreuung	diversion
vorstellen	to represent	zeugen	to generate
die Vorstellung	representation	die Zeugung	generation
der Wahn	delusion	das Ziel	gaol
der Wahnsinn	delirium	der Zierat	ornamentation
der Wahnwitz	mania	die Zucht	training, discipline
die Wahrnehmung	perception	der Zufall	chance, contingency
die Weisheit	wisdom	zufällig	contingent, fortuitous
der Welturheber	author of the world	die Zufriedenheit	contentment
das Werk	work	zumuthen	to demand, to expect
das Werkzeug	tool, instrument	zusammen-stimmen	to accord, to harmonise
der Wert	worth, value	die Zusammen-stimmung	accordance, harmony
das Wesen	essence	der Zwang	coercion
der Widerstand	resistance	der Zweck	end, purpose
der Widerstreit	conflict	zweckmäßig	purposive
der Wille	the will	die Zweckmäß-igkeit	purposiveness
um . . . willen	for the sake of . . .	die Zweck-verbindung	purposive connection
die Willkür	free choice	zweckwidrig	counter-purposive
wirklich	actual		
die Wirkung	effect		
das Wohlbefinden	well-being		
das Wohlgefallen	delight		

English–German

abyss	der Abgrund	command	das Gebot
adherent	adhärierend	common sense	der Gemeinsinn
admiration	die Bewunderung	communicable	mitteilbar
aesthetic	ästhetisch	communicability	die Mitteilbarkeit
aesthetic	die Ästhetik	to communicate	mitteilen
to affect	affizieren	concept	der Begriff
affect	der Affekt	condition	die Bedingung
to agree	übereinstimmen	to condition	bedingen
agreeable	angenehm	conflict	der Widerstreit
the agreeable	das Angenehme	conformable	
agreement	die Übereinstimmung,	to law	gesetzmäßig
	die Einhelligkeit	conformity to law	die Gesetzmäßigkeit
allegory	die Allegorie	contemplation	die Betrachtung, die
animation	die Belebung		Kontemplation
aping	die Nachäffung	to contend	streiten
to appear	erscheinen	contentment	die Zufriedenheit
appearance	die Erscheinung	to convince	überzeugen
approbation	die Billigung	to copy	nachmachen
approval	der Beifall	copying	die Nachmachung
to approve	billigen	creation	die Schöpfung
to arouse	erregen	creature	das Geschöpf
archetype	das Urbild	culture,	
architecture	die Baukunst	cultivation	die Kultur
art	die Kunst	delight	das Wohlgefallen
assent	die Beistimmung	delirium	der Wahnsinn
astonishment	die Verwunderung	dependent	anhängend
attribute	das Attribut	design	die Zeichnung
author of the		designation	die Bezeichnung
world	der Welturheber	desire	die Begierde
aversion	das Mißfallen	determinate	bestimmt
belief	der Glaube	to determine	bestimmen
body	der Körper	determining	die bestimmende
body politic	der Staatskörper	power of	Urteilskraft
bound	die Grenze	judgement	
boundlessness	die Grenzlosigkei	determination	die Bestimmung
cause	die Ursache	determining	der Bestimmungs-
charm	der Reiz	ground	grund
check	die Hemmung	dignity	die Würde
claim	der Anspruch	disapprobation	die Mißbilligung
clue	der Leitfaden	disgust	der Ekel
cognition	die Erkenntnis	disinterested	uninteressiert
cognitive		displeasure	die Unlust
judgement	das Erkenntnisurteil	to dispute	disputieren
to cognize	erkennen	diversion	die Zerstreuung

drive	der Trieb	genius	das Genie
duty	die Pflicht	gaol	das Ziel
effect	die Wirkung	gratification	das Vergnügen
elevation	die Erhebung	gulf	die Kluft
end	der Zweck	handicraft	das Handwerk
endowment	die Anlage	happiness	die Glückseligkeit
to enjoy	genießen	to harmonize	übereinstimmen
enjoyment	der Genuß	harmony	die Übereinstim-
to enliven	beleben		mung
enthusiasm	der Enthusiasmus	health	die Gesundheit
essence	das Wesen	helplessness	die Ohnmacht
to estimate	schätzen	the highest good	das höchste Gut
estimation	die Schätzung	horrible	gräßlich
example	das Beispiel	human being	der Mensch
exemplary	exemplarisch	humanity	die Humanität,
existence	die Existenz,		die Menschheit
	das Dasein	humorous	launicht
to expect	ansinnen, zumuten	humour	die Laune
expression	der Ausdruck	idea	die Idee
faculty	das Vermögen	ill-humoured	launisch
faculty of desire	das Begehrungs-	image	das Bild
	vermögen	imagination	die Einbildungskraft
faculty of	das Erkenntnis-	imitation	die Nachahmung
cognition	vermögen	to imitate	nachahmen
faculty of	das Erkenntnis-	imitator	der Nachahmer
knowledge	vermögen	impartiality	die Unparteilichkeit
faith	der Glaube	impulse	der Trieb
fanaticism	die Schwärmerei	to impute	ansinnen
fantasy	die Phantasie	incentive	der Triebfeder
favour	die Gunst	inclination	die Neigung
fear	der Furcht	indemonstrable	indemonstrabel
fearful	furchtbar	indifferent	gleichgültig
to feel	fühlen	inexponible	inexponibel
feeling	das Gefühl	inspiration	die Eingebung
feeling of life	das Lebensgefühl	inspired	geistreich
field	das Feld	instrument	das Werkzeug
figure	die Gestalt	intentional	absichtlich
figural	figürlich	interest	das Interesse
final cause	die Endursache	intuition	die Anschauung
final end	der Endzweck	irresistibility	die Unwiders-
finery	der Schmuck		tehlichkeit
following	die Nachfolge	to judge	beurteilen
to form	bilden	judgement	das Urteil,
formation	die Bildung		die Beurteilung
formative art	die bildende Kunst	judgement	das Geschmacks-
free choice	die Willkür	of taste	urteil

jurisdiction	die Gesetzgebung	to play	spielen
kingdom	das Reich	to please	gefallen
knowledge	die Erkenntnis	pleasure	die Lust
to know	erkennen, wissen	poetry	die Dichtkunst
labour	die Arbeit	precept	die Vorschrift
law	das Gesetz	pre-eminence	die Überlegenheit
leap	der Sprung	to present	darstellen
legislation	die Gesetzgebung	presentation	die Darstellung
limit	die Grenze	principle	das Prinzip,
limitlessness	die Unbegrenztheit		der Grundsatz
machine	die Maschine	property	die Eigenschaft
magnitude	die Größe	proposition	der Satz
man	der Mensch	prudence	die Klugheit
mania	der Wahnwitz	purpose	der Zweck
mark	der Charakterismus	purposive	zweckmäßig
maxim	die Maxime	purposiveness	die Zweckmäßigkeit
means	das Mittel	rationalizing	vernünftelnd
member	das Glied	the real	das Reale
middle term	das Mittelglied	realm	das Gebiet
might	die Macht	reason	die Vernunft
mind	das Gemüt	idea of reason	die Vernunftidee
model	das Muster	reflection	die Reflexion
moment	das Moment	reflective	reflektierend
the monstrous	das Ungeheure	remunerative art	die Lohnkunst
morality	die Moralität	to represent	vorstellen
morally practical	moralisch-praktisch	representation	die Vorstellung
morals	die Sitten,	resoluteness	die Entschlossenheit
	die Sittlichkeit	respect	die Achtung
natural end	der Naturzweck	reverence	die Ehrfurcht
natural		rule	die Regel
endowment	die Naturanlage	self-esteem	die Selbstschätzung
nature	die Natur	self-preservation	die Selbsterhaltung
object	der Gegenstand,	semblance	der Schein
	das Objekt	sensation	die Empfindung
organ	das Organ	sense, meaning	der Sinn
organism	der Organismus	the senses	die Sinne
organization	die Organisation	sensibility	die Sinnlichkeit
originality	die Originalität	sensible,	
ornamentation	der Zierat	sensuous	sinnlich
participation	die Teilnehmung	sensuous	
passion	die Leidenschaft	rendering	die Versinnlichung
peculiarity	die Eigentümlichkeit	sensuous	
perception	die Wahrnehmung	semblance	sinnlicher Schein
perfect	vollkommen	sentimentality	die Empfindelei
perfection	die Vollkommenheit	sign	das Zeichen
play	das Spiel	skill	die Geschicklichkeit

sophistical	vernünftelnd	tendency	der Hang
soul	die Seele	territory	der Boden
source	die Quelle	terror	der Schreck
species	die Art	tool	das Werkzeug
spirit	der Geist	totality	die Totalität
spontaneity	die Spontaneität	transition	der Übergang
standard	der Maßstab	the unconditioned	das Unbedingte
stimulus	der Anreiz	understanding	der Verstand
subject	das Subjekt	universal	allgemein
sublime	erhaben	universality	die Allgemeinheit
the sublime	das Erhabene	universally valid	allgemeingültig
substrate	das Substrat	unmeasurability	die Unermeßlichkeit
subtlety	die Vernünftelei	useful	nützlich
to suffer	leiden	the useful	das Nützliche
sum	der Inbegriff	valid	gültig
supersensible	übersinnlich	validity	die Gültigkeit
to surpass	übertreffen	violence	die Gewalt
symbol, symbolic	das Symbol, symbolisch	vocation	die Bestimmung
		well-being	das Wohlbefinden
talent	das Talent	will	der Wille
taste	der Geschmack	work	das Werk
taste of the palate	der Gaumengeschmack	work of art	das Kunstwerk
technic	die Technik	worth	der Wert
technically-practical	technisch-praktisch		

ANALYTICAL INDEX

abstraction from content of judgement of taste 112; from concept of object 60, 62; from the agreeable 47

actual definition of 229

actuality of what is only possible according to ideas 277

admiration definition of 102; contrasted with astonishment 193

advantageousness as purely relative purposiveness 195

aesthetic aesthetic quality defined 23; transcendental aesthetic deals only with pure judgements 100; the aesthetic faculty is legislative 177; aesthetic and mathematical estimation of magnitude contrasted 82; all estimation of magnitude ultimately aesthetic 82

aesthetic ideas meaning of 142; justification of the expression 142; spirit as faculty of presenting such ideas 142; as counterpart to rational ideas 143; contrasted with intellectual ideas 143; faculty of such ideas best displayed in poetry 143; serve rational ideas in place of logical presentation 144; beauty as an expression of such ideas 149; main intention of sculpture is expression of such ideas 151; fine art derives its rule from such ideas 178; distinguished from rational ideas of determinate ends 178; play of aesthetic ideas in relation to laughter and music 160

aesthetic judgement difficulty of discovering *a priori* principle of such judgement 4; reveals relationship between faculty of knowledge and feeling of pleasure 5; such judgement defined 29; compared with teleological judgement 29; compared with logical judgement 36; pleasure in such judgement 54; division of aesthetic judgement 54; does not afford confused knowledge of objects 59; subjective reference of aesthetic judgement 59; the *ought* in aesthetic judgement 68; logical peculiarities of aesthetic judgement 111; arises through delight predicated of the object 118; contrasted with cognitive judgement 117; as itself both object and law 118; dialectic of aesthetic judgement 165

affect physiological aspects of 13 n; freedom from 102; of strenous or languid type 102 f.

agreeable definition of 37; interested delight in the agreeable 37; it not merely pleases, but gratifies 38; compared with the good 39; contrasted with delight in the beautiful 39, 44, 47; it rests entirely on sensation 39; contrasted with the beautiful and the good 40, 44, 67; difference of opinion about the agreeable tolerated 45; abstraction from the agreeable 57; contrasted with the beautiful, the sublime, and the good 96; as motive of desire always the same in kind 96; difference amongst people concerning the agreeable 121; empiricism confuses it with aesthetic delight 174; music and jest are agreeable rather than fine art 134

agreement necessity of agreement concerning the beautiful 68; between different judging subjects 70; judgement of taste demands agreement from everyone 70; as a duty 125; the agreement of all ages and nations as empirical criterion 62

analogue of art and life contrasted 202

analogy between art and expression 149; as means of presenting concepts 179; analogy underlying related words 180; points of analogy between the beautiful and the good 181; names applied to beautiful objects on analogy with the morally good 181; analogy between purposiveness of reflective judgement and practical purposiveness 16; imagination building up another nature on the basis of an analogy 143; natural beauty regarded on the analogy of art 76; conception of an end read into the nature of things by analogy 188; organization of nature has nothing analogous to any causality known to us 217; geometrical analogy 210; art considered as basis of nature by analogy 217; analogy to artistic instinct in lower animals 270, 293 n; attributes of the Supreme Being only conceived by analogy 285, 292; inference by analogy as a theoretical argument 292; nature of arguments from analogy 292 n; supersensible being conceived on analogy 314

anatomy comparative anatomy 247

Anaxagoras 191

ancients works of the ancients as models 112; a later age will hardly dispense with works of the 63 n., 183

anthropology rational psychology a mere anthropology of inner sense 289

anthropomorphism latent in our representations of God 285, 288 n

antinomy of judgements of taste 165; solution of this antinomy 166; alternatives for avoiding it 173; forces us to look beyond the sensible world 169; the three antinomies of pure reason and how they arise 172; the antinomy of reflective judgement 213; exposition of this antinomy 214; its solution 216

apprehension pleasure connected with it when not referable to objects 24; it precedes any concept 27

archaeologist of nature 248

archaeology as a science 257 n

archetype of taste 62; as set by nature 65

architect God as the supreme architect 238

architectonic the causality of an architectonic understanding 216; the architectonic of an intelligent author of the world 266

architecture as a plastic art 151; design as the essential feature of architecture 56

art judgements on products of art claim universal agreement 26; function of imagination in 27; as realization of an antecedent concept of an object 28; application of principle of purposiveness to 31; beauty of art limited by its required agreement with nature 76; beautiful nature conceived after analogy of 77; sublime not to be sought in art if judgement to be pure 83; interest in fine art no evidence of moral disposition 128; delight in fine art not immediate 128; imitation of nature in art 130; general discussion of 132;

distinguished from nature 131; as skill distinguished from science 133; distinguished from handicraft 133; as free 133; regarded as play 134; requires a mechanical aspect 133; as merely mechanical 134, 136, 139; general discussion of fine art 134; how far it avails itself of science 134; aesthetic art defined and distinguished from agreeable art 134; fine art, though devoid of end, advances interests of social communication 135; reflective judgement, not sensation, as its standard 135; only beautiful when it appears like nature 135; nature only beautiful when it appears like art 135; fine art pleases in mere act of judgement 136; always aimed at the production of something 136; how product of art may seem like nature 135; fine art is the art of genius 136; nature gives rule to art through genius 137; presupposes rules 137; limit to its progress 138; thought of something as end always present to 139; genius supplies material for 139; its form depends on discipline 139; genius required for its production 139; beauty of art and nature contrasted 140; requisites for judging beauty of art and nature 140; involves reference to perfection 140; superior in its ability to furnish beautiful description of what is ugly in nature 141; requires more than mere conformity to taste 141; its form must not appear calculated 142; combination of taste and genius in products of 154; beautiful or inspired art 148; concept of object necessary in 148; division of fine arts 149; conjunction of understanding and sensibility in fine art must appear spontaneous 150; combination of fine arts in the same product 154; its fate if not combined with moral ideas 154; respective worth of different arts 155; the nature of the individual, not a set purpose, gives the rule to 172; no rule or precept can serve as standard 171; the purposiveness of 174; attainment of ends only a determining ground of judgement in mechanical art 178; must derive its rule from aesthetic ideas 178; element of science in art an indispensable condition 182; there is only a manner, not a method, for teaching art 182; the propaedeutic to fine art 182; effect in nature regarded as product of art 194; superiority of nature to 202; natural beauty as analogue of 203; analogy of art does not explain intrinsic natural perfection 203, 204; organization surpasses art 212; introduced on an analogy as basis of nature 218; has objective reality as a causality through ends 224; fine art and sciences as contribution to our higher vocation 262; on analogy with artistic instinct in animals 270, 292 n; analogy of intelligence as source of works of art 294

artist God as supreme artist 266

assent (*see also* AGREEMENT) necessity of universal in aesthetic judgement 70

assimilation its character as organic process 199

association imagination borrows material supplied according to the law of 143; laws of 71, 99

assumption matters of faith only an 299; in interests of practical employment of reason 300

assurance that produced by the teleological proof 290; that produced by a practical faith 295; that is free 298 n

astonishment defined 193

attributes aesthetic attributes defined 144; logical attributes 144; examples
　　of the use of aesthetic attributes 145; of deity 273 f., 285, 309 f., 313 f.
autonomy of the higher faculties 31; does not belong to imagination itself 71;
　　judgement of taste grounded on autonomy 178; mistaken for heteronomy 217
Batteux as art critic 114
beautiful analytic of the 35; definition of the 97; definitions resulting from
　　the moments of taste 42, 56, 66, 71; pleases in the mere judging and reflection
　　122, 135 f.; independent of any determinate concept 39, 60, 122; contrasted
　　with the agreeable, the sublime, and the good 41, 44–6, 75, 96; points of
　　agreement and difference between the beautiful and the sublime 75, 77 f.,
　　86, 88 f., 94 f.; mind in restful contemplation when judging the beautiful
　　78, 88, 91; we dwell on the contemplation of it 54; charms compatible with
　　it 75; one captivated by inclination and appetite cannot judge it 91; delight
　　in it connected with the representation of quality 75; implies a necessary
　　reference to delight 67; as presentation of an indeterminate concept of the
　　understanding 75; delight in it is positive 99; requires a certain quality of
　　the object 97; its ground as sought in what is external to ourselves 77; mere
　　formal purposiveness the ground for judging it 57; what is required for
　　calling an object beautiful 36 f.; difference of opinion not tolerated when
　　anything described as 70; no criterion or objective rule for determining
　　what is 62; no science of the beautiful 134, 182; deduction of judgements
　　concerning it 109; pleasure in it attends a process of judgement encoun-
　　tered in the commonest experience 122; pleasure in it must depend for
　　everyone on the same conditions 122; relationship of the faculties requisite
　　for perception of it 122; mistakes in the judgement of it 122; how far cul-
　　ture is required for its appreciation 95; it cultivates us 97; immediate plea-
　　sure in it cultivates liberality of mind 99; its purposiveness with regard to
　　morality 98; can represent the conformity to law of action done from duty
　　97; only pleases universally in reference to morality 180; beautiful repre-
　　sentation of an object defined 141; beautiful objects distinguished from
　　beautiful views of objects 74; examples of beautiful objects 39
beauty not a property of the object 51, 111 f.; distinction between free and
　　dependent 60; as expression of aesthetic ideas 149; purposiveness here
　　grounded in the form and figure of the object 109; consists in the form of
　　mutual subjective purposiveness of the faculties of imagination and under-
　　standing 115 f.; why scattered abroad so lavishly 109; intellectual beauty an
　　inadequate expression 101; the mind cannot dwell on the beauty of nature
　　without finding its interest engaged 130; beauty of nature superior to
　　that of art in that it awakens an immediate interest 128; as symbol of moral-
　　ity 179 f.; has significance only for human beings as beings at once rational
　　and animal 41; of birdsong contrasted with imitation 73 f.; of human
　　beings 60; as formal subjective purposiveness 189; intellectual beauty
　　wrongly applied to geometrical properties 193; natural beauty as analogue
　　of art 203; beauty of nature furthers moral disposition 274, 311 n; moral

interest probably first drew attention to 287 f., ends of nature excite admiration for 311 n

beaver constructive work of beavers and human beings compared 293 n

being an intelligent being produces with design 219; an intelligent original being not objectively substantiated 226; the concept of an absolutely necessary being 230; concept of a supreme being affords no explanation 238; concept of an original being and its attributes 265, 272 f.; one that has formed human beings with an end in view 274; idea of a supreme being rests on the practical employment of reason 267, 285; moral need for the representation of a supreme being 274 f.; understanding and will not ascribed to such a being on theoretical grounds 287; anthropomorphic representation of a supreme being 288; the possibility of a supersensible being 295

birds as free beauties of nature 60; birdsong 73 f., 131

Blumenbach his theory of epigenesis 253

building 35; palace 36, 60; hut 36; church 60 f.; summer-house 60; temples, arches, columns, mausoleums 151

Burke views on the sublime 107 f.

Camper 133

caricature 66 n

categories the basis of experience in general 18; no pleasure arises from the coincidence of our perceptions with categories 22; misapprehension of the argument of the *Critique of Pure Reason* with regard to the categories 311; the category of causality 312

causality final and efficient causality the only two kinds of 200 f.; possibility of causality of ends cannot be perceived *a priori* 204; teleology does not introduce special ground of 211, 218; of architectonic understanding 216; of an understanding 225; of natural causes subordinated to that of final causes 218; special kind of 217 f., 221 f., 224 f., 263; union of two types of causality 251; causality by means of ideas 281; freedom as a particular kind of causality 297; category of causality 312 f.

cause final and efficient cause contrasted 200 f., 207, 277; intelligent cause 217, 272, 277, 299; organisms judged on principle of final cause 217; a world-cause acting according to ends a mere idea 217; final cause as a substance 221; a cause distinct from nature 225, 245; genesis of organisms unintelligible without final cause 249; supreme cause 251, 269, 273, 283; system of final causes 272; supreme cause governing the world according to moral laws 275

certainty as a quantum 294

chance blind chance 44, 287

charm dwelling on 54; pure judgement of taste independent of it 54, 154, 156, 182; abstraction from it where judgement is to serve as universal rule 124; cannot enhance beauty of form 55 f.; may lend further interest where taste is immature 56; its absence a test of the correctness of ideal beauty 66; beauty compatible with charm 75; charm repugnant to the sublime 76; charms of nature belong to modifications of light and sound 131;

charm (*cont.*): interest in the charm of nature is empirical 128; charms attract in society before forms 127; taste facilitates transition from charm to habitual moral interest 181 f.

Christianity introduced the idea of faith 300 n; a wonderful religion with respect to purer conceptions of morality 300 n

circle its formal purposiveness 190

civilization its development connected with the appreciation of beauty 127; how fine art and the sciences contribute to it 262

co-existence how it may be intuited 89

cognition field, territory, and realm of our cognition 10; the one kind of representation valid for everyone 49

cognitive faculty its bearing on the feeling of pleasure 5; presented with an unbounded field 11; purposiveness in relation to our cognitive faculty 22, 28 f.; pleasure expressing conformity of object to our cognitive faculty 24 f.; accord of the object with respect to our cognitive faculty is contingent 20 f.; harmony with the cognitive faculty 27; its harmonious accord 31; table of the cognitive faculties 32; its free play 49; the accord of the cognitive powers 69

colossal defined 83

colour as objective sensation 38; difference of opinions concerning 43; charm of colour 55; when it is considered beautiful 55; Euler's theory 55; beautiful colour in organic nature 175; the seven colours and their associations 131; names ascribed to colour on analogy with moral considerations 181; the art of colour 153

Columbus the problem of the egg 133

common sense (*see also* SENSUS COMMUNIS) with respect to the necessity in aesthetic judgement 68; meaning of common sense 68; ground for supposing such a sense 68; subjective necessity represented as objective on the presupposition of a common sense 70; not grounded on experience 70; a mere ideal norm 70; constitutive or regulative 70; elements of the faculty of taste are united in common sense 70 f.

communicability of sensation 121; of moral feeling 121; of pleasure in the sublime 122; of pleasure in the beautiful 122; of thoughts 125; of cognitions and judgements 69; cognition alone capable of universal communicability 48; of the accord of the cognitive faculties 69; universal communicability of a feeling presupposes a common sense 68; universal communicability of a pleasure proves it to be one of reflection 135; free play of cognitive faculties must admit of universal communicability 49; the only feeling which apart from concepts admits of universal communicability is freedom in the play of our cognitive faculties 135 f.; this play is purposive 135; pleasure in the object derives from universal communicability of representational state of the mind 48; what sensation is universally communicated in judgement of taste 50; and in the case of the sublime 105; empirical pleasure in communicability deducible from our tendency to sociability 49; universal communicability of our feeling appears to carry an interest 126; universal communicability a source of interest in society 105, 127; a concern for universal communicability required of everyone 126; value of sensations with regard to universal communicability 127

communicable the way in which genius arrives at its ideas not communicable 137; artistic skill not communicable 138; what is communicable in the judgement of taste 48; why this is so 49

communication mode of communication in speech as guiding the division of the arts 149; power of communicating one's inmost self implied by 'humanity' 183; reciprocal communication between the cultivated and the uncultivated 183; fine art advances the interest of social communication 135

community symbolic representation of the community as an organic body 179; civil community 261

concept division of concepts into those of nature and those of freedom 7 f.; their respective field, territory, and realm 10; transition from concept of nature to that of freedom 31; manifold modifications of transcendental concepts of nature 15; concepts not required to enable us to perceive beauty 58 f.; concepts cannot be determining ground of judgements of taste 59; judgement of taste upon object precedes any concept 26, 119; confused and clear concepts 59; abstraction from concepts 60 f.; material beyond what is included in a concept 145; presentation of concepts occasioning a wealth of thought 155; concepts of the understanding are immanent as opposed to transcendent 169; concepts of the understanding are always demonstrable 170

conceptus ratiocinans 223

contemplation 41

contingency of nature 188; apparent contingency of what displays formal purposiveness 192; relative purposiveness contingent with respect to the thing itself 195 f.; contingency of form makes us look to ends of reason 198; contingency of coincidence 198; unity of an end not thinkable apart from contingency 221; natural end implies both contingency and necessity 224; possibility, necessity, and contingency 230; duty implies contingency 231; the particular contains something contingent in respect of the universal 232; conformity to law on the part of the contingent is termed purposiveness 232; contingency of the constitution of our understanding 233, 236 f.; contingency of variety in a given particular 234; contingency makes it difficult to reduce multiplicity of nature to unity of knowledge 234; contingency of synthesis 235; contingency of purpose to which empirical ends refer 269; the contingent points towards an unconditioned ground 277

contradiction principle of 295; what the moral law postulates can be thought without contradiction 300 n

conversation the art of, described 135

conviction contrasted with persuasion 291; proof tending toward conviction 292

cosmopolitan whole development of civil communities in this direction 261

creation *see* FINAL END

criterion beauty has no universal 62; universal communicability as 62

critique of pure reason 3 f., 14; in the narrow sense: why judgement and reason are excluded 3; in the wider sense: why it is incomplete unless judgement is treated 4; of practical reason 4; of judgement specifically 4; not directed to the culture of taste 5; as a theory of judgement 6; it shows how different legislations are compatible 11; critique of judgement connects both parts of philosophy 12; general statement of its nature and functions 12; has no realm and is not a doctrine 12; divisions of critique of pure reason 14; why critique of judgements of taste is necessary 26; ground of the twofold division of such a critique 26 f.; the division between aesthetic and teleological judgement 28; aesthetic part of the critique of judgement essential 28; position of aesthetic judgement in the critique 29; as propaedeutic 29; critique of taste as art and as science 116; transcendental critique 116; dialectic belongs to the critique of taste, not taste itself 165

crustacea as examples of free beauty 60

crystals formation of 248; crystallization as example of the free formation of nature 176

culture of taste not the object of the critique 5; how far required for judging the beautiful and the sublime 95; promoted by fine art 135; stability of judgement guarantees progressive culture 148; music more a matter of enjoyment than culture 157; adopted as standard 158; its progress 183; propaedeutic to fine art 182 f.; true standard of taste as mean between the higher and modest worth of nature 183; constraint of culture united with the truth of nature 183; promoted by beautiful forms 208 n; as an end 258; skill as a form of culture 260; requires discipline 260; how war serves it 260

cypher through which nature speaks to us figuratively 130

dance its combination of arts 154

decoration 152

deduction of principle of purposiveness 18; of pure aesthetic judgements 109; where it is obligatory 109; only necessary for judgements on the beautiful 109; what suffices for a deduction in aesthetic judgements 110 f.; method of deduction for judgements of taste 110; the problem of deduction of such judgements 117; deduction of judgements of taste 119 f.; as principle for deriving products from their causes 188

definition transcendental 13 n

Deism 180

deity (*see also* ATTRIBUTES, BEING, CAUSE, GOD) physical teleology cannot afford adequate conception of deity 265; as supreme cause 273; no theoretical proof of the existence of a deity 295

delight as disinterested 36, 41; comparison of its different kinds 41; as related to inclination, favour and respect 41; as universal 42; taste gains from the combination of intellectual and aesthetic delight 61; contrasted with that in the good 71; in the way a figure strikes the eye 72; as combined with knowledge 72; not a predicate of the object 118; in moral action 122

Democritus his system of accidentality 219

demonology 288

Descartes his view of animals as machines 293 n

descent of different species from a common parent 247; of man in relation to crude matter 247 f.

design as essential element in formative arts 56 f.; nature not to be credited with causes acting designedly 187 f.; teleological judgement of nature as a whole silent on question of design 207; physics ignores the question 210; the purposiveness of nature considered as if designed 211; in relation to matter 211; technic of nature as designed and undesigned 219; idealism denies intentional design 220; Spinoza eliminates all trace of design 220; problematic character of the concept 224; cause that pursues design 225, 274; design as basic for investigating organized products 255 f.; ends not observed as designed 229; origin of organisms as referred to design 250

desire faculty of desire defined 13 n; the faculty of principles of desire 4 f.; its definition tested by consideration of fantastic wishes 13 n; causal reference of desire 13 n; its reference to interest 36; duty as independent of desire 299 f.

dialectic of aesthetic judgements 165; belongs to the critique of taste, not taste itself 165; of reflective judgement 213 f.

discipline required by culture 260; of the inclinations 261

disgust what excites disgust cannot be represented in fine art 141

disputes in relation to taste 62, 166

division of philosophy 6; of theoretical and practical 7; why Kant's divisions are threefold 32 n; between the beautiful and the sublime 26 f.; between the mathematically and dynamically sublime 78

doctrine principles belonging to it must be determining 29

dominion defined as might superior to the resistance of that which itself possesses might 90

drama as rhetoric combined with pictorial representation 154

dreams function of 208

duty implies contingency 231; our disposition towards duty 274 f.; regarded as a divine command 310

education as fitting us for a higher vocation 262

emotion spirited and tender emotions 102 f.

empiricism in relation to the critique of taste 174

end defined 16; natural end 28; natural beauty and natural ends contrasted 28; no reason assignable *a priori* why there should be objective ends of nature 28; teleological judging of ends of nature 29; actual existence of natural ends not proved by experience 187; concept of end read into the nature of things 187; where experience leads us to concept of an end of nature 194; when a thing possible only as an end 197; implies reference to will 198; requisites for judging a thing in its intrinsic nature as an end 201 f.; nature in general as system of ends 205, 207, 256; distinction between judging a thing as natural end on account of its form, and regarding its existence as an end of nature 206; a categorical end 206; divine end in the ordering of nature 210;

end (*cont.*): idea of end required for cognition of certain objects 211; world-cause acting according to ends a mere idea 216; unity of end not thinkable apart from contingency 221; mere ontological unity not a unity of 221; as a special kind of unity 221; unity of end implies cause possessed of intelligence 222; causality of end different from mechanism 224; objective reality cannot be procured for 224; contingency of thing thought as subject to condition of an 226; end in nature not observed as designed 227; concept of end as designed read into the facts 227; as designed not given in the object 227; directed to production, represented as source of accord with judgement 235; defined as product of a cause whose determining ground is merely the representation of its effect 236; why natural science not satisfied with explanation in terms of ends 236; concept of whole as end not derivable from mechanical generation 236 f.; principle of end does not render production of organisms comprehensible 239; implies means 242; mechanism ultimately subordinated to causality according to ends 243 f.; correlation of ends does not help mechanical explanation 245 f.; where this concept applies to things 246 f.; difficulty in question of the genesis of a thing that involves an 249; relation of substance to consequence regarded as 250; question of end for which organisms exists 254; origin according to ends not inherently inconsistent with mechanical generation 257 f.; certain laws of unity only be represented through ends 258; nature strives after higher ends than it can itself afford 262; supreme good of the world as highest end 264; unconditional legislation in respect of ends 264; end of nature must first be given if we are to infer world-cause 265; ends of nature oblige us to look for final end 265; all ends in the world empirically conditioned 269; of the existence of nature 272; man exists for an end which implies a being with that end in view 274; moral law directs us to strive towards universal highest end 275; harmony of the world with moral end 276; relative and absolute end contrasted 278; ends certainly are found in the world 282; principle that there is nothing in the world without an end 282; connecting natural and ethical end 283; ends of nature sufficiently prove intelligent world-cause for reflective judgement 284 f.

enjoyment those intent on it would gladly dispense with all judgement 38; an obligation to enjoyment is an absurdity 40; the nature of its pleasure 121; pleasure in the beautiful not a pleasure of enjoyment 122; value of life measured solely by enjoyment 262 n

enlightenment defined 124

ens rationis ratiocinantis 296

ens realissimum as ontological concept 305

entertainment of the mental faculties 72 f.; taste and social entertainment 44

enthusiasm its sublimity 102; compared with fanaticism 105

Epicurus on the corporeal basis of pain and gratification 107, 159, 163; on chance 220; his purely mechanistic concept of nature 220

epigenesis theory of 251; advantages of the theory 253; merits of Blumenbach's theory 253

ether example of a matter of opinion in science 296

ethics a theological ethics is impossible 314

Euler his theory of colour 55

evolution organization must be assumed for evolution of new structures 246 f.; contrasted with theory of individual preformation 251; tracing back from man to polyp, even to mosses and lichens 247

examples function of illustration by examples 115 f.; as intuitions verifying reality of empirical concepts 178

existence taste indifferent to the existence of objects 36; ontological argument for existence of God 302; can only be conceived as magnitude 313

experience cannot prove existence of ends of nature 187; furnishes the occasion for adopting principle of judging internal purposiveness 204

explanation (*see also* DEDUCTION, INSIGHT) not provided by teleology 187 f.; geometrical analogies not a ground of explanation 210; mechanism affords no explanation of organisms 216, 241 f.; systems attempting an explanation of the purposiveness of nature 220; how concept of God renders purposiveness intelligible 227; of origin of organized beings without reference to design 227 f.; general explanatory digression 228; mechanical and teleological modes of explanation are not inconsistent 237; nature not explained by reference to supreme architect 238; purposiveness not explained by appeal to final cause 238; mechanistic explanation excludes teleological 240; basis of explanation contrasted with basis of exposition 240; defined as derivation from a principle 240; we do not know how far mechanical explanation can reach 243; mechanical explanation not helped by teleology 245 f.; subordination of mechanism to teleology in explanation of natural ends 246; critical principles bring us no nearer to explanation of origin of things 265

expression nature and function of 146; beauty as expression of aesthetic ideas 149; in words and tones 149

fact matters of 296 ff., 298 n; object of freedom as matter of fact 297, 302 f.; philosophy must lay foundations of all assurance here 304; matters of fact fall under the concepts of nature or the concept of freedom 304

faculty the three faculties of the mind 13; table of the higher faculties 32; of intellectual and aesthetic judgement compared 129; when faculties can be considered pure 14; the peculiar constitution of our cognitive faculty 225 f., 229 f.; as peculiar to the human race 228 f., 231 f.; as source of teleological representation 265; theological concepts relative to our cognitive faculty 285

faith type of assurance produced by practical faith 295 f.; matters of faith 296 f.; highest good a matter of faith 297; historical belief 298; faith defined 300; distinguished from credulity 300 f.; doubtful faith 301; contrasted with knowledge 304

fanaticism compared with enthusiasm 105

fatality Spinoza's system of 219

fear of nature 91; access to fear through the imagination 99; contrasted with awe 99

feeling of pleasure and displeasure the middle term between faculties of cognition and desire 4; of pleasure and displeasure in relation to the enigma of judgement 5; constitutive principle in respect of feeling 31; aesthetic judgement decides questions of taste by reference to feeling 29; the purely subjective element in a representation of feeling 24 f., 35, 38; the feeling of respect 53; taste as a faculty of judging the communicability of feeling 130; lack of taste distinguished from lack of feeling 95; our feeling for beautiful nature 132

fiction logical 223

field field of concepts defined 10

figure geometrical figures 190 ff., 276, 297; geometrical figures traced in sand 198

final end contrasted with other ends 196 f.; of nature 206; the unconditioned condition 206; contrasted with ultimate end 255; of creation 263 f.; defined 263; unconditioned 263; of an intelligent cause 264; of creation is not happiness 264 f.; ends of nature oblige us to look for 265; must be presupposed if world is to have a worth 271; in relation to good will 272; man as subject to moral laws is 274, 277 f.; proposed by us in the world 276; happiness the subjective condition of 278; presupposes moral world-cause 279; the furtherance of happiness in agreement with morality 280; existence of God assumed for us to conceive possibility of final end 281; idea of final cause has practical reality 281 f.; not to be found in nature 282; idea of final end resides in reason 282; practicability of 283, 299 f.; nature must assist us to make its realization possible 283; how far future life required by 290; not the foundation of duty 299 f.

flower as example of free beauty 39, 60, 63; contrasted with implements 67; contrasted with fabricated objects 128 f.

form reflection on the form of an object apart from any concept 26; form of aesthetic judgement implies abstraction from all content 111; of subjective purposiveness 115 f.; character of the pleasing form in works of art 141; the form of fine art must not appear sought after 142

formative arts division and definition of 150; analogy to gesture 152; contrasted with arts of tone 158; painting pre-eminent amongst such arts 158 f.

formative impulse in the organized body 253

freedom world of freedom meant to have influence on that of nature 11 f.; causality through nature and through freedom 30; imagination regarded in its 71; fine art impossible without 182; problem of uniting constraining force and 183; presupposed by reason in practical sphere 231; not objectively determined as a form of causality 232; of political states 261; a supersensible faculty in man 264; nomothetic of 276 f.; harmony of world of nature and world of 276 f., 282 f.; moral law the formal condition of 278; the highest good possible in the world through 278; as a matter of fact 297, 303;

formerly regarded as mere negative condition 301; a basis of knowledge of the supersensible from practical point of view 303; concept of freedom contrasted with that of nature 304; how its reality is revealed 304

furniture classed under painting 152

future life (*see also* IMMORTALITY, SOUL) our hope of a future life 289; Spinoza's view on 280

gardening as an ornamental art 151

general his aesthetic pre-eminence over the statesman 93

genius definition of 136, 146, 171; fine art as art of 136; its relation to taste 140 ff., 148 f.; derivation of the word from guardian spirit 137; originality of 137; its models exemplary 137, 146 f.; cannot indicate how it brings about its product 137; prescribes rules to art, not to science 137; opposed to spirit of imitation 137 f.; not something that can be learned 137 f., 146 f.; its function of supplying material 139; out of place in province of rational investigation 139; faculties of the mind which constitute 142, 145; freedom of 147; its union with taste in fine art 148; taste the discipline of 148; to be sacrificed rather than taste 148; poetry owes its origin almost entirely to 155; as the nature of the subject 136, 171; stifled by uncritical imitation of a master 182; special relation of the mental powers in 66 n

geometry (*see also* FIGURE) geometrically regular figures 72; Plato's conception of its importance 191

gesture in the formative arts 149, 152

God all knowledge of God is symbolic 180; the fear of God 91; our proper attitude before God 93; introduction of the concept into natural science 209; lifeless or living 220 n; purposiveness made intelligible to us by reference to 227; attributes of 273; moral proof of existence of 276 f.; use of moral argument for the existence of 288; effect of belief that there is no 280; assumption of God's existence involves no contradiction 281; steps in inference to existence of 284; objective reality of idea of 285; type of assurance provided by teleological proof for existence of 290; no theoretical proof of existence of 292; curiosity regarding intrinsic nature of God is senseless 294; existence of God a matter of faith 298; relativity of concept of God to object of our duty 299; respective value of moral and other arguments for existence of 304; ontological proof of existence of 304; metaphysical-cosmological argument for existence of 305; teleological argument for existence of God worthy of our respect 306; physico-teleological proof of existence of 306; relation of moral and physico-teleological arguments for existence of 307; how determinate concept of God is obtained 311

good defined 39 f., 41; contrasted with the agreeable, the beautiful, and the sublime 39–41, 43 f.; happiness as a 40; the beautiful independent of representation of the 57; affects purity of judgement of taste 61; union of the beautiful and the 61; delight in it associated with interest 39; moral good carries with it the highest interest 40; analogy between beauty and the morally good 181; the moral good to be aesthetically represented as sublime not beautiful 101

grass possibility of the generation of blade of grass 206, 228, 238; no Newton to explain it 228

gratification the agreeable gratifies 37 f., 39; nature of gratification 159; free play of sensations always a source of gratification 159

grotesque taste for what borders on the grotesque 73

ground supersensible ground 30; clear and distinct grounds of judgement 58 f.; as ultimate and purely negative concept 295

guiding-thread transcendental purposiveness as 20; concept of final causes as 217

habitat of organisms as provided by a teleological system 256

handicraft distinguished from fine art 133

happiness precepts for attaining 9; not unconditionally a good 40; as an end 258; quite possible as effect of mechanism of nature 264; not final end of creation, or even its ultimate end 264 n; a consequence of harmony 264 n; absolute worth not to be valued by 271; as subjective condition of final end 279; empirically conditioned 282; its relation to final end 279 f., 299 f.

harmony (*see also* COGNITIVE FACULTY, IMAGINATION) of nature with our judgement 174 f.; in music 153

health as a good 40; the feeling of health 159 ff.

highest good highest good possible in the world through freedom 278; concept of the original being in relation to the 273; as matter of faith 298

hindrances opposed by nature 30; on the part of sensibility 97

history natural history of the earth 257; as a matter of fact 298; credulity in matters of history 300

Homer contrasted as poet with Newton as scientist 138

humanity saved from humiliation by the might of nature 92; concept of humanity implies feeling of sympathy and power of communication 183; the development of humanity 262

Hume his comparison of critics and cooks 115; his comparison of English and French works of art 148 n; his views criticized 249

humility sublimity of humility 94

humour defined 164; examples of jests and amusing tales 161 f.

hybrid cannot be explained by system of preformation 252

hylozoism contrasted with theism 219 f.; does not perform what it promises 222

hypothesis allowable with respect to nature as a whole 242; of evolution 248; grounded on theoretical argument 292; possibility of object must be certain to ground a hypothesis 295

hypotyposis schematic or symbolic 179; examples of the latter 180

idea (*see also* AESTHETIC IDEAS, REALITY) defined 63, 169 f.; regulative function of 3; have only practical reality 11; the normal idea of the human form 64; presentation of ideas not possible in the logical sense 98; reason interested in the objective reality of 130; terms corresponding to distinction between an idea and a concept of understanding 169; palm given to painting because it penetrates far into the region of 158 f.; the underlying possibility of natural product 205; world-cause acting according to ends a mere 216; of reason 229, 296; of unconditional necessity of original ground of nature 231; something to which no commensurate object can be given in experience 232; difference between underlying natural end and other ideas 233; of a possible understanding different from the human 233; of divine author as ground 245 f.; underlying idea of final cause 254; causality by means of ideas 281; practical reality of 284; reason restricted in respect of idea of the supersensible 288; idea of reason incapable of presentation 296; freedom the only idea of reason the object of which is a matter of fact 297

ideal defined 63; art always has an ideal in view 182; ideal of beauty 62; how we arrive at the latter 63; objects to which ideal of beauty is or is not applicable 63 f.; testing correctness of this ideal 66; judgements according to the ideal not pure judgements of taste 66

idealism *see* PURPOSIVENESS

ideality of purposiveness 174; of sensuous objects as phenomena 178

idolatry defined 288

illusion produced by dialectic of reflective judgement 214

imagination in its harmony with the understanding 25 f., 49 f.; mutual relation of imagination and understanding requisite for every empirical cognition 26; as employed in presentation 28; it refers the object to the subject 35; in conjunction with understanding requisite for cognition 49; its power to recall and reproduce 64; taste is a free conformity of the imagination to law 71; productive as distinct from reproductive 71; forms such as it would project in conformity to the law of the understanding 71; the understanding at the service of imagination 73; its scope for unstudied and purposive play 73; what it grasps 74; its straining to use nature as a schema for ideas 95; its function in mathematical representations 192 f., 194

imaginative power what is required for great 66

imitation contrasted with mere following 137 ff.; of nature to the point of deception 128 f., 131; of nature in fine art 131; spirit of imitation is opposed to genius 137, 147; learning as mere imitation 137; when it becomes aping 147; examples of a master not to be imitated without criticism 182

immortality of the soul 298, 301

impression aesthetic judgement should refer to sensuous impressions 100

inclination aroused by what gratifies 38; discipline of the inclinations 261 f.

infinite as the absolutely great 85

insight complete insight only possible into what we can produce through our own concepts 212; we have none into the nature of things apart from the mechanistic principle 238; or into the supersensible substrate of nature 277 n

inspiration where it is not required 141

instinct in animals 29

intelligence Spinoza divests original ground of all 221; effect of a final cause must be by virtue of 221; supreme intelligence as cause of the world 222;

intelligence (*cont.*): existence of intelligent original being cannot be substantiated 226 f.; concept of intelligent world-cause subjective 265; we have no determinate concept of a higher intelligence 267; art-intelligence controlled with wisdom 269; determined by simple necessity of its nature by analogy to art-instinct 270; final end of an intelligent cause 274 f.; intelligent world-cause, if there is such 275; highest possible intelligence 309; not ascribed to ultimate source 313

interest defined 36; delight in the good associated with 39; moral good carries the highest 40; presupposes a need 42; of inclination in case of the agreeable 42; pure practical laws carry an 43; detachment from 43; contemplative pleasure does not bring about an 53; vitiates judgements of taste 54; empirical interest in the beautiful 126; cannot be determining ground of pure judgement of taste though it may be combined with it 126; can only be indirectly combined with it 126; consists in pleasure at existence of the object 126; empirical interest in the beautiful only exists in society 126; empirical interest in the beautiful affords very doubtful transition from the agreeable to the good 127; intellectual interest in the beautiful discovers a link in the chain of our faculties *a priori* 127; intellectual interest in the beautiful 127 f.; in the beautiful regarded as mark of good moral character 128; in the beautiful of art no evidence of good moral disposition 128; in charms of nature no evidence of good moral disposition 128; thought that the object is nature's handiwork is basis of intellectual interest in the beautiful 128 f.

intuition contrasted with thought 229 f.; a factor in knowledge 234; intellectual intuition 237; one different from our own sensuous intuition 246 f.

involution theory of 252

Iroquois sachem anecdote concerning eating-houses 36

judgement middle term between understanding and reason 4, 13; as synonymous with sound understanding 4; difficulty of discovering *a priori* principle of 4; especially in case of aesthetic judgements 5; when necessary as *a priori* principle in logical judging of nature 5; no reference to feeling of pleasure in logical judging of nature 5; why the critique needs a separate division for 5; territory of principle of 13; presumption that judgement effects transition from realm of nature to that of freedom 14; defined 15; determining and reflective judgement contrasted 15; reflective judgement compelled to ascend from particular to universal 15; transcendental principle of reflective 15 ff.; maxims of 17, 119; law of specification makes us proceed on principle of conformity of nature to our faculty of cognition 21, 23; aesthetic judgement on purposiveness of the object 24; singular empirical judgement claims universal assent 26; function of judgement when object is given 27; connects legislations of understanding and reason 29 ff.; provides mediating concept 31; provides constitutive *a priori* principle for feeling of pleasure and displeasure 31; grounds of judgement as clear or confused 59; mathematically determining and reflective judgement contrasted 80; of experience 117; cognitive judgement contrasted with aesthetic 118; specific distinction between determining and reflective 213, 233; teleological judging is reflective not determining 188, 203; teleological judgement not warranted by relative purposiveness 196; antinomy of 213; transcendental 213; principle of reflective judgement not objective 213; maxims of reflective judgement 213 ff.; does not need special principle for applying *a priori* laws 214; two antithetical maxims of reflective judgement 214 f.; maxim of judgement contrasted with objective principle 218; maxim of judgement indispensable 227; principle of judgement for applying understanding in the abstract to possible objects of experience 233; accord of things in nature with our power of 235; method of applying teleological judgement 245 ff.; principles of reflective judgement tell us nothing as to the origin of things 257; no room for opinion in *a priori* judgement 294

judgement of taste a subdivision of aesthetic judgements 54 f.; is aesthetic 35; defined 35 n; involves reference to the understanding 35; not a cognitive judgement 35, 60; affords no knowledge of anything 168; a special faculty for judging by rule and not by concepts 29; is reflective not determining 29; is contemplative 41; compared with empirical judgements 26; rests on *a priori* grounds 53; hence requires a critique 26; is both synthetic and *a priori* 118 f.; constitutive principle in respect of feeling of pleasure and displeasure 31; can only have its ground in the subjective condition of a judgement in general 116; what is asserted in a 119; how we become conscious of accord in 50; relative priority of feeling of pleasure and judgement of the object in 48; should be grounded on autonomy not heteronomy 178, 181; contrasted with logical judgements 115 f., 120; logical peculiarities of 111 f., 113 f.; not determinable by grounds of proof 113, 166; its logical quantity as singular 46, 75, 119; not determined by interest 36, 126; should be disinterested 37; may be combined with interest 126; what is *a priori* represented in such a judgement is not pleasure but its universal validity 119; universality of delight in such a judgement only represented as subjective 45; speaks with a universal voice 47; the view that it cannot claim any necessity 173; how expected as a sort of duty 125; as a faculty of communicating even our feelings to others 126; pure judgement of taste independent of charm or emotion 54; not pure if conditioned by determinate concept 60; its purity affected by association with the agreeable or the good 61; pure when judging a free beauty 60; independent of concept of perfection 57; interest may be combined with a pure 126; how false judgement of taste is possible 47 f.; conflict in relation to 165 f.; deduction of 109; key to enigma of judgement of taste supplied by indeterminate idea of the supersensible 168; rational concept of the supersensible underlies 167; its universal validity explained by reference to rational concept of the supersensible 167; perhaps the supersensible substrate of humanity is determining ground of 168

knowledge aesthetic judging contributes nothing to 5; dependent upon universal communicability 69; division of matters as possible objects of 295 f.; theoretical knowledge contrasted with practical faith 304

landscapes *see* VIEWS

laughter in general 160 ff.; physical character of its cause 160; something absurd always lies behind it 161; agreeable art of inducing air of gaiety with jest and laughter 135

law contrasted with rules and precepts 8; conformity to law without law 71; the moral law as our highest vocation 94; ends of nature cannot be conceived as possible in accordance with natural laws 197

legislation of reason and the understanding 10; the non-interference of these different legislations 11

Lessing as art critic 114

life judgement of taste refers to feeling of life in the subject 36; the technic of nature as analogue of life 203; value of life measured by enjoyment 262 n; hope of future life 289; materialism cannot determine question of future life 289

line aimlessly intertwining lines as example of free beauty 39

link intellectual interest in the beautiful discovers link in the chain of faculties 127; mediating link between concepts of nature and freedom 31

Linné his theory of classification 255

logic contrasted with philosophy 7

logical judgement compared with aesthetic judgement 36; analogy of judgement of the beautiful with logical judgement 43; how the former is converted into the latter 115; only such judgement yields knowledge 59; as distinguished from judgement of taste 116

logical presentation 144

logical quantity of aesthetic judgements 46, 75, 98, 111

logical universality compared with aesthetic universality 45 f.

logical validity defined 24

luxury defined 261

machine 194 n; has only motive, not formative power 202; Descartes's view of animals as machines 293

magnitude its mathematical and aesthetic estimation 81 f.; how it is represented 84

man beauty has significance only for man as both rational and animal 41; ideal of beauty only possible in the case of man 64; as ultimate end of creation 255, 258; titular lord of nature 259; only ultimate end by referring to an end independent of nature 259; as noumenon the final end of creation 264; only as a moral being the final end of creation 264 f.; creation would be a wilderness without man 271; the final end as subject to moral laws 274, 277 f.

mannerism a mode of aping 147

Marsden his description of Sumatra 73

master can only teach by illustration 182; not to simply be imitated without criticism 182

materialism cannot determine question of future life 289; psychology saved from materialism 289

mathematics as pure not concerned with actual existence of things 194

matter organic matter alone involves concept of natural end 207; design as referred to matter 211; lifelessness its essential characteristic 222; formative force of matter 253

maxims of judgement 17 f., 19; of common human understanding 124; of unprejudiced thought 124; of broadened thought 124; of consistent thought 125; of aesthetic judgement 167

mechanism concept of nature as mechanism enlarged to that of nature as art 77; something mechanical required in fine art 139; of nature 175, 204; blind mechanism 205; impossibility of production of organisms in accordance with mechanism unprovable 216, 222; unable to furnish explanation of production of organisms 216; its inner ground beyond our ken 222; distinction between mechanism and technic may arise from our type of understanding 231 f.; conception of whole as end not explicable by reference to 236; union of teleological principle with principle of mechanism in the technic of nature 238; no insight into nature of things apart from 238; its subordination to teleology in explanation of natural end 246; mechanical explanation to be pursued as far as possible 246 f.; of nature subordinated to architectonic of an intelligent author of the world 266; possible identity of ground of mechanism and nexus of final causes 218, 241, 250

metaphysics projected system of metaphysics 4; requires a preliminary critique 4; divisible into that of nature and of morals 6; metaphysical principle 16 f.; universal theory of purposiveness and question of design belongs to it 210; fundamentally directed to problems of God, freedom, and immortality 301

method of applying theory of teleological judgement 245 ff.

methodology of taste 182

might power to resist great hindrances 90; sublime represented as might 102

misanthropy when it appears sublime and when not 105 f.

misery splendid 261

modality of judgement of taste 67

models exemplary models 62; in arts of speech 63 n; criticism of models displays taste 62 f.; works of the ancients regarded as models 112; exemplary models of genius 137; how they aid genius 139; models of the ancients indispensable 183

moments of judgement of taste grounded on the logical functions of judgements 35 n; why quality considered first 35 n; of quality 35; of quantity 42 f; relation 51; of modality 67; modality of the sublime 94 f.

monstrous defined 83

moral disposition the beautiful and sublime purposive in respect of moral disposition 95 f.; union of feeling for the beautiful with moral disposition 128; communicability of moral dispositions 121; harmony of moral disposition and sensibility necessary for genuine taste 183; how natural beauty encourages moral disposition 274

moral ideas alone attended with self-sufficing delight 154; respect for them raises us above necessity for gratification 163; taste as faculty of judging the

moral ideas (*cont.*): rendering of moral ideas in sensuous terms 183; beauty in human figure consists in expression of moral ideas 66

moral judgement pleasure in such judgement is practical 53; analogy between moral judgement and judgement of taste 130

moral law as object of pure intellectual delight 101; as basis of communicability of feeling of the sublime 122; represented as divine command 231; the formal condition of freedom 278; confidence in the promise of 300 n; human beings as subject to 274, 277; directs us to strive towards universal highest end 275; pays no regard to ends 279 f.

morality beauty as symbol of morality 178 f.; taste in relation to morality 42; absolutely impossible as result of natural causes 264; gains by representation of a supreme being 275; we are *a priori* assured of its possibility 282; one of the factors of final end 282; and religion 288 f.; without theology 314

music at banquets 135; nature of 153 f., 157 f.; combined with poetry in song 154; compared with other arts 158; its lack of urbanity 158; nothing is thought in music 160; physical character of its enlivening effects 160 f.; play here proceeds from sensations to aesthetic ideas 160; an agreeable rather than fine art 158; annoyance caused by hymn-singing 158 n

natural end (*see also* END, ORGANISM) existence of natural ends not proved by experience 187; distinctive character of things considered as 197; represented as both cause and effect of itself 199; preserves itself generically 199; produces itself as an individual 199; reciprocal dependence of parts in 199 f.; things so considered are organisms 200; first requisite of thing considered as 201; distinguished from art-product 201; every part of it an organ 201; as organized and self-organizing being 202; concept of thing as intrinsically natural end only available for reflective judgement 203; distinction between judging a thing a natural end on account of its form and regarding its existence as an end of nature 206; mechanism discloses no foundation for distinctive character of 215 f.; this concept a stranger in natural science 218; concept of natural end subsumes nature under causality only thinkable by the aid of reason 223; concept of natural end unprovable 224; involves reference to the supersensible 224; why we must judge a natural end in the light of a causality different from mechanism 224; as designed not given in the object 227; we must ascribe its possibility to an intelligent being 228; indulging this idea differs from other ideas 233; mechanistic explanation inadequate for 243; mechanism subordinated to teleology in explanation of 246; autocracy of matter in natural ends is unmeaning 249; how natural ends afford confirmation to theology 273; end connecting natural and ethical ends 283

nature purposiveness of 16; multiplicity of 18; might baffle our understanding 20; law of specification of 21; harmony of nature in its specific laws with our cognitive faculties appears contingent 20 f., 23; universal laws of the understanding necessarily accord with 21 f.; pleasure derived from uniting empirical laws of 22; extent of its purposiveness indeterminate 23; aesthetic representation of purposiveness of 23 f.; beauty and purposiveness of nature defined 28; no *a priori* grounds why there should be objective ends of nature 28; only cognized as phenomenon 31; free beauties of 60; comparison of wild and regular beauty of 73 f.; art restricted by its required agreement with 76; object of nature may properly be called beautiful but not sublime 76; its self-subsisting beauty reveals a technic of nature 76 f.; conception of nature as mechanism enlarged to that of nature as art 77; which of its phenomena described as sublime 85; why the sublime not to be sought in nature 80; sublimity applied to it by subreption 87 f.; nature as might 90; self-preservation that cannot be assailed by 92; in its totality thought as a presentation of something supersensible 98; phenomenal nature a presentation of a nature in itself 98; as imitated by art 131; the language of nature 131; art distinguished from 131 f.; natural beauty distinguished from that of art 140; requisites for judging the beauty of art and of nature 140 f.; genius as nature in the subject 171; nature in the subject as supersensible substrate 171 f.; ideality of purposiveness of 174; beautiful forms in organic nature suggest realism of purposiveness 175; free formations of 176; names given to beautiful objects of nature implying analogy with the morally good 181; examples of beauty of 60, 175; subjective purposiveness of nature in its particular laws 187; universal idea of nature does not lead us to assume that things serve one another as means to ends 187; organizes itself 202; its organization has nothing analogous to any causality known to us 203; not given as organized as a whole 226; aggregate conceived as an animal 222; aggregate conceived as a system 207; as a teleological system 269; nature as a whole referred to design by an allowable hypothesis 243; ultimate end of nature as a teleological system 258; final end of 206; we must look beyond nature for the end of its existence 207; mechanism of 216, 246; hint given by 218; blind necessity of nature in Spinoza 221; supersensible substrate of 238; intelligible substrate of 247; strives towards higher ends than it can itself afford 262; teleologically subordinated to final end 264; prospect beyond the horizon of 265; accord of nature with conditions of human happiness 271; final end not found in 282; concept of nature and that of freedom 304

necessity of the reference of the beautiful to delight 67; exemplary 67; subjective necessity of judgement of taste 68; a common sense as ground of necessity 68; necessity of universal assent subjective, but represented as objective 70; deduction only required where judgement claims necessity 110; of judgements of taste 111

Newton his work compared with products of artistic genius 138; who would explain the genesis of a blade of grass 228

noumenon as substrate 85; man as noumenon the final end of creation 264

objective subjective necessity represented as 70

occasionalism 251

ontological argument criticized 304 f.; exerts no influence on popular thought 305

opera elements of 154

opinion difference of opinion not tolerated when something described as beautiful 70; as probable 292; no room for opinion in *a priori* judgements 294; matters of 296

oratorio 154

organ every part of a natural end is an 201 f., 205

organism (*see also* NATURAL END) things considered as natural ends are organisms 200; not a mere machine 202; intrinsic natural perfection of 203; affords objective reality to concept of an end of nature 204; principle for judging the intrinsic purposiveness of the organism 204; definition of 204; only cognizable on principle of ends 211; mechanism does not afford explanation of 216, 228; judged on principle of final causes 217; its possibility must be referred to causality by ends 237 f.; cannot be subjected to investigation except under concept of end 243 f.; its purposive form unthinkable without assuming a fundamental organization 248; teleological system in extrinsic relations of the 253 f.; extrinsic purposiveness implies reference to organisms as ends 253 f.; question of end for which it exists 254; a creative understanding taken to account for intrinsic purposiveness of the 254; design not easily dissociated from concept of 254; idea of final cause underlying the organism 254

organization of body politic 203; fundamental 247 f.; inscrutable principle of primordial 253; of the sexes 254

origin of blade of grass 206, 228; principles of reflective judgement say nothing regarding origin of things 257; critical principle brings us no nearer an explanation of natural things 265

originality is not throwing off all restraint of rules 139; of genius 137, 139

ornamentation as adjuncts and *parerga* 57

ought judgement containing an 68, 70

pain 159

painting design the essential thing here 56; contrasted with plastic art 150; as a formative art 151; aesthetic 151 f.; its superiority amongst the formative arts 158 f.

pantheism 250, 268

patterns in free beauty 39

peace possible degrading effects of continuing peace 93

peculiarity first peculiarity of judgement of taste 111 f.; its second peculiarity 113 f.

perfection judgement of taste independent of this concept 57, 167 f.; defined as internal objective purposiveness 57; held by some to be convertible with beauty 58; as thought in a confused way 58; qualitative and quantitative contrasted 58; requires representation of an end 58; beauty involves no thought of perfection of the object 59; involved in dependent beauty 60; does not gain by beauty or vice versa 61; definition of 140; must be considered when judging the beautiful in art 140; antinomy of taste irresolvable if beauty grounded on 169; also otiose 173

personality continuance after death 289

persuasion as object of rhetoric 155; contrasted with conviction 291

phenomenon legislative authority of understanding confined to 10 f., 14; contrasted with things in themselves 11; implies possible form of intuition different from ours 233; material world as 237; supersensible the basis of nature as 241; presupposes supersensible ground 241; self-subsistent being of which we only know the phenomenon 251

philosophy defined 7; realm of 10; of nature and morals contrasted 7; divided into theoretical and practical 7–10; this division justified 12 f.; can prove but not demonstrate 170; coextensive with applicability of *a priori* concepts 10; trichotomous divisions of 32 n; critical duty of 214; schools have tried every possible solution to problem of purposiveness 220 n; its concepts enriched by Christianity 300 n; speculative negative results of 303; foundations of 304; its arguments for the existence of God 304 f.

planets their inhabitation a matter of opinion 296

plastic arts contrasted with painting 150; division of 151

Plato his idea of original constitution of things 191; banished from his school those ignorant of geometry 191

play of cognitive faculties 31, 48 f., 73, 88 f.; purposive 73; of figures or sensations 56; is agreeable on its own account 133; free play as source of gratification 159; free play in poetry 71; of cognitive faculties 31, 48 f., 73, 88 f.; purposive 73; of figures or sensation 56; is agreeable on its own account 133; art as 133; free play a source of gratification 159

pleasure (*see also* FEELING) associated with concept of purposiveness 21; its subjective quality incapable of becoming a cognition 24; only connected with representation through reflective judgement 25; in judgement of taste dependent on empirical representation 26; its relative priority in judgement of taste 48; what it denotes 51; causal connection with representation not determinable *a priori* 53; where the mental state is identical with 53; is contemplative in aesthetic judgements 54; in the consciousness of formal purposiveness 53 f.; as non-practical 53

poem didactic 154

poetry imagination enjoys free play in 71; requires prosody and measure 134; faculty of aesthetic ideas best displayed in 143; contrasted with rhetoric 149, 155; combined with music in song 154; compared with other arts 155

Polycletus his *Doryphorus* 65

possibility definition of 229; representation of whole as cause of possibility 235; question of possibility must be met sooner or later 239; of things as natural ends 266; possibility of a thing must be certain to ground hypotheses 295

possible distinguished from actual 229 f.

practical practical philosophy contrasted with theoretical 7–9; misuse of the word 7 f.; precepts 8 f.; the morally practical compared with the technically practical 8; reason can only prescribe laws in practical sphere 10; practical function distinguished from theoretical 10; practical reality of ideas 11;

practical (*cont.*): practical purposiveness 17; broadening the mind from practical point of view 85

practical point of view verdict on our vocation only valid from a 289; assurance in matters of faith furnished from a purely 298; meaning of 298 f.; all that is necessary for religion is validity from a 303

prayer superstition at basis of prayer 14 n

predicate pleasure united to concept of object as if it were a predicate 26

pre-establishment theory of pre-established cause 251

prejudice 124

presentation as function of judgement 27; of ideas 98, 143

principle constitutive 3, 31; regulative 3, 31; transcendental or metaphysical 16 f.; principle of judgement independent 4; reference to pleasure the enigma of principle of judgement 5; as technically or as morally practical 8; of the purposiveness of nature 16 f.; one more principle for reducing phenomena to rules 188; regulative contrasted with constitutive 188 f.; regulative principle for judging intrinsic purposiveness 204; concept of objective purposiveness a critical 225; principle of reason as regulative not constitutive 228 f.; subjective principle for use of judgement 232; heuristic 239; mechanistic and teleological principle not to be applied in conjunction 240; the supersensible common to mechanistic and teleological derivation 240; critical principle brings us no nearer explanation of origin of things 265; principle of harmony of nature with the moral law 287; human reason prefers one principle instead of several 290

probability a fraction of possible certainty 294

progress limit to that of art 138; of culture 148

proof grounds of judgements of taste admit no 113 f.; fine art does not appeal to 134; moral 281 f.; should convince us 290; two kinds of 291; theoretical arguments available for 292

propaedeutic culture propaedeutic to fine art 182 f.; development of moral ideas propaedeutic to taste 183; to all philosophy 29

prosody required in poetry 134

prudence rules of prudence mere corollaries to theoretical philosophy 8 f.

psychology modality of aesthetic judgements lifts them out of sphere of 96; critique of taste as an art deals with psychological rules 116; rational psychology an anthropology of inner sense 289 f.

purposiveness defined 16, 51; practical purposiveness differs from that of reflective judgement 16, 22; as transcendental principle of judgement 16–18, 28; empirical nature must be regarded on a principle of 18; transcendental concept of purposiveness of nature neither a concept of nature or of freedom 19; principle of purposiveness of nature recognized as objectively contingent 20; feeling of pleasure associated with concept of 21; is determined by an *a priori* ground 22; this concept takes no account of faculty of desire 22; not a quality of the object itself 24; why attributed to the object 24; objective and subjective purposiveness compared 27; subjective purposiveness rests on pleasure 27; objective purposiveness not concerned with pleasure 27; and natural ends as organic bodies 28; formal purposiveness a principle without which understanding could not find itself in nature 28; leaves question of application in particular cases undetermined 28; as mediating link 31; objective 57; formal 57; of representational state of the subject 58; in the sublime 83; example of stone implements 66–7 n; ideality of 174; realism and idealism of 174; subjective purposiveness of nature in its particular laws 187; beauty as formal subjective purposiveness 188; formal distinguished from material objective purposiveness 190; formal purposiveness of geometrical figures 190; real purposiveness dependent on concept of end 191; material purposiveness 194; intrinsic compared with relative purposiveness 194; extrinsic purposiveness the advantageousness of a thing for other things 196; relative purposiveness does not warrant absolute teleological argument 196; principle of judging intrinsic purposiveness 204; systems dealing with purposiveness of nature 217; as a critical principle 225; rendered intelligible by reference to a God 227; conformity to law on part of the contingent is termed 232; why a necessary concept for judgement 232; representation of purposiveness results from peculiar character of our understanding 235; as undeniably pointing to special type of causality 239; intuition different from ours required to derive it from mechanism 246 f.; extrinsic purposiveness defined 253 f.; extrinsic and intrinsic contrasted 254; creative understanding represented to account for 254; extrinsic purposiveness in relation of the sexes 254; of nature compels us to think a supreme cause 313

pyramids as examples of sublimity 82

quality delight in the beautiful associated with representation of 75; quality of delight in judging the sublime 87; of the feeling of the sublime is a displeasure 89

quantity delight in the sublime associated with representation of 75

race preservation of 249

rationalism in the critique of taste confuses the good and the beautiful 174

realism of the principle of taste 174

reality practical reality of ideas 11; deduction need not justify objective reality of a concept 120; reason interested in objective reality of ideas 130; intuitions required to verify the reality of our concepts 178; objective reality of rational concepts cannot be verified 178 f.; semblance of objective reality of ideas 143; organisms first afford objective reality to concept of an end of nature 204; no insight into objective reality of concept of natural end 223; why objective reality of natural ends not provable 224; necessary to prove objective reality for determining judgement 225; objective reality must be given to concepts of the understanding 228; subjectively practical reality 281 f.; practical reality of an idea 284; of the concept of freedom 304

realm of philosophy defined 10; of our faculty of cognition 10; realm of concept of freedom meant to influence that of concept of nature 12

reason pure reason defined 3; critique of pure reason 3; contains constitutive *a priori* principles solely for faculty of desire 4; critique of practical reason 4; can only prescribe laws in practical sphere 10; legislations of reason and the understanding 10 f.; interest of 54; ideas of reason 87; intervenes to make sensuous representations adequate to ideas 98; the seat of both rational and aesthetic ideas 171; a faculty of principles 228; aims at the unconditional as its goal 228; regulative rather than constitutive principles of 228 f.; becomes extravagant when it advances beyond the reach of the understanding 229; displays itself in ideas 229; concept of absolutely necessary being an indispensable idea of 230; must presuppose freedom in the practical sphere 231; pre-eminent task to prevent poetic extravagance in field of thought 238 f.; how it is sent on a roving expedition 239; demands absolute unity of principle 268; pure practical reason legislates for itself alone 275; determines us to further the highest good as far as lies in our power 282; idea of final end resides in 282; as morally practical and technically practical 284; human reason prefers one principle instead of several 290

refinement connected with communication of feeling 127

Reimarus his physical teleology 306

religion as sublime 93; how and why it is favoured by governments 105; example better than precept in matters of 113, and note; how distinguished from superstition 94; how saved from theurgy and from idolatry 288; true religion defined 289; theology leads to 310; disposition the essential element in 310; validity of argument from practical point of view all that is needful for 303

respect defined 87; aroused by the moral good 101; inclination, favour and 41; the feeling of 53; joined with representation of object as great without qualification 80

rhetoric defined and described 155; contrasted with poetry 149; in drama 154; contrasted with poetry 149; generally 154 f.

Rousseau 36

rule aesthetic judgement a special faculty for judging according to a rule 29; difference of a general and a universal 44; rules for establishing union of taste with reason 61; no objective rule for determining the beautiful 62; normal idea as source of possibility of 65; question of taste not to be settled by appeal to any 114; how a rule is furnished to art 136 f.; *Doryphorus* of Polycletus called the 65; technically or morally practical rules 8; emancipation from all constraint of 139; in fine art cannot be set down in a formula, but must be gathered from the execution of the work 139

sacrifice in representation of the sublime 101; by the imagination 99

sadness insipid contrasted with interesting 106

St. Peter's aesthetic effect of 83

Saussure his reference to insipid sadness 95

Savary his account of Egypt 82

scepticism 69

schema the imagination strains to use nature as schema for ideas 95; contrasted with examples and symbols 179 f.

schematism of judgement 99; objective schematism 50

scholastics their definition of transcendental perfection 221

school origin of a 147; leaders of a newer school 134

science art distinguished from 133; genius prescribes the rule to art not science 137; relative merits of art and 138

sculpture design the essential thing in 56; may only represent unpleasing things indirectly 141; described and contrasted with architecture 151

Segner his use of inscription over the Temple of Isis 145 n

sensation is subjective but belongs to cognition of things 24; double meaning of the term 37; communicability of 121; as the real in perception 121; difference in sensation of different persons 121; passivity of 121; through which we are conscious of reciprocal activity of cognitive powers 50

senses in relation to feeling of pleasure 125; functions of imagination, understanding, and the senses 69

sensus communis (*see also* COMMON SENSE) reason for supposing such a thing 69; taste as a kind of 123; a name given to common human understanding 123; as a public sense 123

sentimentality is a tendency to indulge in tender emotions 103

series progressive and regressive contrasted 200

sex organization of the sexes 254

simplicity of nature in the sublime 105

skill and culture 260; can hardly be developed without inequality among human beings 261

sociability judgement in reference to 44; properties constituting sociability of mankind 183

society sublime not introduced in a mere conventional way into society 95; universal communicability a source of interest in 105; isolation from society regarded as sublime 105; empirical interest in the beautiful only exists in 126

soldier reverence for 93

solitude attractions of 106

soul properties figuratively ascribed to the 286; no theoretical proof of its existence 295; its immortality a matter of faith 298; immortality of the soul in metaphysics and psychology 301

space subjective, but constituent of the knowledge of things 24; measurement of 89; delimitations of space in accordance with arbitrary rules 192; not a quality of things 192; not a real ground of the generation of things 237

species origin of 247 f.

speech division of arts of 149 f.

Spinoza his system of fatality 219; eliminates design 220 f.; criticized 250; his belief that there is no God 280

spirit the animating principle of the mind 142; the faculty of presenting aesthetic ideas 142, 146

spontaneity in the play of the cognitive faculties 31; of some cause 239

statesman compared with a general 93

subjective purposiveness contrasted with objective 27; necessity represented as objective 70; subjective purposiveness necessary if anything is to please disinterestedly 84

sublime ground of the division between the beautiful and the 26 f.; points of agreement and difference between them 75 ff., 86; contrasted with the good 75, 97; delight in it combined with representation of quantity 75; presents an indeterminate concept of reason 76; charms repugnant to the 76; a negative pleasure 76; object of nature not itself 80; concerns ideas of reason 76 f.; theory of the sublime an appendage to the aesthetic judging of nature 77; concerns nature in its chaos 77; distinction of the mathematically and dynamically 78; moments of judgement on the 77 f.; movement of the mind connected with the 78; definition of the 78 f.; feeling of respect produced by the 80; its reference to the supersensible faculty within us 81; estimation of magnitude requisite for the mathematically 81 f.; not to be sought in works of art if judgement is to be pure 83; not based on purposiveness of the form of the object 84; examples of the mathematically 86; quality of our delight in the 87 f.; applied to the object by subreption 87 f.; involves feeling of pleasure and displeasure 88; examples of the dynamically 90 f.; we must be safe to respond to the 92; sublimity of war 93; of a religion 93; of humility 94; culture requisite for appreciation of the 95; modality of judgement on the 78; defined 97 f.; its purposiveness in connection with moral disposition 98; moral disposition required for feeling of the 99; cultivates liberality in our mental attitude 99; delight in it is negative 99; as the might to overcome hindrances 101; freedom from affects represented as 102; isolation from society regarded as 105; no deduction of judgements required 109; exposition suffices 110; nature only supplies the occasion for judgement on the 109 f.; brought into union with beauty in tragedy 154

substance unity of end referred to simple 249 f.; original source of things must be pictured as simple substance 251; causal dependence on one substance changed to unity of inherence in one substance 268

substrate intelligible substrate of nature 247; supersensible 251, 277 n; representation based on final causes refers phenomena to 258

subsumption logical and aesthetic contrasted 120; mistakes in 120 f.

Sumatra Marsden's description of 73

supersensible introduction of idea of the 11; practical reality of concept of freedom brings us no nearer to knowledge of the 11; gulf between the sensible and the 11, 30; ground of unity of the supersensible at basis of nature with freedom 12; in the subject 30; substrate of nature 30 n, 238, 251; freedom a supersensible attribute of the subject 53; reference of sublime to the supersensible faculty in us 81; rational idea of 88; as substrate of nature, principle of purposiveness, and principle of ends of freedom 173 f.; nature employed as schema for 155; union of mechanistic and teleological principles must be placed in the 241; all determination of it purely negative 289

superstition 124; distinguished from religion 94

symbol beauty as symbol of morality 178 f.; contrasted with schema 179

symbolic all knowledge of God is 180

symbolism nature of 179

symmetry 72

sympathy the word humanity implies sense of 183

system of ends 205 f.; every science a 209; dealing with the purposiveness of nature 220 f.; two kinds of system dealing with purposiveness 218 f.; nature in its entirety as a 237; nature as a 241; of sciences 245; teleological system in extrinsic relations of organisms 253 f.; of whole of nature following final causes 256; ultimate end of nature as a teleological system 258, 272 f..

taste (*see also* JUDGEMENT OF TASTE) principle that everyone has his own taste 44, 166; disputes about taste 62; archetype of 63; whether an original faculty 70; English taste in gardens 73; reason for the name 114; a judging not a producing faculty 141 f.; the saying that there is no disputing about taste 165 f.; stiff regularity repugnant to 73

technic of nature 27; nature regarded as possessing capacity for acting technically 188; of nature cannot be treated dogmatically 223; type of our understanding as source of distinction between mechanism and 232; union of mechanistic and teleological principles in the technic of nature 238

technically practical *see* PRACTICAL

teleological judgement contrasted with aesthetic 28 f.; not a special faculty 29

teleology for science organisms suggest concept of 204; as inherent principle of natural science 209; natural teleology as part of physics 210; function of teleological judging in natural science 211; does not convert nature into an intelligent being 211; whether must be treated as branch of natural science 245; not a branch of doctrine but only of critique 246; contains *a priori* principles 246; principle of 249; ethico–teleology does what physical teleology could not 272 f.; moral and teleological arguments cannot be combined in one 308; concept of supreme cause defined by moral 310; moral teleology alone furnishes concept of a unique author of nature 310

Temple of Isis 145 n

territory of concepts defined 10; none in field of the supersensible 11

testimony as ground of belief 298

theism contrasted with hylozoism 219 f.

theology teleology not a branch of 245; physico–theology defined 265; moral or ethico–theology defined 265; physical teleology affords no basis for 266; physico–theology is physical teleology misunderstood 270; ethico–theology 271; how reason advances from teleology to 277; transition from moral teleology to 282; how saved from theosophy and demonology 288; leads to religion 311; ethical theology quite possible 314

theosophy 288

thought all our thoughts associated with bodily movements 162; contrasted with intuition 230

tone art of tone described 156; charm of 55; when to be regarded as beautiful 55

totality required by reason 85

tragedy sublime and the beautiful united in 154

transcendental principle 16 f.; general problem of transcendental philosophy 118; principle of judgement 15; transcendental aesthetic deals with pure judgements 100

transition between the two parts of philosophy 12; concept of purposiveness affords 31; judgement effects a 31; none from concepts to feeling of pleasure 43; intellectual interest in the beautiful discovers transition from sensuous enjoyment to moral disposition 127; that from the agreeable to the good is ambiguous 127; taste makes possible transition from sensuous charm to habitual moral interest 181 f.

ugliness capacity of art for dealing with 141

ultimate end contrasted with final end 255; of nature as a teleological system 258 f.

unbelief dogmatic unbelief not consistent with moral maxim 301

understanding its pretensions restrained by critique 3; comparison of functions of reason and the 29, 30 f., 228; its legislation confined to phenomena 10 f.; supplies constitutive principles for faculty of cognition 3; its pure concepts only touch the possibility of nature 15; an architectonic 216; unable to keep pace with reason 229; why it cannot rival reason 230; our understanding must move from universal to particular 232; idea of a possible understanding differing from the human 233; a faculty of concepts 234; as discursive 234; concept of an intuitive 234; our understanding must advance from the parts 235; discursive understanding needs images 236; original understanding as cause of the world 238; the constitution of our human 242

universal particular not determined by 234; analytic contrasted with synthetic 235

universal validity deduction only necessary where judgement claims such validity 110; of judgements of taste 25; nature of such validity in judgements of taste 111; of pleasure 119

universality of delight in judgement of taste only subjective 45; when it is aesthetic 45 f.; dialectic only arises where judgements lay claim to 165

utility defined as objective external purposiveness 57; delight in the beautiful cannot rest on 57 f.; a relative purposiveness 195

validity (*see also* UNIVERSAL VALIDITY) exemplary 70

views of nature 74, 151 f.

virtuosi moral character of 128

Voltaire his remarks on hope and sleep 162 f.

war sublimity of war and its effect on character 93; how it serves culture 261 f.

watch used as illustration of a machine 202

whole representation of a whole as source of possibility of form 235 f.; mechanical generation of 236; as end 236; parts of space only determinable in relation to 237; a cosmopolitan 261

Wieland Homer and Wieland contrasted with scientists 138

will as a cause 8; defined 51; respect as determination of the will derived from the idea of the moral law 53; end implies reference to a 198; faculty of acting according to ends 198; absolute worth only exists by reference to the good will 272; will and understanding not ascribed theoretically to the supreme being 286

world intelligible world where everything is actual 231; moral author of the 283

worth how absolute worth given to the existence of a person 40; object of fine art must have a certain intrinsic worth 164; assigned to life 262 n; presupposes a final end 271; absolute worth only exists by reference to the good will 272; man alone has a concept of worth 278; intrinsic moral worth depends on formal character of our actions 299

American Literature

British and Irish Literature

Children's Literature

Classics and Ancient Literature

Colonial Literature

Eastern Literature

European Literature

Gothic Literature

History

Medieval Literature

Oxford English Drama

Poetry

Philosophy

Politics

Religion

The Oxford Shakespeare

A complete list of Oxford World's Classics, including Authors in Context, Oxford English Drama, and the Oxford Shakespeare, is available in the UK from the Marketing Services Department, Oxford University Press, Great Clarendon Street, Oxford OX2 6DP, or visit the website at www.oup.com/uk/worldsclassics.

In the USA, visit www.oup.com/us/owc for a complete title list.

Oxford World's Classics are available from all good bookshops. In case of difficulty, customers in the UK should contact Oxford University Press Bookshop, 116 High Street, Oxford OX1 4BR.

A SELECTION OF OXFORD WORLD'S CLASSICS

	Classical Literary Criticism
	The First Philosophers: The Presocrates and the Sophists
	Greek Lyric Poetry
	Myths from Mesopotamia
APOLLODORUS	The Library of Greek Mythology
APOLLONIUS OF RHODES	Jason and the Golden Fleece
APULEIUS	The Golden Ass
ARISTOPHANES	Birds and Other Plays
ARISTOTLE	The Nicomachean Ethics
	Physics
	Politics
BOETHIUS	The Consolation of Philosophy
CAESAR	The Civil War
	The Gallic War
CATULLUS	The Poems of Catullus
CICERO	Defence Speeches
	The Nature of the Gods
	On Obligations
	Political Speeches
	The Republic and The Laws
EURIPIDES	Bacchae and Other Plays
	Heracles and Other Plays
	Medea and Other Plays
	Orestes and Other Plays
	The Trojan Women and Other Plays
HERODOTUS	The Histories
HOMER	The Iliad
	The Odyssey